Working Collaboratively in Second/Foreign Language Learning

Trends in Applied Linguistics

Edited by
Ulrike Jessner

Volume 30

Working Collaboratively in Second/Foreign Language Learning

Edited by
María del Pilar García Mayo

ISBN 978-1-5015-2096-9
e-ISBN (PDF) 978-1-5015-1131-8
e-ISBN (EPUB) 978-1-5015-1124-0
ISSN 1868-6362

Library of Congress Control Number: 2020946347

Bibliographic information published by the Deutsche Nationalbibliothek
The Deutsche Nationalbibliothek lists this publication in the Deutsche Nationalbibliografie;
detailed bibliographic data are available on the Internet at http://dnb.dnb.de.

© 2022 Walter de Gruyter Inc., Boston/Berlin
This volume is text- and page-identical with the hardback published in 2021.
Typesetting: Integra Software Services Pvt. Ltd.
Printing and binding: CPI books GmbH, Leck

www.degruyter.com

This book is dedicated to the loving memory of my mother, María del Pilar Mayo Santos.
Volver para non esquecer.

Foreword

It is with great pleasure that I welcome readers to this collection of scholarly work that views collaboration in second and foreign language (SL/FL) learning through multiple lenses. An advocate for the use of interactive tasks in Spanish EFL classrooms for more than two decades, Dr. García Mayo is exceptionally well-suited to edit this collection. Starting with her early research about the use of form-focused tasks in EFL classrooms, she has continually pushed classroom-based research forward by exploring diverse aspects of collaboration in ecologically-valid instructional settings. Her work has investigated multiple topics related to the design and implementation of collaborative tasks, such as task modality, task repetition, pair formation method, and group size. These empirical studies have addressed key questions that SL/FL instructors confront when deciding how to create and use tasks in their classrooms, especially instructors who work with young learners and adolescents. In addition to task characteristics and implementation factors, she has also examined another key factor in the success of collaborative tasks, namely learners' attitudes toward task-based interaction. As SL/FL instructors can confirm, a perfectly designed and carefully implemented task can fail horribly if learners do not perceive its value and relevance.

The impetus for this edited collection stems in part from the *Oral-Written Connection in Second/Foreign Language Learning* conference (March 2018) organized by Dr. García Mayo in her role as director of the *Language and Speech* research group (www.laslab.org). Funded by grants from the Basque government, the conference explored the various ways that collaboration promotes SL/FL learning. Plenary speakers highlighted how collaboration within and across modalities creates learning opportunities while also acknowledging the importance of learner factors such as motivation. As attested by the diversity of topics across the conference programme, researchers are moving in new directions to refine the construct of collaboration, examine the interface between oral and written language use, and identify areas of convergence and divergence between face-to-face and computer-mediated collaborations.

Reflecting this diversity, this edited collection brings together 10 chapters that collectively explore three main themes about collaboration in SL/FL classrooms. At the forefront of this research is the recognition that asking learners to work in pairs and small groups is no guarantee that they will truly collaborate while carrying out a face-to-face or computer-mediated tasks. Of interest to both instructors and researchers, the quest to understand the factors that either encourage or discourage learners to work together is the focus of several chapters that examine patterns of interaction with different age groups and task types. A second theme evident throughout the volume is the need to further investigate the effects that collaboration has on SL/FL learners. In addition to examining traditional constructs such as language-related episodes and patterns of interaction, these chapters also explore how collaboration affects written text quality, grammatical knowledge, production of lexico-grammatical features, and pragmatic competence. The volume also examines whether the benefits associated with collaborative performance transfer to individual performance. By casting a broader net, these studies expand our view about what aspects of SL/FL performance and knowledge may be impacted by collaboration.

A final theme that unites the chapters is recognition of the need to broaden the empirical basis of collaboration research. The volume brings together collaboration research carried out in multiple countries (e.g., Canada, Indonesia, Spain, United States) that targets different second languages (e.g., English, German, Spanish). Although much collaboration research has been conducted with university students, this volume includes several chapters that report studies with adolescent participants. In many chapters, the researchers situated their research materials in specific learning contexts by exploiting activities from common lessons, tasks vetted by instructors, and activities adopted from course design. Reflecting the growing role of technological tools in SL/FL learning, the volume features studies in which collaboration occurred while co-constructing a text in person using a Moodle platform, asynchronous interaction via Google docs, and a combination of face-to-face interaction followed by asynchronous collaboration. However, reflecting its continuing importance in SL/FL teaching, collaboration during face-to-face interaction is also examined in several chapters. Reflecting both the age and proficiency level of the participants, the analysis of short written texts (approximately 100 words) is explored in several chapters, which is a welcome addition to collaborative writing research that has largely focused on longer texts produced by more proficient writers. By including a variety of languages, countries, and data elicitation tasks, this edited volume makes an important contribution to expanding the boundaries of collaboration research. This collection is sure to be of interest for readers from a wide range of backgrounds.

Kim McDonough

Contents

Foreword —— VII

María del Pilar García Mayo
Introduction —— 1

Neomy Storch
Collaborative writing: Promoting languaging among language learners —— 13

James Scotland
The efficacy of collaboratively completing form-focused tasks: A research synthesis —— 35

Tomas Kos
What exactly is mutuality? An analysis of mixed-age peer interactions on classroom tasks in German secondary school classrooms —— 59

Izaskun Villarreal and Miren Munarriz-Ibarrola
"Together we do better": The effect of pair and group work on young EFL learners' written texts and attitudes —— 89

Monika Geist and Angela Hahn
The effect of collaborative writing on individual writing strategies: A case study of two L2 English writers —— 117

Fauzul Aufa and Neomy Storch
Learner interaction in blended collaborative L2 writing activities —— 151

Izaskun Villarreal, M. Camino Bueno-Alastuey and Raquel Sáez-León
Computer-based collaborative writing with young learners: Effects on text quality —— 177

Marta González-Lloret
Online collaboration through tasks for L2 pragmatic development —— 199

Mimi Li
Participation and interaction in wiki-based collaborative writing: An Activity Theory perspective —— 227

Hyeyoon Cho
Factors mediating small-group interactions during synchronous web-based collaborative summary writing using Google Docs —— 249

Index —— 275

María del Pilar García Mayo
Introduction

Collaborative learning has played an important role in the second language (L2) classroom since the times of communicative language teaching (Savignon 1991). Research on collaborative work has been informed by both cognitive (Long 1983, 1996) and sociocultural (Vygotsky 1978) theories. Cognitive theories highlight the facilitative role of learner interaction (i.e. the use of language for communicative purposes with a focus on meaning rather than on formal aspects of the target language) in the language learning process (García Mayo and Alcón Soler 2013; Loewen and Sato 2018). Interaction has been claimed to provide not only positive input but also opportunities for learners' 'pushed output' in order to make their message more comprehensible (Swain 2005). During interaction learners can also receive feedback from their interlocutors (teachers and/or peers), which also plays a crucial role in L2 learning. The negotiation of meaning that takes place during interaction has been claimed to trigger cognitive mechanisms (noticing, for example (Schmidt 1990)) crucial for language leaning. Storch (2013:13) points out that "This hypothesis [the interaction hypothesis] provides a rationale for the use of small group and pair work in the language classroom."

Sociocultural theories state that human cognitive development is a socially situated activity mediated by language. Specifically, knowledge is claimed to be socially constructed by interaction with others and then internalized. The gap between current and potential abilities in order to perform a task independently is known as *scaffolding*. Some authors have studied interaction to discover how dialogue is used as a cognitive tool (Donato and Lantolf 1990). As Storch (2016: 389) points out, Swain (2000) reconceptualized her output hypothesis to reflect that "[. . .] production of language, whether speaking or writing, was a communicative and a cognitive activity." More importance was given to the dialogue learners generated while they completed tasks than to output *per se*, Swain (2000) coined this dialogue *collaborative dialogue*, which she claims allows learners to co-construct knowledge and finally internalize it. The unit of analysis used to code learner collaborative dialogue was the language-related episode (LRE), defined as instances in the conversation where learners "talk about the language they are producing, question their language use, or correct themselves or other" (Swain and Lapkin 1998: 326). Collaborative dialogue is seen as language learning

---

María del Pilar García Mayo, Universidad del País Vasco (UPV/EHU)

https://doi.org/10.1515/9781501511318-001

mediated by language and has been shown to lead to learning in both second and foreign language contexts (Alegría de la Colina and García Mayo, 2007; Basterrechea and García Mayo 2013; Calzada and García Mayo, 2020a, 2020b; García Mayo 2002, 2014; Imaz Agirre and García Mayo; 2020; Kim 2008). Research has shown that the solutions reached by learners working collaboratively during task completion are mainly correct and lasting in time (see review in Storch 2013) so there is a clear pedagogical implication of this type of research. More recently, Swain (2006) introduced the term *languaging* to capture the process in which learners verbalize their thinking. She maintains that learners benefit from languaging because first they externalize their thoughts and then these thoughts provide them with objects to reflect on: "Learners are expected to learn through the process and the product of their languaging." (Ishikawa 2018: 51). In short, languaging contributes to L2 learning.

Collaborative work can be carried out with tasks that lead to oral production or with tasks that also incorporate a final written product. Research in L2 acquisition has traditionally favored spoken discourse but is now turning its interest towards writing and the interconnection between the two modalities. The impact of task modality on L2 interaction has been the subject of recent research in the second language acquisition field with most studies showing that tasks that encourage oral interaction tend to focus learners' attention on meaning, whereas those that incorporate a writing component focus learners' attention on form (García Mayo and Azkarai 2016). Although there are many differences between the two modalities, one of the most important has to do with time: in oral tasks there is more online processing by the learners, who have little time to react immediately to their partner's questions/concerns. When a written component is included, learners have more time to process feedback received by peers and to refine the L2 output they produce, focusing on formal aspects of the language they are learning.

A task that combines both modalities is collaborative writing. Storch (2019:40) defines collaborative writing as "an activity that requires the co-authors to be involved in all stages of the writing process, sharing the responsibility for and the ownership of the entire text produced." There has been a growing interest in collaborative writing among researchers and educators in recent years, which she attributes to the importance of writing in teams in the workplace and to the advent of Web 2.0 applications (blogs, wikis, Google Docs . . . etc), which have transformed what used to be an individual activity in the language classroom into one in which learners co-construct their knowledge while writing. The use of collaborative writing tasks reflects a move from a traditional learning-to-write perspective to one which combines writing-to-learn and learning-to-write (Manchón 2011). Whereas traditionally language learners were taught how to reproduce a model text in the target language, the process of collaborative writing is an opportunity for learners not only to compose texts in the L2 but also to learn about its lexicon and grammar.

Against this backdrop, the main aim of this volume is to share with the reader ten chapters that illustrate the benefits of collaborative dialogue in second/foreign language classrooms and to contribute to research in the field in several ways. The data featured in the different chapters enlarge the empirical database about collaborative work and written tasks providing information about research carried out in different countries (Australia, Germany, Indonesia, the US, Spain), with learners with different first languages (Arabic, Basque, Chinese, English, German, Japanese, Korean and Spanish) and learning English as a second or a foreign language and other foreign languages. This volume also includes studies in collaborative writing conducted with young learners, an under-researched cohort in research on collaborative writing (Storch 2013). The three chapters by Kos, Villarreal and Munarriz-Ibarrola and Villarreal, Bueno-Alastuey and Sáez-León report on studies conducted with adolescent and young learners collaborating in the completion of oral tasks and oral tasks that incorporate a written component. The empirical data in the chapters are analyzed from Vygotsky's Socio-cultural theory (Vygotsky 1978), Engeström's Activity Theory (Engeström 1990) and Conversation Analysis (Sidnell 2010).

Another contribution of the volume has to do with the analysis of factors that (de)motivate learners to collaborate face-to-face (FTF), online and in blended environments. As McDonough mentions in her foreword, teachers and researchers should not assume that learners will adopt a collaborative mode just because they are performing a collaborative task and, therefore, it is important to assess the variables that play a role. The chapters by Storch, Kos, Villarreal and Munárriz-Ibarrola, Aufa and Storch, Li and Cho consider some of those variables such as agency, attitudes, beliefs, goals, hesitation to provide peer feedback, mutuality, ownership, patterns of interaction, self-perceived and other-perceived roles.

The various chapters provide a wealth of examples showing the reader how learners use language when they collaborate to complete different types of tasks in diverse environments (FTF and online) in second and foreign language settings. They also offer insights about the effects of collaboration on language learning opportunities, operationalized as LREs, patterns of interaction, the nature of the learners' written product, grammatical knowledge, pragmatic competence and even on first language writing skills. Some of the chapters feature small scale studies or case studies (Geist and Hahn, González-Lloret, Li, and Cho) whose findings cannot be generalized but which provide interesting suggestions for further research on the basis of the results reported. As Storch (2013: 169) observed:

> Detailed microgenetic investigations of what transpires during collaborative writing activities can provide researchers with insights into how learning is happening and why learning may or may not happen during collaborative work. Such insights can be used to inform instructors on how to implement collaborative writing activities more effectively and thus improve learning outcomes

In her contribution "Collaborative writing: Promoting languaging among learners", **Storch** provides a critical review of research on collaborative writing. The review highlights that although collaborative writing may provide learners with opportunities for two forms of languaging (collaborative dialogue and private speech), it is collaborative dialogue that may be more conducive to L2 learning. The main focus of this chapter, however, is on factors that have been shown to impact on learners' languaging opportunities. These factors include both learner and context related factors. In this chapter, Storch focuses in particular on learners' sense of textual ownership, a construct that to date has received scant attention in L2 research. She then proposes a range of pedagogical strategies that may enhance learners' sense of ownership and thus encourage them to contribute to the task and engage with each other's contributions. These recommendations are important because, as Storch argues "[. . .] as researchers and teachers we need to consider how to implement collaborative writing tasks more effectively in order to maximize the learning opportunities these tasks afford to learners."

In Chapter 2 "The efficacy of collaboratively completing form-focused tasks: A research synthesis", **Scotland** examines both the designs and the findings of eleven studies that have explored whether collaborative work is more effective than individual work when employing form-focused tasks to promote the development of specific L2 grammatical features. The learning of grammar is central to language learning (Nassaji 2017) and recent research has pointed out the need for effective grammar pedagogy (Kasprowicz and Marsden 2018). Whether or not collaborative work is appropriate to facilitate the development of L2 grammar is worth investigating. Scotland used the following set of criteria in the selection of the studies analyzed: the study intentionally targeted at least one pre-specified grammatical feature, it had at least one participant group which worked collaboratively in pairs or small groups to complete at least one form-focused task, and potential gains in grammatical accuracy were measured using at least one pretest and at least one posttest. The author reviews those eleven research studies carried out from psychological or sociocultural perspectives, highlights some of their methodological limitations and suggests how those limitations could be addressed in future research. On the basis of his review and considering the methodological shortcomings found in previous research, we have to conclude that more studies are needed in order to be able to claim that form-focused tasks completed in collaboration lead to sustained gains in grammatical knowledge (Calzada and García Mayo 2020b).

The following six chapters focus on collaborative work in foreign language settings. They include empirical studies which illustrate how learners in this low-input setting, where few opportunities for meaningful language exchanges exist in and outside the school context, interact while completing tasks in collaboration both FTF, online or in a blended environment. In Chapter 3, "What exactly is mutuality? An analysis of mixed-age peer interaction on classroom tasks in German secondary schools", **Kos** investigates the oral interactions of 20 adolescent learners of English as a foreign language (EFL) in Germany in a mixed-age (MA) classroom, that is, a classroom composed of two or three different grades. He is interested in analyzing the construct of mutuality, defined by Storch (2002) as the level of engagement learners have with each other's contributions. The ten dyads were audio-recorded when interacting in regular classroom tasks completed collaboratively and which were part of a unit of work lasting two and a half months. The researcher also conducted interviews with the participants in their first language so that he could triangulate data from the audio-recordings and the interviews. Kos provides very detailed definitions of three levels of mutuality (high, moderate and low) identified in the learners' interactions and illustrates them with different excerpts. The findings indicate that most pairs engaged in interactions which were moderate or high on mutuality and that mutuality affected the number of LREs generated. This study contributes to refining the construct 'mutuality', in which social, cognitive and emotional dimensions intertwine and, suggests that multidimensional measures of engagement should be used to assess it (Philp and Duchesne 2016). Moreover, the interaction of the under-research population of teenagers in an MA classroom is documented in a longitudinal design and the relationship between the dyads' degree of mutuality and actual learning opportunities created during peer interaction is assessed.

In Chapter 4, ""Together we do better": The effect of pair and group work on young EFL learners' written texts and attitudes", **Villarreal and Munarriz-Ibarrola** consider the effects of type of learner setup (pair and small group) on learners' engagement (operationalized as LREs), the written output and the attitudes toward writing of 21 groups of 12–13 year old Basque-Spanish EFL learners. Collaboration among young foreign language learners is still an underexplored area in spite of the fact that this population has increased worldwide (Enever 2018). No study to date has examined how learner grouping affects the writing process of young learners, whether they engage in language-focused discussions and, if they do, how successful they are at solving them.

The participants wrote a narrative text individually (pre-test) and a week later a second narrative text in pairs or small groups of three, and their interactions were recorded for the analysis of LREs. They also completed a satisfaction questionnaire about writing, group work, collaborative work and the quality of the collaborative text. The researchers analyzed the written texts for accuracy, fluency, mechanics and lexical range and global scales. The findings showed that groups created more opportunities for discussing grammar and lexical issues but pairs arrived at more target-like solutions. Regarding the nature of the texts produced, pairs and small groups wrote better texts than individuals but learner setup had an impact on different constructs. Thus, writing in pairs led to greater fluency but writing in small groups led to better scores in lexical and grammatical accuracy and global scales. Regarding learners' attitudes to collaborative work, Villarreal and Munarriz-Ibarrola's findings supported those in previous research because these young leaners were very positive about the collaborative experience. As the authors state "Writing together is, therefore, an opportunity for the meaningful integration of the four skills that cannot be missed in F(oreign)L(language) settings."

Chapter 5, "The effect of collaborative writing on individual writing strategies. A case study of two L2 English writers", presents a case study of two German EFL learners taking a university language course at the language center of a large German university. The participants differed in their proficiency level in English (A2 and B2). **Geist and Hahn** offer a detailed qualitative analysis of the two learners' individual writing and problem-solving strategies at two points in time. The study focuses on how a collaborative writing experience influences the writing process of individuals rather than the co-authored written product. It seeks to answer the question of whether there is a transfer of composing strategies and focus on form from collaborative to individual writing tasks, and which aspects are transferred to individual writing. The research design was comprised of three writing tasks (individual, collaborative, individual) on different topics in the same genre. Document sharing technology with a recording facility was used to record the composing activity in both the individual and the collaborative writing sessions. In addition, the spoken interactions in the collaborative writing session were audio-recorded and stimulated-recall interviews were conducted after the individual writing sessions in order to gain deeper insights into composing strategies, the focus of LREs and the choice and use of problem-solving strategies. The data gathered were analyzed qualitatively with respect to observable effects of the collaborative writing task on the composing strategies of individuals. Areas of interest in the analysis include the individual phases of the writing process and composing strategies, including planning, monitoring, revising, noticing and focus on form (as demonstrated in LREs) and the use of problem-solving strategies. The findings showed that collaborative writing might not only influence the written product but that it may also influence L2 writing and problem-solving strategies relevant for individual writing. The findings of this small scale study identify areas worth of future investigation and the kind of research tools (e.g. think-aloud protocols) and design (longitudinal) to be used in such future studies.

In chapter 6, "Learner interaction in blended collaborative L2 writing activities", **Aufa and Storch** examine the patterns of interaction formed during the blended (FTF and online – Google Docs) collaborative prewriting activities of Indonesian EFL learners and the LREs generated during those activities. This study is the first to investigate the nature of collaboration when the collaborative writing activity is implemented in a blended approach. Over the course of a 16-week semester, 27 undergraduate students at a university in Indonesia completed six different text genres in three dyads and seven triads. The researchers collected qualitative data from classroom observation, recorded group talk, computer log files, and the jointly produced texts. Drawing on Storch's (2002) model and other studies on patterns of interaction in the online mode, the authors identified five typical patterns: collaborative, cooperative, facilitative/cooperative; facilitative/cooperative/cooperative and cooperative/passive/passive; all illustrated in detail in different excerpts in the chapter.

The findings showed that most groups displayed variations with regard to their patterns of interaction in the blended setting across modes. Most groups approached the task in the two modes differently: in the FTF the pairs and triads tended to form a cooperative pattern with one member taking a leading role and facilitating interaction, whereas in the online mode the pattern became cooperative or cooperative/passive/passive, with no member taking a leading role to move the task along. The collaborative pattern in both modes produced the highest number of LREs, that is, the pattern of interaction affected the quantity of LREs generated. Mode also impacted on the quantity and the resolution of LREs, with more frequent and correctly resolved LREs in the FTF mode than online, but not their focus, which was mainly lexical in both modes. The study showed that the mode and the interactional patterns the learners formed seemed to influence whether learners engaged in languaging.

In chapter 7 "Computer-based collaborative writing with young learners: Effects on text quality", **Villarreal, Bueno-Alastuey and Sáez-León** explored the effect of different groupings (individual vs. collaborative) and different writing modes (FTF vs. online) on the quality of texts written by 28 young (12–13) first year secondary school students. The researchers analyzed a total of 56 texts, which were assessed quantitatively for accuracy and fluency and qualitatively using holistic scales assessing content and language use. The findings point to a positive role of collaboration for accuracy, fluency and holistic measures and support the benefits of technology-based collaborative writing. As for mode, most of the results favored paper-based written texts, which were more accurate and had an overall better quality. The authors reflect on the possible lack of learner collaboration skills in the online mode and on how teachers should raise learner awareness of the increased opportunities for interactive and meaningful practices offered by technology-based collaborative writing.

Chapter 8 "Online collaboration through tasks for L2 pragmatic development" presents another study in a foreign language setting, this time with Spanish as a foreign language at a US university, but also considers tasks developed via synchronous text-based computer-mediated communication (CMC). Unlike other studies that have employed LREs as units of analysis, González-Lloret employs Conversational Analysis to analyze the interaction of two pairs of university students, one student from a US university and another from a Spanish university, and a group of three students (two from the US and one from Spain), while they engage in tellecollaboration. The US students were learners of L2 Spanish and the Spanish students were learners of L2 English. She presents a detailed analysis of how conversational closings change throughout the six weeks of the study and how they develop to be more similar to those of the expert speakers in the amount of turns, length, and sequential structure within the affordances of the medium. The study demonstrates how technology-mediated tasks can facilitate collaborative engagement that results in the development of the learners' L2 pragmatics, specifically, the study shows how L2 learners' closings change when interacting with an expert speaker in a telecollaborative online environment.

The two final chapters in the volume report on work carried out in English as a second language (ESL) contexts and they are both framed within an Activity Theory Perspective. In Chapter 9, "Participation and interaction in wiki-based collaborative writing: An Activity Theory Perspective", **Li** analyzes peer interaction and explains interconnected components (tools, rules, community, division of labor, objects and outcome) within a wiki group writing activity. Specifically, the chapter focuses on two small groups (each with three members) in an English for Academic Purposes course at a public university in the US. They jointly worked on two collaborative wiki writing tasks (research proposal and annotated bibliography) and were required to communicate in the L2. Li shows that the two groups demonstrated distinctive patterns of interaction: Expert/novice for Group A (mid-low equality, high mutuality) and cooperating-in-parallel (high equality, low mutuality) for Group B. She then discusses interconnected components that afford and/or constrain these ESL students' participation and learning, namely, mediating tools (wiki), object (collaboration in the wiki writing task), division of labor, rules (MLA formatting and no L1 allowed) and community, and identifies contradictions embedded in the system. Li concludes that the wiki proved to be a good tool allowing for L2 learning but that training is essential in computer-mediated collaborative writing so that students can take full advantage of technology.

In the final chapter, "Factors mediating small group interactions during synchronous web-based collaborative summary writings using Google Docs", **Cho** investigates why small group interactional patterns vary in the context of web-based collaborative writing. In her study she compares two separate synchronous modes of CMC to assess whether and how they foster different types of collaboration. The participants, six ESL learners (all from East Asia) divided into two groups of three members each, were recruited from an English debate club at a Canadian university. They collaboratively wrote debate summaries (about an hour each) three times using web-based tools: Google Docs and voice chat (Skype). All participants completed a one-hour stimulated-recall interview in which they commented on the collaboration process. Cho identifies collaborative and leader/participants patterns, although the former was predominant. She also examines how participant goals prompted different actions and individual goals influenced group interaction patterns. Moreover, she identifies five factors that mediated small group collaboration: voice chat, matching self-perceived and other-perceived roles, hesitation to provide peer-feedback, understanding of task requirements and task familiarity. Cho concludes by providing some insights for teachers who want to use web-based collaborative writing activities, including the concept of co-ownership.

The discussion and investigation of issues related to collaborative work will make this volume a worthy contribution to the current debates on the value of such a pedagogical approach for language learning, and will hence advance the research agenda. All the issues covered in the different chapters will appeal to a wide audience interested in second/foreign language learning and teaching, mainly to researchers, graduate (MA, Ph.D.) students, and stakeholders/educators. It will be of interest to researchers and students because further studies will be fostered by the contributions in the volume. Future investigations may also benefit from deploying different research tools to complement existing ones. These tools may include key stroke logging and eye tracking data (Leijter and Van Waes 2013; Li, Dursun and Hegelheimer 2017). The volume will also be of interest to stakeholders/educators because they will find ideas for pedagogical practice. In fact, a call for research-informed, evidence-based pedagogic recommendations is currently being made in the second language acquisition field (Boers 2017; Marsden and Kasprowicz 2017).

I am sincerely grateful to the series editor, Ulrike Jessner, and to the following colleagues for their invaluable help in reviewing the chapters in this volume: Rebeca Adams, Agurtzane Azkarai, Ana Fernández Dobao, Marta González-Lloret,

Mimi Li, Rosa M. Manchón, Katie Nielson, Caroline Payant, Rhonda Oliver, Julio Roca de Larios, Masatoshi Sato, Neomy Storch and Parvaneh Tavakoli. I am also grateful to the external reviewer for all the feedback provided. The financial support of the Basque Government (grant number IT904-16) and of the Spanish Ministerio de Economía y Competitividad (grant number FFI2016-79450-P, AEI/FEDER/EU) is hereby gratefully acknowledged.

References

Alegría de la Colina, Ana, and María del Pilar García Mayo. 2007. "Attention to Form across Collaborative Tasks by Low-proficiency Learners in an EFL Setting." In *Investigating Tasks in Formal Language Learning*, edited by María del Pilar García`Mayo, 91–116. Clevedon: Multilingual Matters.

Basterrechea, María, and María del Pilar García Mayo, 2013. "Language-related Episodes during Collaborative Tasks: A Comparison of CLIL and EFL Learners." In *Second Language Interaction in Diverse Educational Contexts*, edited by Kim McDonough and Alison Mackey, 25–43. Amsterdam: John Benjamins.

Boers, Frank. 2017. "Between Rigour and Reality." *Language Teaching Research* 22: 5–9.

Calzada, Asier and María del Pilar García Mayo. 2020a. "Child Learners' Reflections about EFL Grammar in a Collaborative Writing Task: When Form is not at Odds with Communication." *Language Awareness* https://doi.org/10.1080/09658416.2020.1751178

Calzada, Asier and María del Pilar García Mayo. 2020b. "Child EFL Grammar Learning through a Collaborative Writing Task." In *Languaging in Language Learning and Teaching*, edited by Wataru Suzuki and Neomy Storch, 19–40. Amsterdam: John Benjamins.

Donato, Richard, and James P. Lantolf. 1990. "The Dialogic Origins of L2 Monitoring." *Pragmatics and Language Learning* 1: 83–97.

Enever, Janet. 2018. *Policy and Politics in Global Primary English*. Oxford: Oxford University Press.

Engeström, Yrgö.1990. *Learning, Working, and Imagining: Twelve Studies in Activity Theory*. Helsinki, Finland: Orienta-Konsultit Oy.

García Mayo, María del Pilar. 2002. "The Effectiveness of Two Form-focused Tasks in Advanced EFL Pedagogy." *International Journal of Applied Linguistics* 12: 156–175.

García Mayo, María del Pilar. 2014. "Collaborative Tasks and Their Potential for Grammar Instruction in Second/Foreign Language Contexts", in *The Grammar Dimensions in Instructed Second Language Learning: Theory, Research and Practice*, edited by Alessandro Benati, Cécile Laval and María J. Arche, 82–102. London/New York: Continuum.

García Mayo, María del Pilar and Eva Alcón Soler. 2013. "Negotiated Input and Output Interaction", in *The Cambridge Handbook of Second Language Acquisition*, edited by Julia Herschensohn and Martha Young-Scholten, 209–229. Cambridge: Cambridge University Press.

García Mayo, María del Pilar and Agurtzane Azkarai. 2016. "EFL Task-based Interaction. Does Task Modality Impact on Langauge-related Episodes?, in *Peer Interaction and Second Language Learning. Pedagogical Potential and Research Agenda*, edited by Masatoshi Sato and Susan Ballinger, 241–266. Amsterdam: John Benjamins.

Imaz Agirre, Ainara and María del Pilar García Mayo. 2020. "The Impact of Agency in Pair Formation on the Degree of Participation in Young Learners' Collaborative Dialogue." In *Using Tasks in Diverse Contexts*, edited by Craig Lambert and Rhonda Oliver, 307–324. Bristol: Multilingual Matters.
Ishikawa, Masako. 2018. "Written Languaging, Learners' Proficiency Levels and L2 Grammar Learning." *System* 74: 50–61.
Kasprowicz, Rowena and Emma Marsden. 2018. "Towards Ecological Validity in Research into Input-based Practice: Form Spotting can Be as Beneficial as Form-meaning Practice. *Applied Linguistics* 39: 886–911.
Kim, Youjin. 2008. "The Contribution of Collaborative and Individual Tasks to the Acquisition of L2 Vocabulary." *The Modern Language Journal* 92:114–130.
Leijter, Mariëlle and Luuk Van Waes. 2013. Keystroke Loggin in Writing Research: Using Inputlog to Analyze and Visualize Writing Processes. *Written Communication* 3: 358–392.
Li, Zhi, Ahmet Dursun and Volvker Hegelheimer. 2017. Technology and L2 Writing. In *The Handbook of Technology and Second Language Teaching and Learning*, edited by Carol A. Chapelle and Shannon Sauro, 77–92. Hoboken, NJ: Wiley.
Loewen, Shawn and Masatoshi Sato. 2018. Interaction and Instructed Second Language Acquisition. *Language Teaching* 51: 285–329.
Long, Michael. H. 1983. "Native Speaker/Non-Native Speaker Conversation and the Negotiation of Comprehensible Input." *Applied Linguistics* 4: 126–141.
Long, Michael.H. 1996. "The Role of the Linguistic Environment in Second Language Acquisition", in *Handbook of Second Language Acquisition*, edited by William C. Ritchie and Tej K. Bathia, 413–468. New York, NY: Academic Press.
Manchón, Rosa M. 2011. *Learning-to-Write and Writing-to-Learn in an Additional Language*. Amsterdam: John Benjamins.
Marsden, Emma and Rowena Kasprowicz, R. 2017. "Foreign Language Educators' Exposure to Research: Reported Experiences, Exposure via Citations, and a Proposal for Action." *The Modern Language Journal* 101: 613–642.
Nassaji, Hossein. 2017. "Grammar Acquisition", in *The Routledge Handbook of Instructed Second Language Acquisition*, edited by Shawn Loewen and Masatoshi Sato, 205–223. New York: Routledge.
Philp, Jenefer and Susan Duchesne. 2016. "Exploring Engagement in Tasks in the Language Classroom." *Annual Review of Applied Linguistics* 36: 50–72.
Savignon, S. J. 1991. "Communicative Language Teaching: State of the Art." *TESOL Quarterly* 25: 261–277.
Schmidt, Richard. 1990. "The Role of Consciousness in Second Language Learning." *Applied Linguistics* 11: 192–196.
Sidnell, Jack. 2010. *Conversation Analysis: An Introduction*. London: Wiley-Blackwell.
Storch, Neomy. 2002. "Patterns of Interaction in ESL Pair Work." *Language Learning* 52: 119–158.
Storch, Neomy. 2013. *Collaborative Writing in L2 Classrooms*. Bristol: Multilingual Matters.
Storch, Neomy. 2016. "Collaborative Writing". In *Handbook of Second and Foreign Language Writing*, edited by Rosa M. Manchón and Paul K. Matsuda, 387–407. Berlin: De Gruyter.
Storch, Neomy. 2019. "Collaborative Writing". *Language Teaching* 52: 40–50.
Swain, Merrill. 2000. "The Ouput Hypothesis and Beyond: Mediating Acquisition through Collaborative Dialogue. In *Sociocultural Theory and Second Language Learning*, edited by James Lantolf, 97–114. Oxford: Oxford University Press.

Swain, Merrill. 2005. "The Output Hypothesis: Theory and Research". In *Handbook of Research in Second Language Teaching and Learning*, edited by Eli Heinkel, 471–483. Mahwah, NJ: Lawrence Erlbaum Associates.

Swain, Merrill. 2006. "Languaging, Agency and Collaboration in Advanced Language Proficiency. In *Advanced Language Learning: The Contribution of Halliday and Vygotsky*, edited by Heidi Byrnes, 95–108. New York: Continuum.

Swain, Merrill and Sharon Lapkin. 1998. "Interaction and Second Language Learning: Two Adolescent French Immersion Students Working Together". *The Modern Language Journal* 82: 320–337.

Vygotsky, Lev S. 1978. *Mind in Society: The Development of Higher Psychological Processes*. Cambridge, MA: Harvard University Press.

Neomy Storch
Collaborative writing: Promoting languaging among language learners

1 Introduction

Interest in collaborative writing tasks has increased over the past two decades, as a growing body of research (see review in Storch 2013, 2019a) has shown the language learning benefits of such tasks. This research has provided ample empirical evidence that collaborative writing tasks encourage second language (L2) learners to engage in deliberations about the target language, deliberations that have been referred to as *languaging*, as well as some evidence that such deliberations lead to language (and writing) development. This research has also identified some of the factors that may influence the quantity, quality and outcome of these deliberations. Therefore, what we need now is a greater understanding of these factors and to consider strategies that could promote languaging in order to maximise the language learning opportunities afforded by these tasks. In this chapter I focus on these factors and strategies, extending on previous discussions (Storch 2013, 2017) by drawing on more recent research in the field of L2 writing and beyond. In particular, I focus on learners' sense of ownership, an aspect of collaborative writing that to date has received scant attention.

The chapter begins with an overview of research on collaborative writing and its theoretical underpinnings. It then proceeds to critically discuss research on factors that have been identified as impacting on the occurrence and nature of languaging, including that of ownership. A discussion of a range of pedagogical strategies follows, including strategies that may promote among learners a sense of collective ownership which is germane to collaboration. In discussing these factors and strategies I also identify areas that need additional investigation. As such, the chapter seeks to address the interests of both L2 writing teachers and researchers.

2 An overview of research on collaborative writing

Collaborative writing is defined as the co-authoring of one text by two or more writers (for a more elaborate definition see Storch 2013). It is important to note

---

Neomy Storch, The University of Melbourne

https://doi.org/10.1515/9781501511318-002

that the distinguishing traits of this co-authoring activity is a sense of a shared responsibility and ownership of the text and hence substantive involvement of all co-authors in all the stages in the production of the joint text. This means that in creating the joint text, the co-authors need to negotiate and agree about what ideas to include, how to organise these ideas, and how best to express these ideas (see Niu 2009). Thus, collaborative writing by combining writing and communication throughout the text composing process offer second language (L2) learners not only the language learning benefits associated with writing tasks (e.g., slow pace, visible output, see Williams 2012) but also the benefits associated with speaking tasks (e.g., the availability of an audience and immediate feedback). In other words, collaborative writing may provide more opportunities for language learning than speaking or writing tasks alone.

Research interest in collaborative writing tasks has grown substantially in the past two decades (see Storch 2019a). In early research (e.g., Storch 2001, 2002), the collaborative writing activities took place in the physical classroom, with learners communicating with each other orally, face-to-face (FTF). In more recent research (e.g., see review in Li 2018 and studies reported in this volume), collaborative writing activities have been predominantly computer-mediated, using online platforms such as wikis and Google Docs. In computer-mediated collaborative writing, learners can communicate in written form via text chats, in oral form using voice chats, or a combination of both. There are now also emerging studies (see Aufa and Storch this volume) which combine FTF and computer mediated modes of interaction

Most of the research on collaborative writing has been informed by Vygotsky's (1978) sociocultural theory (SCT). This theory views development of all higher order human cognitive capacities, including language learning, as socially co-constructed. Development occurs in interaction between experts and novices, where the expert (e.g., parents, teachers, more knowledgeable peers) provides appropriate assistance to the novice. The provision of assistance is mediated by a range of tools. These tools can be material artefacts (e.g., computers, toys) or symbolic (e.g., gestures, language). For assistance to be appropriate and effective it needs to be dynamic and graduated, aligning with the novice's evolving capacities rather than existing capacities. The difference between these two types of capacities is encapsulated in the construct the Zone of Proximal Development (ZPD) and the carefully calibrated assistance has been referred to in the literature as *scaffolding* (Wood, Bruner, and Ross 1976). From a sociocultural perspective, learning is viewed as the internalization of socially co-constructed knowledge.

In L2 classrooms, Vygotsky's SCT and its focus on interaction has resonated with task based approaches to language instruction. Research on the nature of interaction in group and pair work soon revealed that assistance can also be provided by peers of similar L2 proficiency, whether adults (e.g., Ohta 2001, van Lier 1996) or younger learners (e.g., García Mayo and Lázaro 2015, see also studies in this volume). Furthermore, Donato (1994) found evidence of learners pooling their linguistic resources during small group work, in a process he labelled *collective scaffolding*. This process enables the learners to perform beyond their existing capacity. Thus in collaborative writing tasks, depending on the L2 proficiency of the co-authors, the assistance may be provided by more proficient peers or by peers of similar L2 proficiency but with different areas of relative expertise, with learners pooling their linguistic resources to co-construct new knowledge. Such pooling of expertise rests on the simple yet profound premise put forward by the philosopher Lévy (1997, 13–14) that "No one knows everything, everyone knows something, all knowledge resides in humanity".

The construct that has been used in research informed by SCT to describe task-based L2 interaction is *languaging* (see Suzuki and Storch 2020). Swain (2000, 2006), a leading sociocultural theorist, defines languaging as the act of using language as a tool to deliberate about and talk through a problem in order to solve the problem, including language related problems. In L2 classes, the language used as a tool can be the learners' first (L1) or second language. Swain distinguishes between two forms of languaging: *private speech* which is speech directed to oneself and which is therefore usually sub-vocal and *collaborative dialogue* which is vocalised other-directed speech. Swain (2006) argues that both forms of languaging are means of acquiring new knowledge or consolidating existing knowledge. In other words, languaging is where learning occurs.

In collaborative writing tasks both forms of languaging take place. However, because in collaborative writing private speech occurs in the presence of others, it is externalised; that is, it is audible and can thus elicit a peer response. This immediate source of potential assistance is one of the key advantages of collaborative writing compared to individual writing. Another advantage is that deliberations during collaborative writing can provide opportunities for learners to pool their linguistic resources and co-construct new knowledge – a process not available during individual writing. The following excerpts, taken from studies conducted in different L2 learning contexts, illustrate these distinct language learning advantages available during collaborative writing.

Excerpt 1 comes from a large scale study conducted by Fernández Dobao (2012) with intermediate learners of Spanish in the USA. The excerpt comes from the talk of a pair working collaboratively on a jigsaw task. The long pauses and repetitions in Line 1 suggest that Rosie is having difficulties remembering the word for ship in Spanish. Her vocalised deliberations (self-directed talk) culminate in a request for assistance. Tori responds, offering the equivalent L2 word but is uncertain (Line 2). Rosie then confirms that it is the correct L2 word (Line

3) and Tori agrees. The vocalised deliberations in the context of collaborative writing thus provided these students language learning opportunities: for Rosie the opportunity to learn a new word, for Tori the opportunity to consolidate her existing knowledge after receiving Rosie's positive feedback (confirmation).

Excerpt 1: Languaging triggered by a need for assistance

1	Rosie:	querían: e:h . . . e:h querían ir en un: ship? [they wanted eh . . . eh they wanted to go by: ship?]
2	Tori:	barco? [ship?]
3	Rosie:	barco! heh sí [ship! heh yes]
4	Tori:	sí [yes]

Excerpt 2 comes from the study by Rouhshad and Storch (2016), which was based on Rouhshad's PhD study conducted with ESL learners in a pre-university English for Academic Purposes (EAP) course. Here deliberations about language were triggered by an other-correction by Peter for verb choice (Line 2), followed by an other-correction by Shawn for verb form (Line 3). Peter initially seems uncertain about whether to accept the correction (Line 4), and Shawn then sounds out two forms of the verb (Line 5) – another example perhaps of private speech. Hearing the two alternative forms may have helped Peter to decide which is the correct form (Line 6), a decision accepted by Shawn (Line 7). The deliberations in this excerpt represent collective scaffolding (Donato 1994) where the two learners pool their linguistic resources to co-construct a correct resolution. The process leads to the production of a joint text that is perhaps more accurate than the version that either learner could have produced on his own.

Excerpt 2: Languaging and collective scaffolding

1	Shawn:	According to the reasons mentioned in the paragraph we can decide that
2	Peter:	Or, we have decide
3	Shawn:	We have decided
4	Peter:	Uhm
5	Shawn:	We have to decide, decided
6	Peter:	We have decided to release
7	Shawn:	Yeah

As these excerpts show, the two forms of languaging, self- and other-directed talk, occur in collaborative writing and it may not always be possible to clearly distinguish between the two. Moreover, these excerpts also suggest that other-directed forms of languaging provide learners with more opportunities for language learning than self-directed languaging. Vocalised deliberations by one learner in the pair may trigger peer feedback in the form of suggestions, explanations, confirmations as well as a pooling of resources. The extracts also show that the peer feedback offered during collaborative writing has a number of important characteristics that align with attributes of effective assistance (for a more detailed discussion see Storch 2019b). The feedback is timely and directly responsive to the learners' identified needs. It is also accessible, devoid of complex grammatical terminology and draws on a shared L1 when available. Moreover, the feedback is not only corrective but also positive (reassuring).

Research has shown that the resolutions learners reach during languaging episodes are predominantly correct (e.g., García Mayo and Imaz Agirre 2019, see also review in Storch 2013) and are remembered (Brooks and Swain 2009, Storch 2002). More importantly, a small number of studies have shown that the knowledge co-constructed during collaborative writing results in learning, including learning to write better texts (e.g., Bikowski and Withanage 2016, Shehadeh 2011) and language learning (e.g., Fernández Dobao 2014, Kim 2008, Storch 2002). As the excerpts above suggest, the interaction during collaborative writing can lead to new knowledge (Excerpt 1) and/or a consolidation of existing language knowledge (Excerpts 1 and 2).

However, it is important to note that the productive interactions depicted in these excerpts show all co-authors involved in the deliberations, working together through the problem encountered. This does not mean that simply assigning students to co-author a text will necessarily ensure that the learners will be willing to engage and contribute to the deliberations that arise. When humans interact, they do not merely exchange information, but also bring into the activity their agency; that is, their emotions, their goals, beliefs and desires and these affective factors will determine the kind of relationship they form. In my earlier research (Storch 2001, 2002) I reported on four distinct patterns of dyadic relationships which are distinguishable in terms of the learners' contribution and control over the task (termed equality) and engagement with each other's contribution (termed mutuality). These four patterns are: collaborative, dominant/dominant or cooperative, dominant/passive and expert/novice. What distinguished collaborative and expert/novice patterns from the other patterns is the high level of engagement with each other's contributions and more evidence of deliberations about language (i.e., languaging). Other studies, conducted in different L2 learning contexts, including collaborative writing implemented using online collaborative writing platforms such as wikis and Google Docs, found similar patterns (e.g., Bradley, Lindström, and Rystedt 2010; Li and Zhu 2017a, 2017b; Tan, Wigglseworth, and Storch 2010), as well as additional distinct patterns such as expert/passive (e.g., Watanabe and Swain 2007), dominant/withdrawn (Li and Zhu 2013), and dominant/defensive (Li and Zhu 2017a, 2017b). Furthermore, the names used to describe these patterns were slightly altered to capture patterns of interaction among small groups rather than pairs, as in the original Storch model (2002). For example, Li and Zhu (2017a, 2017b) distinguished between collaborative triads and collective triads. In the collective triad all three members participated fully in contributing and amending the joint wiki text; in the collaborative triad, only two of the three members collaborated.

Research on learner interaction in computer-mediated collaborative writing tasks suggests that learners are more likely to form cooperative rather than collaborative relationships. For example, studies in which the same learners engaged in collaborative writing tasks in FTF and computer mediated forms (e.g., Rouhshad and Storch 2016; Tan, Wigglesworth, and Storch 2010) reported more instances of cooperation than of collaboration. When learners cooperate, they tend to divide roles (e.g., composer, scribe) or divide the task and the joint text is an aggregate of individual contributions. Excerpt 3 (from Rouhshad and Storch 2016) depicts a cooperative pattern of interaction with a distinct division of labour: Tina dictated the text to Feri who acted as the scribe (e.g., Line 36, 38, 42). As the excerpt shows, and as found in the study, in a cooperative pattern there was little evidence of the two learners engaging with each other's suggestions or deliberating about language choices throughout the co-writing process. I believe that fleeting attention to language choice (e.g., Lines 39–42) does not accord with the definition of languaging (see Storch and Shuraidah 2020)

Excerpt 3: Cooperative relationship
36   Tina: I think the 3rd sentence is more clearly
               ok keep going
               and will continue her job once she is free
               delete "so she keep up to date"
37   Feri: I start to talk 2nd reason
38   Tina   Ok
               Stop
               2ndly . . . Ahhh wat is the 2nd reason
39   Feri: The personality?
40   Tina: Her good behavior
41   Feri: Oh

42	Tina	Whatever . . . . But briefly
		Ok 2nd the future
		Add 'the' . . .
		Spelling "moreOver"
		Full stop after mother

Patterns of interaction learners form when co-authoring a text, whether FTF or online, are important. There is now fairly convincing evidence (see review of studies in Storch 2013) that when learners collaborate or form expert/novice patterns of interaction (i.e., with high to medium levels of mutuality) they are more likely to engage in languaging and collective scaffolding. In other words, this research suggests that mutuality or level of engagement may be a more important trait than equality because of its impact on the nature of languaging (e.g., Li and Zhu 2013, 2017a, 2017b). Groups that collaborate have also been shown to be more likely to persist in trying to resolve their deliberations, drawing on all available resources (e.g., Kim and McDonough 2008; Li and Zhu 2013; Rouhshad and Storch 2016). This research also suggests that collaborative relationships are associated with a greater retention of the knowledge co-constructed during languaging (Storch 2002), with a greater learner satisfaction with the activity (e.g., Li and Zhu 2013; Watanabe 2008) and the production of better quality joint text (Li and Zhu 2017a).

The important question to consider, then, is what can explain why some learners form particular types of relationships and what encourages learners to engage in languaging with their peers. In the next section I review a number of factors, identified by a relatively small number of studies, that have attempted to explain observed learner behaviour when completing collaborative writing tasks, both in FTF and computer mediated modes. I also discuss in greater detail a factor that has hitherto received little L2 research attention, namely the sense of textual ownership that co-authors experience during collaborative writing activities.

3 Factors that may explain patterns of interaction and the nature of languaging

A number of factors have been identified in the literature as possibly explaining why some learners collaborate and others do not when assigned to work on a joint writing task, with a flow-on effect on the frequency and quality of languaging. These factors can be categorised as learner-related and task-related factors. Whereas learner related factors relate to the traits of the learners such as L2 proficiency, attitudes and goals; task related factors include variables concerning the design and implementation of collaborative writing tasks such as type of writing task and group composition (see also Storch 2013, 2017).

I begin with discussing learner-related factors which are perhaps more complex and require much more research attention, particularly the notion of ownership. Throughout this discussion, what becomes clear is that these factors are confounded by the mode of communication; that is, whether the collaborative writing tasks are implemented FTF or in the online mode.

3.1 Learner-related factors

A number of learner-related factors have been identified in the literature on collaborative writing. One such learner-related factor is the L2 proficiency of group members. Leeser's (2004) study was the first to consider the impact of the relative proficiency of learners forming pairs when completing a collaborative form-focused task (dictogloss). Using Language Related Episodes (LREs) (Swain and Lapkin 1998) to capture instances where learners attended to language choice, Leeser found that pairs composed of high proficiency learners generated the most LREs (and resolved these correctly), followed by mixed proficiency pairs. The smallest number of LREs was generated by pairs composed of low proficiency learners. These findings suggested that relatively low L2 proficiency learners should be paired with higher proficiency learners to maximise opportunities to language. However, subsequent studies have suggested that it is not only L2 proficiency which is an important factor in explaining the incidence of languaging in collaborative writing tasks, but the relationships learners form (e.g., Storch and Aldosari 2013) and the learners' perceived L2 proficiency (Watanabe and Swain 2007). For example, Storch and Aldosari (2013), in a study conducted in Saudi Arabia with English as a Foreign Language (EFL) students working on a range of collaborative writing tasks FTF, found that pairs composed of learners with similar L2 proficiency (high-high and low-low) were more likely to collaborate and engage in languaging than mixed proficiency pairs (high-low). Mixed proficiency pairs tended to form a dominant/passive relationship, with very little input by the passive (the low proficiency learner) and thus little incidence of languaging. In a study conducted with younger learners in a Spanish/English immersion program in the USA, Young and Tedick (2016) reported that groups of similar proficiency working collaboratively on reading and writing tasks, showed relatively equal contribution whereas in mixed proficiency groups, the less proficient learners were often marginalised and their contributions disregarded by their more proficient peers. The researchers found that in such mixed proficiency groups, instead of scaffolding there was relentless correction. Overall, what these findings suggest is that the impact of proficiency pairing on languaging is difficult to predict.

Learners' goals and attitudes to an activity they are assigned to complete seem to better explain why learners form a particular type of relationship and in turn the nature of languaging. In my study (Storch 2004), in-depth interviews with learners revealed that pairs who formed a collaborative or expert/novice relationship viewed the activity and peer feedback very positively and valued each other's suggestions. The collaborative pairs saw the activity as an opportunity to learn from each other; the novice in the expert/novice pair saw it as an opportunity to learn from the expertise of his more proficient partner. In contrast, learners who formed dominant/dominant and dominant/passive relationships preferred to write individually rather than in pairs and their goals were to complete this dispreferred activity quickly and expediently. Some were also driven by a desire to display their superior linguistic knowledge. Similar findings have since then been reported by a number of studies (e.g., Cho 2017; Li and Zhu 2017a, 2017b) where the collaborative writing activities were implemented online. Sato and Viveros (2016), who used the term collaborative mindset to capture learners' attitudes towards the task and their peers in a collaborative oral task, found that this mindset affected the learners' readiness to pay attention to and accept the peers' feedback. Interestingly, this attitude was also found to be more important than proficiency differences in explaining the learners' gains following the task performance.

Li and Zhu (2017b) attribute the formation of different patterns of interaction in wiki collaborative tasks not only to learners' goals but also to their sense of agency. Drawing on the work of Duff (2012), the researchers define agency as learners' ability to make choices whilst pursing their goals, and distinguish between individual and collaborative agency. Whereas individual agency drives the learner to take actions in pursuit of individual goals; collaborative agency drives a group towards a team goal. Li and Zhu observed that the group identified as pursuing group goals also had positive feelings about the activity. This reference to individual and collaborative agency seems closely related to notions of different forms of ownership, discussed in a number of research fields.

3.1.1 Ownership

The construct of ownership has received relatively little attention in research on L2 learning, including task based instruction and collaborative writing. This is somewhat surprising given that it features prominently in research on cooperative group work in psychology, organisational behaviour and higher education, particularly in investigations of wiki group work (e.g., Caspi and Blau 2011; Dawkins, Wei Tian, Newman, and Martin 2017; Pierce and Jussila 2010). In this literature, ownership is perceived as a psychological phenomenon with important emotional, attitudinal and behavioural effects. I note, however, that although there is much discussion in this literature of what ownership means and how it is manifested, there are no suggestions as to how to promote a sense of ownership that is conducive to successful group work.

Two forms of ownership have been identified: individual and collective ownership. Whereas collective ownership confers a desire to achieve a common set of goals or outcomes by members of a group who recognise each other's contribution and ownership of the cultivated object (e.g., co-authored text); individual ownership confers a feeling of individual territoriality and even superiority and a desire to achieve individual goals and self-efficacy (Pierce, Kostova, and Dirks 2001; Raban and Rafaeli 2007). Some of the markers of ownership are the choice of pronoun (i.e., we versus I), how suggestions are made, and the presence/absence of affective comments.

Collaborative writing, by its very definition, assumes a collective sense of textual ownership. It is this sense of collective ownership that encourages members of the pair or small group to contribute to the composing activity, to value each other's contribution and engage with these contributions; that is, to language. In pairs or small groups that form a collaborative or expert/novice pattern, this sense of collective or co-ownership is present, evident in the use of first person plural pronouns (e.g., Storch 2001, 2004), in learners' willingness to contribute to the task and offer assistance (Storch 2002), and in the positive comments often made during the activity and in post-task interviews about the experience of working collaboratively (e.g., Li and Zhu 2013, 2017a, 2017b; Storch 2004). For example, in Li and Zhu's study (2017b, 111), Feng who worked collaboratively reflected with pleasure about his experience of writing collaboratively with his group, noting that "we respect each other's work, we are very friendly."

In computer-mediated collaborative writing, the sense of collective versus individual ownership seems to manifest itself most clearly in whether learners edit the posted contributions of other members of the group and the nature of such editing changes. The literature on L1 collaborative writing reports quite extensively on learners' reluctance to amend the contributions of others and that such amendments are often discouraged and are not welcome (e.g., Lund 2008). Similar findings have been reported in a small number of L2 studies, with researchers noting a greater incidence of self-edits than other-edits (Elola and Oskoz 2010; Li and Zhu 2017a); that is, learners being more willing to amend their own contributions to the join text than the contributions made by other members of their small group. For example, in Li and Zhu's (2017a) study, whereas the members of the triad which worked as a collective edited their own and their peers' contributions; in the dominant/defensive pattern amendments were predominantly self-corrections (13 of the 14 corrections found in the data).

We also see evidence of this sense of individual ownership in the following excerpt from Cho's (2017) study, in which three ESL learners worked in a small group on a collaborative writing task using Google Docs. As Excerpt 4 shows, Joey seeks permission to amend the contribution Haru made to the joint text (Line 1). The request and hesitation (Line 3) suggest that Joey views Haru's contribution as being owned by Haru rather than being owned collectively. Joey amends the text only when permission is granted. The amendments made are minor and superficial and do not encourage the learners to language.

Excerpt 4: Evidence of individual ownership
1   Joey: Can I?
2   Haru: Yes!
3   Joey: Uh . . .
4   Haru: You can, you can edit
5   Joey: Yeah, edit here actually. Instead of the . . . we need comma here and yeah.
            [Text changes: 'A' to 'a' and replaces a period with a comma]
6   Haru: Okay

In studies which identified groups working collaboratively using wikis (e.g., Bradely, Lindström, and Rystedt, 2010; Li and Zhu 2017a, 2017b; Strobl 2014) or Google Docs (Steinberger 2017), the co-authors made direct amendments to the evolving text and this may suggest a sense of collective ownership. However, as Bradely, Lindström, and Rystedt (2010) noted, these direct amendments were not accompanied by instances of languaging. Despite the availability of chat and comment functions in these online platforms, learners seem reluctant to use these facilities to make counter-suggestions, provide explanations for amendments made, or offer positive feedback to the same extent as in FTF collaborative writing (see Rouhshad and Storch 2016). Yamuda's (2009) study may explain learners' reluctance to language in computer mediated collaborative writing. The study compared L2 learners' oral interaction in four groups: using videoconferencing, audioconferences, text chats with and without images. The study found that the presence of the partner's image seemed to motivate learners to communicate. Questionnaire data showed that learners perceived the combination of image displays and voice-based communication, available in videoconferencing, as playing an important role in enhancing their interaction because it provided them with the kind of non-verbal cues and the immediacy of vocalised responses found in FTF interaction. The lack of social presence in online collaborative writing platforms may explain why studies are continuing to report on learners' reluctance to participate in collaborative dialogue.

Admittedly, it may be that in computer-mediated collaborative writing learners engage in a self-directed form of languaging when providing or noting the changes made to the evolving text, but the incidence of such languaging is difficult to ascertain. More importantly, and as I noted earlier, self-directed forms of languaging may not provide the kind of rich learning opportunities that other-directed forms of languaging afford learners. As Excerpts 1 and 2 illustrated, languaging in the form of other-directed talk provides learners with opportunities to receive explanations, consider alternative suggestions and to build on each other's expertise. It is such episodes of languaging that are likely maximise language learning opportunities.

3.2 Task-related factors

In addition to learner-related factors, a number of task-related factors have also been identified in the literature as potentially influencing the incidence and quality of languaging. These task related factors may also influence learners' sense of ownership. One such task-related factor is the type of task. For example, Li and Zhu (2017b) in a study of collaborative writing using wikis found that their triads engaged in less interaction and attention to language on an annotated bibliography task requiring learners to summarise a set of studies than a research report task. Perhaps what can explain this observed learner behaviour is that an annotated bibliography lends itself to a division of labour, with each learner summarising an assigned study. Such a division of labour is likely to cultivate an individual sense of ownership and thus encourage self- rather than other-corrections. However, a number of studies have found that the same task may be successful in promoting languaging in FTF but ineffective when performed online (e.g., Baralt, Gurzynski-Weiss, and Kim 2016; Rouhshad and Storch 2016), suggesting that it is mode of communication that may have a greater impact on languaging than the type of task.

The size of the group may also have an impact on languaging. Fernández Dobao (2012) found more evidence of languaging in groups of four than in pairs, suggesting that larger groups may be better than pairs in terms of a greater pool of available linguistic resources. However, L2 researchers (e.g., Elola and Oskoz 2010; Kost 2011) still promote the use of small groups (from two to four members), even in online environments that can technically accommodate larger groups. The concern in larger groups is a diffusion in the sense of personal responsibility to the task, referred to in the literature on cooperative learning as social loafing (e.g., Johnson and Johnson 2009). It is perhaps also harder to cultivate a sense of collective textual ownership in larger groups. In Kessler and Bikowski's (2010) study, for example, the researchers found that in a very large group wiki project, learners shirked their responsibility to contribute to the task and there was very little evidence of languaging.

Group membership, both in terms of learners' familiarity with each other and the relative L2 proficiency of group members, is another important consideration and has implications for whether students should self-select or be allocated to the group by the teacher. In one of the few studies to investigate learners' preferences, Hassaskhah and Mosaffari (2015) reported that their learners expressed a strong preference for self-selecting group members. A number of researchers (e.g., Bikowski and Vithanage 2016; Li and Zhu 2017a, 2017b) indeed allow learners to self-select. However, the researchers admit that they then adjust the group membership to ensure some heterogeneity in L2 proficiency and L1 background, assuming that heterogeneity would encourage more interaction and languaging. What has not been investigated is the impact of self-selection and familiarity on learners' sense of ownership.

Given the importance of languaging for language learning, in the section that follows I suggest how teachers can encourage learners to engage in other-directed forms of languaging when implementing collaborative writing tasks, whether in FTF or in the computer mediated mode.

4 Strategies to encourage learners to language

A number of recommendations have been made in the literature about how to encourage learners to language (see review in Storch 2013, 2017; Bikowski and Vithanage 2016). These recommendations relate to how collaborative writing tasks should be implemented and assessed. In this section, I critically evaluate some of these recommendations and consider new strategies.

4.1 Implementation decisions

As mentioned in the previous section, group formation is an important factor to consider when implementing collaborative writing tasks. One decision concerns whether to allow learners to self-select their group members. One of the advantages of teacher allocation, particularly in second language contexts, is ensuring that the groups include students from different L1 backgrounds who need to use the shared L2 in order to communicate with each other. However, the advantage of self-selection is that familiarity between members of the group may promote a sense of collective ownership and thus a greater willingness to offer corrective feedback and contribute to languaging deliberations. Mozaffari (2017), one of the few studies to investigate the impact of the allocation factor, found that his Iranian EFL learners preferred collaborating with self-selected group members and there was more attention to language form in self-selected than teacher assigned pairs. However, the study also found that self-selected groups spent more time on off-task talk than teacher assigned pairs, a finding also reported by Garcia Mayo and Agirre (2019) with young L2 learners. A number of alternatives suggestions have been put forward, including allowing students to choose group members but providing students a set of guidelines (Bikowski and Vithanage 2016), or requiring students to change partners when implementing a series of collaborative writing tasks (Shehadeh 2011). However, the impact of these different group formation strategies on languaging and sense of ownership have not been investigated.

Groups may also be assigned or encouraged to select a leader (Arnold and Ducate 2006). The role of the leader is to monitor and facilitate the activity, encouraging all members of the group to contribute to the activity. However, Li and Zhu (2017a, 2017b), who deployed this strategy, reported that not all the groups, despite having a group leader, worked collaboratively. In the study by Young and Tedick (2016), mentioned earlier, the assigned leader seemed to exacerbate the power relationship in the group, often assuming a dominant teacher role and silencing students perceived to be less proficient. One other concern with having group leaders is that it may encourage cooperation rather than collaboration, with the group leader assigning sub-tasks or distinct roles (as reported in Li and Zhu 2017a, 2017b), thus encouraging learners to develop a sense of individual rather than collective ownership.

A novel way to encourage learners to participate more fully in collaborative writing tasks is to make them aware of their level of their contribution. For example, Cooperpad, developed by Liu, Calvo, Pardo and Martin (2015), continuously gathers and analyses group members' contributions to a collaborative writing task and the kind of changes (e.g., additions, deletion, copy/paste) they each make to the evolving text. This information is then presented visually, showing each participant's engagement intensity in comparison to other members of their group. Unlike other data visualisation tools such as DocuViz (Yim and Warschauer 2017), the advantage of Cooperpad is that it is a web-based system which provides a collaborative writing platform (with online chat and document creation tools, similar to Googe Docs) as well as data collection and visualisation tools all within the one system. The window on which the students compose their joint text displays in real time the individual engagement intensity of each member of their group. Liu, Liu and Liu's large scale study (2018) evaluated this tool. The study, conducted with Engineering students in China, compared students' engagement with and without access to Cooperpad. Using a range of engagement measures, the study found that groups that used Cooperpad showed greater engagement in the group writing tasks than groups without access to the tool. Data collected via a perception survey also found that the majority of the participants in the experimental group found that the engagement intensity information motivated them to participate more actively in the group writing task. The authors attribute their findings to the ability of Cooperpad to raise members' awareness of their group functioning and their individual contribution to the group's effort. In other words, the tool encouraged group members to develop a sense of responsibility to their group functioning and thus encouraged collective ownership. This is an interesting development and future research needs to investigate the use of this tool with different cohorts of L2 learners.

Augmenting collaborative writing tasks with collaborative processing of feedback may also enhance opportunities to language and encourage the formation of collective ownership. Such feedback can be provided by the teacher, by peers, or be computer generated. Studies that have investigated learners' collaborative processing of feedback they receive on their jointly written feedback (e.g., Brooks and Swain 2009; Storch and Shuraidah 2020; Storch and Wigglesworth 2010) suggest that this activity encourages learners to language, as they try to understand the intent of the feedback and the source of their errors. It may also encourage learners to develop a sense of collective ownership, as they decide whether to accept or reject the feedback provided on their joint text. To date studies that have extended the collaborative writing activity to include collaborative processing of feedback have been relatively few in number and small scale. They have also been conducted only in the FTF mode.

Above all, the implementation of collaborative writing tasks needs to be preceded by carefully designed training sessions. Such training sessions need to present students with information about the potential benefits of collaboration and languaging for learning, giving students opportunities to discuss any concerns they may have about the activities, and to include perhaps a model of collaborative dialogue (e.g., see Kim and McDonough 2011). Although pre-task training is at times mentioned by researchers who implement online collaborative writing tasks, (e.g. Bikowski and Vithanage 2016; Ducate, Lomicka

Anderson, and Moreno 2011), the nature of the training is not elucidated or tends to focus only on training students to use the functionalities of the online platform (e.g., Such 2019). A number of researchers acknowledge in discussing the limitations of their study that their learners needed more training in collaboration, given that learners are often not familiar with such tasks (e.g., Bikowski and Vithanage 2016; Such 2019). In a study by Lin and Kesley (2009) conducted in an L1 context, it was only after the researchers provided more systematic instructions about how learners should engage with each other's contributions that the participating students were observed to interact more effectively with their peers in the wiki project.

Learners' readiness to engage in languaging may require not only training but also time. For example, Bikowski and Vithanage (2016) observed that of their nine groups, five could be labelled as 'budding collaborators' who needed to overcome their initial difficulties and tendencies to work independently rather than collaboratively. The sense of individual ownership is well entrenched in our education system, and encouraging collective ownership may take time to develop. Thus it is also important not only to train students but also to implement collaborative writing activities on more than one occasion.

4.2 Assessment decisions

Different approaches to assessing collaborative writing activities may also work to encourage learners to not only contribute to the text but also to language. A number of such suggestions are discussed by Storch (2013, 2017). For example, one suggestion is to award students grades not only for their contribution to the joint text but also for their engagement with each other's contribution. The use of Cooperpad may facilitate such a grading scheme. Another suggestion is a grading scheme which combines a grade for individual contributions and a group grade for the quality of the joint text. For example, Such (2019), in a study conducted in the USA with college ESL learners working in small groups on a series of collaborative writing tasks using wikis, used an assessment rubric that included criteria such as the presence of group discussions, the cohesiveness of the final product, as well as the length and accuracy of the text produced. However, despite the use of these assessment criteria, the study found that collaboration was inconsistent over time, and that all groups experienced problems with participation. The assessment rubrics did not seem to cultivate among the learners a sense of collective ownership. The learners seemed to communicate with each other only because the assignment required them to do so. The researcher attributes these findings to the lack of familiarity of the learners with each other and with collaborative writing tasks, lending support for suggestions made earlier concerning group formation. Clearly more research is needed about the impact of different assessment schemes on learners' sense of ownership, contributions and willingness to engage with each other's contributions.

5 Concluding remarks and research directions

The pedagogical rationale for implementing collaborative writing tasks in L2 classes is that these tasks encourage learners to language; that is, to engage in deliberations about language with their peers, and that languaging is a site for language learning. However there is evidence that not all learners engage in languaging when completing collaborative writing tasks, and that a number of learner and task related factors affect whether and to what extent learners engage in languaging. One such under-researched factor is that of the sense of ownership learners experience when working in pairs or small groups, whether FTF or in computer mediated mode, on collaborative writing tasks. As researchers and teachers we need to consider how to implement collaborative writing tasks more effectively in order to maximise the learning opportunities these tasks afford learners.

In this chapter I considered a number of suggested strategies that may encourage learners to engage in languaging. However, many of these suggestions have not been sufficiency investigated. More pedagogically driven research is now needed to assess the efficacy of these suggested strategies. Such research needs to be conducted in a range of educational settings and with different cohorts of learners, because what may be effective for adult L2 learners may not be appropriate for younger learners. Such investigations need to be conducted particularly in computer mediated collaborative writing tasks, as this is where we observe an absence of a shared sense of ownership and a reluctance to offer peer feedback and to engage in languaging and yet this is the mode that is increasingly adopted in many writing (L1 and L2) classes.

References

Arnold, Nike, and Lara Ducate. 2006. "Future Foreign Language Teachers' Social and Cognitive Collaboration in an Online Environment." *Language Learning & Technology* 10 (2006): 314–342.

Baralt, Melissa, Laura Gurzynski-Weiss, and Youjin Kim. 2016. "Engagement with the Language: How Examining Learners' Affective and Social Engagement Explains Successful Learner-generated Attention to Form." In *Peer Interaction and Second Language Learning: Pedagogical Potential and Research Agenda*, edited by Masatoshi Sato and Susan Ballinger, 209–240. Amsterdam/Philadelphia: John Benjamins.

Bikowski, Dawn, and Ramyarshani Vithanage. "Effects of web-based collaborative writing on individual L2 writing development." *Language Learning & Technology* 20 (2016): 79–99.

Bradley, Linda, Berner Lindström, and Hans Rystedt. 2010. "Rationalities of Collaboration for Language Learning in a Wiki." *ReCALL* 22: 247–265.

Brooks, Lindsay, and Merrill Swain. 2009. "Languaging in Collaborative Writing: Creation and Response to Expertise." In *Multiple Perspectives on Interaction in SLA*, edited by Alison Mackey and Charlene Polio, 58–89. Mahwah, NJ: Lawrence Erlbaum.

Caspi, Avner, and Ina Blau. 2011. "Collaboration and Psychological Ownership: How does the Tension between the Two Influence Perceived Learning?" *Social Psychology of Education*, 14: 283–298.

Cho, Hyeyoon. 2017. "Synchronous Web-based Collaborative Writing: Factors Mediating Interaction among Second-Language Writers." *Journal of Second Language Writing* 36: 37–51.

Dawkins, Sarah, Amy Wei Tian, Alexander Newman, and Angela Martin. 2017. "Psychological Ownership: A Review and Research Agenda." *Journal of Organizational Behavior* 38: 163–183.

Donato, Richard. 1994. "Collective Scaffolding in Second Language Learning." In *Vygotskian Approaches to Second Language Research*, edited by James P. Lantolf and Gabriela Appel, 33–56. Norwood, NJ: Ablex.

Ducate, Lara, Lara Lomicka Anderson, and Nina Moreno. 2011. "Wading through the World of Wikis: An Analysis of Three Wiki Projects." *Foreign Language Annals* 44: 495–524.

Duff, Patsy. 2012. "Identity, Agency, and SLA. In *Handbook of Second Language Acquisition*, edited by Alison Mackey and Susan Gass, 410–426. London, UK: Routledge.

Elola, Idoia, and Ana Oskoz. 2010. "Collaborative Writing: Fostering Foreign Language and Writing Conventions Development." *Language Learning and Technology* 14: 51–71.

Fernández Dobao, Ana. 2012. "Collaborative Writing Tasks in the L2 Classroom: Comparing Group, Pair, and Individual Work." *Journal of Second Language Writing* 21: 40–58.

Fernández Dobao, Ana. 2014. "Vocabulary Learning in Collaborative Tasks: A Comparison of Pair and Small Group work." *Language Teaching Research* 18: 497–520.

García Mayo, María del Pilar, and Ainara Imaz Agirre. 2019. "Task Modality and Pair Formation Method: Their Impact on Patterns of Interaction and Attention to Form among EFL Primary School Children." *System* 80: 165–175.

García Mayo, María del Pilar, and Amparo Lázaro. 2015. "Do Children Negotiate for Meaning in Task-based Interaction? Evidence from CLIL and EFL Settings." *System* 54: 40–54.

Hassaskhah, Jaleh, and Hamideh Mozaffari. 2015. "The Impact of Group Formation Method (Student-selected vs. Teacher-assigned) on Group Dynamics and Group Outcome in EFL Creative Writing." *Journal of Language Teaching and Research* 6: 147–156.

Johnson, David, and Roger Johnson. 2009. "An educational psychology success story: Social interdependence theory and cooperative learning." *Educational Researcher* 38: 365–379.

Kessler, Greg, and Dawn Bikowski. 2010. "Developing Collaborative Autonomous Learning Abilities in Computer Mediated Language Learning: Attention to Meaning among Students in Wiki Space." *Computer Assisted Language Learning* 23: 41–58.

Kim, Youjin. 2008. "The contribution of collaborative and individual tasks to the acquisition of L2 vocabulary." *The Modern Language Journal* 92: 114–130.

Kim, Youjin, and Kim McDonough. 2008. "The Effect of Interlocutor Proficiency on the Collaborative Dialogue between Korean as a Second Language Learners." *Language Teaching Research* 12: 211–234.

Kim, Youjin, and Kim McDonough. 2011. "Using Pretask Modelling to Encourage Collaborative Language Learning Opportunities." *Language Teaching Research* 15: 183–199.

Kost, Claudia. 2011. "Investigating Writing Strategies and Revision Behaviour in Collaborative Writing Projects." *CALICO Journal* 28: 606–620.

Leeser, Michael. 2004. "Learner proficiency and focus on form during collaborative dialogue." *Language Teaching Research* 8: 55–81.

Lévy, Pierre. 1997. *Collective intelligence: Mankind's emerging world in cyberspace.* New York: Plenum Publishing Corporation.

Li, Mimi. 2018. "Computer-mediated collaborative writing in L2 contexts: An analysis of empirical research." *Computer Assisted Language Learning* 31: 882–904.

Li, Mimi, and Wei Zhu. 2013. "Patterns of Computer-mediated Interaction in Small Writing Groups using Wikis." *Computer Assisted Language Learning* 26: 61–82.

Li, Mimi, and Wei Zhu. 2017a. "Good or Bad Collaborative Wiki Writing: Exploring Links between Group Interactions and Writing Products." *Journal of Second Language Writing* 35: 38–53.

Li, Mimi, and Wei Zhu. 2017b. "Explaining Dynamic Interactions in Wiki-based Collaborative Writing." *Language Learning & Technology* 21: 96–120.

Lin, Hong, and Kathleen Kesley. 2009. " Building a Networked Environment in Wikis: The Evolving Phases of Collaborative Learning in a Wiki Book Project." *Journal of Educational Computing Research* 40:145–169.

Liu, Ming, Leping Liu, and Li Liu. 2018. "Group awareness increases student engagement in online collaborative writing." *The Internet and Higher Education* 38: 1–8.

Liu, Ming, Rafael Calvo, Abelardo Pardo, and Andrew Martin. 2015. "Measuring and visualising students' behavioural engagement in writing activities." *IEEE Transactions on Learning Technologies* 82: 215–224.

Lund, Andreas, 2008. "Wikis: A Collective Approach to Language Production.*" ReCALL* 20: 35–54.

McDonough, Kim, William Crawford, and Jindarat De Vleeschauwer. 2016. "Thai EFL learners' interaction during collaborative writing collaborative writing" tasks and its relationship to text quality." In *Peer Interaction and Second Language Learning: Pedagogical Potential and Research Agenda*, edited by Masatoshi Sato and Susan Ballinger, 185–208. Amsterdam/Philadelphia: John Benjamins.

Mozaffari, Hamideh. 2017. "Comparing Student-selected and Teacher-assigned Pairs on Collaborative Writing." *Language Teaching Research* 21: 496–516.

Niu, Ruiying. 2009. "Effect of Task-inherent Production Modes on EFL Learners' Focus on Form." *Language Awareness* 18: 384–402.

Ohta, Amy. 2001. *Second Language Acquisition Processes in the Classroom. Learning Japanese*. Mahwah, NJ: Lawrence Erlbaum.

Pierce, Jon, and Iiro Jussila. 2010. "Collective Psychological Ownership within the Work and Organizational Context: Construct Introduction and Elaboration." *Journal of Organizational Behavior* 31: 810–834.

Pierce, Jon, Tatiana Kostova, and Kurt Dirks. 2001. "Toward a Theory of Psychological Ownership in Organizations." *Academy of Management Review* 26: 298–310.

Raban, Daphne, and Sheizaf Rafaeli. 2007. "Investigating Ownership and the Willingness to Share Information Online." *Computers in Human Behaviour* 23: 2367–2382.

Rouhshad, Amir, and Neomy Storch. M 2016. "A focus on mode: Patterns of Interaction in Face-to-Face and Computer-mediated Modes." In *Peer Interaction and Second Language Learning: Pedagogical Potential and Research Agenda*, edited by Masatoshi Sato and Susan Ballinger, 267–290. Amsterdam/Philadelphia: John Benjamins.

Sato, Masatoshi, and Paula Viveros. 2016. "Interaction for Collaboration? Group Dynamics in the Foreign Language Classroom." In *Peer Interaction and Second Language Learning: Pedagogical Potential and Research Agenda*, edited by Masatoshi Sato and Susan Ballinger, 91–112. Amsterdam/Philadelphia: John Benjamins.

Shehadeh, Ali. 2011. "Effects and Student Perceptions of Collaborative Writing in L2." *Journal of Second Language Writing* 20: 286–305.

Steinberger, Franz. 2017. Synchronous Collaborative L2 Writing with Technology. Interaction and Learning. Unpublished PhD dissertation, Ludwig-Maximillians University, Munich, Germany.

Storch, Neomy. 2001. "How Collaborative is pair work? ESL Tertiary Students Composing in Pairs." *Language Teaching Research* 5: 29–53.

Storch, Neomy. 2002. "Patterns of Interaction in ESL pair work. " *Language Learning* 52: 119–158.

Storch, Neomy. 2004. "Using Activity Theory to Explain Differences in Patterns of Dyadic Interactions in an ESL class." *The Canadian Modern Language Review* 60: 457–480.

Storch, Neomy. 2013. *Collaborative Writing in L2 Classrooms*. Bristol, UK: Multilingual Matters.

Storch, Neomy. 2017. "Implementing and Assessing Collaborative Writing Activities in EAP Classes." In *Teaching Writing for Academic Purposes to Multilingual Students: Instructional Approaches*, edited by John Bitchener, Neomy Storch and Rosemary Wette, 130–144. New York & London: Routledge.

Storch, Neomy. 2019a. "Time Line on Collaborative Writing." *Language Teaching* 52: 40–59.

Storch, Neomy. 2019b. "Collaborative Writing as Peer Feedback." In *Feedback in Second Language Writing: Contexts and Issues (2nd Ed)*, edited by Ken Hyland and Fiona Hyland, 143–162. Cambridge: Cambridge University Press.

Storch, Neomy, and Ali Aldosari. 2013. "Pairing Learners in Pair-work Activity." *Language Teaching Research* 17: 31–48.

Storch, Neomy, and Ali Shuraidah. 2020. "Languaging when providing and processing peer feedback." In *Languaging in language learning and teaching: A collection of empirical studies*, edited by Wataru Suzuki and Neomy Storch. 111–128. Amsterdam,: John Benjamins.

Storch, Neomy, and Gillian Wigglesworth. 2010. "Learners' processing, uptake and retention of corrective feedback on writing: Case studies." *Studies in Second Language Acquisition* 32: 303–334.
Strobl, Carola. 2014. "Affordances of Web 2.0 Technologies for Collaborative Advanced Writing in a Foreign Language." *CALICO Journal* 31: 1–18.
Such, Brenda. 2019. "Scaffolding English language learners for online collaborative writing activities." *Interactive Learning Environments*. DOI: 10.1080/10494820.2019.1579233
Suzuki, Wataru, and Neomy Storch. 2020. "Introduction." In *Languaging in language learning and teaching: A collection of empirical studies*, edited by Wataru Suzuki and Neomy Storch. 1–15. Amsterdam: John Benjamins.
Swain, Merrill. 2000. "The Output Hypothesis and Beyond: Mediating Acquisition through Collaborative Dialogue." In *Sociocultural Theory and Second Language Learning*, edited by James Lantolf, 97–114. Oxford: Oxford University Press.
Swain, Merrill. 2006. "Languaging, Agency and Collaboration in Advanced Second Language Learning." In *Advanced Language Learning: The Contributions of Halliday and Vygotsky*, edited by Heidi Byrnes, 95–108. London, UK: Continuum.
Swain, Merrill, and Sharon Lapkin. 1998. "Interaction and second language learning: two adolescent French immersion students working together." *The Modern Language Journal* 82: 320–337.
Tan, Liana, Gillian Wigglesworth, and Neomy Storch. 2010. "Pair interaction and Mode of Communication: Comparing Face-to-Face and Computer Mediated Communication." *Australian Review of Applied Linguistics* 33: 1–24.
Van Lier, Leo. 1996. *Interaction in the Language Curriculum: Awareness, Autonomy and Authenticity*. London: Longman.
Vygotsky, Lev. 1978. *Mind in Society: The Development of Higher Psychological Processes*. Cambridge: Harvard University Press.
Watanabe, Yuko. 2008. "Peer-peer Interaction between L2 Learners of Different Proficiency Levels: Their Interaction and Reflections." *The Canadian Modern Language Review* 64: 605–635.
Watanabe, Yuko, and Merrill Swain. 2007. "Effects of Proficiency Differences and Patterns of Pair Interaction on Second Language Learning: Collaborative Dialogues between Adult ESL Learners." *Language Teaching Research* 11: 121–142.
Williams, Jessica. 2012. "The potential role(s) of writing in second langauge development." *Journal of Second Langauge Writing* 21: 321–331.
Wood, David, Jerome Bruner, and Gail Ross. 1976. "The Role of Tutoring in Problem-solving." *Journal of Child Psychology and Psychiatry and Allied Disciplines* 17: 89–100.
Yamuda, Masanori. 2009. "The role of social presence in learner-centered communicative language learning using synchronous computer-mediated communication: Experimental study." *Computers & Education* 52: 820–833.
Yim, Soobin, and Mark Warschauer. 2017. "Web-based collaborative writing in L2 contexts: Methodological insights from text mining." *Language Learning & Technology* 21: 146–165.
Young, Amy. I. and Diane J. Tedick. 2016. "Collaborative Dialogue in a Two-way Spanish/English Immersion Classroom: Does Heterogeneous Grouping Promote Peer Linguistic Scaffolding?" In *Peer Interaction and Second Language Learning: Pedagogical Potential and Research Agenda*, edited by Masatoshi Sato and Susan Ballinger, 135–160. Amsterdam: John Benjamins.

James Scotland
The efficacy of collaboratively completing form-focused tasks: A research synthesis

1 Introduction

This chapter is a research synthesis. It explores the designs and the results of the small number of second language acquisition (SLA) studies which have attempted to investigate completing form-focused tasks collaboratively and the longer-term learning of specific grammatical features. This chapter is intended to help the reader to make better sense of the current research which pertains to how efficient it is to complete tasks in collaboration for form-focused targets.

Numerous studies have shown how collaboratively completing form-focused tasks provides learners with cognitive spaces in which they can contribute to the resolution of grammatical problems, co-construct new linguistic knowledge, and gain access to a larger pool of knowledge and resources (e.g., De Guerrero and Villamil 2000; Donato 1994; Fernández Dobao 2012, 2014; Storch 1999, 2007; Swain 2000). Participating in such spaces is then expected to result in more accurate language use in subsequent individual performance. However, expectations of learning need to be empirically verified. When it comes to participating in the collaborative completion of form-focused tasks, there is currently limited empirical evidence on learners' retention of grammatical knowledge; nevertheless, some evidence does exist.

The study eligibility criteria revolve around meeting the experimental condition of working in collaboration with peers as well as the measurement of learning gains for a form-focused target. Specific criteria for selection are as follows: the study intentionally targeted at least one pre-specified grammatical feature, contains at least one participant group which worked collaboratively in pairs or small groups to complete at least one form-focused task, and potential gains in grammatical accuracy were measured using at least one pretest and at least one posttest. Here, a form-focused task is operationalized as a task which is meaning orientated but is given to learners with the intent of increasing their awareness of at least one pre-specified grammatical form; examples include: cloze, dictogloss, jigsaw, and text-editing. Due to their lexico-grammatical nature, studies which have used phrasal verbs as their target structure are included in this review. Excluded in this review are studies which have explored the learning of grammar

James Scotland, Qatar University

https://doi.org/10.1515/9781501511318-003

during collaborative tasks but did not trace retention beyond the limits of interaction through the use of posttest instruments (e.g., Fernández Dobao 2014; García Mayo 2002a, 2002b; Storch 1999). Also excluded are studies which employed a dyad-specific posttest but not in conjunction with a pretest. This is because designs without a pretest are considered to be pre-experimental, and as such, they do not provide evidence of cause-effect relationships (Cohen, Manion and Morrison 2007, 283). Further exclusions include studies which explored the retention of co-constructed knowledge but did not focus exclusively on grammatical forms (e.g., Shehadeh 2011; Swain and Lapkin 1998). Finally, study quality was not a criterion for study eligibility. The studies included in this review are: Adams (2007), Adams, Nuevo, and Egi (2011), Eckerth (2008), Kuiken and Vedder (2002), Lapkin, Swain, and Smith (2002), McNicoll and Lee (2011), Nassaji and Tian (2010), Reinders (2009), Spielman-Davidson (2000), Swain and Lapkin (2001), and Teng (2017). Although eleven studies are not enough to provide any definitive conclusions (Norris and Ortega 2006), exploring patterns within the current findings is a first step in ascertaining the efficiency of completing tasks in collaboration for form-focused targets; additionally, and perhaps more importantly, highlighting methodological weaknesses within the current body of knowledge should help to stimulate and improve the quality of future research in this area.

Previous research has been conducted from two distinct epistemological perspectives. The interactionist approach is located within a psycholinguistic perspective of language learning. As well as drawing upon the work of other researchers, the most recent version of the interactionist approach has its roots in Krashen's Input Hypothesis (Krashen 1977, 1980), Long's Interaction Hypothesis (Long 1983, 1985, 1996), Swain's Output Hypothesis (Swain 1985, 1993), and Schmidt's Noticing Hypothesis (Schmidt 1990, 1993). Storch (2013, 7) explains that in theories which are located within an interactionist approach, "the learner's existing mental capacity is the source of their own learning". Thus, interactionist research focuses "on what triggers learner internal cognitive processes" (Storch 2013, 7). The core components of the interactionist approach are "interactionally modified input, having the learner's attention drawn to his/her interlanguage and to the formal features of the L2, opportunities to produce output, and opportunities to receive feedback" (Mackey, Abbuhl, and Gass 2012, 10). Conversation repair acts which occur as a result of some kind of communication breakdown are deemed to be especially beneficial for L2 development. Theories which are located within an interactionist approach focus on "how learner-internal cognitive mechanisms (such as attentional control and working memory capacity) mediate the relationship between interaction and L2 learning [italics in original]" (Mackey, Abbuhl, and Gass 2012, 10).

The sociocultural approach has its roots in the work of Lev Semenovich Vygotsky (1896–1934). From a sociocultural perspective, social interaction is the primary source of an individual's mental development, and individuals need to internalize the concepts and processes which are embodied within socially rooted speech (Vygotsky 1978). Consequently, the sociocultural approach focuses on how knowledge and mental processes, including those which pertain to language learning, which are initially social become internalized by an individual (Lantolf and Thorne 2006). SLA researchers which have adopted a sociocultural approach have tended to investigate "how the use of language in social interaction mediates language learning" (Storch 2013, 7). These investigations have centered around how "[l]anguage functions as a tool for thinking as well as communication" (Philp, Adams, and Iwashita 2014, 23), including how language is used by learners as a psychological cognitive tool with which to organize and structure their thinking (Alegría de la Colina and García Mayo 2009; Antón and DiCamilla 1999; Gánem-Gutiérrez 2008; Swain and Lapkin 1998); how language is used by more capable others to enable learners move from assisted performance towards independent performance (De Guerrero and Villamil 2000; Donato 1994); and how language is used by learners to collaboratively solve problems and build knowledge (Ohta 1995; Swain 2000; Swain and Lapkin 2002). As well as focusing on language use, research framed using a sociocultural approach has also focused on how activity and practice appear in a learner's own performance and how those activities are internalized and automated over time (Brooks, Swain, Lapkin and Knouzi 2010). A sociocultural approach to second language research primarily revolves around how knowledge and mental process manifest themselves in shared social activity before being internalized by a learner. This synthesis includes studies from both epistemological domains of the interactionist approach and the sociocultural approach.

The first part of this synthesis is interrogative. It summarizes each of the selected studies and then reflects on their findings. The second part of this synthesis is more critical. It highlights some of the methodological limitations inherent within the existing research and suggests how they could be addressed.

2 The current body of research

The designs and results of the eleven studies which together form the current body of knowledge are now summarized. A general summary of each study is given to avoid commenting on decontextualized methodologies and findings. As well as attempting to measure learning gains, many of these studies contain additional elements, for example an analysis of the learners' interactions. However, exploring these elements is beyond the scope of this chapter.

Although some of the selected studies share variants of the same task type, they have used different terminology. In this chapter, text reconstruction (Eckerth 2008; McNicoll and Lee 2011; Reinders 2009) and writing task (Teng 2017) will be referred to as a dictogloss task (Wajnryb 1990); and text repair task (Eckerth 2008; McNicoll and Lee 2011), reconstruction editing (Nassaji and Tian 2010), and editing task (Teng 2017) will be referred to as a text-editing task.

2.1 Eleven studies

Spielman-Davidson (2000) employed a Vygotskian sociocultural lens to investigate whether completing tasks collaboratively led to greater gains in linguistic accuracy in comparison to completing a regular classroom curriculum. French conditionals were targeted. Two samples of eight students took part in the study. All were between 13–14 years old, spoke English as their L1, and were studying in French in an immersion setting in Canada. After the initial pretest, the experimental group completed twelve treatment sessions over a four-week period. The treatment sessions, which were audio-recorded, consisted of explicit grammatical instruction, two main writing activities, peer editing, a comic strip, and two dictogloss tasks. The comparison group "received their teacher's regular instruction based upon his 17 years of experience" (Spielman-Davidson 2000,41).Testing consisted of a cloze test, a paragraph writing task, and an interview. The experimental group also received tailor-made test items designed to assess the learning of the forms which participants had received feedback on during their interactions. Spielman-Davidson's (2000, 53) tailor-made test items took the form of grammaticality judgement tests, and were administered in weeks three, four, and five. After the treatment ceased, an immediate posttest was given; the delayed posttest took place eleven weeks later. In the delayed posttest, the experimental group completed a fourth tailor-made posttest created with items from the three previous tailor-made tests (Spielman-Davidson 2000, 53). An analysis of covariance found a statistically significant difference between the pretest and posttest results in favour of the experimental group on the paragraph writing task and the interview. Additionally, Spielman-Davidson (2000) found the experimental group correctly answered between 81–87% of the tailor-made posttest items. No statistically significant differences were found between the pretests and the delayed posttests of the two groups. By attempting to link peer dialogues to the learning of a linguistic feature over a relatively long duration, Spielman-Davidson's (2000) study represents a starting point in the attempt to empirically verify the belief that collaboratively completing form focused tasks results in the longer-term retention of grammatical knowledge.

Drawing upon the concepts of the output hypothesis and collaborative dialogue (Swain 2000), Swain and Lapkin (2001) were interested in better understanding which task types provided a greater focus on form (Swain and Lapkin 2001). French pronominal verbs were targeted. The participants were 65 grade eight mixed-proficiency French immersion students who spoke English as their L1. Data was collected over a five-week period. In week one, the participants completed a pretest. The pretest contained three item types. In type A learners matched masculine or feminine articles to the target structure; type B was a grammatical judgement test which involved a certainty scale; type C was a picture stimulus followed by multiple-choice answers. In week two, the participants were familiarized with their respective task type. In week three, the participants were shown a 5-minute "pre-recorded mini-lesson on French pronominal verbs" (Swain and Lapkin 2001, 102). Then, in dyads, the participants completed either a jigsaw task ($n = 35$) or a dictogloss task ($n = 30$). These treatment sessions were audio-recorded. The mean time on task was 10.2 minutes for the jigsaw task and 10.2 minutes for the dictogloss task (Swain and Lapkin 2001, 107). In week five, posttesting took place. Similar to Spielman-Davidson (2000), tailor-made posttest items were created from the participants' interactions. The posttest contained all pretest items in addition to the new tailor-made items. A two-tailed test found no statistically significant differences between both the pretest and delayed posttest scores for each class and the pretest and delayed posttest scores for each task, indicating that neither class (i.e., the jigsaw or dictogloss task) made any measurable gains. As direct pretest to posttest comparisons are possible only with the "core items" (Swain and Lapkin 2001, 108), the researchers excluded the tailor-made test items from the posttest statistical analysis and explained that when completing the tasks, the participants discussed relatively few pretest items. Swain and Lapkin's (2001) research highlights the difficulty of designing a study which can successfully anticipate the linguistic items that learners will focus on when they work collaboratively.

Drawing upon the concepts of noticing (Schmidt 1990, 1993) and the output hypothesis (Swain 1985, 1993), Kuiken and Vedder (2002, 346) investigated the effect of interaction between learners during a form-focused task and the acquisition of the passive form. The participants (N = 34) were 16–18-year-old Dutch high school students who were in their fifth year of learning English. After the initial pretest, they were randomly assigned to two groups who completed two dictogloss tasks, either individually ($n = 14$) or in groups of three or four ($n = 20$). As well as a pretest, Kuiken and Vedder (2002) also administered an immediate posttest, and two weeks later a delayed posttest. Testing consisted of a 32-sentence detection test with passive voice structures which the participants were asked to underline. An analysis of covariance (ANCOVA) found no statistically significant differences between the pretest and posttest results nor between the pretest and delayed posttest results of the two groups. A strength of Kuiken and Vedder's (2002) study is that it contains random group allocation.

Referencing the sociocultural concept of collaborative dialogue (Swain 2000) and the concept of noticing (Schmidt 1990), Lapkin, Swain, and Smith (2002) attempted to trace the grammatical knowledge discussed by peers over to its attempted use in a subsequent individual performance task. The participants were eight grade seven mixed proficiency French immersion students who spoke English as their L1. Lapkin et al. (2002) targeted French pronominal verbs and collected data over a two-week period. After watching a 5-minute mini-lesson on pronominal verbs, dyads either collaboratively completed a dictogloss task ($n = 4$) or a jigsaw task ($n = 4$) (30 minutes). Two days later, the dyads collaboratively discussed their text in relation to a reformulated model (10 minutes).Then two days later, the dyads completed a stimulated recall activity during which they reflected on their noticing (40 minutes). The first treatment session (i.e., collaboratively writing a text) served as the pretest. The posttest was administered four days after the final treatment session and involved individually rewriting the text which was initially collaboratively written (15 minutes). Lapkin et al. (2002) found that 66% of the reformulated verbs were correct or improved upon. This research design was able to trace grammatical knowledge discussed by peers over to subsequent independent performance. However without a pretest which is completed individually, it is not possible to ascertain the extent to which each participant improved.

Located within the interactionist approach, a study by Adams (2007) investigated whether the learning of second language forms is promoted by learner-learner interactions. Twenty-five adult intermediate learners of English with a variety of L1 backgrounds took part in the study that focused on three linguistic features: past tense, question formation, and locative preposition collocations. Over the course of a week, participants collaboratively completed three treatment sessions. Each treatment session consisted of three tasks (a spot the difference task, a jigsaw task, and discussing a seating plan), each targeting one of the three linguistic features. All interaction sessions were audio-recorded. The posttest was administered five days after the last interaction session. Similar to Spielman-Davidson (2000), Adams (2007) employed tailor-made test items to measure learning. Each tailor-made posttest consisted of nine acceptability judgment tests and three to five picture labelling items. Test items were only given for errors that occurred more than once and errors that were self-corrected were excluded (Adams 2007, 50). Adams (2007) found that 59% of the tailor-made posttest items were answered correctly. One consideration of employing tailor-made test items is that because the test items emerge naturally from learner interactions no pretesting is possible (Adams 2007, 50). Consequently, "it is not possible to determine whether the learners did not know the correct linguistic forms before the interactions" (Adams 2007, 50).

Taking a psycholinguistic approach to the study of language learning, Eckerth (2008) investigated the extent to which dyadic consciousness-raising tasks resulted in the learning of transitive prepositional verbs, passive voice, and reflexive prepositional verbs. Fourteen adult lower intermediate and 17 upper intermediate learners of German with a variety of L1 backgrounds took part in the study with five treatment/test cycles. Each week, learners worked in pairs to complete either a dictogloss task or a text-editing task. Learner-learner interactions were audio-recorded. Tests included a pretest immediately before each of the five treatment sessions, a posttest immediately after each treatment session, and a delayed posttest seven days later. Each cycle's tests were identical and "had the format of discrete-item sentence-assembly tasks" (Eckerth 2008, 126). Similar to Spielman-Davidson (2000) and Adams (2007), Eckerth (2008) also employed tailor-made test items. Each time a dyad's views diverged about a non-targeted L2 feature, Eckerth (2008, 129) categorized the discourse sequence as a "controversial language-related episode". Within each controversial language-related episode, "individual students' views were labelled 'Individual Learner Hypotheses'" (Eckerth 2008, 130). From these learner hypotheses, tailor-made test items were then composed. Each tailor-made delayed posttest encompassed both open and closed questions and was administered seven days after its corresponding task. A repeated measures two-factorial ANOVA found a statistically significant difference between both the pretest and posttest results and the pretest and delayed posttest results with a large effect size. Eckerth (2008) did not break down the results for each target structure or for each task type. Regarding the tailor-made test items, Eckerth (2008) compared the answer of each test item to its respective individual learner hypothesis. 1% of the individual learner hypotheses were revised in ways not conforming to the norms of the target language; 38% of the individual learner hypotheses "not conforming to L2 norms were replaced by L2-conform representations" (Eckerth 2008, 132); and 61% of the individual learner hypotheses were not revised. It is important to note that a learner's individual hypothesis could conform to target language norms when it was initially spoken during a treatment session. Incorporating three target structures, two levels of learner proficiency, two types of treatment task, a pretest-posttest-delayed posttest design, tailor-made test items, and five treatment/test cycles, Eckerth's (2008) study is relatively complex. In addition, of the eleven studies reviewed in this synthesis, Eckerth's (2008) is the only one to have provided an effect size.

Adopting a cognitive approach, Reinders (2009) investigated the effects of three types of production activities on the acquisition of negative adverbs with subject-verb inversion. The 28 participants were adult upper-intermediate learners of English with a variety of L1 backgrounds. Three treatment sessions were completed over a three-week period, each consisting of one task. The participants were randomly assigned to one of three conditions: individual dictation ($n = 9$), individual dictogloss task ($n = 8$), or collaborative dictogloss task($n = 11$). Tests included: a pretest, a posttest immediately after the final treatment session, and a delayed posttest one week later. Each test consisted of a timed grammatical judgement test containing 50 items, of which, 20 pertained to the target structure. The posttest and delayed posttest were the same test as the pretest but with the order of the items changed. An analysis of variance (ANOVA) found that "the treatments had no effect on the acquisition of negative adverbs a measured by overall gain scores on the GJTs" (Reinders 2009, 215). Reinders' (2009) study attempts to take into account the effects of task complexity. He hypothesised that the individual dictogloss task was more complex than the other two tasks as it "requires participants to remember a relatively long stretch of text" and as the activity is completed individually "cognitive resources cannot be pooled" (p. 208). Reinders (2009, 217) suggests that the lack of statistical significance may have been caused by the inductive nature of the tasks.

Drawing on the interactionist approach as well as a Vygotskian sociocultural perspective, Nassaji and Tian (2010) investigated the effect of collaborative output on the learning of phrasal verbs. The participants were 26 low-intermediate adult learners of English with a variety of L1 backgrounds. In order to control for individual differences, Nassaji and Tian (2010) employed a within-subject design. Over a two-week period, all the participants completed a reconstruction cloze task and a text-editing task both dyadically and individually. Before each treatment session, learners received an input-based mini-lesson (i.e., a vocabulary-matching task) relating to the target words. Participants were then given eight minutes to complete each task, no post-task feedback was provided and all pair work was audio recorded. Before each treatment session, a pretest was given and four days after a treatment session a delayed posttest was administered. Each test consisted of a vocabulary knowledge scale (VKS) five-point self-report test. A repeated measures ANOVA found no statistically significant differences between time and condition; however, Nassaji and Tian (2010, 397) found that from the pretest to the posttest the text-editing task led to significantly more gains than the cloze task. Nassaji and Tian (2010, 402) utilized a within-subject design, which requires all participants to complete all task types both collaboratively and individually, and thus enables individual differences to be controlled (Cohen et al. 2007, 282).

Adopting an interactionist lens, Adams et al. (2011, 42) investigated "how different types of feedback and responses to feedback promote learning of English past tense and locatives". Seventy one high intermediate adult learners of English, who predominately spoke Spanish as their L1, took part in the study. The participants were randomly assigned to either a collaborative group or a control group (i.e., a group which did not complete the treatment tasks either collaboratively or individually). Over a three-day period, the participants in the collaborative group completed three treatment sessions; each treatment session consisted of three tasks: a spot the difference task, a jigsaw task, and discussing a seating plan (Adams et al. 2011, 49). Approximately 40 minutes were given for each treatment session and no post-task feedback was provided. Three tests were administered: a pretest immediately before the first treatment task, a posttest immediately after the final treatment session, and a delayed posttest one week later. The tests comprised of oral performance tests and untimed grammaticality judgement tests. Three versions of the oral performance test and three versions of the untimed grammaticality judgement test were created and all tests were counterbalanced among the participants. In summary, this study used a pretest-posttest-delayed posttest design, two target structures (i.e., past tense and locatives), two groups (i.e., experimental and control), and two types of test (i.e., oral performance tests and untimed grammaticality judgement tests). The learners who completed the treatment sessions did not significantly outperform the control group on two of the tests, for the locatives between the oral performance pretest and posttest, and for the past tense between the grammaticality judgement pretest and posttest. On the six other tests, the treatment group significantly outperformed the control group (Adams et al. 2011, 51).

McNichol and Lee (2011) quasi-replicated Eckerth's (2008) study. The participants were 20 South Korean high school graduates whose English was of pre-intermediate and intermediate level. McNichol and Lee (2011) targeted the following grammatical features: simple past/interrogatives, present perfect/simple past, modals of ability and probability, and past perfect. There were four treatment/test cycles. Each week, learners worked in pairs to complete either a dictogloss task or a text-editing task. Grammatical form was not taught or discussed and learner-learner interactions were audio-recorded. Tests included a pretest immediately before each treatment session, a posttest immediately after each treatment session, and a delayed posttest seven days later. "Test items were predominately discrete-item sentence-assembly tasks (McNichol and Lee 2011,130)." Similar to Eckerth (2008), McNichol and

Lee (2011) created tailor-made test items each time a dyad's views diverged about a non-targeted L2 feature (McNichol and Lee 2011, 131). These tailor-made items were added to the corresponding delayed posttests. A Wilcoxon signed-rank test found no statistically significant difference for the results of the dictogloss task, but it did find a statistically significant difference between the pretest and posttest results and the pretest and delayed posttest results for the text-editing task. Finally, "in roughly half of the negotiations between the dyads, non-conforming views of the TL were replaced with conforming L2 (English) norms" (McNichol and Lee 2011,132). McNichol and Lee (2011, 131) opted to use the non-parametric Wilcoxon signed-rank test due to the small sample size of their study. Small samples (i.e., below 25) often do not yield a normal sampling distribution of the mean (Hopkins, Hopkins, and Glass 1996, 159). As non-parametric statistical tests make no assumptions about the normality in the data (Cohen et al. 2007, 503), they are often an appropriate choice when analysing data sets containing small sample sizes.

In a study similar to Nassaji and Tian (2010), Teng (2017) investigated the effect of collaborative output tasks on the learning of phrasal verbs. The participants were 72 low to intermediate adult learners of English whose native language was Chinese. Teng (2017) employed a within-participant design. Over a three-week period, the participants completed a reconstruction close task, a text-editing task, and a dictogloss task. The tasks were completed individually, in pairs, and in groups of three. Learners received input-based instruction related to the target words before each treatment session; then, 30 minutes were given to complete each task. Corrective feedback was provided by the teacher. A pretest was administered one day before its corresponding treatment session, and a delayed posttest six days after that treatment session. Similar to Nassaji and Tian (2010), each test consisted of a vocabulary knowledge scale (VKS) five-point self-report test. Teng (2017) found that learners who worked in groups tended to produce significantly higher mean scores than learners who worked in pairs, and learners who worked in pairs tended to produce significantly higher mean scores than learners who worked individually. Teng (2017) also found that the dictogloss task led to a greater number of significant gains than the text-editing task, and the text-editing task led to a greater number of significant gains than the reconstruction close task. Building upon Nassaji and Tian's (2010) earlier study, Teng (2017) included the additional condition of completing the treatment tasks in groups of three. In comparison to working in pairs, working in small groups can offer "more opportunities for elaborate engagement with the target structure" (Fernández Dobao 2014, 182). Learning outcome differences between the conditions of working in pairs and working in small groups need to be investigated further.

2.2 What can we say?

Over the past 20 years, the studies which have investigated a possible relationship between completing tasks collaboratively and the longer-term learning of specific grammatical features have utilized a wide variety of designs which in turn, have been implemented in a wide variety of contexts. These differences in design can be partly accounted for by differing theoretical perspectives. One important difference is the length of participant exposure to the target structure(s). For example, Spielman-Davidson's (2000) treatment sessions lasted for several weeks; however, Nassaji and Tian (2010) focused on one single task. The studies also differ in the way in which they have measured learning. For example, Kuiken and Vedder (2002) employed a detection test; in contrast, Lapkin et al. (2002) measured learning through a written production task. Another important difference is the timing of the delayed posttests. With the exception of Spielman-Davidson (2000) who administered posttests eleven weeks after her final treatment session, the delayed posttests of previous studies were administered within a range of four days (Lapkin et al. 2002; Nassaji and Tian 2010) to two weeks (Kuiken and Vedder 2002; Swain and Lapkin 2001) of the completion of the corresponding treatment session(s). Finally, it is important to note that many studies have omitted key information, for example, whether pre-task input and/or post-task feedback was given. This omission of information hampers interpreting the findings of these studies. Inevitably, choices in design will have enhanced or curtailed a study's likelihood of registering gains in learning.

The results of the studies can be categorized into three broad groups. Firstly, two studies did not analyse their results through the use of inferential statistics. Adams (2007) and Lapkin et al. (2002) employed descriptive statistics and both studies found that the collaborative condition showed posttest gains of around 60%. Secondly, four studies analysed their results through the use of inferential statistics but did not include a comparison condition within their design. These four studies analysed their results by comparing the collaborative condition's knowledge prior to the treatment session(s) with their knowledge after the treatment session(s). Three of these studies report *non-significant* findings (Adams et al. 2011; McNicoll and Lee 2011; Swain and Lapkin 2001); and three *significant* findings (Adams et al. 2011; Eckerth 2008; McNicoll and Lee 2011). The concurrent statistical significance and non-significance reported by Adams et al (2011) and McNicoll and Lee (2011) can be partly attributed to the implementation of complex designs. Adams et al. (2011) used more than two target structures in combination with two types of data collection instrumentation and McNicoll and Lee (2011) employed two types of treatment task. Finally, five studies included a comparison condition and analysed their results through the use of inferential statistics. These five studies were able to investigate whether collaboratively completing form-focused tasks was significantly more effective than completing those same, or similar, tasks individually. Four of these studies report *non-significant* findings within their results (Kuiken and Vedder 2002; Nassaji and Tian 2010; Reinders 2009; Spielman-Davidson 2000); and two report *significant* findings (Spielman-Davidson 2000; Teng 2017). The concurrent statistical significance and non-significance reported by Spielman-Davidson (2000) can be partly attributed to the use of more than one type of test. Taken together, the results of these studies suggest that collaboratively completing form-focused tasks can, but does not always, result in statistically significant gains in the learning of L2 form, and that when learning L2 form, the condition of working collaboratively and working individually tend to lead to comparable degrees to learning.

The length and intensity of the treatment may impact on learning. To illustrate, both Kuiken and Vedder (2002) and Nassaji and Tian (2010) focused on one single task and did not find a statistically significant difference between time and condition. In contrast, Spielman-Davidson (2000) found statistically significant differences in favour of her experimental group; however, her study involved twelve treatment sessions over a four-week period. Here, a further distinction needs to be made between the length of a study and the duration of its participants' exposure to the targeted grammatical structure(s). Of the studies for which total exposure to the target structure(s) can be calculated, the durations are as follows: 15.2 minutes (Swain and Lapkin 2001), 32 minutes (Nassaji and Tian 2010), 85 minutes (Lapkin et al. 2002), 90 minutes (Teng 2017), 120 minutes (Adams et al. 2011), and 800 minutes (Spielman-Davidson 2000). From this data, a tentative pattern emerges. The two studies which provided the least amount of target structure exposure to their participants (Nassaji and Tian 2010; Swain and Lapkin 2001) found their results to be of statistical non-significance. In contrast, the three studies which provided the most target structure exposure to their participants (Adams et al. 2011; Spielman-Davidson 2000; Teng 2017) found their results to contain statistical significance. Lapkin et al. (2002) did not employ inferential statistics.

The choice of task type may impact on learning. Many of the eleven studies have either not matched their test results to specific task types or not analysed their results by task type. However, there is not strong evidence which suggests that collaboratively completing either cloze tasks, jigsaw tasks, or dictogloss tasks results in significant learning gains in L2 form, either in comparison to learners' knowledge prior to task completion or in comparison to gains made by learners who completed the same, or similar, task(s) individually. However, limited evidence exists which suggests that when used for the purposes of learning L2 form, collaboratively completing text-editing tasks is superior to collaboratively completing cloze tasks (Nassaji and Tian 2010; Teng 2017) and dictogloss tasks (McNicoll and Lee 2011). If the instructional goal is for students to learn targeted L2 form, it still remains to be seen which types of language task are the most effective when they are completed collaboratively.

Overall, some studies found statistically significant learning gains within their results, some others did not, and the results of a third group contain findings which are both significant and non-significant. However, most of the previous studies, whether comparing pretest to posttest performance or collaborative to individual task performance, have failed to find statistically significant evidence which suggests that completing form-focused tasks collaboratively is more effective than completing the same, or similar tasks, individually. Considering the theoretical rationales which underpin collaborative work (i.e., the interactionist approach and sociocultural theory), this is unexpected. Unsurprisingly, SLA researchers have repeatedly requested more empirical evidence which shows the extent to which working collaboratively with peers affects the longer-term development of a learner's linguistic system (García Mayo 2014; Kim and McDonough 2008; Storch 2001, 2007; Swain, Brooks, and Tocalli-Beller 2002). Part two of this chapter addresses the ways in which the existing body of research could be strengthened.

3 Current limitations and future research

A selection of the methodological limitations inherent within the existing research are now explored. This selection is not exhaustive.

3.1 The extent of linguistic gains

Most of the previous studies which have investigated the effectiveness of collaboratively completing form-focused tasks have overlooked the degree to which the linguistic knowledge of their participants may have developed. Viewed from a sociocultural perspective, language development can be observed at two distinct levels: actual performance (i.e., what an individual can perform without assistance) and potential performance (i.e., what an individual can perform with assistance) (Vygotsky 1978, 86). Over time, potential performance develops into independent performance.

However, the transition from potential performance to independent performance takes time and is subject to fluctuations (Lantolf and Thorne 2007, 200). With the exceptions of the use of five-point self-report tests (Nassaji and Tian 2010; Teng 2017), the use of a certainty scale (Spielman-Davidson 2000; Swain and Lapkin 2001), and the acceptance of improved upon answers (Lapkin et al. 2002), most previous studies have neglected to pay attention to the incremental improvements that their participants may have made. This is problematic because a participant may have developed their knowledge of the linguistic feature on which they were tested but just not to the extent that their improvement registers on the data collection tools used in the study. Consequently, the development of emergent grammatical knowledge may have gone undetected and the treatment sessions used in these studies may have been more effective than initially thought.

Emanating from a sociocultural perspective, dynamic assessment attempts to address the problem that although different learners may perform at a similar level on a test, their underlying grammatical knowledge may be vastly different. In dynamic assessment, assistance is provided by an expert in an attempt to deliberately guide the learner towards development (Swain, Kinnear, and Steinman 2011, 128).The amount and nature of assistance required to successfully accomplish the task or a test item is then recorded. By exceeding a learner's independent performance through the use of assistance, an assessor can gain a deeper insight into the extent of the knowledge and/or abilities in question. The two kinds of mediation that researchers can employ when administering dynamic assessment are interventionist and interactionist (Poehner 2008, 18). Although both kinds of mediation provide leaners with contingent and graduated help, one tends to be more interpretive (interactionist) and the other tends to be more quantitative (interventionist). Interventionist dynamic assessment is of interest here as it has the potential to generate standardized, comparable numerical scores for each participant (Poehner 2008, 43). Uses of interventionist dynamic assessment within an SLA context include: diagnosing language aptitude (Guthke, Harnisch, and Caruso 1986) and investigating L2 reading and listening comprehension (Poehner, Zhang, and Lu 2014). Interventionist dynamic assessment may offer a more accurate methodology when measuring the extent to which a participant may have developed their knowledge of the linguistic feature on which they are being tested.

3.2 A meaningful amount of exposure

The participants of some studies may not have been provided with a meaningful amount of exposure to the target language. Although short duration times have been found to be effective (Norris and Ortega 2000, 472), Alegría de la Colina and García Mayo (2007, 28) argue that a single task may not have immediate effects but, rather, "triggers a process, so repeated exposure is needed to consolidate gains". Future studies should give their participants sustained exposure to the target structures in question. However, the length of exposure required as well as its intensity is still unclear.

3.3 Control and comparison groups

With the exception of Adams et al. (2011), all previous studies did not employ a control group. This means that most studies did not isolate the condition of collaboratively learning L2 form from the SLA context in which the study took place. The inclusion of a control group would give strength to claims that any reported linguistic gains were due to the treatment condition of working collaboratively rather than the concurrent experiences of a study's participants (e.g., the language courses that a study may be situated within).

Only five of the studies included a comparison group or utilized a within-subject design (Kuiken and Vedder 2002; Nassaji and Tian 2010; Reinders 2009; Spielman-Davidson 2000; Teng 2017). The decision as to whether to include a comparison group, or not, is important as it affects how the results can be analyzed. Researchers who include a comparison condition have the option of conducting a between group analysis; gains made by the collaborative condition can be compared to gains made by the individual condition. This comparison would then enable a researcher to better isolate the collaborative condition, and thus, provide a better indication of whether gains experienced by the collaborative condition are due to working collaboratively or due to completing the tasks. As well as a control group, future studies should also include a comparison group.

3.4 Longevity of linguistic gains

The studies reviewed in this chapter have measured relatively short-term linguistic gains. As the acquisition of grammatical form is complex and takes time (Ellis 2012, 82–98), it is questionable as to whether the durations which have been employed are long enough to ascertain whether the gains reported in these studies are durable or not. If linguistic gains which are thought to have been brought about by the act of collaboratively completing form-focused tasks lack longevity, then it is possible that peer interaction may be less effective at promoting the development of specific L2 grammatical features than currently thought. Conversely, if linguistic gains take time to better materialize, then peer interaction may be more effective than currently thought.

Administering a delayed posttest will allow researchers to more accurately ascertain whether the treatment effects last. However, retesting may lead to inflated results due to a practice effect (Cohen et al. 2007, 160). In order to account for the posttest results being influenced by a possible practice effect, researchers could add another control group to the design which does not experience the pretest (Cohen et al. 2007, 277). Alternatively, researchers could embed control items into the pretests and posttests (e.g., Eckerth 2008, 127). Another way in which researchers can gain further insights into the durability of the learning which may have taken place is through complementing a delayed posttest with a transfer task. By imposing "different cognitive demands" upon a learner (Ammar and Hassan 2018, 74), a transfer task provides learners with an opportunity to transfer and re-contextualize knowledge to a more complex and demanding situation. Complementing a delayed posttest with a transfer task would help to provide evidence that the gains made by learners when working collaboratively are more stable over the longer term.

3.5 Sample size

Previous studies have tended to use a small sample size. Of the studies which used inferential statistics to analyze their results, the number of participants ranges from 16 (Spielman-Davidson 2000) to 72 (Teng 2017).Thus, the number of participants in each of the studies is relatively small. This is problematic because *p*-values are not independent of sample size (Cohen et al. 2007, 520). A statistically significant result can be obtained either by "having a large coefficient together with a small sample or having a small coefficient together with a larger sample" (Cohen et al. 2007, 520). In other words, small sample sizes limit the power of statistical analyses. Some studies did not find a statistically significant difference between the collaborative and individual treatment conditions, even when the collaborative treatment condition resulted in superior task performance (e.g., Nassaji and Tian 2010; Reinders 2009). It is possible that statistically significant differences were not detected in these studies due to their use of a relatively small number of participants. This is known as a Type II error (Cohen et al. 2007, 145).

The sample size used in a study needs careful consideration. The APA Manual 6th edition (2011, 31) suggests that researchers "use calculations based on a chosen target precision (confidence interval width) to determine sample sizes".

Cohen et al. (2007,104) provide a guide for sample size relative to confidence levels and confidence intervals. Usually, larger sample sizes increase the accuracy of the results. When planning their design, future researchers should carefully consider the size of their sample in relation to the population they may wish to generalize to and the statistical analyses they plan to perform.

3.6 Omission of key statistical information

The inferential statistical tests which the previous studies have employed may have been inappropriate for their respective data set. Each of the previous studies did not report key statistical information about their data which underpins their choice of inferential statistical test. For example, in order to analyze their results, four studies employed some form of analysis of variance (ANOVA) (Eckerth 2008; Nassaji and Tian 2010; Reinders 2009; Teng 2017). Among other things, an ANOVA assumes that the dependent variable is measured at the interval or ratio level, the data generated is approximately normally distributed, and the distributions of data in the groups being compared have the same shape (Laerd Statistics, n.d.). However, these four studies did not report the distribution or variance of their data. For studies which omit key statistical information, it is impossible to independently verify whether their choice of inferential statistical tests is appropriate. Depending on the statistical model adopted, future research should consider the: normality, homogeneity of variance, and homogeneity of regression (APA Manual 6th edition 2011, 30). Additionally, researchers should report the standard deviation with all means, exact t values, exact F values, exact p values, and all statistical tests used to compare means (Plonsky 2014, 465). Failing to thoroughly report key information about data limits the interpretability of results (Plonsky 2014, 451).

Effect size provides an alternative to significance levels. As previously explained, statistical significance (p-value) depends on both sample size and the strength of the correlation. Thus, statistical significance can be achieved by having either a large correlation combined with a small sample, or a weak correlation combined with a large sample. Effect sizes can address this problem. The effect size is "a measure of the effectiveness of the treatment" (Coe 2000, 1 as cited in Cohen et al. 2007, 521). In other words, it signals to the reader "the magnitude or importance of a study's findings" (APA Manual 6th edition 2011, 34). The APA Manual 6th edition (2011, 33) emphasizes that as well as completely reporting all tested hypotheses, reporting "estimates of appropriate effect sizes and confidence intervals are the minimum expectations for all APA journals". However with the exception of Eckerth (2008), all of the studies which employed inferential statistical tests did not report their effect sizes. Norris and Ortega (2000) advocate the reporting of confidence intervals, effect sizes, as well as the minimal information to calculate an effect size.

3.7 Complexity of design

Many studies have either a design which includes more than one treatment task, more than one target structure, or more than one proficiency level. These design choices make it difficult to determine which aspect of the design was effective. In addition, the possibility of interaction effects add to the opaqueness of the findings. An interaction effect occurs when the effect of one variable is influenced by the effect of another variable. For example, lower proficiency learners may especially benefit from a longer task duration (Ammar and Hassan 2018, 70). The results of each study may have been affected by the existence of an unknown interaction between one or more of the variables. Norris and Ortega (2000, 497) recommend that SLA researchers should "[u]tilize simple designs that investigate only a few variables at most; interactions of variables should be investigated systematically across multiple experiments, not within single experiments". Studies which utilized simpler designs would result in a better understanding of under which specific conditions working collaboratively is most effective, and thus provide clearer guidance about how to implement working collaboratively within a classroom setting. If a researcher did wish to include more than one independent variable within their design, they should consider employing a factorial design in order to better understand how the independent variables influence the dependent variable and interact (Cohen et al. 2007, 280; Mackey and Gass 2010, 151).

3.8 Summary of limitations

The existing body of research contains a wide array of methodological limitations. These limitations include: neglecting to pay attention to the extent of a participant's gains, providing a relatively short amount of exposure time to the target structure(s), not including a control or a comparison group, neglecting to test longer-term linguistic gains, having a relatively small sample size, omitting key statistical information about the data, not providing effect sizes, and implementing designs which are relatively complex. In addition, although some studies have randomly distributed the participants into groups (Adams et al. 2011; Kuiken and Vedder 2002; Reinders 2009) or used a within-subject design (Nassaji and Tian 2010; Teng 2017), all the studies which make up the current body of knowledge did not conduct random sampling from a well-defined population. Finally, only Adams et al. (2011) and Spielman-Davidson (2000) have measured learners gains through the use tests which require oral production. Oral production tests are useful as they have the potential to tap into SLA knowledge which is more implicit in its nature (Ellis 2012, 889). Many of the above methodological limitations can be attributed to the practical realities of conducting research. For example, conducting studies with intact classes limits both sample sizes and the opportunity to randomize participants (Mackey and Gass 2010, 141–142). Although using intact classes enhances ecological validity (Cohen et al. 2007, 138), it also imposes methodological constraints.

4 Conclusion

Currently, there is a lack of research on how efficient it is to complete tasks in collaboration for form-focused targets. Furthermore, much of the previous research which has investigated working collaboratively and the longer-term learning of specific grammatical features, whether they have compared pretest to posttest performance or collaborative to individual task performance, has failed to find statistically significant evidence which suggests that completing form-focused tasks collaboratively is more effective than completing the same, or similar tasks, individually. Thus, the expectations of learning which accompany the use of collaborative form-focused tasks in L2 classrooms have yet to be empirically verified. However, the studies which make up the existing body of research are relatively few in number, lack a shared methodology, and have designs with methodological shortcomings. In addition, some of the studies have omitted key information in their account of what took place. It is understood that the availability of a small number of studies prevents this synthesis from being able to provide any definitive answers (Norris and Ortega 2006). Nevertheless, for those who are interested in the efficacy of collaboratively completing form-focused tasks in L2 classrooms, this chapter provides a reflection point on the current state of the knowledge accumulated.

Form-focused instruction can have a positive effect on learners' grammatical accuracy (Ellis 2012, 900; Nassaji and Fotos 2011, 136; Norris and Ortega 2000), and the collaborative completion of form-focused tasks can provide a meaningful context in which to draw learners' attention to aspects of L2 form (De Guerrero and Villamil 2000; Donato 1994; Fernández Dobao 2012, 2014; Storch 1999, 2007; Swain 2000). DeKeyser (1998,42) stated that "some kind of focus on form is useful to some extent, for some forms, for some students, at some point in the learning process . . . Beyond that basic, tentative agreement, however, uncertainty looms large". Regarding the efficacy of collaboratively completing form-focused tasks, this observation is still as true as when it was initially made.

References

Adams, Rebecca. 2007. "Do Second Language Learners Benefit from Interacting with Each Other." In *Conversational Interaction in Second Language Acquisition*, edited by Alison Mackey, 29–51. Oxford: Oxford University Press.
Adams, Rebecca, Ana Maria Nuevo, and Takako Egi. 2011. "Explicit and Implicit Feedback, Modified Output, and SLA: Does Explicit and Implicit Feedback Promote Learning and Learner–learner Interactions?" *The Modern Language Journal* 95:42–63.
Alegría de la Colina, Ana and María del Pilar García Mayo. 2007. "Attention to Form across Collaborative Tasks by Low-proficiency Learners in an EFL Setting." In *Investigating Tasks in Formal Language Learning*, edited by Maria del Pilar García Mayo, 91–116. Clevedon, UK: Multilingual Matters.
Alegría de la Colina, Ana and María del Pilar García Mayo. 2009. "Oral Interaction in Task-based EFL Learning: The Use of the L1 as a Cognitive Tool." *International Review of Applied Linguistics in Language Teaching* 47: 325–345.
American Psychological Association. 2011. *Publication Manual of the American Psychological Association*. 6th ed. Washington, D.C.: American Psychological Association.
Ammar, Ahlem, and Rania Mohamed Hassan. 2018. "Talking It Through: Collaborative Dialogue and Second Language Learning." *Language Learning* 68:46–82.
Antón, Marta, and Frederick J. DiCamilla. 1999. "Socio-cognitive Functions of L1 Collaborative Interaction in the L2 classroom." *The Modern Language Journal* 83:233–247.
Brooks, Lindsay, Merrill Swain, Sharon Lapkin, and Ibtissem Knouzi. 2010. "Mediating between Scientific and Spontaneous Concepts through Languaging." *Language Awareness* 19:89–110.
Coe, Robert. 2000. *What is an effect size?* CEM Centre: University of Durham.
Cohen, Louis, Lawrence Manion, and Keith Morrison. 2007. *Research Methods in Education*. 6th ed. London: Routledge.
De Guerrero, Maria C. M. and Olga S. Villamil. 2000. "Activating the ZPD: Mutual Scaffolding in L2 Peer Revision." *The Modern Language Journal* 84: 51–68.
DeKeyser, Robert. 1998. "Beyond Focus on Form: Cognitive Perspectives on Learning and Practicing Second Language Grammar." In *Focus on Form in Classroom Second Language Acquisition*, edited by Catherine Doughty and Jessica Williams, 42–63. Cambridge: Cambridge University Press.
Donato, Richard. 1994. "Collective Scaffolding in Second Language Learning." In *Vygotskian Approaches to Second Language Research*, edited by James P. Lantolf and Gabriela Appel, 33–56. Norwood, NJ: Ablex.
Eckerth, Johannes. 2008. "Investigating Consciousness-raising Tasks: Pedagogically Targeted and Non-targeted Learning Gains." *International Journal of Applied Linguistics* 18:121–145.

Ellis, Rod. 2012. *The Study of Second Language Acquisition*. 2nd ed. Oxford: Oxford University.
Fernández Dobao, Ana. 2012. "Collaborative Writing Tasks in the L2 Classroom: Comparing Group, Pair, and Individual Work." *Journal of Second Language Writing* 21:40–58.
Fernández Dobao, Ana. 2014. "Attention to Form in Collaborative Writing Tasks: Comparing Pair and Small Group Interaction." *Canadian Modern Language Review* 70:158–187.
Gánem Gutiérrez, Adela. 2008. "Microgenesis, Method and Object: A Study of Collaborative Activity in a Spanish as a Foreign Language Classroom." *Applied Linguistics* 29:120–148.
García Mayo, María del Pilar. 2002a. "Interaction in Advanced EFL Pedagogy: A Comparison of Form-focused Activities." *International Journal of Educational Research* 37:323–341
García Mayo, María del Pilar. 2002b. "The Effectiveness of Two Form-focused Tasks in Advanced EFL Pedagogy." *International Journal of Applied Linguistics* 12:156–175.
García Mayo, María del Pilar. 2014. "Collaborative Tasks and Their Potential for Grammar Instruction in Second/foreign Language Contexts." In *The Grammar Dimension in Instructed Second Language Learning*, edited by Alessandro G. Benati, Cécile Laval, and María Arche, 82–102. London: Bloomsbury.
Guthke, Jürgen, A Harnisch, and Mario Caruso. 1986. "The Diagnostic Program of "Syntactical Rule and Vocabulary Acquisition" – a Contribution to the Psychodiagnosis of Foreign Language Learning Ability." In *Human Memory and Cognitive Capabilities, Mechanisms and Performances*, edited by Friedhart Klix and H. Hagendoft, 903–911. Amsterdam: Elsevier.
Hopkins, Kenneth D., Bruce R. Hopkins, and Gene V. Glass. 1996. *Basic Statistics for the Behavioural Sciences*. 3rd ed. Boston, M.A.: Allyn & Bacon.
Kim, YouJin, and Kim McDonough. 2008. "The Effect of Interlocutor Proficiency on the Collaborative Dialogue between Korean as a Second Language Learners." *Language Teaching Research* 12:211–234.
Krashen, Stephen. 1977. "Some Issues Relating to the Monitor Model." In *On Tesol, 77*, edited by H. Douglas Brown, Carlos A. Yorio, and Ruth H. Crymes, 144–158. Washington D.C.: TESOL.
Krashen, Stephen. 1980. "The Input Hypothesis." In *Current Issues in Bilingual Education*, edited by James Alatis, 168–180. Washington D.C.: Georgetown University Press.
Kuiken, Folkert, and Ineke Vedder. 2002. "The Effect of Interaction in Acquiring the Grammar of a Second Language." *International Journal of Educational Research* 37:343–358.
Laerd Statistics. n.d. "One-way ANOVA in SPSS statistics." statistics.laerd.com. https://statistics.laerd.com/spss-tutorials/one-way-anova-using-spss-statistics.php (accessed April 21, 2020).
Lantolf, James P., and Steven L. Thorne. 2006. *Sociocultural Theory and the Genesis of Second Language Development*. Oxford: Oxford University Press.
Lantolf, James P., and Steven L. Thorne. 2007. "Sociocultural Theory and Second Language Learning." In *Theories in Second Language Acquisition*, edited by Bill VanPatten and Jessica Williams, 201–224. Mahwah, NJ: Lawrence Eribaum.
Lapkin, Sharon, Merrill Swain, and Monika Smith. 2002. "Reformulation and the Learning of French Pronominal Verbs in a Canadian French Immersion Context." *The Modern Language Journal* 86:485–507.
Long, Michael H. 1983. "Native Speaker/non-native Speaker Conversation and the Negotiation of Comprehensible input1." *Applied Linguistics* 4:126–141.

Long, Michael H. 1985. "Input and Second Language Acquisition Theory." In *Input in Second Language Acquisition*, edited by Susan Gass and Carolyn Madden, 377–393. Rowely, NA: Newbury.

Long, Michael H. 1996. "The Role of the Linguistic Environment in Second Language Acquisition." In *Handbook of Second Language Acquisition*, edited by William C. Ritchie and Tej K. Bhatia, 413–468. New York: Academic Press.

Mackey, Alison, Rebekha Abbuhl, and Susan M. Gass. 2012. "Interactionist Approach." In *The Routledge Handbook of Second Language Acquisition*, edited by Susan M. Gass and Alison Mackey, 7–23. New York: Routledge.

Mackey, Alison, and Susan M. Gass. [2005]2010. *Second Language Research: Methodology and Design*. New Jersey: Routledge.

McNicoll, Josh, and Jang Ho Lee. 2011. "Collaborative Consciousness-raising Tasks in EAL Classrooms." *English Teaching: Practice and Critique* 10:127–138.

Nassaji, Hossein, and Sandra S. Fotos. 2011. *Teaching Grammar in Second Language Classrooms: Integrating Form-focused Instruction in Communicative Context*. New York: Routledge.

Nassaji, Hossein, and Jun Tian. 2010. "Collaborative and Individual Output Tasks and Their Effects on Learning English Phrasal Verbs." *Language Teaching Research* 14: 397–419.

Norris, John M., and Lourdes Ortega. 2000. "Effectiveness of L2 Instruction: A Research Synthesis and Quantitative Meta-analysis." *Language Learning* 50:417–528.

Norris, John M., and Lourdes Ortega. 2006. "The Value and Practice of Research Synthesis for Language Learning and Teaching." In *Synthesizing Research on Language Learning and Teaching*, edited by John M. Norris and Lourdes Ortega, 3–50. Amsterdam: John Benjamins Publishing.

Ohta, Amy Snyder. 1995. "Applying Sociocultural Theory to an Analysis of Learner Discourse: Learner-learner Collaborative Interaction in the Zone of Proximal Development." *Issues in Applied Linguistics* 6:93–121.

Philp, Jenefer, Rebecca Adams, and Noriko Iwashita. 2014. *Peer Interaction and Second Language Learning*. New York: Routledge.

Plonsky, Luke. 2014. "Study Quality in Quantitative L2 Research (1990–2010): A Methodological Synthesis and Call for Reform." *The Modern Language Journal* 98:450–470.

Poehner, Matthew E. 2008. *Dynamic Assessment: A Vygotskian Approach to Understanding and Promoting L2 Development*. Springer Science & Business Media.

Poehner, Matthew E., Jie Zhang, and Xiaofei Lu. 2014. "Computerized Dynamic Assessment (C-DA): Diagnosing L2 Development According to Learner Responsiveness to Mediation." *Language Testing* 32: 337–357.

Reinders, Hayo. 2009. "Learner Uptake and Acquisition in Three Grammar-oriented Production Activities." *Language Teaching Research* 13:201–222.

Schmidt, Richard W. 1990. "The Role of Consciousness in Second Language Learning." *Applied Linguistics* 11:129–158.

Schmidt, Richard W. 1993. "Awareness and Second Language Acquisition." *Annual Review of Applied Linguistics* 13:206–226.

Shehadeh, Ali. 2011. "Effects and Student Perceptions of Collaborative Writing in L2." *Journal of Second Language Writing* 20:286–305.

Spielman-Davidson, Sylvia Justina. 2000. *Collaborative Dialogues in the Zone of Proximal Development, Grade Eight French Immersion Students Learning the Conditional Tense*.

Unpublished doctoral dissertation, Ontario Institute for Studies in Education of the University of Toronto.
Storch, Neomy. 1999. "Are Two Heads Better Than One? Pair Work Grammatical Accuracy." *System* 27:363–374.
Storch, Neomy. 2001. "How Collaborative Is Pair Work? ESL Tertiary Students Composing in Pairs." *Language Teaching Research* 5:29–53.
Storch, Neomy. 2007. "Investigating the Merits of Pair Work on a Text-editing Task in ESL Classes." *Language Teaching Research* 11:143–159.
Storch, Neomy. 2013. *Collaborative Writing in L2 Classrooms*. Multilingual Matters: Bristol, UK.
Swain, Merrill. 1985. "Communicative Competence: Some Roles of Comprehensible Input and Comprehensible Output in Its Development." In *Input in Second Language Acquisition*, edited by Susan M. Gass and Carolyn G. Madden, 165–179. Rowely, NA: Newbury House Publishers.
Swain, Merrill. 1993. "The Output Hypothesis: Just Speaking and Writing Aren't Enough." *Canadian Modern Language Review* 50:158–64.
Swain, Merrill. 2000. "The Output Hypothesis and Beyond: Mediating Acquisition through Collaborative Dialogue." In *Sociocultural Theory and Second Language Learning*, edited by James P. Lantolf, 97–114. Oxford: Oxford University Press.
Swain, Merrill, and Sharon Lapkin. 1998. "Interaction and Second Language Learning: Two Adolescent French Immersion Students Working Together." *The Modern Language Journal* 82:320–337.
Swain, Merrill, and Sharon Lapkin. 2001. "Focus on Form through Collaborative Dialogue: Exploring Task Effects." In *Researching Pedagogic Tasks: Second Language Learning, Teaching and Testing*, edited by Martin Bygate, Peter Skehan, and Merrill Swain, 99–118. London: Routledge.
Swain, Merrill, and Sharon Lapkin. 2002. "Talking It through: Two French Immersion Learners' Response to Reformulation." *International Journal of Educational Research* 37:285–304.
Swain, Merrill, Lindsay Brooks, and Agatha Tocalli-Beller. 2002. "9 Peer-peer Dialogue as a Means of Second Language Learning." *Annual Review of Applied Linguistics* 22:171–185.
Swain, Merrill, Penny Kinnear, and Linda Steinman. 2011. *Sociocultural Theory in Second Language Education: An Introduction through Narratives*. Bristol, UK: Multilingual Matters.
Teng, Mark Feng. 2017. "The Effectiveness of Group, Pair and Individual Output Tasks on Learning Phrasal Verbs." *The Language Learning Journal*, 1–14.
Vygotsky, Lev Semenovich. 1978. *Mind in Society: The Development of Higher Psychological Processes*. Cambridge, MA: Harvard University Press.
Wajnryb, Ruth. 1990. *Grammar Dictation*. Oxford: Oxford University Press.

Tomas Kos
What exactly is mutuality? An analysis of mixed-age peer interactions on classroom tasks in German secondary school classrooms

1 Introduction

Classrooms, which are composed of two or three different grades, are called mixed-age (M-A) classrooms (sometimes referred to as *multi-grade, mixed-grade* or *composite classes*). It follows that a three-grade classroom can be made up by grades ranging from the 1st to the 3rd, from the 4th to the 6th and from the 7th to the 9th grade. The supporters of M-A classrooms usually claim that age differences among children can be beneficial to their intellectual development (Hoffman 2002; Kalaoja and Pietarinen 2009; Little2007) and that the younger learners benefit from being tutored or mentored by their older peers, while the older learners benefit from teaching the younger ones (Little 2007; Wagener 2014). In addition, grouping children across ages and grades reduces antisocial behavior (Hoffman 2002) and promotes cooperative behavior, sharing, help and self-directed learning (Campagna-Schleusener 2012; Wagener 2014). In contrast, research also suggests that M-A is not always based on the shared interests of children in an interaction, and may even contain instances of older children acting out authority and control over younger children (Huf and Raggl 2015).

Due to the high degree of heterogeneity in terms of age and language proficiency in M-A language classrooms, teacher-centred sessions are limited and a great deal of work must be done either by students themselves, in pairs or groups which are often composed of learners of differing ages *and* language proficiencies. Unfortunately, we know very little from the L2 research about peer-interactions among learners in M-A classrooms (Kos 2017). Using data from an English as a foreign language (EFL) M-A classroom, this chapter presents findings that were part of a larger study that sought to fill that gap in research into M-A peer interactions. This chapter has three main aims. The primary aim is to explore the degree of mutuality among M-A young adolescent learners in an EFL classroom and the factors that influence it. Mutuality is an important index that has been used to examine and to understand the relationship established within pairs as well as the

Tomas Kos, University of Leipzig

https://doi.org/10.1515/9781501511318-004

degree of collaboration in peer interaction (Storch 2002). Such exploration is important as it can for example reveal to what extent and how M-A pairs engage with each other's contributions and ideas, and how they assist one another or negotiate agreement when interacting on classroom tasks. The second aim is to discuss some of the challenges to determine the degree of mutuality in the analysis of peer interactions. The third aim is to highlight the relationship between the degree of mutuality and actual learning opportunities created during M-A peer interactions, operationalized in this study as language-related episodes (LREs) (Swain and Lapkin 1998).

2 Literature review

Research has shown that an important factor that affects second language learning and development is the quality of the partners' engagement (Damon and Phelps 1989; Dao and McDonough 2018; Philp and Duchesne 2016) and the patterns of interaction established by the learners (Li and Zhu 2017; Storch 2002). Damon and Phelps (1989) explain the quality of engagement in pair work in terms of equality and mutuality. Both partners are engaged equally if the control over the direction of a task is equal. Interaction is high on equality when learners frequently take directions from one another and their contribution to the task is equal. Interaction is high on mutuality when both learners regularly engage with each other's contributions, provide a rich reciprocal feedback and share ideas (p.13). Grounding her research in sociocultural theory (Vygotsky 1978; 1986), Storch (2002) explored the nature of pair interaction in an adult English as a second language (ESL) classroom. Storch mainly inquired into how learners approach the task, what roles they assume, to what extent each individual learner is involved in and contributes to the task (p.126). She found four patterns of interaction (collaborative-dominant/passive-dominant /passive-expert/novice) which were determined in terms of equality and mutuality based on the study by Damon and Phelps (1989). In order to indicate the extent of mutuality and equality among learners, and of collaboration, Storch (2002) coded the patterns of interaction for the following traits: 1) pattern of contribution 2) decision-making behaviour 3) nature of assistance 4) discourse and linguistic features. She proposed that the collaborative pattern of interaction contributes most to learning because both learners help each other, engage with each other's contributions, work together throughout the whole task and experience a feeling of shared endeavour.

Storch's (2002) framework of patterns of interaction has been particularly significant because it highlights the important role of mutuality as a major contributing factor to successful task-based interaction between peers. According to Storch (2001a), a discourse high on mutuality is marked with a high occurrence of requests, questions, explanations, repetitions, instances of collaborative completions, simultaneous talk or use of phatic utterances. Based on Storch (2002), there has been an increasing number of researchers (Li and Zhu 2017; Moranski and Toth 2016; Sato and Ballinger 2012; Toth, Wagner and Moranski 2013) who have underlined the important role of mutuality in creating optimal conditions for peer interaction and provided evidence that social and cognitive engagement between peers, that is listening to one another, pooling their skills and ideas, and providing feedback to one another is beneficial to learning.

For example, in their investigation of small-group meta-analytic talk and Spanish L2 development among adolescent learners of Spanish as a foreign language, Moranski and Toth (2016, 306) showed that learners learned from one another as they pooled their linguistic resources such as by discussing form-meaning connections. Moranski and Toth (2016) used the term *analytic mutuality* which was made visible by the reciprocal nature of learners' discussion as they built on the other's turn, by "the roles of expert and novice being taken up by both learners at different points" and "by the equality in the number and length of the turns taken by each" (307).

Li and Zhu (2017) referred to mutuality as the degree of engagement with each other's ideas and each other's wiki texts and providing scaffolding in producing wiki joint writing. Mutuality was explored through integrating *language functions* (agreeing, disagreeing, questioning, etc. grouped under two main categories *initiating* and *responding*), *writing change functions* (adding, rephrasing, correcting), and *scaffolding strategies* (affective involvement, contingent responsivity, direction maintenance, intersubjectivity, recruiting interest) (p.5). Importantly, when necessary, Li and Zhu (2017) considered *learners' roles/stances* because their individual roles in the pursuit of their goals influence the extent of their engagement with each other's contributions (see also Cumming 2012; Storch 2004).

Overall, studies suggest that mutuality implies that learners are engaged with each other and with each other's contributions, they create shared meaning and support one another. Mutuality can be made visible through measures such as turn-taking, language functions, scaffolding strategies or by looking at learners' roles/stances. However, because the vast majority of studies were conducted in adult ESL classrooms and/or in contexts involving computer-mediated interaction, it is important to investigate why and how young adolescent learners engage with one another in foreign language classrooms, in particular during interactions among learners of differing age and language proficiency. This classroom-based research study investigated the degree of mutuality among M-A young adolescent learners in an English as a foreign language (EFL) classroom. Further, it explored the factors that influence the degree of mutuality. Finally, it considered whether there is a relationship between the degree of mutuality and actual learning opportunities created during M-A peer interactions. This chapter attempts to answer the following interrelated research questions.

3 Research questions

RQ 1. What is the degree of mutuality among M-A young adolescent learners in an English as
a foreign language (EFL) classroom?
RQ 2. What are the factors that influence the degree of mutuality among these learners?
RQ 3. Is there a relationship between the degree of mutuality and actual learning opportunities created during M-A peer interactions?

4 Methodology

4.1 Context and participants

This classroom-based study examined peer interactions in three M-A EFL secondary school classrooms at an alternative school in Germany, which is a kind of school that has a special curriculum and offers a more flexible program of study than a traditional school. The classrooms are simultaneously mixed-proficiency classrooms. Due to wide differences in learners' age and language proficiencies, one of the school's main aims is to implement an individualized and learner-centred approach to teaching and learning. Consequently, learners are allowed to learn at their own speed and level, and teachers strive to develop individual learning paths. Learners are encouraged to accomplish tasks either individually, with a partner, in small study groups, or with the teacher's help, depending on their needs and abilities. The English curriculum at the school involves three lessons a week of which two were teacher-led lessons and one was *self-study time* (Studiezeit).

Twenty-two learners served as participants in this study. They attended three M-A classes composed of grade 7 (age 12–13), grade 8 (13–14) and grade 9 (14–15) learners and formed eleven mixed-age pairs. However, as Table 1 shows, only data from 20 learners will be analysed due to some of the participants' illness and attrition. Pseudonyms are used throughout the study. The majority of learners had known each other for a long time, some were very close friends and some were acquaintances. All participants had learned English since grade 3. The participants' relative proficiency was measured employing two classroom achievement tests, which were taken in the first term. However, the assessment practices were grade-specific and, therefore, the description is relative to the particular grade, and not an estimate relative to overall proficiency. Table 1 also shows the relative proficiency score:

Table 1: Participant characteristics.

Pair number	Name	Age	Gender	Grade	Relative proficiency
Pair 1	Lara	15	F	9	H
	Ella	14	F	8	H
Pair 2	Emilia	15	F	9	A
	Stella	12	F	7	A
Pair 3	Irena	14	F	7	A
	Sara	13	F	8	A
Pair 4	John	15	M	9	H
	Will	13	M	7	H
Pair 5	Lea	15	F	9	H
	Jess	14	F	8	A
Pair 6	Lilliana	13	F	7	H
	Leni	14	F	8	A
Pair 7	Riki	14	F	8	A
	Lyn	13	F	7	L
Pair 8	Gussi	14	M	8	H
	Jossi	13	M	7	H
Pair 9	Lenka	14	F	8	A
	Lucy	13	F	7	A
Pair 10	Alena	14	F	8	H
	Enna	13	F	7	H

H: high proficiency/A: average proficiency/L: low proficiency (relative to year group as assessed by the first term assessment practices)

4.2 Data collection

Data were collected during everyday common classroom lessons over one unit of work lasting two and a half months in total. The researcher was the teacher of the participants. Each time pairs worked on pedagogic tasks and exercises, they were audio-recorded. However, the data reported in this chapter were gained from recordings which were made by learners themselves during the study time lessons, during which learners worked on tasks included in their *study plan* (Fachplan). These lessons were supervised by another teacher and the teacher/researcher was not present.

The study plans contained pedagogical tasks and exercises (see Table 3) which were to be completed with a self-selected partner, as long as he/she was of a different age/grade. The reason for this step was that allowing learners to choose their partner is the usual practice in these classrooms, as revealed in the interviews that had been conducted with other language teachers. The rationale for the choice was that selecting a partner is more likely to result in more motivation to complete the tasks at hand and in well organized learning when the teacher is absent.

Audio-recordings on tasks which took place in the middle and towards the end of the whole period were chosen for analysis because students will by then have had a chance to become used to the use of microphones/digital recorders, which were provided to the students for the whole period of the unit of work.

After the unit of work, mainly within the first two days after the last task had been completed, interviews with all participants were conducted (see Kos 2017 for interview questions). The interviews aimed at understanding participants' feelings and perceptions of their interactions with an older/younger classmate over the whole period. They were held in the learners' L1 (German) and lasted for about forty-five minutes. The transcriptions of the interviews were compared with the audio recordings of the interactions for data triangulation, but a detailed description of learners' perceptions is not possible due to space constraints. Excerpts are included here as they provide some important insights into factors influencing mutuality, which may not be detectable from the audio-recordings only. Finally, student's pieces of writing and students' notes were examined and compared with the transcriptions of the audio-recordings. Table 2 below provides an overview of all data sources.

Table 2: Data sources.

Audio-recordings	Interviews	Artefacts
92 interactions (8–10 per pair)	18 interviews	students' notes
16 individual interviews	60 pieces of writing	
2 interviews with 2 learners	classroom tests	

Table 3: A description of language tasks and exercises.

Task	Description
Comic	Students jointly read the comic and worked out the meaning of the story. Then, they jointly completed a grammar exercise (pre-task phase) to practice the backshift of tenses before engaging in the main task. Later, they wrote the comic as a story and read their story to the class. In the subsequent 45 minute lesson (post-task phase) learners were asked to complete related exercises individually. (135 minutes).
Text-Reconstruction task	Students jointly identified and filled in the missing targeted linguistic features. Later, they were asked to replace the identified features with different words. (40 minutes)
Looking for help?	Students jointly read a text concerning a teenager looking for help and three replies of an agony aunt or uncle who are online experts, providing confidential advice and guidance. Then, they summed up the main text, determined the replies and talked about what they would do in a similar situation. (30 minutes)
Grammar exercises	Students jointly completed two grammatical exercises to practice and consolidate their knowledge of *phrasal verbs* and *infinitive with/without to*. (45 minutes)

4.3 Tasks and exercises

Tasks included mainly collaborative tasks, which combined speaking, writing and reading. However, learners also collaboratively carried out two grammatical exercises, which were aimed at the practice of certain linguistic items. Some tasks implemented were consistent with some general frameworks of task-based language teaching and learning according to which *a task* involves *holistic language use*, achieves *one or more meaningful outcomes*, or is made up of *different phases* (see for example, Samuda & Bygate 2008). To achieve ecological validity, tasks and exercises provided in the text-book were used. These were a part of the 8th and

9th grade syllabus and were included in the 8th and 9thgrade textbooks named Orange Line 4 and 5. However, since 7th grade learners also completed the tasks in the 8th and 9th grade syllabus, when necessary, these tasks were simplified to accommodate for their abilities. Thus, while for the 7th and 8th graders the majority of tasks in this unit were meant to expose and practice new grammatical forms, for the 9th graders the tasks served as an opportunity to gain increased control over forms that had already been encountered and practiced in the previous year.

5 Data analysis

The approach to analysis aimed at obtaining multiple perspectives such as participants' feelings, attitudes, intentions, and behaviors as well as at a detailed understanding of meaning-making actions. This will become evident when discussing the excerpts later in this chapter.

The first step of the analysis was to segment data into on- and off-task talk (Storch 2001a). Only on-task talk, in which learners were engaged in the task was further analysed. However, episodes of off-task talk, during which learners were engaged in talk not relevant to the task, were also counted and considered in further stages of analysis. Within the on-task talk, learners talked mainly about 1) the task at hand, 2) language use and choices, and 3) other task-related content. Episodes in which learners talked about how to go about completing the task at hand, negotiated or assigned roles, announced or negotiated the next stage in the task (Storch 2001a) are referred to as *task-related episodes* (TREs). Excerpt 1 provides an example of a TRE from the data, in which one learner helps the other to understand the task by checking on her understanding of it and then by inviting her to speak English. Words and sentences in italics included in square brackets are translations from learners' L1 German.

Excerpt 1: Task-related episode (TRE)
Li: [*So, now we've done the first task and now we're going to do the next one. I'm going to read it.*] What makes a person friend for you? What qualities are important?
Li: [*What does it mean, Leni?*] (saying as a teacher).
Le: [*Well, what a friend is to you*]. (overlap).
Li: [*Exactly!*] (saying as a teacher) [*What is important to you?*]
Li: [*Shall we speak in English?*]
Le: [*Yes, I think so.*]

Episodes, during which learners talked about language use and their choices are referred to as *language-related episodes* (LREs). LREs were coded based on Swain and Lapkin's (1998, 326) definition as "any part of a dialogue where language learners talk about the language they are producing, question their language use, or correct themselves or others" (see Excerpt 2 below). Episodes, during which learners perform the task but do not talk about the task or about language use are referred to as *content-related episodes* (CRE). In these episodes, learners talk about characters, events, etc. These three types of episodes (TREs, LREs, and CREs) were used as units of analysis.

The next step in the analysis was to derive a taxonomy of mutuality while attempting to preserve the emerging aspects of the term. Coding for mutuality is a challenging task because the construct implies cognitive, affective and social dimensions of peer interaction (Li and Zhu 2017; Moranski and Toth, 2016; Storch 2002). Mutuality was operationalized as the quality and degree of engaging with each other's ideas and contributions as well as assistance provided within pairs during task-related, content-related and language-related episodes. It became evident during the process of reading the transcripts that similarly to previous research, the degree of mutuality among pairs was mainly visible in *language functions* (agreeing, suggesting, etc.) and in the way and the extent learners requested and provided *assistance* to one another (co-construction, explanation, other-correction, etc.). Table 4 below shows definitions and examples from the data.

Table 4: Codes and examples from data.

	Language functions	
Suggesting	Offering suggestions/ recommendations about language or task.	E: that Jaden finished the mural?
Questioning	Asking questions that one is not clear about.	A: Did you say *has to* or *had to*?
Agreeing	Expressing agreement with others' viewpoints.	Good idea. So, let's write in German first.
Disagreeing	Expressing disagreement with other's viewpoints.	I don't think so.
	Ways of assistance	
Request for information	A request eliciting lexis, morpho-syntax or spelling. (Storch, 2001a)	L: What means fortführen?

Table 4 (continued)

Request for explanation	A request eliciting responses such as explanations or opinions.	Can you tell me what are we supposed to do here, please?
Co-construction	"The joint creation of an utterance, whether one person completes what another has begun, or whether various people chime in to create an utterance." (Foster and Ohta 2005, 420)	L: Well, look is not an irregular verb E: So then, looked L: (repeats and writes the sentence down). L: Sandy told others that the mural . . . (saying while writing the sentence down). E: looked great
Other-correction	An utterance which "involves a peer correcting his or her partner." (Foster and Ohta 2005, 420)	L: Sandy tells others . . . **E: told!**
Explanation	Refers to instances, during which learners explain language-related or task or language-related issues.	J: He let them down and that is why they are mad at him.
Other-repetition	A repetition of other's utterances with or without some type of expansion or modification	E: guilty A: **guilty** but his lovely girl wasn't too impressed.
Teacher-like assistance	Teacher-like assistance involved types of comments, including *continuers* and *active listening*. *Continuer* is an "instance where an interlocutor takes an interest in the speaker's utterance and encourages him/her to continue" (Foster and Ohta 2005, 420). Continuers may also occur when a speaker indicates to the interlocutor that the utterance is incomplete by rising intonation *Active listening*; a listening strategy where trained learners become skillful partners in giving feedback by using verbal/non-verbal methods of active participation in the conversation, such as back-channeling and the use of "wh" questions to help the speakers to continue (what?, where?, who?, when?, why?) (Gagné and Parks 2013, 207)	E: But Jaden explained that he . . . that he . . . that he . . . **S:** had? E: Yes, yes, great. Le: So we have done the first task and now we're going to do the next one. I'm going to read it. "What makes a person friend for you? What qualities are important?" Li: **What does this mean Le?** (sounding as a teacher).

Table 4 (continued)

Other indicators of mutuality	Turn-taking, time on task, number of conversational turns, LREs/ conversational turn frequency, learner's roles within LREs, TREs and CREs, aspects such as laughter, tone and pragmatic discursive function of each utterance

For example, with regards to language functions, peers frequently used suggestions, asked questions, sought agreements or expressed disagreements with one another. Suggestions were very common in the data. According to Wells (1999), a suggestion is a move that draws the other member of the pair into the decision-making process and therefore indicates high mutuality. Furthermore, instances of disagreements or challenging each other using disagreements were also common. Disagreements with each other were expressed via other-corrections (e.g., *No . . . His girlfriend was angry!* [argumentative tone] or requests for explanation (e.g., *Why is that?* [argumentative tone]). Moreover, disagreements sometimes remained unresolved. Storch (2001a) claimed that this indicates a lack of a shared perspective of the task. This lack of shared perspective is according to her (see also Antón and DiCamilla 1999) suggestive of low mutuality. However, unresolved disagreements in the data did not necessarily imply low involvement with each other's contributions. They seemed to have indicated that learners challenge one another as they grapple with a new language that appears to point to high mutuality. In contrast, instances during which learners displayed a lack of responsiveness to the propositional content of the partners' utterances were considered as an indication of low mutuality.

In relation to assistance, the most salient ways of requesting assistance found in the data were *request for information* and *request for explanation*. Learners provided assistance to one another mainly using *co-constructions, explanations, other-correction* and *other-repetitions*. Co-constructions in the data resemble Donato's (1994) notion of collective scaffolding, which implies that although prior to the co-construction each individual member of the pair lacked the necessary knowledge to produce a grammatically correct form, each member of the group contributed from his/her particular knowledge to the problem solution (see Table 4 above). And because during co-constructions learners pool their linguistic resources in order to form an utterance that neither of the learners is capable of forming individually, it follows that a co-construction requires a high degree of mutual engagement and is therefore indicative of mutuality.

Other instances of assistance suggestive of mutuality included *continuers* or *checking partner's understanding* which resemble strategies used by teachers (Davin and Donato 2013; Foster and Ohta 2005) and were therefore termed *teacher-like assistance*. Furthermore, Storch (2001a; 2001b) argued that *linguistic features* such as the first-person plural pronouns [*we, our*], or the use of [*let's, could you? do you think that?*] are features indicative of mutuality and joint ownership of the task, while a predominance of first- and second-person pronouns indicates low mutuality and non-collaborative orientation. However, it became clear during the analytical process that it was crucial to pay particular attention to the tone and the pragmatic discursive function of each particular utterance in order to understand the speaker's intention which in turn was important to determine the level of her/his willingness to engage with the task and the partner. For example, the pronoun *we* as in "*We must use simple past here!*" can have a different connotation depending on the intention of the particular speaker. When uttered in a bossy way, it can be intended to embarrass or ridicule a partner. When uttered in a friendly tone, however, it can serve the function of clarifying or even inviting the partner into a joint pursuit of the task at hand. In a similar vein, emotional aspects of each particular interaction such as instances of joy, laughter, anger ridiculing one another, etc. were taken into account in order to determine mutuality.

To determine the degree of mutuality and to better understand the mediating factors, all episodes (TREs, LREs and CREs) were further analyzed for the role played by each member of the pair in each episode (Moranski and Toth 2016). For example, some learners tended to initiate episodes while others were attentive listeners and stepped in only when a problem needed to be resolved. Excerpt 2 provides an example of learners' roles. During this interaction on the text-reconstruction task learners attempt to replace the word *kids* with a word of similar meaning. In this example, Alena initiates the LRE by requesting confirmation of her suggestion. Enna responds to Alena's request by suggesting the word *learners*. Alena then resolves the LRE by explaining that the word *learners* means *Schüler* and by providing the right word *children*.

Excerpt 2: Language related episode (LRE) – Initiation, Response, Resolution

A: Und kids ist people oder so? [*And kids is people or something like that?*] **initiation**
E: Learners? **response**
A: E: Aber learners ist doch Schüler aber ne Kinder oder? [*But learners is pupils but not children, right?*] . . . children! **resolution**

Finally, measures such as *time on task, turn-taking, number of conversational turns, LREs/conversational turn frequency* (see Table 6 above) were taken into consideration because they imply that learners are engaged with each other's contributions. The codes were then imposed back on the data and further analysed. Based on the analysis, indicators of the degree of mutuality were identified (see Table 5 below). Based on theseindicators, the degree of mutuality for each pair was determined and identified as high, moderate and low. This classification is, however, not straightforward, as there are numerous overlaps between the categories high, moderate and low, as interactions often displayed features of more categories. What is more, some pairs displayed differing degrees of mutuality within one task or across tasks suggesting that the degree of mutuality may vary. Therefore, after the codes had been imposed back on all transcripts and analysed, the overall degree of mutuality across tasks was determined for each pair.

Table 5: Degree of mutuality and its indicators.

HIGH MUTUALITY
Learners frequently engage with each other's contributions regarding the task and language. Learners listen to each other and display a willingness to offer and engage with each other's ideas. Learners take an interest in each other's utterances, encourage each other or even praise each other. Learners negotiate and establish an agreement with one another with regards to means of their joint activity, events, and goals of a task. Disagreements may occur but there is a willingness to resolve them. The talk is marked by short turns, speaker change is smooth and avoidance of longer gaps between turns. The discourse is rich in suggestions, questions, an agreement seeking behavior, repetitions, instances of simultaneous talk or use of phatic utterances. Discourse contains instances of joy, laughter or joking about language. Assistance is predominantly bidirectional and the distribution of assistance among learners is similar or even. Learners frequently request assistance and assist one another using collaborative completions, elaborate explanations, and constructions. Assistance is valued and accepted. Learners frequently engage in LREs and/or LREs/conversational turn ratio is high. Learners experiment with language and LREs tend to be elaborate.

MODERATE MUTUALITY
Although both learners contribute to the task, their willingness or ability to fully engage with each other's ideas and contributions regarding the task and the language is moderate or tends to vary. Learners negotiate an agreement with one another with regards to means of their joint activity, events, and goals of a task. Disagreements may occur but there is some willingness to resolve them. The talk is generally marked by short turns but occasionally contains longer gaps between turns. The discourse contains suggestions, questions, and agreement seeking behavior. Assistance is predominantly bidirectional, but the distribution of assistance among learners may vary throughout the task. Learners display some degree of willingness to assist each other. Explanations and co-construction occur, but they tend to be short and less elaborate. Other-corrections are frequent but are often not justified. LREs appear but are less elaborate. LREs/conversational turn ratio is moderate.

Table 5 (continued)

LOW MUTUALITY
Learners are not willing or unable to fully engage with each other's ideas and contributions regarding the task and language. Learners do rarely negotiate an agreement with one another with regards to means of their joint activity, events, and goals of a task. The discourse is poor in suggestions, questions, and agreement seeking behavior. Learners display low responsiveness. The talk is marked by long turns, speaker change is occasional and there are very few or no overlaps. Learners display low willingness to assist each other and rarely request and assist one another. LREs are rare, short and simple. Learners' discourse may contain argumentative tone, instances of anger, despair or even ridiculing one another.

Table 6: Degree of mutuality across language tasks and exercises.

Pair (Degree of mutuality)		Pair (Degree of mutuality)	
1.	Lara & Ella (MODERATE)	6.	Lilliana & Leni (HIGH)
2.	Emilia & Stella (HIGH)	7.	Riki & Lyn (LOW)
3.	Irena & Sara (MODERATE)	8.	Gussi & Jossi (MODERATE)
4.	John & Will (MODERATE)	9.	Lenka & Lucy (MODERATE)
5.	Lea & Jess (HIGH)	10.	Alena & Enna (HIGH)

Finally, in order to highlight the relationship between mutuality and actual learning opportunities created during interactions, LREs were analysed in terms of their occurrence and resolution across pairs. All LREs were classified as correctly resolved, incorrectly resolved, or unresolved. Excerpt 2 above provides an example of a correctly resolved LRE.

5.1 Coding and analysis of interviews

The insights into learners' perceptions were gained during interviews conducted after the unit of work. The interviews were analysed for the following categories adapted from Watanabe's (2008) study: (1) *overall perceptions about the pair interactions*, (2) *perceptions towards the degree of contribution, and* (3) *perceived learning outcomes* (see Kos 2017 for interview questions).

5.2 Inter-and intra-rater reliability

A second rater took part in two training sessions with the researcher. Concerning the degree of mutuality, we reached a consensus in 80 % of the instances. Our disagreements were related mainly to the language functions and ways of assistance. There were no disagreements concerning coding interviews. With regards to LREs we reached a consensus in 92 % of the instances. Later, we discussed differences and similarities concerning any episodes which remained unresolved and reached agreement. Intra-rater reliability was achieved by revisiting the data several times in later stages of the analysis and revising some codes. The revised codes were then imposed back on the data.

6 Findings and discussion

This section will provide findings and discussion in relation to each research question.

6.1 RQ1. What is the degree of mutuality among M-A young adolescent learners in an English as a foreign language (EFL) classroom?

As shown in Table 6, most pairs displayed either moderate (five pairs) or a high degree of mutuality (four pairs). It had been anticipated that when older (more proficient) and younger (supposedly less proficient) learners work together, their interactions would likely be moderate or even low on mutuality. These expectations were not met as only one pair displayed a low level of mutuality. And because mutuality plays an important role as a major contributing factor to successful task-based interaction between peers (Philp and Duchesne 2016), it follows that interactions of nine out of ten pairs in the current study were likely beneficial to learning. Moreover, learners within these pairs were engaged with each other, without the older or higher proficiency learners dominating the interaction or accomplishing the large part of the work. What is more, they were willing to engage their younger/less knowledgeable partner. It needs to be mentioned that although the degree of mutuality remained fairly stable across tasks and exercises, there were some slight variations, which could have been related to the linguistic demands of the task at hand. For example, on slightly more challenging tasks such as the Comic and a grammatical exercise that focused on phrasal verbs, some older/more proficient learners tended to take more initiative in completing linguistic problems on their own than in less linguistically demanding tasks. It seems that in such cases the older/more proficient learners' linguistic resources were necessary to complete the task which was above the other learner's level. This had an impact on the degree of mutuality.

6.2 RQ2. What are the factors that influence the degree of mutuality among these learners?

The following sections provide a more detailed description of selected pairs in order to highlight the degree of mutuality and the mediating factors. Although not typical for the data, the next section provides an example of high mutuality and illustrates some important factors that may influence the level of mutuality, namely learners' goals and perceptions of the partner's proficiency. In addition, this example illustrates that even younger learners can take on the role of an 'expert' and this role can be accepted and valued by the older partner.

6.2.1 High mutuality

Pair 6 Lilliana (7th grade, high proficiency) and Leni (8th grade, average proficiency)
In their interaction (Excerpt3) on the text-reconstruction task, it is surprising that the younger but more proficient learner, Lilliana, assists her older but less proficient partner Leni. Lilliana clearly plays the role of an expert. She leads Leni throughout the task and offers different forms of assistance, which are sensitive to the difficulties her partner is experiencing. In fact, she engages in forms of assistance which, according to the research, resemble those used by teachers such as *continuers, active listening* or *checking understanding* (Davin and Donato 2013; Foster and Ohta 2005). Lilliana frequently encourages Leni to complete her utterances (turns 136, 138) and patiently waits for her to do so. Lilliana often checks her understanding of the text (turns 131, 133, 140), as well as her understanding of grammar, or vocabulary (turn140). She mainly uses L1 to achieve this (turns 131, 133, 136, 139). What is more, Leni not only receives assistance when she directly asks for it but also when she doesn't (turn 131). Importantly, Lilliana does not merely provide Leni with correct answers but allows her first to read the text (turn 128), and to work out the answers on her own (turn 130). She also often praises Leni for her contributions (turns 129, 135, 142). However, it has to be said that the quality of Lilliana's assistance seems to have slightly varied across the tasks and could have been related to the linguistic demands of the task at hand.

Excerpt 3: Interaction of high mutuality
128   Le: After that I decided that it was dangerous to be a director. (reading and completing the sentence with the word *director*)
129   Li: Hmmm. (saying in prolonged pronunciation, praising and giving a sign to continue)
130   Le: than to be a policeman so I became a detective (reading and completing)
131   Li: [*Did you understand the story?*] (checking understanding)
132   Le: [*Well . . .*] (Leni is not sounding certain)
133   Li: [*Or at least the ending?*](checking understanding)
134   Le: [*Well, that the father was killed.*]
135   Li: Hmmm. (saying in prolonged pronunciation, indication of praisingLeni's correct utterance)
136   Li: [*And then?*] (inviting to continue, checking understanding)
137   Le: *silence*
138   Li: [*thinks*]
139   Le: [*thinks about*]
140   Li: [*Ok, and then he decided on what?*] (inviting to continue, checking understanding)
141   Le: [*something dangerous*]
142   Li: yes! (praising)

We can see that Lilliana is willing to assist her friend, can assist Leni at the right level and can explain the language in ways familiar to her partner. Although she lacks the adult expertise, Lilliana is able to draw Leni's attention and participation. It seems that she succeeds because Leni is not shy, and is very interested in the task, and in learning the language. It is very likely that being closer in knowledge and status than the adult teacher, Leni may feel freer to express her opinions, ask questions, and risk speculations, which contributes to the liveliness, and "mutuality" of the discourse (Damon and Phelps 1989). Damon and Phelps (1989, 11) refer to such discourse as *peer tutoring*. They explain that although such tutoring is low on equality it can be very high on mutuality. The variation in mutuality is, however, related to the tutor's interpersonal skill and training as well as to the tutee's receptiveness to learning (Damon and Phelps 1989, 11). It can be said that Lilliana shows receptiveness to Leni's learning. It appears that this quality contributed to a joint orientation to their work, willingness to share their ideas and a high degree of intersubjectivity established and maintained across tasks.

The establishment and maintenance of intersubjectivity is according to Antón and DiCamilla (1999) a necessary condition without which assistance may be hindered. As Antón and DiCamilla (1999, 240–241) explain, asking questions implies that "interlocutors operate on the cognitive plane with ideas and the social plane, as they actively engage another in solving a problem." They further explain that "to suggest or to propose that X is the case is to offer X for the listener's consideration and thereby invite the listener's active participation in the task" (240–241). In a similar vein, Leni's frequent use of questions, and suggestions seemed to have stimulated Lilliana's willingness to provide her with assistance, and thus contributed to the establishment and maintenance of intersubjectivity and thus to a high degree of mutuality of this pair. In fact, Leni was slightly more active speaking than her partner, taking 226 conversational turns compare to Lilliana's 224 across four tasks. Moreover, a high extent of assistance provided between these two learners is also indicated by a high number of LRE turns per conversational turns (see Table 7 below). Leni's active participation also greatly contributed to the fact that 48 out of 53 LREs were resolved correctly, although it was Lilliana who initiated and resolved the majority of them.

Table 7: Occurrence of LREs and their resolution across tasks.

Pair	MUT	RP	LRE	COR	INC	UNR	LRE turn/ conv turn	Ratio
Lara9/Ella8	M	H/H	57	58%	25%	18%	381/501	0.76
Emilia9/Stella7	H	A/A	64	72%	19%	9%	575/728	0.79
John9/Will7	M	H/H	9	67%	11%	22%	61/162	0.37
Lilliana 7/Leni8	H	H/A	53	91%	5%	4%	370/447	0.83
Lea9/Jess8	H	H/A	35	83%	0%	17%	218/356	0.61
Gussi8/Jossi7	M	H/H	60	83%	3%	13%	241/380	0.63
Lenka8/Lucy7	M	A/A	48	50%	25%	25%	300/453	0.66
Irena8/Sara7	M	A/A	30	63%	17%	20%	203/292	0.69
Alena8/Enna7	H	H/H	53	75%	8%	7%	267/359	0.74
Riki8/Lyn7	L	A/L	24	67%	33%	0%	77/120	0.64
N			433	317	58	58		
Percentage			43.3	73	13	13		
M				31.7	5.8	5.8		
Range			9–64	6–64	0–14	0–12		

RP – relative proficiency, LRE – Language Related Episode, COR – Correctly Resolved LRE, INC – Incorrectly Resolved LRE, UNR – Unresolved LRE

The interaction between Leni and Lilliana reveals two important aspects that appear to influence the level of mutuality, namely the learners' goals (Li and Zhu 2017, 3) and perceptions of the partner's proficiency (Watanabe 2008). As a result of her continuous pair work with her partner, Leni said that she learned a lot from Lilliana and considerably improved her English skills such as speaking skills as she was fully concentrated on English, worked intensively, and spoke only English during pair work. During the interview, she responded that she greatly valued collaborative work with Lilliana and expressed a positive attitude to pair work as such, and to its benefits for learning. Her words suggest that her goal was not to simply perform and complete a task, but a willingness to master new language and knowledge, to extend her abilities and to gain greater control over her learning (Li and Zhu 2017, 3). In line with previous research (Cumming 2012; Li and Zhu 2017; Storch 2004), this suggests that the level of commitment of individual learners to the shared goals as well as their individual roles in the pursuit of these goals impacts on how and to what extent learners engage with each other's contributions. As Li and Zhu (2017, 3) rightly say, "group/pair work is a goal-directed action in which one's aims or objects or efforts, or desired results mediate group/pair interaction."

In addition to learners' goals, Leni's words [*She is an English specialist. She helped me a lot with the tasks. And I have learned a lot from her.*] suggest that her perceptions of her partner's proficiency also influenced her engagement with Lilliana. In addition, her words point to the importance of taking learners' perceptions of partner's proficiency into consideration when setting up pair work in M-A classrooms because pairs are composed of learners of different ages and proficiencies. For example, perceiving a partner as a novice with low abilities could result in dominant behaviour by the older/more proficient learner and with the younger/less proficient learner taking a rather passive role (Watanabe 2008).

6.2.2 Moderate mutuality

Pair 8 – Gussi (8th grade, high proficiency) and Jossi (7th grader, high proficiency)

The following excerpt comes from the pair talk of Gussi, a high proficiency 8th grader, and Jossi, a high proficiency 7th grader, translating the text of the Comic task. It illustrates a connection between learners' emotions and the degree of mutuality. Importantly, it reveals the necessity to closely examine contextual aspects of interactions in order to determine mutuality.

Excerpt 4: Interaction of moderate mutuality

1	J:	Ok. It wasn't easy to plan the mural but on Sunday they started to work. (reading the first sentence in English, as if he was recruiting G.'s interest in the task as G. is involved in off-task behaviour with another student)
2	G:	Saturday.
3	J:	On Saturday.
4	G:	Es war nicht einfach das für die zu plannen. Doch am Samstag geht's mit der Arbeit los (translating from English).
5	J:	I have a date. I nearly forgot. (reading)
6	J:	[*I had a date.*] (translating)
7	G:	[*No, I have.*] (correcting)
8	J:	[*No, I have . . .*] (correcting, inaudible)
9	G:	[*Yes, I have forgotten or something like that.*] (contra-suggestion)
10	J:	[*Yes, I have . . .*] (insisting on his solution)
11	G:	[*No, he has forgotten it!*]maybe because he has no time now for this Graffiti. (correcting in an argumentative tone and explaining)
12	J, G:	The blue colour was a great idea Fetch. (overlap, reading) laughter
13	J, G:	Diese blaue Farbe war eine gute Idee, Zach. (jointly translating the previous sentence) laughter . . . . .
20	G:	*wasn't too impressed.* No idea. Chloe wasn't . . .
21	J:	But . . .
22	G:	I think, war nicht sehr beeindruckt (translating *wasn't very impressed*) . . . laughter

As excerpt 4 shows, both learners contribute to the translation, displaying an equally high degree of control and authority over the task and its direction. However, despite being the younger student in the pair, already at the beginning of the task, Jossi has to recruit Gussi's interest in the task as he is involved in off-task talk with another student (turn1). Although both learners engage with each other's suggestions they do so predominantly by very explicit other-corrections (turns 3, 7, 9), and by offering counter suggestions (6, 8, 10) without providing any justification. Moreover, both learners frequently challenged one another engaging in disagreements which were sometimes uttered in an argumentative tone (e.g., *No, he has forgotten it!*), which were not necessarily resolved. Also, despite the lack of explicit requests, questions, suggestions which according to research (Storch 2001a) suggests low mutuality, they seemed to have enjoyed all tasks, spent a relatively long time on them, listened to each other, joked about the language, laughed about each other's utterances while experimenting with a new language. In addition, they produced a relatively high number of co-constructions, lengthy LREs and their LRE/conversational turn ratio was high. Moreover, this pair showed little evidence of the first-person plural which according to Storch's (2002) framework indicates that this pair lacks joint ownership of the task and is therefore low on mutuality. However, both learners often exchanged views and opinions about the task and language while using the first person singular (e.g., I think, war nicht sehr beeindruckt [translating *wasn't very impressed*]). Furthermore, both learners' enjoyment of tasks, instances of laughter, joking about language and about each other's utterances indicate that positive emotions of these learners are connected with their joy of exploration or working together as well as their interest in and pursuit of the task (van Lier 1996). This observation also reflects Vygotsky's (1978, 1986, see also Swain 2013) proposals that cognition and emotion are interconnected as well as Imai's (2010) explanation that emotions are "socially constructed acts of communication that can mediate one's thinking, behavior, and goals" (276). What is ore, they can be "co-constructed as an event progresses" (Swain 2013, 196). On first sight, this pair's mutuality would likely be considered as low. However, a closer examination of learners' emotions is more likely to result in classifying this pair's degree of mutuality as moderate.

6.2.3 Low Mutuality

Pair 7 – Riki (8th grader, average proficiency) and Lyn (7th grader, low proficiency)

Excerpt 5 provides an example of low mutuality. It comes from an interaction between Riki, an average proficiency 8th grader, and Lyn, a low proficiency 7th grader on a grammatical exercise, which was targeted to deepen their knowledge of *present perfect*. Students had to decide whether the temporal words are related to *present perfect* or *past simple*. As the excerpt reveals, Riki shows a willingness to encourage Lyn to participate in the task. Riki assists Lyn by providing explanations (turn 1), by inviting her to produce an utterance (turns 3, 5, 7), by providing implicit feedback via rising intonation, which indicates that Riki's utterance may not be correct (turn 9), and by translating the target words into L1 with the follow-up question (turn 11). However, Lyn's replies are merely limited to short replies, or guesses without any reasoning for her choices (turns 4, 8, 10, 12). The only exception is seen in turn six, where she provides some reasoning for her choice.

Excerpt 5: Interaction of low mutuality
1   R: [*So, the first exercise is, what is finished and what is not finished, yet*]
2   L: Ok
3   R: [*So*] two days ago? (checking understanding)
4   L: [*is not finished, yet*]
5   R: Two days ago (stress on ago) ago . . . war [*was*] . . .
6   L: waren [*was, so it is finished*]
7   R: [*So, ok. always, finished or not?*] (checking understanding)
8   L: [*finished*] (only guessing)
9   R: always [*finished?*] (checking again)
10 L: [*No*] (guessing, not giving a reason)
11 R: [*so this year*] (translating for her) [*Is it in the past?*]
12 L: [*not finished*] (from now on L. doesn't say much and tends to merely write down what R. says)

Despite being a hardworking and responsible student, the younger/less proficient learner within this pair, Lyn, simply lacked the linguistic resources to engage with her older/more proficient partner's (Riki) contributions and thus to contribute to the task. At the same time, Riki did not seem to be capable of providing the necessary assistance for Lyn in order for her to participate more. Although she was willing to help Lyn to participate more, Riki simply has no other choice than complete the task without Lyn. It can be said that Lyn's limited linguistic resources greatly influenced the degree of mutuality of this pair. This case suggests that there is a threshold in terms of participation of younger lower-level learners. The question arises as to whether younger lower-level learners are likely to benefit from interactive work with an older/more proficient partner as they may not be developmentally ready to engage in discussions about some linguistic problems.

Overall, this section has indicated that the degree of mutuality within M-A pairs is mediated by a variety of factors including learners' goals, emotions, proficiency, perceptions of each other and partner's proficiency and linguistic difficulty of the task. It follows that to understand why learners engage with each other during their interactions the way they do, we need to obtain a variety of measures that allow for an examination of the above-mentioned dimensions as intertwined rather than distinct. In other words, the findings lend some support to studies that have argued for multidimensional measures of engagement which include not only learners' cognitive responsiveness but also social and emotional aspects (Lambert, Philp and Nakamura 2017; Philp and Duschene 2016; Swain 2013). Moreover, it lends some support to studies that investigate the elements that make up mutuality/engagement as autonomous constructs (Philp and Duschene 2016). Importantly, our attention has to be given to learners' perspectives to understand their perceptions, goals, and feelings.

6.3 RQ3. Is there a relationship between the degree of mutuality and actual learning opportunities created during M-A peer interactions?

This section complements the analysis and presents findings related to the occurrence of LREs and their resolution across pairs to highlight the relationship between the degree of mutuality and actual learning opportunities created during interactions as measured by LREs. The findings of the analysis of LREs are based on the analysis of interactions on three tasks and one grammatical exercise. As Table 7 below reveals, there were great variations in the LREs produced across pairs ranging from 9 to 64, the average score (M) 43. 3 and the median being 48. LREs tended to be resolved correctly across pairs and tasks and all pairs resolved 50% or more LREs correctly with the range being 6–64 (i. e. 50% to 91%).

However, most pairs left a number of LREs unresolved (range from 0–12, i. e. 0% to 25%) or resolved incorrectly (range 0–12, i. e. 0% to 33%). Table 7 shows that with the exception of John/Will, pairs frequently engaged in LREs despite the differences in age and language proficiencies. It also shows that even the pair that was low on mutuality engaged in LREs, although the number of LREs was very low, LREs were mostly short and a high percentage remained unresolved or resolved incorrectly. When looking at each individual pair, Table 7 reveals that pairs that were high on mutuality did not necessarily produce more LREs than moderate pairs. In other words, at first glance, the findings suggest that LREs tended to be engaged in and resolved regardless of whether mutuality was high or moderate. However, when we calculate the average number of LREs for pairs coded as displaying medium mutuality and those displaying high mutuality (see Figure 1 below), we can see that pairs that were higher on mutuality produced on average a higher number of LREs than pairs of medium mutuality. In other words, the level of mutuality did affect the number of LREs generated.

These findings can be interpreted from two different perspectives. On the one hand, they point to the limits of M-A peer interactions in terms of resolving linguistic problems and to the importance of the teacher's role to provide direct assistance to the learners. In other words, the findings suggest that although teachers may benefit from implementing M-A pair work, they should not assume that the older or higher ability students will, as a matter of fact, engage with the contributions of their younger or lower ability peers and help them to

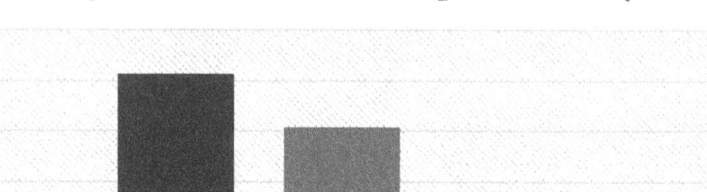

Figure 1: *Average number of LREs across degrees of mutuality.*
HM- High Mutuality, MM- Moderate Mutuality, LM- Low Mutuality

resolve linguistic problems in a way that a teacher does, and that no additional teacher's assistance is required.

Another possible interpretation is that despite the relatively high number of unresolved or incorrectly resolved LREs, the process of engagement with LREs without teacher's assistance might have allowed learners the freedom to explore and experiment with the language, to pool their language resources to complete difficult tasks and to try out different alternatives (Philp et al. 2014). According to Philp et al. (2014), such experience is highly valuable and may evoke positive feelings towards trying out new things, may help reduce anxiety about being corrected and may even lead towards increased autonomy (p. 25). It can also be said that the production of correct LREs may not be the ultimate pedagogical goal. Instead, the goal of itself might be the "verbalization of thoughts that makes learners to become aware of the limits of their knowledge, to predict linguistic needs, and to set goals for further learning" (Swain 2005 cited in Philp et al. 2014, 23). However, while allowing learners to grapple with difficult language, the teacher's task is to assist the younger or weaker students and to make sure that the older learner will not leave out her/his partner from the interaction (Kowal and Swain 1994), or complete the task for them.

Overall, the findings indicate that there was a relationship between the degree of mutuality and actual learning opportunities created during M-A peer interactions in this study. We have seen that nine out of ten pairs engaged in interactions that were moderate or high on mutuality. Both learners within these pairs appeared to be willing to offer and engage with each other's contributions, helped one another and were able to contribute to the task work (Storch 2002). They also frequently engaged with LREs and their interactions appeared to be conducive to learning (Storch 2002). This suggests that there is pedagogical value for older or more proficient students to be paired with younger or less proficient ones. Nonetheless, the analysis of LREs has also shown that while the majority of LREs were correctly resolved, a relatively high proportion of them remained either unresolved or was incorrectly resolved. This points to the necessity of the presence of the teacher to monitor interactions; in particular of pairs composed of low proficient learners in order to provide them with necessary assistance.

Finally, it has to be mentioned that the nature of peer interaction and assistance among pairs in this study was mediated by the context and the nature of learning at the alternative school which they attend. In fact, most learners in this study have known each other for a long period of time, and have had many opportunities to learn together and do assignments together. It also seems that having been taught according to the principles of learner autonomy afforded some students with abilities to grapple with tasks and language which were above their level. It must be acknowledged that the tasks and exercises applied in this study did by their own nature elicit focus on form, and trigger more deliberations about form than other tasks (Alegría de la Colina and García Mayo 2007). Therefore, they had an impact on the occurrence of and learners' engagement with LREs.

7 Conclusion

So what exactly is mutuality? This chapter confirms Damon and Phelp's (1989) and Storch's (2002, 2013) original definition of mutuality that suggests that mutuality is the quality and degree of engagement with each other's ideas and contributions and of mutual assistance during an interaction. The study confirms that mutuality is a complex construct that necessarily contains social, cognitive and emotional dimensions. In other words, to understand why some pairs are higher on mutuality than others, we need to pay closer attention to social, cognitive and emotional aspects of each particular interaction. For instance, we can say that in terms of social aspects, an interaction is high on mutuality when learners establish an interpersonal relationship, when they negotiate and establish an agreement with one another (intersubjectivity) with regards to means of their joint activity, events and goals of a task when they help each other and share ideas. However, mutuality can only be high if learners are able to negotiate and process the language as well as the objectives and content of the task at hand. This points to the cognitive dimension of mutuality and can be made visible in learners' engagement within LREs, TREs, and CREs. Finally, an interaction is more likely to be high on mutuality if learners are interested in the task or/and experience joy of exploration or working together. On the contrary, if learners are afraid to contribute to the task (Kowal and Swain 1994), are not responsive and/or try to save their face without causing one another embarrassment (Philp and Tognini 2009) the level of mutuality is likely to be low. This points to the emotional dimension of mutuality and reveals the importance of emotions in interpreting learners' utterances and in coding for mutuality. In theoretical terms, the construct as such reflects Vygotsky's (1978, 1986) proposal that knowledge and cognition are constructed through social interaction and that cognition and emotion are interconnected, thus greatly influencing language development (see also Swain 2013).

Contributing to the available body of EFL research by providing a picture of actual peer collaborative dialogue among young adolescent learners in an under-researched context of M-A classrooms, the current study aimed at laying the foundations for future research on M-A peer interactions in L2 M-A classrooms. Based on previous studies on peer interactions, the current study analyzed interactions of M-A pairs in terms of mutuality (Damon and Phelps 1989), which has been claimed to be a useful index to examine and to understand the degree of collaboration in peer interaction. Examining the factors that influence the M-A pairs' degree of mutuality and challenging the up to date approach to determining mutuality, this study contributes by deepening our understanding of what mutuality means and how do we go about analyzing it. It also sheds more light on why some M-A peer interactions are higher on mutuality than others. It proposes that the degree of mutuality is mediated by a variety of factors encompassing learners' goals, emotions, proficiency, perceptions of each other and partner's proficiency and linguistic difficulty of the task. Finally, it suggests a relationship between the degree of mutuality and actual learning opportunities created during M-A peer interactions.

While the study aimed to describe the naturally occurring peer interactions within M-A classrooms, it is likely that students' behaviour was influenced by the fact that the researcher was their teacher. For example, knowing that the teacher would listen to their recordings could have impacted on how they interacted while performing the tasks. Furthermore, the fact that the participants were mostly female (16 out of 20) obscures a genuine picture of M-A classroom interactions including both genders. The reason for this imbalance is that some male students, who had agreed to participate in the study, withdrew from it when they fully realized what they were expected to do. In addition to this, the small number of participants does impact on the validity of the quantitative analysis.

Another limitation of the current study is that it did not empirically evaluate L2 learning and development as a result of M-A pair work. Building on this study, future studies could investigate the potential of M-A peer interactions to foster second language development. Future research could also compare the nature of M-A peer interactions across different ages and contexts.

References

Alegría de la Colina and García Mayo, María del Pilar. 2007. "Attention to form across collaborative tasks by low proficiency learners in an EFL setting. " In Investigating tasks in formal language learning, edited by García Mayo, María del Pilar, 91–116. Clevedon: Multilingual Matters.

Antón, Marta, and Frederick Dicamilla. 1999. "Socio-Cognitive Functions of L1Collaborative Interaction in the L2 Classroom."*The Modern Language Journal* 83: 233–247.

Campagna-Schleusener, Sabine. 2012. *Kinder unterstützen Kinder* [Children Assist Children]. Bern: Haupt.

Cumming, Alister. 2012. "Goal Theory and Second-language Writing Development, Two Ways." In *L2 Writing Development: Multiple Perspectives*, edited by Rosa María Manchón Ruiz, 135–164. Berlin: Walter de Gruyter, Mouton.

Damon, William, and Erin Phelps. 1989. "Strategic Uses of Peer Learning in Children'sEducation." In *Peer Relationships in Child Development*, edited by Thomas J. Berndt and Gary W. Ladd, 135–157. NewYork: Wiley.

Dao, Phung, and Kim McDonough. 2018. "Effect of Proficiency on Vietnamese EFL Learners' Engagement in Peer Interaction." *International Journal of Educational Research* 88: 60–72.

Davin, J. Kristin, and Richard Donato. 2013. "Student Collaboration and Teacher-directed Classroom Dynamic Assessment: A Complementary Pairing."*Foreign Language Annals* 46: 5–22.

Donato, Richard. 1994. "Collective Scaffolding in Second Language Learning." In *Vygotskian Approaches to Second Language Research*, edited by James P. Lantolf and Gabriela Appel *Vygotskian Approaches to Second Language Research*, 33–56. Norwood, NJ: Ablex.

Foster, Pauline, and Amy Snyder Ohta. 2005. "Negotiation for Meaning and Peer Assistance in Second Language Classrooms." *Applied Linguistics* 26: 402–430.

Gagné, Nathalie and Susan Parks. 2013. "Cooperative learning tasks in a Grade 6 intensive ESL class: Role of scaffolding." *Language Teaching Research*, 17: 188–209.

Hoffman, Jo. 2002. "Flexible Grouping Strategies in the Multiage Classroom." *Theory into Practice* 41: 47–52.

Huf, Christina, and Andrea Raggl. 2015. "Social Orders and Interactions among Children in Age-mixed Classes in Primary Schools – New Perspectives from a Synthesis of Ethnographic Data."*Ethnography and Education* 10: 230–241.

Imai, Yasuhiro. 2010. "Emotions in SLA: New Insights from Collaborative Learning for an EFL Classroom." *The Modern Language Journal* 94: 278–292.

Kalaoja, Esko, and Janne Pietarinen. 2009. "Small Rural Primary Schools in Finland: A Pedagogically Valuable Part of the School Network." *International Journal of Educational Research* 48: 109–116.

Kos, Tomas. 2017. "Peer Assistance among Mixed-age Pairs in Mixed-age EFL Secondary School Classrooms in Germany." *European Journal of Applied Linguistics*. 0(0): -. Retrieved 2 Dec. 2018, from doi:10.1515/eujal-2017-0013.

Kowal, Maria, and Merill Swain.1994. "Using Collaborative Language Production Tasks to Promote Students' Language Awareness." *Language Awareness* 3: 73–93.

Lambert, Craig; Philp, Jenefer, and Nakamura, Sachiko. 2017. "Learner-generated Content and Engagement in Second Language Task Performance." *Language Teaching Research* 21: 665–680.

Li, Mimi, and Wei Zhu. 2017. "Explaining Dynamic Interactions in Wiki-based Collaborative Writing." *Language Learning & Technology* 21: 96–120.

Little, Angela W. 2007. *Education for all and Multigrade Teaching: Challenges and Opportunities*. Springer:Dordrecht.

Moranski, Kara, and Paul, D. Toth. 2016. "Small-group Meta-analytic Talk and Spanish L2 Development." In *Peer Interaction and Second Language Learning: Pedagogical Potential and Research Agenda*, edited by Masatoshi Sato and Susan Ballinger, 291–316. Amsterdam: John Benjamins.

Philp, Jenefer, and Susan Duchesne. 2016. "Exploring Engagement in Tasks in the Language Classroom." *Annual Review of Applied Linguistics* 36: 50–72.

Philp, Jenefer, Adams, Rebecca, and Iwashita, Noriko. 2014. *Peer interaction and second language learning*. New York: Taylor & Francis.

Philp, Jenefer, and Rita Tognini. 2009. "Language Acquisition in Foreign Language Contexts and the Differential Benefits of Onteraction. "*International Review of Applied Linguistics* 47: 245–266.

Sato, Masatoshi, Susan Ballinger. 2012. "Raising language Awareness in Peer Interaction: A Cross-context, Cross-method Examination." *Language Awareness* 21: 157–179.

Storch, Neomy. 2001a. "*An Investigation into the Nature of Pair Work in an ESL Classroom and its Effect on Grammatical Development*." PhD thesis, Department of Linguistics and AppliedLinguistics. The University of Melbourne.

Storch, Neomy. 2001b. "How collaborative is Pair Work? ESL Tertiary Students Composing in Pairs." *Language Teaching Research* 5: 29–53.

Storch, Neomy. 2002. "Patterns of interaction in ESL pair work." *Language Learning* 52:119–158.

Storch, Neomy.2004. "Using Activity Theory to Explain Differences in Patterns of Dyadic Interactions in an ESL Class."*The Canadian Modern Language Review* 60: 457–480.

Storch, Neomy. 2013.*Collaborative Writing in L2 Classrooms*. Bristol, UK: Multilingual Matters.

Swain, Merill. 2013. "The Inseparability of Cognition and Emotion in Second Language Learning." *Language Teaching* 46: 195–207.

Swain, Merill, and Sharon Lapkin. 1998. "Interaction and Second Language Learning: Two Adolescent French Immersion Students Working Together." *The Modern Language Journal* 82: 320–337.

Toth, Paul D., Elvis Wagner, and Kara Moranski. 2013. "Co-constructing Explicit L2 Knowledge with High School Spanish Learners through Guided Induction." *Applied Linguistics* 34: 255–278.

van Lier, Leo. 1996. "*Interaction in the Language Curriculum: Awareness, Autonomy, and Authenticity*. Harlow, UK: Longman.

Vygotsky Lev Semyonovich. 1978. *Mind in Society: The Development of Higher Psychological Processes*. Cambridge, MA: Harvard University Press.

Vygotsky Lev Semyonovich. 1986. *Thought and Language*. Cambridge, MA: MIT Press.

Wagener, Matthea. 2014. *Gegenseitiges Helfen.Soziales Lernen im jahrgangsgemischten Unterricht*[Helping Each Other. Social Learning in Age-mixed Lessons]. Wiesbaden: Springer VS.

Watanabe, Yuko. 2008." Peer-Peer Interaction between L2 Learners of Different Proficiency Levels: Their Interactions and Reflections." *The Canadian Modern Language Review*64: 605–635.

Wells, Gordon. 1999. *Dialogic Inquiry: Towards a Sociocultural practice and Theory of Education*. Cambridge, UK: Cambridge University Press.

Izaskun Villarreal and Miren Munarriz-Ibarrola

"Together we do better": The effect of pair and group work on young EFL learners' written texts and attitudes

1 Introduction

Many teachers are leveraging the learning opportunities offered by group work in the classroom because group work enables teachers and students to develop and employ knowledge and skills in authentic and meaningful tasks. However, pair and group activities have unevenly been introduced in foreign language (FL) classrooms. While group and pair activities involving oral interactions are common (García Mayo and Lázaro Ibarrola, 2015; García Mayo and Zeitler 2017), collaborative writing activities, understood as the co-authoring and co-ownership of a single text by two or more writers (Storch 2013, 2018), are relatively unusual.

Writing at schools has traditionally been situated within the learning-to-write approach rather than the writing-to-learn a language perspective, in which writing serves as a vehicle for language learning (Manchón 2011). Young learners with emerging language skills have been afforded fewer opportunities to write rather than speak because a certain threshold language proficiency is presupposed below which writing activities might be barren. Besides, young learners' metalinguistic awareness and ability to metatalk are often underestimated (Muñoz 2017).

Moreover, students and teachers tend to perceive writing tasks negatively. Students conceive writing as a boring and difficult activity and they usually rank it as the most boring language skill to practice (Murtiningsih 2016). Teachers, on the other hand, avoid encouraging writing because they feel overwhelmed with corrections and unsure as to how to give feedback on the written text (McDonough, De Vleeschauwer, and Crawford 2018). However, existing research on students' beliefs about writing collaboratively has underscored that learners enjoy writing together and consider collaborative writing advantageous for writing and language learning (see Storch 2013 for a summary).

Additionally, research has found that pair work increases engagement and facilitates language learning (Storch 2013). Adult learners have been shown to be able to help peers move towards a more proficient state by providing timely attuned support (De Guerrero and Villamil 2000; Donato 1994; Ohta 1995; Swain 2000, 2006). In fact, recent research has shown that pair and group work

Izaskun Villarreal, Miren Munarriz-Ibarrola, Public University of Navarre

https://doi.org/10.1515/9781501511318-005

improve one or more components of CAF (Complexity, Accuracy and Fluency, e.g., Fernández Dobao, 2012, 2014a; McDonough and García Fuentes 2015; Wigglesworth and Storch 2009) and also some global qualitative measures including content, organization, vocabulary and grammar (Storch 2005; Shehadeh 2011; Villarreal and Gil-Sarratea 2020). The impact that learner setup has on the purported benefits of collaboration, however, is still an underexplored area of research (Fernández Dobao 2012, 2014a).

The limited research that has been carried out has addressed pre-university learners (e.g., Kim and McDonough 2011; Kuiken and Vedder 2002) and mixed findings have been obtained. While in a study with 15–16-year olds completing a dictogloss task benefits were only attested for students whose classroom dynamics already included plenty of pair work (Basterrechea and García Mayo 2013), Bueno-Alastuey and Martínez de Lizarrondo (2017) and Villarreal and Gil-Sarratea (2020) obtained more competent texts from all collaborating students when completing a description task (12–13-year olds) and a composition task (17–18-year olds), respectively.

All in all, writing has been shown to be valuable for learning languages (Manchón, 2011) and pair and group work have been reported to improve written texts on quantitative and qualitative measures (e.g., Fernández Dobao 2012; Villarreal and Gil-Sarratea 2020) and to elicit positive responses from teachers and students alike (Fernández Dobao and Blum 2013; McDonough, De Vleeschauwer, and Crawford 2018). Therefore, situated within the writing to learn language approach (Manchón 2011), the current study seeks to explore the linguistic and motivational effects of writing conditioned by group type. This study adds to the Second Language Acquisition (SLA) literature by exploring the effects of collaboration among young learners, a population which remains underexplored in spite of constituting one of the largest (and fastest growing) groups of English learners in the world (Enever 2018; García Mayo 2017, 2018; Lázaro-Ibarrola and Villarreal 2019).

2 Literature review

The social constructivist perspective of learning (Vygotsky, 1978) establishes that cognitive and linguistic development occur through scaffolded interaction. The use of pair and group work in second language (L2) teaching and learning processes hinges on this view, as it has been shown that peers can provide each other with carefully attuned support that pushes their learning forward (De Guerrero and Villamil 2000; Donato 1994). Following this approach, researchers applying sociocultural theory to the study of L2 learning maintain that learners can have a positive impact on each other's development and even achieve a higher level of performance by working collaboratively, as they can offer each other scaffolded assistance and even counterbalance their weaknesses with their strengths (Storch 2011; Swain 2000).

Existing research has suggested that cognitively immature young learners do not make full use of their metalinguistic awareness abilities because these cognitive processes are relatively effortful and resource-intensive (Tellier and Roehr-Brackin 2017). Metalinguistic awareness is activated as students try to understand material, analyse input, or attempt to solve production or comprehension problems (Tellier and Roehr-Brackin 2017) and it has been claimed to change and evolve as learners grow in cognitive maturity (Muñoz 2014). In fact, spelling and word combinations appear as early concerns for young English language learners, while more grammatical concerns appear as they grow older (Muñoz 2014).

To date, few studies have investigated the merits of collaboratively written tasks for young EFL secondary learners, a population that has frequently been deprived of the opportunity to write together because their capacity for mutual scaffolding has often been underestimated (Muñoz 2017).

2.1 Language focused episodes

When students collaborate in the co-construction of meaning, they encounter linguistic difficulties which create meaningful and authentic opportunities to interact in and about language (Storch 2013; Swain and Watanabe 2012). These language focused discussions are known as language-related episodes (LREs) (Swain and Lapkin 1998) and refer to episodes where there are interactional modifications as a result of students' attention to form (Long 1996). These LREs are considered opportunities for language learning and development, because they help students to gain and co-construct new knowledge or consolidate existing knowledge (Storch 2013; Swain and Watanabe 2012).

An increasing number of studies have reported that students mostly discuss grammar and vocabulary (e.g., Fernández Dobao 2012; Wigglesworth and Storch 2009). Mechanics seem to attract less attention from participants, probably because the learner writing the text ultimately decides on spelling, punctuation, and capitalization (Fernández Dobao 2012). The outcome or resolution of the LREs generated has also been investigated (Leeser 2004; Swain 1998). Students seem to solve correctly most of the LREs generated (Alegría de la Colina and García Mayo 2007; Fernández Dobao 2012; García Mayo and Azkarai, 2016;

García Mayo and Imaz Agirre, 2019; Storch and Aldosari 2013), which has been associated with enhanced linguistic performance (Kim 2008; Swain 1998).

As mentioned above, most of the studies target university students and few studies have addressed pre-university cohorts. Villarreal and Gil-Sarratea (2020) investigated 17–18-year-old intermediate English as a foreign language (EFL) secondary learners writing an argumentative text. They found that students focused similarly on lexical and grammatical aspects (42.03% and 44.93%, respectively), while considerably less attention was given to mechanical aspects, around 13%. The correct resolution rate, however, was similar for the three types of episodes, and pairs resolved them correctly approximately 90% of the times. Similarly, Basterrechea and García Mayo (2013), in a study conducted with 15–16-year-old lower intermediate EFL learners completing a dictogloss (Wajnryb 1990), also reported that students attended to grammar and lexis at parallel rates (around 50%, but mechanics was not measured). Students were successful at solving them about 75% of the time. Different results were obtained by Kim and McDonough (2011) with a group of young learners (13–14 year-olds) completing a dictogloss task. They observed that although the rate of positive resolution was once again high across categories (approximately 75%), students discussed lexical aspects more frequently than grammatical ones.

Relatively rare are studies that have contrasted pair and group LREs in an attempt to explore which condition fosters more learning opportunities, and those that have done so involve university learners. Fernández Dobao (2012, 2014b, 2014a), for instance, examined the pair and group deliberations of English university students learning Spanish as a foreign language when completing a composition. She concluded that the number of participants in the interaction did not have much influence on the focus of the LREs, but groups created more LREs and were more successful at solving them. Similar findings were obtained by García Mayo and Zeitler (2017) in a partial replication of Fernández Dobao (2014b). They reported (non-significant) advantages for groups over pairs on the occurrence and outcome of lexical LREs (grammar LREs were not analysed). Both studies emphasized that the success achieved by the groups was the consequence of a positive effect of the number of participants: more learners meant a larger pool of knowledge and subsequently more chances to solve problems satisfactorily. No study to date has examined how learner grouping affects the writing process of young learners and in particular, whether they engage in language-focused discussions and how successful they are at solving them, a task we take up here.

2.2 Texts written individually vs in pairs and in groups

2.2.1 Quantitative measures

Studies conducted predominantly among university students have provided converging evidence for the positive effects of collaboration on the accuracy and fluency of written texts. Regarding fluency, pairs and groups have been reported to write shorter texts than individuals, probably due to insufficient writing time (Fernández Dobao 2012) or length restrictions imposed by task design features (Villarreal and Gil-Sarratea 2020).

Higher accuracy rates have been consistently reported for advanced L2 learners (e.g. Storch 2005; Wigglesworth and Storch 2009) and for intermediate FL university students (e.g. Fernández Dobao 2012; McDonough and García Fuentes 2015) alike. The more accurate texts have been attributed to deliberations over language and the learners' opportunities to pool their resources. However, contradictory results have been reported in secondary school contexts. Basterrechea and García Mayo (2013), for example, only found accuracy improvements for learners in a content and language integrated learning (CLIL) program, students who were already familiar with a task-based methodology which included extensive group work. The texts written by EFL learners were unaffected and accuracy rates did not improve. In contrast, Villarreal and Gil-Sarratea (2020) found significant accuracy improvements with slightly older learners: students wrote texts that had fewer errors and in particular, fewer grammatical errors, when they wrote in pairs. The authors related the accuracy advantage to the language discussions generated while negotiating meaning and the timely assistance offered by peers. Finally, Bueno-Alastuey and Martínez de Lizarrondo (2017) in a partial replication of Fernández Dobao's (2012) investigation explored collaboration and learner grouping effects on physical descriptions written by 12–13-year-old EFL learners. Descriptions were analysed for complexity, accuracy, and fluency indicators. Similar to Fernández Dobao (2012), the authors reported an overall trend favouring collaborating students, although significant differences were only obtained for the number of error free T-units when individuals were contrasted with dyads and triads. They also suggested that task type might have affected their results, as well as the fact that students were of varying proficiency levels.

2.2.2 Qualitative measures

Recent studies have questioned the ecological validity of employing exclusively discourse analytic measures to estimate the impact of collaboration on written texts (McDonough and García Fuentes 2015; Villarreal and Gil-Sarratea 2020). Rubrics are common among instructors, and more specifically among secondary school teachers, not only because these types of scales enable them to assess learners who are still developing their own language ability, but also because they are aligned with current views on education in which formative assessment is prioritized (Ball, Kelly, and Clegg 2015).

To date the studies that have used rubrics to assess the effect of collaboration have reported mixed findings, probably due to the different text types represented, and also due to the variety of components measured. Some authors have reported no differences in writing ratings (McDonough and García Fuentes 2015; Storch 2005), while others have found benefits for content, organization, vocabulary, mechanics, and grammar after sustained and prolonged collaboration (Khatib and Meihami 2015; Shehadeh 2011). After a single collaborative task, Villarreal and Gil-Sarratea (2020) reported significant differences only for the structural features of the text.

These inconclusive findings emphasize the need for further studies to understand how collaboration, and in particular, type of grouping, affects the written compositions of young FL learners. It is our belief that by analysing both quantitative and qualitative measures a more reliable representation of the effects of collaboration will be obtained.

2.3 Students' attitudes and perceptions

Previous studies which have canvassed students' attitudes towards composing in collaboration have mostly obtained positive views. Yet, they have mainly investigated university students and have predominantly focused on students writing in pairs (e.g., Shehadeh 2011; Storch 2005, but see Fernández Dobao and Blum 2013 for groups of four).

In a study by Storch (2005), the majority of students found collaboration very helpful, especially for grammatical accuracy and vocabulary learning. They considered that collaboration provided them with opportunities to pool their knowledge together and learn alternative ways of expressing the same ideas. Shehadeh's research (2011) revealed the same positive perception with participants finding collaboration both beneficial and enjoyable. The same impression was gathered by Fernández Dobao and Blum (2013) with university Spanish FL learners. Students believed that when working collaboratively there were more resources to share, which allowed them to write more competently, although they did not consider that it contributed to new language learning.

Currently, most studies investigating collaboration have identified some positive effects on students' written texts and attitudes towards writing. However, little is known about the effects of collaboration and type of grouping on the texts written by young learners as well as on their attitudes towards writing. Considering that, the present study seeks to explore the effects of collaboration and type of grouping on the written texts and on the attitudes towards writing of 54 12–13-year-old Basque-Spanish EFL learners. The following research questions guided this study:

1. Do young learners engage in collaborative dialogue, operationalized as LREs? If so, what type of LREs do they generate? What is the outcome of these LREs?
2. Is there a difference in the texts produced by young EFL secondary school learners in terms of quantitative and quality measures under three grouping conditions?
3. What is the attitude of young EFL secondary students towards writing and towards writing in collaboration, in particular?

3 Methodology

3.1 Participants and instructional context

The participants were 54 12–13 year-old Basque-Spanish EFL learners in a school context in Navarre (Northern Spain). They came from two intact classes studying their first year of compulsory secondary education at a semi-private Basque secondary school.

Students were taught by two different teachers who shared the syllabus and followed identical teaching materials as well as assessment criteria and tools. The methodology used in the English classroom, as well as in the rest of the classes, was a constructivist, action-based approach. As a result, communicative and basic interaction in English was common and pair and group work was frequent. However, the teachers confirmed that pair and group writing was new to students as learners always wrote texts individually.

At the time of data collection, all learners had been learning English at the same school for 6–7 years, with five 50′ English lessons per week every year. According to school internal observations, most students had a beginner proficiency level as described by the Common European Framework of Reference for Languages. An independent English placement test (UCLES 2017) the students completed confirmed that most students were beginners except for two that were low intermediate.

3.2 Instruments

Four instruments were used for data collection: (a) a pre-test: an individual narrative text; (b) an experimental task: a second narrative text written either in pairs (n=9) or groups of three students (n=12); (c) the recordings of the conversations of the pairs and groups; (d) a questionnaire which gathered students' attitudes and perceptions towards writing in collaboration.

The pre-test and the experimental tasks were specifically designed by the researchers and their suitability was confirmed by both teachers. The tasks were typical narrative texts (a common genre in the primary and the secondary education curriculum) which targeted the narration of personal experiences: for the individual writing, the students had to write about something funny that happened last summer, and for the text written in pairs or groups, about a scary moment in their lives. Both prompts followed a similar structure and provided similar instructions. Students were asked to write about 100 words.

The recordings of the students' interactions formed the third source of information. The pairs and groups recorded their own interactions by using their personal cell phones and transferred their files to the second author at the end of the session.

Finally, students were administered an individual and anonymous questionnaire. The survey was based on Fernández Dobao and Blum (2013), Shehadeh (2011), and Storch (2013) and elicited participants' attitudes and perceptions regarding the collaborative writing task. It consisted of 17 questions which combined close-ended and open-ended questions. The survey canvassed students' opinions on writing, group work, the relative difficulty of writing collaboratively, the quality of the collaborative text, the improvement of specific language aspects or skills, and the amount of English learnt from peers and from the teacher. It also assessed students' perceptions of what the quality of the content, vocabulary, and grammar of the text would have been if they had written the text individually. Students' writing preferences were also surveyed. Finally, students were asked about what the source of difficulty was when writing with a peer.

When learners were given a rating scale question, they were also required to justify their answer. Questions were written in English and in Basque to ensure it would be understandable for all students and to avoid reported difficulties when collecting personal opinions in a FL (Shehadeh 2011).

3.3 Procedure

The study involved six sessions and was carried out as part of the regular coursework over a period of three weeks. In the first session, students were asked to complete a language background questionnaire. The outcomes of the questionnaire discarded any meaningful contact with the language outside school and thus its results will not be further analysed here.

In the second session, participants took the Cambridge English Placement Test (UCLES 2017). The pairs and groups were formed by parallel proficiency level students as previous studies indicate that collaboration tends to occur mainly among similar language ability pairs (Storch 2005). The teacher and the second author formed the groups, which were established with three criteria in mind: the placement test results, the results from the individual writing, and a fluent relationship with their partners. This resulted in the creation of 9 pairs (18 students) and 12 small groups (36 students). Students were assigned at random to the pair or group conditions.

In the third session, students played a game for 35 minutes to revise and reinforce their prior knowledge about the structure and characteristics of narrative texts. In the fourth session, participants were given 30 minutes to write the first narrative essay individually. This individual essay served as a pre-test against which to compare the results from the collaborative writing activity in order to observe whether collaboration had any effect on the written texts.

In the fifth session, a week later, students were asked to write a second narrative essay. As this was the experimental task, teachers assigned students to one of the conditions: pairs or groups of three. This time, students were given 40 minutes to compose their writings based on the finding that pairs and groups take usually longer to complete tasks (Fernández Dobao 2012; Storch 2005; Wigglesworth and Storch 2009). Participants' voices were recorded using cell phones while they performed the task.

In the sixth session, participants were asked to complete an online survey about their perceptions on the advantages and/or disadvantages of collaboration.

3.4 Data analysis

The data gathered in this study included three different sets of data: 1) 49[1] individual texts, 9 texts written in pairs, and 12 texts written in groups of three; 2) the recordings of the oral interactions (a total of 225.3 minutes) by 7 pairs and 6 groups while they were completing the experimental task (which were later

---

[1] Five participants were excluded from the first writing counting (n=49) because 4 did not write the individual text and one wrote an unintelligible text. However, not to compromise further the already small sample size in the experimental task, those students were considered for the experimental task (n=54).

transcribed verbatim). Due to technical difficulties, 8 recordings out of 21 were discarded; and 3) 51[2] questionnaires about students' perceptions on the collaborative task.

3.4.1 Criteria for the analysis of the pair dialogues

First, the recordings were scrutinized for LREs, that is to say, for extracts in which students explicitly focused their attention on language, questioning their language use or correcting themselves or others. These LREs were later categorized for focus and classified as (i) lexis-focused episodes (L-LRE) if learners focused on vocabulary (Example 1); (ii) form-focused (F-LRE) if learners discussed grammatical aspects (Example 2); and (iii) mechanics-focused (M-LRE) if aspects like spelling and punctuation were targeted (Example 3).

Example 1
P4.1: by the . . . *nola esaten da 'ventana'?* [how do you say "window"?]
P4.2: by the window.

Example 2
G4.1: on the lunch we went to a restaurant.
G4.2: okay.
G4.1: and . . . we went to the restaurant and a *camarer* [meaning waiter].
G4.3: to a restaurant or to the? To a restaurant.
G4.2: to a restaurant, because the restaurant is when you have to go e *aldi gehiagotan* [more than once].
G4.1: To a restaurant and we . . .

Example 3
G2.1: *nola idazten da* Halloween? [how do you spell Halloween?]
G2.2: *con dos e.* [with double *e*]
G2.3: *h-rekin.* [with *h*]
G2.2: *no sin h.* [no without *h*]
G2.3: *con h.* [with *h*]

---

2 For various reasons, 3 students did not complete the final survey (n = 51).

Finally, the LREs generated were also considered on the basis of their outcome (García Mayo and Azkarai, 2016; Leeser 2004; Swain 1998) and were tallied as correctly resolved (Example 4), incorrectly resolved (Example 5), or unresolved (Example 6).

Example 4
G3.1: a lot of gums.
G3.2: no, gum is *chicle* [gum].
G3.1: with a lot of *goxokiak* [sweets]!
G3.2: sweets!

Example 5
G2.2: no, in her house, *porque hemos puesto aquí* . . . [because here we've written . . .]
G2.1: there in her house . . .
G2.3: no, no! In shes house.
G2.1: in shes house. Shes o she?
G2.3: shes.

Example 6
G1.1: *a la última planta. Finally* plant. [to the last floor] (they mean penthouse)
G1.2: Finally plant, *ez.* Finally *da nola "lo último"*.
G1.1: *pues eso*. [that's it]
G1.2: *baina es que* finally *da nola* .. *¿sabes*? [but, I mean, finally is how . . . do you get it?]
(They wrote penthouse in brackets)

3.4.2 Criteria for the analysis of compositions

Firstly, the essays were analysed in terms of quantitative measures of accuracy and fluency (Fernández Dobao 2012; Storch 2005; Wigglesworth and Storch 2009). The quantitative analysis of lexical and complexity measures was discarded as the shared communicative goal of the compositions might not require any complexity growth (Pallotti 2009), and in addition, the limited word length (100 words) might prevent it (Villarreal and Gil-Sarratea 2020). Fluency was measured by the total number of words produced in each text. Accuracy of the texts was analysed by focusing on grammatical, lexical, and mechanical errors. Grammatical errors included syntactic and morphological errors; lexical errors included confusion of word choice; and mechanical errors included spelling, punctuation, and capitalization. Totals, means, and the standard deviations were calculated for the analysis of the error types.

Secondly, a qualitative evaluation of the written texts considered holistic measures of adequacy, coherence, cohesion, grammatical accuracy, lexical range, and mechanics. An analytic rubric using a three-point scale, created by the second author, was used to assess the writings, 3 being good, 2 average, and 1 poor (see Appendix 1 for the full rubric). The rubric was based on the ones used at the school students attended and on the writing scale by Hedgcock and Lefkowitz (1992).

To ensure coding reliability, 10% of the data were independently coded by the two researchers. The transcripts were compared and differences discussed until a total intercoder agreement was reached. Finally, the remaining data were coded by the second author.

3.4.3 Criteria for the analysis of the questionnaire

A mixed-method research design combining quantitative and qualitative data was used. Quantitative data were obtained from the close-ended questions. Likert-scale ratings were grouped into two categories: positive (yes) vs. negative (no) attitudes, and percentages were calculated for all the students.

Qualitative data were obtained from the open-ended questions and the justifications of the close-ended questions in the survey. Responses were compared, and recurrent themes identified.

4 Results

4.1 Language-related episodes (LREs)

Table 1 features the results regarding the frequency of LREs. It can be seen that groups created more LREs than pairs, 16.33 on average for groups and 12.57 for pairs. Moreover, groups discussed F-LREs more frequently, while groups and pairs focused their attention similarly on lexis and mechanics. Differences were not significant for any of the comparisons.

Regarding the length of each recording, Table 1 also shows that pairs and groups spoke for a similar amount of time, approximately 17 minutes.

Table 2 displays information about the outcome of LREs and it shows that there is a high correct resolution rate for both groupings when total LREs outcomes are contrasted, while incorrect and unresolved instance rates are fairly low. However, the picture is somewhat different when the type of LRE is

Table 1: Frequency and length of LREs by types in pairs and groups.

Condition	Pairs			Groups		
	N	M	SD	N	M	SD
F-LREs	24	3.4	2.4	39	6.5	3.8
L-LREs	37	5.3	2.8	36	6.0	3.2
M-LREs	27	3.9	3.4	23	3.8	3.4
Total LREs	88	12.57	4.39	98	16.33	8.24
Minutes	119.27	17:03:51	7:31:24	106.03	17:40:40	3:30:36

Table 2: Outcome of LREs by type for pairs and groups.

	Outcome	Pair				Groups			
		N	M	SD	%	N	M	SD	%
F-LRE	Correct	21	3.0	1.5	87.5%	31	5.2	2.6	79.49%
	Incorrect	3	0.4	1.1	12.5%	8	1.3	1.4	20.51%
	Unresolved	0	0	0	0%	0	0	0	0%
	Sub-total	24	3.4	2.4	27.27%	39	6.5	3.8	39.8%
L-LRE	Correct	20	2.9	3	74.07%	16	2.7	2.2	44.44%
	Incorrect	8	1.1	0.7	21.62%	6	1	0.9	16.67%
	Unresolved	10	1.4	1.5	27.03%	14	2.3	1.8	38.89%
	Sub-total	37	5.3	2.8	41.05%	36	6	3.2	36.73%
M-LRE	Correct	22	3.1	2.9	81.48%	18	3	3.1	78.26%
	Incorrect	5	0.7	0.8	18.52%	5	0.8	1.2	21.74%
	Unresolved	0	0	0	0%	0	0	0	0%
	Sub-total	27	3.9	3.4	30.68%	23	3.8	3.4	23.47%
TOTAL -LRE	Correct	63	9	1.57	71.59%	65	10.83	6.08	66.33%
	Incorrect	16	2.29	1.60	18.18%	19	3.1	2.4	19.39%
	Unresolved	10	1.42	1.51	8.8%	14	2.3	1.75	14.29%
	Total	88	12.57	4.39	100%	98	16.33	8.23	100%

considered: pairs arrive at correct solutions more frequently than groups for every type of LRE analysed, although the difference is not significant. When incorrect resolution rates are contrasted, it seems that both groups and pairs reach lexical and mechanical incorrect solutions at a similar rate, but groups do so significantly more for grammar (z = −2.053; p = 0.040). Unlike with L-LREs, pairs and groups did not leave any mechanical or grammar difficulty unresolved. Pairs left 27.06% of their L-LREs unresolved, while groups did this at a higher rate (38.89%), although statistically significant differences cannot be reported.

4.2 Accuracy and fluency of texts written individually and in collaboration

Table 3 displays information about the fluency and accuracy rates by grouping. The fluency means are (non-significantly) higher for pairs. Pairs wrote the longest texts while groups wrote the shortest. Accuracy results remained quite stable across groupings, although groups seemed to make fewer lexical, grammatical, and total errors than pairs and individuals. Although the difference was small, individual texts contained the highest mean of grammatical errors (mean 14.3 vs 14.2 for pairs and 13.7 for groups) and the lowest of mechanical errors (8.1 vs 8.3 for groups and 9.2 for pairs). No accuracy comparison, however, yielded significant differences.

Table 3: Fluency (number of words) and Accuracy (number of errors) rates by grouping.

Dimensions	Aspect	Individual (pre-test, n = 49)			Pairs (experimental task, n = 9)			Groups (experimental task, n = 12)		
		N	M	SD	N	M	SD	N	M	SD
Fluency	Number of words	4432	90.4	25.3	935	103.9	24.3	1081	90.1	19.4
Accuracy	Grammatical errors	701	14.3	5.8	128	14.2	3.8	164	13.7	5.5
	Lexical errors	178	3.6	2.8	32	3.6	2.6	42	3.5	2.5
	Mechanical errors	399	8.1	6.2	83	9.2	6.7	100	8.3	5.4
	Total errors	1278	26.1	10.5	243	27	11.1	107	21.4	10.1

4.3 Global measures of adequacy, coherence, cohesion, grammar, mechanics, and vocabulary

Table 4 shows that there seems to be a small increase in the global scores after collaboration. When students wrote in pairs and groups, they obtained higher scores than when they wrote individually for all the global measures and the total scores. However, only the difference for vocabulary turned out to be significant favouring groups ($z = -2.000$; $p = 0.046$). Yet, when the two learner groupings were contrasted, pairs obtained higher means than the groups in all the global measures and total scores (11.8 for pairs and 11 for groups), except for mechanics and adequacy. Groups and pairs obtained the same means for adequacy (2.4), while groups only exhibited an increase of 0.1 over pairs for mechanics.

Table 4: Global measures by grouping condition.

		Individual			Pairs			Groups		
		N	M	SD	N	M	SD	N	M	SD
Task	Adequacy	81	1.7	0.8	22	2.4	0.7	29	2.4	0.8
	Coherence	71	1.4	0.6	18	2	0.9	22	1.8	0.7
Language	Cohesion	80	1.6	0.7	19	2.1	0.8	21	1.8	0.6
	Grammar	67	1.4	0.6	15	1.7	0.7	18	1.5	0.5
	Mechanics	82	1.7	0.6	15	1.7	0.9	22	1.8	0.6
	Vocabulary	63	1.3	0.6	17	1.9	0.9	20	1.7	0.5
Total		444	9.1	3.1	106	11.8	4.2	132	11	3.1

4.4 Attitudes and perceptions towards writing in collaboration

Table 5 features students' perceptions about writing in English and about the perceived benefits of collaboration.

When students were asked about whether they enjoyed writing in English, only 52.94% answered affirmatively. Collaboration, however, spurred motivation for writing and elicited very positive responses. Specifically, 86.27% responded that they enjoyed writing in collaboration. Students described writing in collaboration as a fun and helpful task and highlighted the help they were able to give and receive from peers as an important factor.

Table 5: Attitudes in percentages.

	Yes	No
I like writing in English	52.94%	47.06%
I like writing in collaboration	86.27%	13.73%
My group worked well and we all participated equally	84.31%	15.69%
It was easier to write in groups than individually	80.39%	19.61%
The text written collaboratively was better than the individual text	74.51%	25.49%
Collaboration helped me solve some doubts	78.43%	21.57%
Collaboration helped me improve other skills	62.75%	37.25%
I learnt more English in collaboration	70.59%	29.41%
I learnt more from my peers than from the teacher	45.1%	54.9%

When asked to reflect on the impact of collaboration on the accuracy of their written text, students noted that collaboration helped them to learn more English as well as to improve speaking, reading, and listening. Overall, most of them considered that the collaborative texts were better than the individual ones (74.51%).

Moreover, most of them (above 80%) stated that they had participated equally and worked well together (Example 7). What is more, they considered that writing in groups was easier than writing individually (80.39%). However, their attitude was less positive (45.1%) when asked whether they thought they learnt more from their peers than from the teacher.

Example 7: *Bat idazten zuelako bestea ideiak eman eta bestea istorioan itzegiten zuelako* [sic]. [One wrote the text, another one gave ideas and the other one spoke in the story].

Only about 15% of students expressed some resistance to collaboration, while approximately 25% did not consider collaboration helpful to develop their English. The negative comments were related to boredom, group management issues including the need to agree (Example 8), unbalanced work share or preference for individual work. Also frequent were the expressions of mistrust about their peers' knowledge (Example 9) which contrasted with overly positive appraisals of self-worth and of self-efficacy for writing (Example 10 and Example 11).

Example 8: *Denak ez gaudelako ados* [we couldn't reach an agreement].

Example 9: *Zuk baino hiztegi gehiago jakiten baldin badu, zalantzak ongi argitzen dizu, baina ingelesez maila "gutxiagoa" baldin badu, ez da oso erreza zalantzak argitzea* [sic]. [If she/he has a wider vocabulary than you do, then she/he can help you out with doubts, if his/her level is "lower", however, it is not very easy to solve problems].

Example 10: Because I was teachin they [sic].

Example 11: Becuse writing I more better [sic].

Table 6 shows that about a third of the students considered that the content, vocabulary, and grammar of the texts would have been poorer if they had written them individually:

Table 6: Perception percentages about how texts would have been if they had written them individually.

If individually	Better	Similar	Worse
Content	23.53%	41.18%	35.29%
Vocabulary	13.73%	47.06%	39.22%
Grammar	11.76%	54.9%	33.33%

They stated that collaboration helped them to solve their doubts about spelling and vocabulary, and to create a better structured text with more sentences and ideas (Example 12). The top-ranked reasons for preferring to write individually were their self-concept (Example 13) and their belief that their suggestions had not been considered (Example 14).

Example 12: *Hainbat hitzetan, ideietan, esaldi kopuruetan.* [With some words, ideas and sentence number].

Example 13: *Oso ondo eramaten zaidalako* [sic]. [I'm good at it].

Example 14: Because they didn't listen to me.

Table 7 presents students' responses when canvassed about their willingness to keep on writing collaboratively.

Table 7: Future writing preferences in percentages.

	Yes	Maybe	No
I would like to write more in collaboration in the future (Yes, No)	88.24%	n/a	11.76%
I would write better if we continued writing in collaboration (Yes, Maybe, No)	62.75%	25.49%	11.76%
	Individually	In pairs	In groups
Which writing condition would you choose in the future	9.8%	35.29%	54.9%

Students provided very positive responses: almost 90% indicated that they would like to write in pairs or groups in the future. When asked about the potential long-term learning benefits of collaboration, the majority of students (62.7%) seemed really positive about its effect on learning. Only 6 participants (11.7%) thought that they would not get better if they continued working collaboratively and 13 students (25.5%) stated that they were not sure.

Students were also questioned about the main difficulties they had experienced when writing in collaboration (Table 8):

Table 8: Frequency of students' main difficulties when writing collaboratively.

Aspect mentioned	Mentions
Vocabulary	37.74%
Ideas/topic	15.09%
Writing	13.21%
Reaching consensus	11.32%
None	7.55%
Insufficient English knowledge	5.66%
Group members	3.77%

Over a third of the difficulties mentioned by students highlighted lexis. Students noted that when they could not retrieve the English word, searching for synonyms was difficult (Example 15), and they resorted to Spanish or omitted the word altogether.

Example 15: *Hitz bat ez bazenekien beste bat bilatzea.* [To search for a different word when you didn't know the word you needed].

Difficulties with generating ideas or with the topic (15.09%) and difficulties experienced with writing in English (13.21%) were mostly related to spelling difficulties. Students had difficulties when deciding what to include in the story (Example 16) and when writing in English (Example 17).

Example 16: Decide the story.

Example 17: *Itzak nola idatzi* [sic]. [Spelling of words].

Eight instances included aspects related to group work: 2 (3.77%) referred to putting up with other group members (Example 18) and 6 (11.32%) mentioned the difficulties they had experienced when trying to reach a consensus.

Example 18: *Taldeko pertsonekin arremanatu* [sic]. [Getting on with the other group members].

5 Discussion and conclusions

The purpose of this study was to explore the effects of collaboration and learner setup, in pairs or in groups of three, on the narratives written by young secondary school learners, a population which has been subject to comparatively meagre investigation. The project also aimed to explore their attitudes towards writing through the examination of students' collaborative dialogues, post-test performance, and attitudes.

The first research question addressed whether secondary school learners engage in collaborative dialogue and whether there were differences in the frequency and outcome of LREs conditioned by grouping. Fernández Dobao (2012, 2014a, 2014b) obtained significant differences favouring groups. In her study, groups created more LREs and were more successful at solving them. García Mayo and Zeitler (2017) partially supported these results: although they did not find differences in LRE frequencies, they reported slight advantages for groups considering the correct resolution of LREs. Our results, however, are inconsistent with regard to those of previous studies and reveal the opposite: groups created more opportunities for discussing language, and in particular for grammar and lexical discussions, but pairs arrived at correct solutions more frequently, specifically for L-LRE (over 30%). In fact, groups came up with incorrect F-LRE outcomes significantly more than pairs.

This apparently contradictory finding could be related to the fundamental differences between our young learners and the adult learners in the previous studies whose cognitive and personal traits are already fully developed. Young learners' metalanguage awareness abilities are developing, and scaffolding each other's language might be challenging and costly (Muñoz 2014; Tellier and Roehr-Brackin 2017) as they may experience difficulties to verbalise rules (as in Example 6) (Muñoz 2017). Our findings, like those in Kim and McDonough (2011), show that vocabulary and spelling attract a lot of attention from young learners. We hypothesize that students' focus will shift to more grammatical aspects as their language proficiency increases (e.g., Wigglesworth and Storch 2009), but also as they grow in cognitive maturity or after an extended classroom focus on form (Muñoz 2014; Tellier and Roehr-Bracking 2017).

The more frequent incorrect outcomes by students working in groups might be related to an additional difficulty young learners experience which is inherent to group work. Children do not automatically develop group work skills and appropriate training might be needed to help them deal with these difficulties independently (Baines, Blatchford, and Webster 2015). In fact, the most frequent complaint about group work was related to the difficulties experienced when trying to agree on different aspects (as in Example 8). Such young learners might still experience difficulties when coping with disagreements and when trying to solve conflicts, and chances are that the student with more determination, and not necessarily more linguistic knowledge, decides on the ultimate linguistic form that appears in the text, in an attempt to help the group move on with the task.

The second research question dealt with quantitative and qualitative differences in the texts produced by individuals, pairs, and groups. Studies contrasting pairs and groups have established that while collaboration benefits accuracy (e.g., McDonough and García Fuentes 2015; Villarreal and Gil-Sarratea 2020), fluency tends to remain unaffected. Fernández Dobao (2012) concluded that small groups were more accurate writing down the picture story than pairs or individuals, and although individuals wrote the longest texts, groups wrote more than pairs. However, more accurate but also fluent texts were written by the pairs and the groups in Bueno-Alastuey and Martínez de Lizarrondo's study (2017). The authors attributed this to the type of task, a description of a person, which, unlike in Fernández Dobao (2012), strictly guided the content that needed to be included, but, possibly, fostered a stronger focus on details by the pairs and groups. In line with earlier studies, the pairs and groups in the present study also wrote better texts than individuals. However, learner setup affected the measures investigated differently. Writing in pairs promoted greater fluency, while writing in groups hindered it. This might be caused by the difficulties in overcoming students' hesitations as to how to select the best ideas for their narrative text.

For the remaining measures, including lexical and grammar accuracy rates and the global scales, groups obtained a slight advantage over pairs and individuals. As argued by Fernández Dobao (2012) and García Mayo and Zeitler (2017), this finding might be the result of a larger pool of knowledge to draw from as a consequence of there being more members in the group. Language focused discussions proved advantageous and resulted in higher accuracy rates as students drew their attention to form when they negotiated meaning (Villarreal and Gil-Sarratea 2020). Unlike in previous research (e.g., Fernández Dobao 2012; Villarreal and Gil-Sarratea 2020; Wigglesworth and Storch 2009), deliberations about mechanics held a prominent place and approximately 30% of the LREs addressed such issues. Unexpectedly, mechanical error rates were lowest for individuals and collaboration did not boost mechanics. These results might be due to their developing language awareness abilities and the instability of the English language of these beginner learners, as suggested by Muñoz (2014), but this is a topic in need of further research. Overall, quantitative and qualitative measures seem to complement and support collaboration as a valuable pedagogical tool to improve writing. The distinct grouping effect calls for pedagogical interventions that combine dyads and triads to unlock the full potential of collaborative writing.

The third and final research question addressed students' attitudes and perceptions towards collaborative writing. The results confirmed those obtained in previous research (Fernández Dobao and Blum 2013; Shehadeh 2011; Storch 2005): participants were positive about the collaborative writing experience. Moreover, unlike the adult learners in Fernández Dobao and Blum (2013), young learners highly valued collaboration for its language learning value. Students appreciated the opportunities afforded by collaboration to learn from each other's ideas, to have a larger pool of resources to draw upon, or to receive linguistic assistance from other group members (Du 2018; Fernández Dobao and Blum 2013; Shehadeh 2011; Storch 2005). The unfavourable perceptions (about 12%) were predominantly driven by an underestimation of their classmates' knowledge and capacity to help. Students seemed to consider that only a more knowledgeable peer could help them improve (Fernández Dobao and Blum 2013). The idea that more improvement is made with a more knowledgeable other is also reflected in the fact that 45.1% of the students considered they learnt more from the teacher than from their peers.

Students' spoken extracts and written texts, however, have shown that beginner level students can and do assist each other effectively (over 66% of the time) by providing timely and carefully attuned support (De Guerrero and Villamil 2000; Donato 1994; Ohta 1995; Swain 2000, 2006). Thus, learners' awareness of the potential and actual benefits of collaborative activities should be fostered as it can shift students' opinions (Du 2018; Fernández Dobao and Blum 2013), develop cognition and personality (Muñoz 2014) and promote their metalinguistic abilities contributing to optimising the language learning process (Tellier and Roehr-Brackin 2017).

Overall, collaboration clearly addresses the negative beliefs held about writing in English. Students have fun and consider that it benefits all skills. Writing together is, therefore, an opportunity for the meaningful integration of the four skills that cannot be missed in FL settings.

Group management issues were mentioned frequently. This might have been partially mitigated if students had received certain guidelines about effective group work strategies (Baines, Blatchford, and Webster 2015). Writing to learn a language (Manchón 2011) seems, therefore, to be optimised by writing together, even among young learners as they have convincingly shown that "together we do better".

This study has some shortcomings that should be acknowledged. The number of students is small and there is no comparison group performing the post-test individually. Furthermore, students might have responded more positively to questions because of the novelty of the task and, thus, sustained written collaboration could lead to a waning of the enthusiasm and purported benefits. Additionally, further research should explore whether subsequent written texts reflect the positive consequences of a deeper level of noticing (Storch 2008). Therefore, our results need to be taken with caution and further research should be carried out to confirm or contradict our findings. Notwithstanding this, our findings lend support to the introduction of collaborative practices, combining pair and group activities, in EFL secondary classes to foster young learners' language development and positive attitudes towards writing.

Appendix 1

Appendix 1: Rubric for marking the compositions.

		MARKS		
		3	2	1
TASK	ADEQUACY	All the points in the instructions are mentioned; all the parts of a story are included (beginning, body, ending); the length of the text is appropriate.	Just some points in the instructions are mentioned; most of the parts of a story are included; the text is too short (ideas are not fully developed).	Notable omission of the content points and/or considerable irrelevance of some of them.
	COHERENCE	A clear text, easy to understand.	Easy to understand, although there are some incoherent points that confuse the reader	Difficult to understand.
LANGUAGE	COHESION	Ideas are well organised (use of paragraphs). Cohesive devices linking sentences and paragraphs. No serious mistakes.	Ideas are organised. Some cohesive devices linking sentences and paragraphs. There may be some mistakes.	There is a lack of organisation or linking devices.
	GRAMMATICAL ACCURACY	Very few, irrelevant, or no grammar errors at all. Good command of grammar; use of Past tense.	Some acceptable grammar errors. Fair command of English grammar; use of Past tense (with some mistakes)	Serious and numerous grammar mistakes.
	MECHANICS	Most words are written correctly, only some occasional mistakes.	Some spelling mistakes (between 3 and 6), some of them in basic vocabulary.	Many spelling mistakes. Invents words.
	LEXICAL RANGE	Rich and varied vocabulary.	Basic vocabulary, enough to convey the message.	Limited range of vocabulary. Some words are in Basque-Spanish.

Acknowledgements: The authors would like to thank the school Paz de Ziganda Ikastola in Atarrabia (Navarre) for granting permission to conduct the study and to the school teachers for donating their precious class time. Our most heartfelt gratitude to the students for their enthusiasm and help. The first author would like to acknowledge grants FFI2016-74950-P (Spanish Ministry of Economy and Competitiveness, National Research Agency and European Regional Development Fund- AEI/FEDER/EU) and IT904-16 (Basque Government), and I-Communitas, Institute for Advanced Social Research (Public University of Navarre).

References

Alegría de la Colina, Ana, and María Pilar García Mayo. 2007. "Attention to Form across Collaborative Tasks by Low-Proficiency Learners in an EFL Setting". In *Investigating Tasks in Formal Language Learning*, edited by María del Pilar García Mayo, 91–116. London: Multilingual Matters.

Baines, Ed, Peter Blatchford, and Rob Webster. 2015. "The Challenges of Implementing Group-Work in Primary School Classrooms and Including Pupils with Special Educational Needs." *Education 3-13: International Journal of Primary, Elementary and Early Years Education* 43 (1): 15–29.

Ball, Phil, Keith Kelly, and John Clegg. 2015. *Putting CLIL into Practice*. Oxford: Oxford University Press.

Basterrechea, María, and María Pilar García Mayo. 2013. "Language-Related Episodes during Collaborative Tasks: A Comparison of CLIL and EFL Learners". In *Interaction in Diverse Educational Settings*, edited by Kim McDonough and Alison Mackey, 25–44. Amsterdam: John Benjamins.

Bueno-Alastuey, María Camino, and Patricia Martínez de Lizarrondo. 2017. "Collaborative Writing in the EFL Secondary Education Classroom Comparing Triad, Pair and Individual Work." Huarte de San Juan. Filología y Didáctica de La Lengua, no. 17: 254–75. https://dialnet.unirioja.es/servlet/articulo?codigo=6408523.

De Guerrero, María, and Olga S. Villamil. 2000. "Activating the ZPD: Mutual Scaffolding in L2 Peer Revision." *The Modern Language Journal* 84: 521–68.

Donato, Richard. 1994. "Collective Scaffolding in Second Language Learning." In *Vygotskian Approaches to Second Language Research*, edited by James P. Lantolf, and Gabriela Appel, 33–56. Norwood: Ablex.

Du, Fangyuan. 2018. "Comparing Students' Perceptions and Their Writing Performance on Collaborative Writing: A Case Study." *English Language Teaching* 11 (12): 131–137. https://doi.org/10.5539/elt.v11n12p131.

Enever, Janet. 2018. *Policy and Politics in Global Primary English*. Oxford: Oxford University Press.

Fernández Dobao, Ana. 2012. "Collaborative Writing Tasks in the L2 Classroom: Comparing Group, Pair, and Individual Work." *Journal of Second Language Writing* 21 (1): 40–58. https://doi.org/10.1016/j.jslw.2011.12.002.

Fernández Dobao, Ana. 2014a. "Attention to Form in Collaborative Writing Tasks: Comparing Pair and Small Group Interaction." *Canadian Modern Language Review* 70 (2): 158–87. https://doi.org/10.3138/cmlr.1768.
Fernández Dobao, Ana. 2014b. "Vocabulary Learning in Collaborative Tasks: A Comparison of Pair and Small Group Work." *Language Teaching Research* 18 (4): 497–520. https://doi.org/10.1177/1362168813519730.
Fernández Dobao, Ana, and Avram Blum. 2013. "Collaborative Writing in Pairs and Small Groups: Learners' Attitudes and Perceptions " *System* 41 (2): 365–78. https://doi.org/10.1016/j.system.2013.02.002.
García Mayo, María del Pilar (ed.). 2017. *Learning Foreign Languages in Primary School. Research Insights*. Bristol: Multilingual Matters.
García Mayo, María del Pilar. 2018. "Child Task-Based Interaction in EFL Settings. Research and Challenges". *International Journal of English Studies* 18: 119–143.
García Mayo, María del Pilar, and Agurtzane Azkarai. 2016. "EFL Task-Based Interaction: Does Task Modality Impact on Language-Related Episodes?" In *Peer Interaction and Second Language Learning. Pedagogical Potential and Research Agenda*, edited by Masatoshi Sato and Susan Ballinger, 241–266. Amsterdam: John Benjamins.
García Mayo, María del Pilar, and Ainara Imaz Agirre. 2019. "Task Modality and Pair Formation Method: Their Impact on Patterns of Interaction and Attention to Form among EFL Primary School Children". *System* 18: 165–175.
García Mayo, María del Pilar, and Amparo Lázaro Ibarrola. 2015. "Do Children Negotiate for Meaning in Task-based Interaction? Evidence from CLIL and EFL settings". *System* 54: 40–54.
García Mayo, María del Pilar, and Nora Zeitler. 2017. "Lexical Language-Related Episodes in Pair and Small Group Work." *International Journal of English Studies* 17 (1): 61–82. https://doi.org/10.6018/ijes/2017/1/255011.
Hedgcock, John, and Natalie Lefkowitz. 1992. "Collaborative Oral/Aural Revision in Foreign Language Writing Instruction." *Journal of Second Language Writing* 1 (3): 255–276. https://doi.org/10.1016/1060-3743(92)90006-B.
Khatib, Mohammad, and Hussein Meihami. 2015. "Languaging and Writing Skill: The Effect of Collaborative Writing on EFL Students' Writing Performance." *Advances in Language and Literary Studies* 6 (1): 203–215. http://dx.doi.org/10.7575/aiac.alls.v.6n.1p.203.
Kim, YouJin. 2008. "The Contribution of Collaborative and Individual Tasks to the Acquisition of L2 Vocabulary". *Modern Language Journal* 92: 114–130.
Kim, YouJin, and Kim McDonough. 2011. "Using Pretask Modelling to Encourage Collaborative Learning Opportunities." *Language Teaching Research* 15 (2): 183–99. https://doi.org/10.1177/1362168810388711.
Kuiken, Forlkert, and Ineke Vedder. 2002. "The Effect of Interaction in Acquiring the Grammar of a Second Language." *International Journal of Educational Research* 37: 343–358. https://doi.org/10.1016/S0883-0355(03)00009-0.
Lázaro-Ibarrola, Amparo, and Izaskun Villarreal. 2019. "Questioning the Effectiveness of Procedural Repetition: The Case of Spanish EFL Primary School Learners." Porta Linguarum 31: 7–20.
Leeser, Michael J. 2004. "Learner Proficiency and Focus on Form during Collaborative Dialogue." *Language Teaching Research* 8 (1): 55–81. https://doi.org/10.1191/1362168804lr134oa.

Long, Michael H. 1996. "The Role of the Linguistic Environment in Second Language Acquisition." In *Handbook of Second Language Acquisition*, edited by William C. Ritchie and Tej K. Bhatia, 413–468. San Diego: Academic Press.

Manchón, Rosa M. 2011. "Situating the Learning-to-Write and Writing-to-Learn Dimensions of L2 Writing." In *Learning-to-Write and Writing-to-Learn in an Additional Language*, edited by Rosa M. Manchón, 3–14. Amsterdam: John Benjamins Publishing Company.

McDonough, Kim, and César García Fuentes. 2015. "The Effect of Writing Task and Task Conditions on Colombian EFL Learners' Language Use." *TESL Canada Journal* 32 (2): 67–79. https://doi.org/10.18806/tesl.v32i2.1208.

McDonough, Kim, Jindarat De Vleeschauwer, and William Crawford. 2018. "Comparing the Quality of Collaborative Writing, Collaborative Prewriting, and Individual Texts in a Thai EFL Context." *System* 74: 109–20. https://doi.org/10.1016/j.system.2018.02.010.

Muñoz, Carmen. 2014. "Exploring Young Learners' Foreign Language Learning Awareness." *Language Awareness* 23 (1–2): 24–40. https://doi.org/10.1080/09658416.2013.863900.

Muñoz, Carmen. 2017. "The Development of Language Awareness at the Transition from Primary to Secondary School." In *Learning Foreign Languages in Primary School: Research Insights*, edited by María del Pilar García Mayo, 49–68. Bristol: Multilingual Matters.

Murtiningsih, Sri Rejeki. 2016. "Collaborative Writing in an EFL Context." *Journal of Foreign Language Teaching and Learning* 1 (1): 82–90.

Ohta, Amy Snyder. 1995. "Applying Sociocultural Theory to an Analysis of Learner Discourse: Learner-learner Collaborative Interaction in the Zone of Proximal Development." *Issues in Applied Linguistics*, 6(2): 93–121.

Pallotti, Gabriele. 2009. "CAF : Defining, Refining and Differentiating Constructs." *Applied Linguistics* 30 (4): 590–601. https://doi.org/10.1093/applin/amp045.

Shehadeh, Ali. 2011. "Effects and Student Perceptions of Collaborative Writing in L2." *Journal of Second Language Writing* 20 (4): 286–305. https://doi.org/10.1016/j.jslw.2011.05.010.

Storch, Neomy. 2005. "Collaborative Writing: Product, Process, and Students' Reflections." *Journal of Second Language Writing* 14 (3): 153–73. https://doi.org/10.1016/j.jslw.2005.05.002.

Storch, Neomy. 2008. "Metatalk in a Pair Work Activity: Level of Engagement and Implications for Language Development." *Language Awareness* 17 (2): 95–114.

Storch, Neomy. 2011. "Collaborative Writing in L2 Contexts: Processes, Outcomes, and Future Directions." *Annual Review of Applied Linguistics* 31: 275–88. https://doi.org/10.1017/S0267190511000079.

Storch, Neomy. 2013. *Collaborative Writing in L2 Classrooms*. Bristol: Multilingual Matters.

Storch, Neomy. "Collaborative Writing: Promoting Languaging among Language Learners" Paper presented at the The Oral-Written Connection International Conference, Vitoria-Gasteiz, Araba, March 2018.

Storch, Neomy, and Ali Aldosari. 2013. "Pairing Learners in Pair Work Activity." *Language Teaching Research* 17 (1): 31–48. https://doi.org/10.1177/1362168812457530.

Swain, Merrill. 1998. "Focus on Form through Conscious Reflection." In F*ocus on Form in Classroom Second Language Acquisition*, edited by Catherine Doughty and Jessica Williams, 64–81. Cambridge: Cambridge University Press.

Swain, Merrill. 2000. "The Output Hypothesis and Beyond: Mediating Acquisition through Collaborative Dialogue." In *Sociocultural Theory and Second Language Learning*, edited by James P. Lantolf, 97–114. Oxford: Oxford University Press.

Swain, Merrill. 2006. "Languaging, Agency and Collaboration in Advanced Second Language Learning." In *Advanced Language Learning: The Contribution of Halliday and Vygotsky*, edited by Heidi Byrnes, 95–108. London: Continuum.

Swain, Merrill, and Sharon Lapkin. 1998. "Interaction and Second Language Learning: Two Adolescent French Immersion Students Working Together." *The Modern Language Journal* 82 (3): 320–37. https://doi.org/Doi 10.2307/329959.

Swain, Merrill, and Yuko Watanabe. 2012. "Languaging: Collaborative Dialogue as a Source of Second Language Learning." *The Encyclopedia of Applied Linguistics*. https://doi.org/10.1002/9781405198431.wbeal0664.

Tellier, Angela, and Karen Roehr-Brackin. 2017. "Raising Children's Metalinguistic Awareness to Enhance Classroom Second Language Learning." In *Learning Foreign Languages in Primary School: Research Insights*, edited by María del Pilar García Mayo, 22–48. Bristol: Multilingual Matters.

UCLES, "Cambridge English Placement Test.", Cambridge Assessment, http://www.cambridgeenglish.org/test-your-english/forschools/

Villarreal, Izaskun, and Nora Gil-Sarratea. 2020. "The Effect of Collaborative Writing in an EFL Secondary Setting". *Language Teaching Research* 24 (6): 874–897. https://doi.org/10.1177/1362168819829017.

Vygotsky, L. 1978. *Mind in Society: The Development of Higher Psychological Processes*. Cambridge: Harvard University Press.

Wajnryb, Ruth. 1990. *Grammar Dictation*. Oxford: Oxford University Press.

Wigglesworth, Gillian, and Neomy Storch. 2009. "Pair versus Individual Writing: Effects on Fluency, Complexity and Accuracy ." *Language Testing* 26 (3): 445–66. https://doi.org/10.1177/0265532209104670.

Monika Geist and Angela Hahn
The effect of collaborative writing on individual writing strategies: A case study of two L2 English writers

1 Introduction

Collaborative writing has gained increasing importance due to its pedagogical value for second language (L2) classrooms. Previous studies have investigated the effects of collaborative writing on language learning based on collaboratively written products (for example, Fernández Dobao 2012), on the subsequent language reflection (concrete linguistic items, Storch 2002), and due to the effect of languaging (for example, Swain 2010) or simply due to the increased use of the L2 during collaborative dialogue (for example, Steinberger 2017). In addition, collaborative writing might constitute a useful pedagogical tool to promote composing and problem-solving strategies of L2 writers. However, the effect of collaborative writing on individual writing and problem-solving strategies has not yet received necessary attention. Individual writing and problem-solving strategies have been investigated in separate studies with focus either on problem-solving behaviors (Cumming 1990) or on the use of online resources, especially language corpora (Yoon 2016).

The aim of this contribution is to take the first step towards the exploration of the influence that collaborative writing might have on individual writing and problem-solving strategies. In this way, the study complements the other studies in this volume which focus on the effects on learners' written texts (Chapters 4 and 7) and attitudes (Chapter 4), as well as L2 pragmatic development (Chapter 8). The analysis of the possible effects of collaborative writing is combined with descriptive accounts of learner interaction, which can be linked to other chapters, focusing on learner interaction in collaborative writing (for example, Chapters 3, 6, 9, 10). As a small scale pilot study, the aim of this research is to present preliminary tendencies and suggest directions in methodological design to ensure a rich data base.

Monika Geist, Angela Hahn, Ludwig-Maximilians-Universität München

https://doi.org/10.1515/9781501511318-006

2 Theoretical background

2.1 Individual and collaborative writing: Theory and research

Writing has gained increased attention in research in recent years due to its potential of facilitating second language (L2) learning (for a review, see Williams 2012). Research so far has shown that in individual writing, self-initiated attention to form occurs and often leads to output modification (see, for example, Swain and Lapkin 1995; Manchón and Roca de Larios 2007; Manchón and Williams 2016). In this way, production of output can serve knowledge internalization (noticing and establishing form-meaning connections), knowledge restructuring (elaborating and refining form-meaning connections based on additional input or negative feedback), or knowledge consolidation (strengthening form-meaning connections through repeated retrieval and deeper processing), see Williams (2012, 322). In collaborative writing, the necessity to negotiate linguistic choices with a partner (or partners) may lead to deeper levels of awareness of the relationship between meaning, form and function, supporting noticing on the level of understanding which in turn is believed to facilitate learning (see Storch 2008). Noticing on the level of understanding as stimulated in collaborative writing can then be seen in the subsequent individual generation of texts.

Based on these theoretical assumptions, collaborative writing has been examined with regard to its effects on the quality and characteristics of the written products (for example, Fernández Dobao 2012; Storch 2005), showing positive effects of the collaborative writing condition on accuracy of the texts produced (Storch 1999, 2005; Wigglesworth and Storch 2009), on selected grammatical features (see Reinders 2009 for negative adverbs) or language acquisition (for example, Kim 2008, on the acquisition of vocabulary; Swain and Lapkin 1998). Apart from investigating the written products with respect to specific language items, the focus of process-product research design is on the transfer of implicit knowledge or form focus from the collaborative writing session into a subsequent individual writing session (for example, Storch 2002; for a review, see Storch 2013, 84–89). The collaborative writing process itself has also received considerable attention with studies investigating the nature of interaction and problem-solving during a collaborative writing task (for example, Fernández Dobao 2012; Steinberger 2017; Storch 2002, 2005). The results so far suggest that collaborative and expert/novice interaction patterns in particular promote the learning and transfer of knowledge into subsequent individual writing and language production, particularly regarding the acquisition of specific linguistic features (Storch 2002; Watanabe and Swain 2007).

So far, little attention has been paid to the effect of collaborative writing on the composing and problem-solving strategies of individual learners. Wigglesworth and Storch (2009, 461) call for more research into the effects of collaboration on individual writing. Even though the process-product studies mentioned above aim at implicit knowledge, they still concentrate on specific linguistic phenomena rather than strategies. Investigating this issue has practical relevance as in real-life contexts, as most writing is done individually (Storch 2013, 171) and collaboration (or better, peer feedback) usually starts when the individual writing process ends, i.e. with a first written draft. For this reason, individual writing and problem-solving strategies and the possibilities of improving them are an important area of research. Collaborative writing might constitute a useful pedagogical tool to promote not only linguistic proficiency, but also composing and problem-solving strategies of L2 writers.

In collaborative writing studies, form-focused tasks such as the dictogloss have been the most common task type used for data elicitation (Storch 2013, 53), even though meaning-focused tasks have also been used (for example, Watanabe and Swain 2007). Most studies are small-scale studies with a limited number of participants, adopting a qualitative research approach, even though there are also larger-scale studies such as Fernández Dobao (2012). The present study uses a meaning-focused task with the aim of having learners produce original pieces of writing instead of reproducing existing texts. In line with most previous studies, it is a small-scale qualitative study.

2.2 Approaches to classifying problem-solving strategies

In order to capture the problem-solving processes of learners in the process of writing, various classifications of problem-solving behaviors and strategies have been taken into account which will be described in the following paragraphs. In our data analysis, we used these classifications to categorize and link writing behaviors in individual and collaborative writing. We take classifications used in analyses of individual writing as our starting point. Even though we are aware that studies into collaborative writing have used similar or slightly different classifications, using classifications from individual writing studies serves our purpose well as our focus is on the effects of collaborative writing on individual writing strategies.

Research into writing focuses on macro-level writing strategies such as planning, generating ideas or revising (for example, Stapleton 2010), or on problem-solving strategies (micro-level), mostly operationalized as language-related episodes (LREs) or related concepts (Cumming 1990; Swain and Lapkin 1995).

Swain and Lapkin (1995, 378) define an LRE as "[. . .] any segment of the protocol in which a learner either spoke about a language problem he/she encountered while writing and solved it either correctly [. . .] or incorrectly [. . .], or simply solved it [. . .] without having explicitly identified it as a problem." The focus of LREs varies in each study, ranging from three basic levels (for example, the lexical, form and discourse levels in Qi and Lapkin 2001) to a differentiated system of levels including spelling, word choice, sentence structure, sentence cohesion, to name just a few (for example, Armengol and Cots 2009).

In addition to the concrete classification of problems, a more abstract classification can be used. Roca de Larios, Manchón, and Murphy (2006) distinguish between compensatory and upgrading problem types, compensatory problems being derived from lack of (automatic) access to linguistic knowledge and upgrading problems resulting from an attempt to upgrade the expression of meaning or to find a better match between intention and expression or both (Roca de Larios, Manchón, and Murphy 2006, 106). Yoon (2016) distinguishes between confirmatory (confirming that the intended solution is correct) and compensatory problem types.

Learners deal with their problems by applying problem-solving strategies. They might draw on their own linguistic and logical resources or make use of an external resource such as a dictionary, the internet, their writing partner or a teacher, if available. Interestingly, there seem to be two strands of research, one of which does not use dictionaries and the internet (including, for example, language corpora), while the other one focuses only on the use of these resources. In studies into individual and collaborative writing, dictionaries are often not available or allowed[1] (for example, Swain and Lapkin 1995; Wigglesworth and Storch 2009). Studies into the use of linguistic resources only take into account these resources and do not analyze other strategies in depth (see, for example, Yoon 2016). An exception is a relatively new study by Gánem-Gutiérrez and Gilmore (2018) which uses methods of screen-recording, eye-tracking and stimulated recall to investigate times devoted to composing processes while allowing the learners to utilize online resources. Similarly, the current study brings these two strands together by allowing and encouraging the learners to use the internet, even though no explicit instruction on possible uses is given to them.

---

[1] Often the studies do not mention whether dictionaries were allowed, but from the analyses presented, it can be concluded that no dictionaries or other resources were available.

Strategies can be classified according to the concrete action that learners take in order to resolve their problem. In this sense, Cumming (1990) divides his heuristic search strategies (i.e. problem-solving strategies) into engaging a search routine; directed translation or code-switching; generating and assessing alternatives; assessing in relation to a criterion, standard, explanation, or rule; relating parts to the whole; setting or adhering to a goal. Swain and Lapkin (1995) identify the following problem-solving behaviours: sounds right / doesn't sound right; makes sense / doesn't make sense; lexical search (via L2); lexical search (via L1 or both L1 and L2); translation (phrase or greater); applying a grammatical rule.

Another way to classify problem-solving strategies is according to the function the strategy fulfills in writing. In the area of speaking, Færch and Kasper (1983, 45) distinguish between reduction strategies, further split into formal reduction (changing the linguistic structure of an utterance) and functional reduction (changing the communicative goal), and achievement strategies (expanding the linguistic repertoire to solve the problem). Hanaoka (2006) utilized this classification for L2 writing. Uzawa and Cumming (1989) distinguish between lower-the-standard and keep-up-the-standard strategies (as compared to the L1 writing standard of a learner).

2.3 Research focus

This study set out to explore whether and in which ways learners might profit from collaborative writing on the level of the writing and problem-solving strategies. Rather than focusing on the linguistic aspects of the compositions (the products), we searched for evidence of learners adopting some of the other learner's composing strategies, be it on the macro or micro level. In order to explore the research interest stated above, this study seeks to answer the following research questions:

1. Which writing and problem-solving strategies do two selected learners of L2 English use when writing individually? In which ways do they differ from each other?
2. How do the two learners interact in a collaborative writing activity? Which strategies do they apply when writing collaboratively?
3. How do the writing and problem-solving strategies change after the collaborative writing activity? Which changes can be traced back to collaborative writing?

3 Methodological approach

3.1 Study context

The study was situated in a university language course at the language center of a large German university. The course is based on a flipped classroom concept where learners follow a course schedule and work mostly at home. Every two weeks they attend an individual coaching session with a language coach where they receive feedback on a piece of writing, ask questions about their home study and complete conversation activities with a coach. One of the coaching sessions is a so-called 'group communication session' in which two students of a similar language level meet and discuss.

The authentic university course setting has the advantage of more practical relevance than a strictly controlled environment. On the other hand, due to the necessity of adapting the research design to the course design, there were restrictions on the data collection schedule and the writing tasks and topics.

3.2 Participants

The participants were two university students with L1 German. These participants volunteered for the study in reaction to an invitation sent to all participants of levels A2, B1 and B2 of the language course mentioned above. Participant 1 (P1) was 44 years old and his level of English was A2 according to the placement test administered by the university language center (Sprachenzentrum der Universität Münster 2019). He did not speak or learn any other foreign languages besides English. Participant 2 (P2) was 26 years old and his level of English was B2 according to the same placement test. Besides English, he also indicated that he had intermediate level in Spanish and beginner level in French. Both participants considered their computer skills rather good, even though in the course of the data collection, it became clear that P2 was faster at typing than P1.

3.3 Data collection

The data collection was embedded into the language course and consisted of five meetings with the researcher for each participant. The procedure is visualized in Figure 1. The first session was an individual meeting in which the participant completed a homework writing task on a computer in the Etherpad module (Moodle-Dev Humboldt-Universität zu Berlin 2019) of the university Moodle platform. In

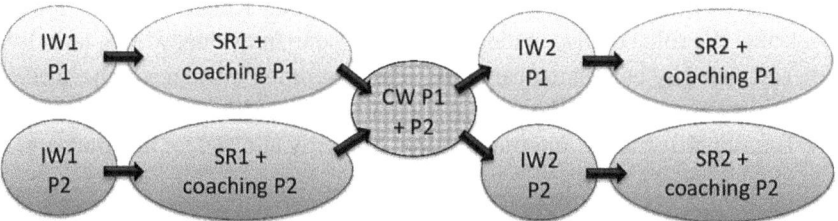

Figure 1: The data collection procedure.

order to also record any screen activities outside of Etherpad, screen recording was done using the OBS Studio (Jim 2012–2019) screen recording software. The second session was a stimulated recall session about the writing task, combined with language coaching which was part of the course syllabus. We opted for stimulated recall interviews because they take place after the writing and therefore will not interfere with the writing process itself in the way think-aloud protocols might. The stimulated recall interviews took place within a week after the individual writing sessions.[2] The researcher used prepared questions which aimed at decision-making processes (for example, asking what the participant was thinking about when making a specific change to the text), strategies (for example, why the participant had decided to use a dictionary) and the learners' focus during the writing task (for example, asking about the participants' thoughts in sections of the screen recording where the participant did not conduct any action). Thus, the topics for the stimulated recall interviews were selected mainly by the researcher. This decision was taken for time and practicability reasons. After the stimulated recall interview, a coaching session took place in which the researcher gave feedback on the linguistic aspects of their written product. Care was taken not to give feedback on writing and problem-solving strategies in order not to interfere with the effects of the collaborative writing session.

After both participants completed the first individual writing task (IW1) and the stimulated recall and coaching session (SR1), a collaborative face-to-face writing session (CW) took place in which the two participants were asked to compose a paragraph together. Each participant had their own computer at their disposal, however, they quickly decided to only use one computer.[3] The collaborative

---

[2] A shorter time span between the individual writing session and the respective stimulated recall interview would have been desirable as recommended in the literature, see Ericsson and Simon (1993, 19), but was not realizable due to time constraints.
[3] There might have been various reasons for this decision. First, if the participants had used two computers, they would have been sitting back to back and face-to-face communication

writing session also took place in Etherpad and was screen-recorded. About a week after the collaborative writing session, a second individual writing task (IW2) was completed by both participants and screen-recorded in the researcher's office, followed by a second stimulated recall interview and coaching session (SR2).[4]

For all writing tasks, internet use was explicitly allowed for any purpose.

3.4 Writing tasks

The writing tasks were adopted from the course design. When selecting the tasks, attention was paid to selecting free writing tasks which elicited opinion on a specific topic. One of the tasks had to take place before the collaborative writing session, the other task after the collaborative writing session. Due to the course setting and the different levels of the participants, the individual writing tasks for each participant were different. For the collaborative writing task, a task from the higher level (B2) course was selected due to its opinion gap character. All writing tasks were meaning-focused essays with a verbal or video prompt. Table 1 lists the different writing tasks.

3.5 Data analysis

The recordings were transcribed, taking into account any writing and editing activities, any activities outside of the text editor (which were mostly searches in an internet dictionary) and verbal comments or conversations (in the course of the writing process or in the stimulated recall interview). Lengthy explanations in stimulated recall interviews were summarized for transcription to better reflect the focus of the explanation.

The transcribed data were segmented into episodes, some of which indicated general writing strategies and behaviors, others being LREs. The coding system is shown in Table 2. Detailed descriptions of the categories including examples are listed in the Appendix. The analytical procedure combined a deductive approach inspired by the existing classifications mentioned in the theoretical background with a data-driven, inductive analytical approach. This approach was chosen to be able to identify any relevant phenomena and not

---

would have been difficult. Second, P1 might have been self-conscious because of his English-language and typing ability, so that he preferred a more passive role in the writing process.

4 The second coaching session was conducted for ethical reasons and in order to comply with the course design. It did not, however, constitute or have any influence on project data.

Table 1: A list of the writing tasks used in the writing assignments.

Participant / Writing task	Task wording
P1 / IW1	Think back to your time at school. What did you like about it, what didn't you like? Which subjects did you have? Then compare your thoughts with what you have read about schools in the UK and the US. (approx. 300 words)
P2 / IW1	At the moment, society is undergoing major changes (political, technological, eating habit . . .). Write a report on which aspect of change you consider the most prominent one. Include your opinion on this aspect and how you think it will develop in the future. (300 words)
P1 + P2 / CW	A common world – Just a dream? Give your opinion on current topics like Trump, Brexit or the AfD. Do those events say anything about today's society? Write an argumentative essay, taking a clear stance. (300 words)
P1 / IW2	Watch the following video to recall the events of 2016: http://link38.flip-englisch.de. Which event of the last year do you consider most important to you personally? Was it a positive or a negative event? Write an essay of about 200 words.
P2 / IW2[5]	Watch the video: http://link40.flip-englisch.de. Now write an essay on your opinion on what you have seen – is this a likely scenario? If so, what could we do to stop it?- Include your own thoughts and suggestions!

miss any interesting links by using a fixed theory-based system of categories. The resulting coding system is a combination of the categorizations elaborated on in the theoretical section of the chapter combined with additional categories which emerged from the data.[6]

Writing strategies and behaviors were coded in order to be able to describe the general stages of the writing process besides the typing itself. The main part of the analysis was devoted to LREs. Four characteristics were coded for each LRE. Problem focus was either on language or content (further differentiated

---

[5] The number of words was not specified for this task in the course syllabus.
[6] Even though the categorizations of strategy types by Cumming (1990) and Swain and Lapkin (1995) were mentioned in the theoretical section due to their importance in research literature on composing strategies, these systems did not fully fit the data and only parts of them were used in our analysis.

Table 2: The coding system developed for data analysis.

Basic category	Code	Sub-code
Writing strategies and behaviors		
	Content discussion / comments	
	Planning	Micro-level
		Macro-level
	Pre-formulating	
	Proof-reading	
LRE: Problem focus	Mechanics	
	Lexis	Does not know word
		Does not like word
		Uncertain about word
		Forgot word
	Grammar + Word order	
	Cohesion	Avoiding repetition
	Content	Addition / specification
		Substitution / reformulation
		Deletion
LRE: Problem type	Confirmatory	
	Upgrading	
	Compensatory	
LRE: Strategy type	Reasoning	
	Rules / knowledge	
	Dictionary	Intuition
		Frequency counts
		Knowledge
		Context

Table 2 (continued)

Basic category	Code	Sub-code
	L1 / Cross-linguistic influence	
	Intuition	
	Writing partner	
LRE: Strategy function	Achievement	
	Formal reduction	
	Functional reduction	

into sub-categories). Problem types refer to the purpose of the LRE. In compensatory problem types, the learners needed to compensate for the lack of linguistic resources. In confirmatory problem types, learners were not sure about the wording or solution they came up with. In upgrading problem types, learners had a word or solution, but were looking for a better alternative. Strategy type refers to the concrete action taken by the learners to resolve their problem. Strategy function refers to the learner's perception of the suitability of their solution for their communicative intention. If a strategy was coded as an achievement strategy, the learner was happy with the solution found (even if the solution was objectively incorrect). Formal reduction strategy denotes that the learner was able to bring over their message, but they did not consider the form ideal. Functional reduction refers to the learner changing or deleting an utterance due to lack of linguistic resources to formulate it.[7]

The category system allowed for a fine-grained analysis due to the different facets of problem-solving strategies it captures. On the other hand, it needs to be noted that not all characteristics were straight-forward to assign to one specific category and that sometimes there were doubts whether categories with partially overlapping definitions (especially problem type and strategy function) should be merged. However, there was not a 100% overlap between these categorizations. As those cases in which the problem type was different from the strategy function (for example, where a participant wanted to upgrade the expression but ended up with formal reduction) were interesting, the coding system was kept in its complexity.

---

[7] Coding strategies in this way is not always straight-forward as it is sometimes unclear how learners perceived their solution. Formal and functional reduction strategies are not always explicitly verbalized.

The coded texts were analyzed with respect to the frequencies of the coded phenomena, their focus and quality, any changes from IW1 to IW2 and possible links with the CW session. The analysis was qualitative, taking into account the specifics of the problem-solving episodes rather than pure numbers and also considering the general characteristics of the participants and their writing processes such as the proficiency level, the speed/fluency of writing as well as the interaction patterns between the two participants in the collaborative writing session.

4 Results and discussion

Due to the character of this study, the results consist of an interpretive account of the writing processes of both participants individually and together. The main objective is to explore how two learners writing collaboratively might influence each other's composing behaviors and strategies, laying a foundation for studies with a larger number of participants. In order to arrive at a meaningful account, both participants' composing strategies will be described and compared, with a special focus on the differences between the first (IW1) and the second (IW2) individual writing. The collaborative writing process and the interactions between the two participants will be described and linked to changes in individual writing in order to arrive at possible influences of the collaborative writing task on individual writing strategies.

Table 3: Comparison of the two study participants regarding their writing strategies, LREs and problem-solving strategies.[8, 9]

	P1	P2
LRE number / writing time	IW1: 50 LREs / ≈ 46 mins IW2: 42 LREs / ≈ 27 mins	IW1: 74 LREs / ≈ 31 mins IW2: 80 LREs / ≈ 36 mins
Words per minute (WPM)	IW1: 5,3 IW2: 6,1	IW1: 11,1 IW2: 7,3

---

[8] Note that this is not a complete list of all results, but rather a selection of the most relevant aspects, especially those where there were differences between the participants.
[9] Note that the LRE numbers sometimes do not add up to the total LRE number as some LREs were coded as having two-fold focus, for example, cohesion / avoiding repetition and content deletion.

Table 3 (continued)

	P1	P2
Writing management	No planning stage No proof-reading	Planning stage (only IW2) Intensive proof-reading
Formulation	Micro-planning on word/phrase level, frequent micro-planning pauses	Micro-planning on clause/sentence level, micro-planning pauses less frequent than P1
Comparatively dominant problem types	Compensatory (IW1, 21 LREs) Upgrading (IW2, 28 LREs)	Upgrading (58 LREs in IW1, 69 LREs in IW2)
LRE focus	Strong focus on lower linguistic levels (mechanics, lexis) + grammar (49 LREs in IW1, 37 LREs in IW2) Very little or no focus on content and cohesion (3 LREs in IW1, 7 LREs in IW2)	Strong focus on content and cohesion compared to P1 (39 LREs in IW1, 44 LREs in IW2) Mechanics, lexis and grammar also in focus (41 LREs in IW1, 51 LREs in IW2)
Lexical problem types	Compensatory (15 LREs in IW1, 11 LREs in IW2) Confirmatory (10 LREs in IW1)	Upgrading (7 LREs in IW1, 15 LREs in IW2) Fewer compensatory (6 LREs in IW1, 7 LREs in IW2)
Grammar problems	Verb forms, regular singular/plural, past participle (IW1), word order (IW2), article use (IW2)	Singular/plural (with vowel change, e.g. cities), articles
Dominant strategy types	Dictionary (IW1, 28 LREs) Intuition (IW2, 27 LREs)	Intuition (63 LREs in IW1, 54 LREs in IW2)
Choice of words from dictionary	Intuition (11 LREs in IW1, 10 LREs in IW2) Known words (12 LREs in IW1, 4 LREs in IW2)	Known words (9 LREs in IW1, 15 LREs in IW2)
Dominant strategy function	Achievement (43 LREs in IW1, 38 LREs in IW2)	Achievement (64 LREs in IW1, 73 LREs in IW2)

4.1 Individual writing processes

Table 3 shows a comparison of both participants regarding their writing process and strategies. A number of differences might be attributed to the different levels between the two participants (fluency of writing, focus of LREs, possibly problem types, the more intensive use of dictionary by P1), other differences might be due to other individual factors such as writing preferences, writing proficiency, typing speed and similar. What both participants had in common was that they mostly used achievement strategies, i.e. they arrived at a result which they accepted as correct and corresponding to their communicative intention.[10] Formal and functional reduction also occurred with both participants, but much less frequently. It should be noted, however, that reduction strategies are not always easy to spot because their recognition depends on whether the participants have verbalized their use.

P1's writing process was not very fluent and he interrupted his flow of writing very often to either resolve a linguistic problem or to think about how to continue his sentence (micro-planning). In IW1, he encountered mainly compensatory problems whereas in IW2, the dominant problem type was upgrading. The focus of his problems was mostly on lower linguistic levels such as spelling or lexis. He also encountered some basic grammar problems such as verb forms of the verbs *to be* and *to have* or 3rd person singular *-s*, regular singular and plural, or past participle. In IW2, the problems were similar, but in addition, P1 encountered one problem with word order, one with article use, but no past participle problems. Problems regarding content and cohesion were rare, but there were more of them in IW2 as compared to IW1. The preferred problem-solving strategy of P1 was the dictionary in IW1 and intuition in IW2. An interesting phenomenon was that P1 also used the dictionary in order to deal with grammar problems such as the different forms of the verbs *to be* and *to have*. From the dictionary output, he selected words intuitively (stating that he selected what sounded or fitted best) or he selected words that he knew. In addition, he used frequency counts as a basis for his decisions, selecting the most frequently used words.

Some phenomena were consistent throughout both individual writing tasks (for example, no planning or proof-reading, focus mainly on lower level problems, compensatory lexical problems), whereas there was a clear shift from IW1 to IW2 regarding other phenomena. Table 4 shows the observed changes.

The most important changes for P1 from the first to the second individual writing concern the problem types (shift from compensatory to upgrading problems types, not dealing with confirmatory lexical problems), a slightly stronger focus on content and cohesion and the shift from reliance on a dictionary to reliance on the writer's own intuition. Possible reasons for these changes will be discussed further below.

---

10 Note that the solutions are correct from the point of view of the participants themselves, but they are not necessarily objectively the "correct" or "best" solutions.

Table 4: Differences between IW1 and IW2 for P1.

IW1	IW2
Compensatory problems dominant	Upgrading problems dominant
A number of confirmatory lexical problems (uncertain about a word)	Only one confirmatory lexical problem (compensatory lexical problems dominant)
Grammar problems: past participle[11]	Grammar problems: word order, article use
No questions of cohesion, three content specifications	Three questions of cohesion, four content specifications
Dictionary as the preferred problem-solving strategy	Intuition and own knowledge as the preferred problem-solving strategies

P2 was a more fluent writer than P1 and encountered a far greater number of LREs compared to P1. His writing process was complex in the sense that P2 had a basic idea in his mind (therefore, there was not as much micro-planning as P1), but he kept reformulating his sentences and deleting or substituting parts of them with the aim of writing as coherent a paragraph as possible. His concern about writing a coherent paragraph is visible from the focus of his LREs (strong focus on content and cohesion in addition to lower linguistic levels) as well as his stimulated recall comments in which he complains about not being able to structure a paragraph in a reasonable way. Due to these concerns, the dominant problem type of P2 was upgrading in both individual writing tasks. P2 created a brief outline in IW2 (he did not create it in IW1, but mentioned in the respective stimulated recall that he usually creates it, so the lack of it in IW1 can be attributed to the data collection situation) and went through an intensive proofreading stage in both individual writing tasks. Besides his concern about content and cohesion, he also encountered a number of LREs in mechanics, lexis and grammar. His lexical LREs were mainly upgrading, i.e. P2 was looking for more suitable alternatives for words, even though he had already come up with a formulation (which he did not consider ideal). In his grammar LREs, he dealt with special cases of singular/plural and with articles (different foci in IW1 and IW2, see below). Even though P2 used a dictionary, he solved most of his problems intuitively. When using a dictionary, he selected words he already knew from the

---

[11] In addition to the grammar problems which differed from IW1 to IW2, there were also grammar problems which occurred in both individual writing sessions. The focus of these grammar problems were verb forms and regular singular / plural.

dictionary output. He also applied reasoning as a strategy in IW2, something P1 did not do.

Most phenomena stayed constant in IW1 and IW2. However, there were a few changes that could be observed (see Table 5). Similar to P1, P2 encountered more upgrading and fewer compensatory and confirmatory problem types in IW2 than he did in IW1. However, the upgrading problem types were dominant in both writing tasks. There was a shift towards upgrading lexical problems from IW1 to IW2. Even though P2 encountered problems with articles in both writing tasks, the focus was different, with decisions about using an article at all in IW1, but decisions about the form of the indefinite article in IW2. In addition, P2 used reasoning as a new problem-solving strategy in IW2.

Table 5: Differences between IW1 and IW2 for P2.

IW1	IW2
Upgrading and compensatory lexical problems with similar frequency	Upgrading lexical problems dominant
Articles: use or no use	Articles: *a* or *an*
No reasoning	Reasoning as a problem-solving strategy

As evident from the above account, self-initiated attention to form (often followed by output modification) occurred in both participants in both individual writing sessions. All three types of possible learning gains (knowledge internalization, knowledge restructuring and knowledge consolidation) can be traced back in the protocols by observing the different problem types (upgrading, compensatory and confirmatory[12]), with different emphases by each of the participants (with P1 being mainly concerned about gaining new knowledge, whereas P2 was more concerned about restructuring and consolidating his knowledge). The outcome being an achievement strategy most of the time, it seems that participants arrive at a solution which either helps them internalize new knowledge, restructure it or consolidate existing knowledge, which might move them forward in their language acquisition process.

---

12 We do not assume a direct correspondence between the possible learning gains and the problem types, but we assume that there is some overlap and the three problem types might point to the different levels of learning gains.

4.2 Collaborative writing process

The collaborative writing task was dominated by the fact that the participants' opinions on the topic in question were very different. For this reason, they spent the first twelve minutes of the writing time discussing content and trying to reach common ground. In this discussion phase, P1 tended to discuss content in a very detailed manner whereas P2 kept reminding P1 that they should try to reach some agreement and create a piece of written work. Possibly in order to achieve this, P2 consciously decided to give up his opinion and accept P1's opinion. This led to clear content dominance by P1 which was also clearly and repeatedly verbalized by P2 (with statements such as "So now YOU would say . . . ", "So the standpoint YOU would like to defend is . . . "[13] which made clear that P2 sought to distance himself from P1's ideas). Still, P2 took charge of the writing process and the formulation of P1's ideas. While still discussing the content issue with P1, he started creating a brief outline and also initiated the writing itself. Most of the time, P2 took over the typing. In the first part of the writing activity (approx. minute 12 to minute 19), P2 was formulating and typing, whereas P1 interrupted him several times either commenting on some content-related issues (without contributing to the formulation) or asking questions about vocabulary. In this part, three sentences were generated. In the second part (approx. minute 19 to minute 29), P2 asked P1 to take over the typing, even though P1 expressed doubt about his abilities. In this phase, P2 dictated most of the text to P1 and P1 used P2 several times to clarify questions of spelling and vocabulary. This dominance was accepted by P1 and is also visible in minute 26 where P1 asks P2, "Have you now finished concerning Brexit?", even though P1 was the one typing at that time. P1's only original contribution was one brief content specification (changing "america first campaign" to "trumps america first campaign"). In these ten minutes, one sentence was generated. At the beginning and at the end of P1's typing phase, there were longer discussions about content, initiated by P1 and interrupted by P2 who took the initiative to further pursue the writing process. In minute 29, P2 offered to take over typing again. In the third writing phase, P1 seemed to be more on topic and actively contributed slightly more to the writing process by making German-language pre-formulations and pointing out insecurities about grammar (for example, the form of an indefinite article). Nevertheless, P2 stayed in charge of the writing process and

---

[13] All statements are translated from German. The participants knew that their mother tongue was German. They did not even consider talking in English to each other. Due to the low proficiency of P1 and that the focus was on writing strategies rather than English language interaction during the CW, the researcher did not try to change the language used.

also clearly expressed disagreement with P1 about linguistic issues. However, he kept accepting P1's content suggestions. In this last writing part, six sentences were generated.

The main phenomena observed in the collaborative writing session are summarized in Table 6. Comparing the problem types with the first individual writing session, fewer compensatory problems are evident. There are some confirmatory problems, but most problems are upgrading. The focus of the

Table 6: An overview of the characteristics of the collaborative writing session.

Area of interest	Description for the collaborative writing session
Number of LREs	65
Participant roles	P1 dominates content P2 dominates language and typing
Writing management	Long content-related discussions Outline created by P2 Proof-reading by P2
Formulation	Micro-planning and pre-formulation done mostly by P2 (even if P1 was typing)
Problem types	Upgrading (52 LREs) Confirmatory (8 LREs) Compensatory (5 LREs)
LRE focus	Lexis (22 LREs) Mechanics (21 LREs) Content (9 LREs) Grammar & Word order (8 LREs) Cohesion & Avoiding repetition (7 LREs)
Lexical problem types	Upgrading (9 LREs) Confirmatory (8 LREs) Compensatory (5 LREs)
Dominant strategy types	Intuition (44 LREs) Writing partner (12 LREs) Dictionary (7 LREs)
Dominant strategy function	Achievement (59 LREs)

problems includes all levels, with lexis and mechanics being dominant.[14] Cohesion and coherence are less frequent in the collaborative writing task than in P2's individual writing task. The reason for this could be that P2 adapts his level to P1 or that he does not have the attentional resources for higher-level problems due to the basic content disagreement and discussion with P1. This adaptation did not seem to have any effect on P2's second individual writing task (he even produced more episodes of this kind in IW2 (n=44) than in IW1 (n=39)).

The strategies used in the collaborative writing task differ from the strategies adopted by each writer individually. An additional resource for clarifying problems is the writing partner. Most frequently, P2 is the resource for P1 (nine times), especially concerning lexical and spelling questions. P2 accepts this role and also corrects P1's English. P2 makes use of P1's suggestions three times and if he asks him for his opinion, it is not language-, but rather content-related. The main strategy for resolving problems is intuition. The dictionary is used much less frequently than in the individual writing sessions. In addition, the participants select only those words from the dictionary output that they already know.

Most of the time, the participants are able to arrive at a solution they are content with, applying achievement strategies. There are four cases of formal reduction (similar to individual writing) and no functional reduction.

As evident from the description above, the participants' relationship in this collaborative writing task according to Storch's model of dyadic interaction (Storch 2002) was somewhere between expert/novice and dominant/passive, with the dominance split across content and language. Scaffolding clearly took place, with P2 being the expert and P1 the novice. Both participants accepted these roles.

As Storch (2016) points out, the success and usefulness of collaborative writing attempts depends on a variety of factors, including proficiency levels and goals of the participants. It is evident from the description above that the participants in this study pursued quite different goals and it required a lot of effort, especially on the side of P2, to find a common ground. Still, tendencies can be traced in the collaborative writing task and the following second round of individual writing which show that there might have been some effect from collaborative writing on individual writing strategies.

Relating the above findings to research on the potential of collaborative writing to support language acquisition, it can be concluded that negotiation of form

---

14 Although it is perfectly understandable that an upgrading orientation may be found in lexical, grammatical and cohesion-related problems, looking at certain mechanical problems as upgrading may seem contradictory. However, this identification fits in with the coding as it was done in this study. Most of these problems were slips of pen, i.e. the participant has spelled a word incorrectly and then corrected the spelling.

and meaning took place and therefore the potential for both participants to notice, establish, elaborate or strengthen form-meaning connections was present. The writing partner served as an additional resource to pose questions about language, discuss them or provide answers. This finding is in line with previous findings (for example, Storch 2008; Watanabe and Swain 2007). Specifically and with regard to the research questions posed in the current study, observable and possible effects of the collaborative writing session on individual writing and problem-solving strategies will be discussed in the following section.

4.3 Possible effects of collaborative writing on individual writing and problem-solving strategies

Several changes from IW1 to IW2 might have occurred due to the interactive experience in collaborative writing and the necessity to share ideas. For example, P1 experienced a clear reduction of dictionary use. In collaborative writing, he did not use a dictionary a single time and used P2 as a source of vocabulary knowledge. This might have affected his reduced dictionary use in the following individual writing task and his increased preference for intuitive solutions. An interesting tendency is also the shift towards upgrading problems for both participants (for P1 generally, for P2 in the area of lexis[15]) from IW1 to IW2. In the collaborative writing session, upgrading problem types were also dominant. The experience from the collaborative writing session might have lead the participants to concentrate more on upgrading rather than on compensatory or confirmatory problems.

A small but still notable change was that P2 started using reasoning as a problem-solving strategy in IW2. A link could be drawn between the necessity to explain his decisions to his partner during the collaborative writing session and the appearance of reasoning strategies in IW2.

A concern about one linguistic phenomenon was quite clearly transferred from the collaborative writing session to IW2 by P2. In IW1, P2 was concerned about articles, but his concern was whether or not to use an article (definite or indefinite) in front of a noun. In the collaborative writing session, the form of the indefinite article was discussed several times and P1 also explicitly formulated the rule about the use of *a* or *an*. It is therefore notable that P2 was not only concerned about using or not using an article in IW2, but also on the form of the indefinite article in two cases.

---

[15] Generally, P2 encountered mainly upgrading problems also in IW1.

All the changes described above might not only have been due to the collaborative writing session, but other factors will have played a role. Both participants got used to the research setting and their confidence increased between IW1 and IW2. Also, there was a time gap of around one month between IW1 and IW2. The learning effort and gain in this time could not be controlled. The writing topic was different for each session (in order to avoid the effects of task repetition and comply with the course syllabus), which means that the writing topic may also have played a role in the selected strategies. Last, some learning might have occurred due to the first stimulated recall interview and the coaching session which took place between IW1 and CW. All these factors might also have led to the other changes which were observed between IW1 and IW2 and could not be traced back to the collaborative writing session (for example, the types of grammar problems addressed or the slight rise in cohesion and content concerns for P1). All in all, no cause-effect relationship can be established based on the limited data set and all changes represent possible directions for further analyses.

As mentioned above, P2 took on the role of a more able peer and was dominant in terms of the writing process management and formulating ideas. Even though the effects of the expert-novice relationship are not directly observable in IW2, the interactions observable in the CW protocol point to several possible learning gains for both participants. These gains can be indirectly traced from the interactions, however, a longer-term study would need to be conducted to find out whether the learners really profit from the interactions in these ways. Whereas P1 might have profited in terms of language (spelling, vocabulary) and possibly content organization,[16] P2 could have profited due to his teacher role. Through having to explain his ideas about the text organization, remind P1 to stay on task and keep to the topic, and explain vocabulary and grammatical items to P1, his awareness of these phenomena was raised (the usefulness of pair-talk for awareness-raising has been shown in research, see Sato and Ballinger 2012). These observations point to a possible long-term effect of collaborative writing on individual writing strategies.

4.4 Possible effects of stimulated recall on writing strategies

Some changes in writing strategies evident from IW1 to IW2 can be traced to the stimulated recall interview rather than the collaborative writing session, even

---

[16] It is questionable, however, whether P1 actually noticed that P2 was trying to organize the content in a meaningful way.

though the researcher did not teach any strategies either in the stimulated recall interview or in the coaching session. For example, P2 mentioned in SR1 that he usually creates a brief outline when writing, something he did not do in IW1. In IW2, he changed this and created an outline before he started writing. In addition, P2 mentioned explicitly that he found the SR sessions useful in order to become aware of his own writing processes and preferences as a starting point for working on them.[17] This finding points to the reactivity of stimulated recall interviews as mentioned in previous research (see Bowles 2010, 2). Stimulated recall served as an awareness-raising instrument (even though it was not used for this purpose in the research design) and for this reason, its effects might not be clearly separable from the effects of the collaborative writing task.

5 Conclusions

The case study presented in this paper explored possible effects of collaborative writing on individual writing strategies. The two participants were different regarding their L2 proficiency as well as their writing and problem-solving strategies. In addition, their opinions on the topic used for the collaborative writing task differed quite strongly. In the collaborative writing task, each of them became dominant in different areas (content for P1, language and writing process and organization for P2) and they developed an expert/novice relationship. There was a shift in strategies used observable in both participants from IW1 to IW2 which can be traced back to the collaborative writing task, but which can also be caused by other factors at play such as increased confidence, familiarity with the research setting, or learning experience between IW1 and IW2. Possible learning gains due to the characteristics of the interaction visible from the CW protocol were also explored.

The results presented in the study show that collaborative writing might not only influence the written product and the L2 proficiency of the participants (as shown in previous studies), but that it may also influence L2 writing and problem-solving strategies relevant for individual writing.

5.1 Limitations and outlook

This small-scale piloting case study is limited in its scope and implications. As mentioned above, the changes observed from IW1 to IW2 might not be only due

---

17 This also corresponds to the decreased fluency of writing in IW2.

to the collaborative writing session, but other factors such as increased confidence or that additional uncontrollable learning opportunities might have been at play. No generalizations are possible based on the data of two specific learners. However, the study has revealed some possible directions for analysis in future studies and necessary adaptations in the methodological approach.

Based on the findings discussed above, future studies should preferably adopt a longitudinal design, including more than one collaborative writing session to allow for more learning processes. Especially in the area of strategies, learners have their ways of approaching tasks and one brief collaborative writing session is not enough to have a strong influence on writing strategies. In addition, conducting several collaborative writing sessions would allow the participants to get used to the research setting, so that the influence of familiarity with the research setting on changes in individual writing strategies could be ruled out. As mentioned in research (Storch 2013, 57–70; Watanabe and Swain 2007), the choice of collaborators – including their numbers – is also an important factor which affects the interaction in collaborative writing and is therefore likely to also affect its learning potential. For this reason, the choice of collaborators should be given enough attention and the way they interact should be considered when interpreting the results. Possibly switching writing partners would be advisable as it was done by Shehadeh (2011) in order to prevent learners from staying in "less productive" interaction patterns.

For the individual writing sessions, think-aloud protocols should be used instead of stimulated recall interviews due to stimulated recall interviews seeming to have initialized additional reflection on part of the participants which apparently did not take place in the writing session itself (which is, for example, visible when P2 reflects on creating an outline in the stimulated recall session). In addition, with think-aloud protocols instead of stimulated recall interviews, the data collection would not be so time-consuming and could be much better integrated into the regular course flow. Conducting both think-aloud protocols and stimulated-recall interviews would also be an option, but it would be very time-consuming. Another argument for the use of think-aloud protocols is that they elicit verbal data similar (though not identical) to the data retrieved in the collaborative writing session.

The collaborative writing session itself should be adapted to better correspond to reality of life. It was found that in the piloting study, if the students are together in one room, they find it unnatural to sit at different computers, especially if the placement of the computers makes face-to-face communication difficult as in this specific case. A future study with a similar design should either opt for a completely online setting, using either text or rather voice chat for communication between participants (Steinberger 2017; as research has shown, participants tend to prefer voice chat and have a more intense exchange in voice chat as compared to text chat, see Cho 2017, this volume), or it can use face-to-face setting where both participants can talk to each other easily (possibly working only on one computer).

In order to find out more about which strategies of the writing partner a learner notices and considers relevant, reflective retrospective interviews about the collaborative writing session would be an option. However, these would have to take place after the second round of individual writing to avoid an awareness-raising effect and thus interference with the effect of the collaborative writing session itself. The same applies to the coaching sessions – a design with a quick sequence of individual and collaborative writing sessions followed by coaching and reflective sessions after the data collection would be an appropriate choice and would also rule out the possibility of additional uncontrollable learning as far as possible.

The pilot study presented in this chapter was an attempt to initiate research into individual writing strategies informed by the intense research into collaborative writing as a process. Collaborative writing and its research offer a number of interesting ideas that can be transferred into individual writing research and vice versa. By applying classifications from studies into individual writing on the collaborative writing session and linking the insights, some preliminary interesting tendencies regarding the possible interaction of individual and collaborative writing processes were found. Linking these two research strands can deliver useful insights regarding composing and problem-solving strategies in individual and collaborative writing and how they influence each other.

References

Armengol, Lurdes, and Josep M. Cots. 2009. "Attention processes observed in think-aloud protocols: two multilingual informants writing in two languages." *Language Awareness* 18.3/4:259–76.

Bowles, Melissa A. 2010. *The Think-aloud Controversy in Second Language Research*. 1st ed. New York / Oxon: Routledge.

Cho, Hyeyoon. 2017. "Synchronous web-based collaborative writing: Factors mediating interaction among second-language writers." *Journal of Second Language Writing* 36. Supplement C:37–51.

Cumming, Alister. 1990. "Metalinguistic and Ideational Thinking in Second Language Composing." *Written Communication* 7.4:482–511.

Ericsson, Karl A., and Herbert A. Simon. 1993. *Protocol analysis. Verbal reports as data*. Cambridge / Mass: MIT Press.

Færch, Claus, and Gabriele Kasper. 1983. "Plans and strategies in foreign language communication." In *Strategies in interlanguage communication*, edited by Claus Færch and Gabriele Kasper, 20–60. Applied linguistics and language study. London / New York: Longman.

FernándezDobao, Ana. 2012. "Collaborative writing tasks in the L2 classroom: Comparing group, pair, and individual work." *Journal of Second Language Writing* 21.1:40–58.

Gánem-Gutiérrez, Gabriela A., and Alexander Gilmore. 2018. "Tracking the Real-Time Evolution of a Writing Event: Second Language Writers at Different Proficiency Levels." *Language Learning* 68.2:469–506.

Hanaoka, Osamu. 2006. "Exploring the Role of Models in Promoting Noticing in L2 Writing." *JACET BULLETIN* 42:1–13.

Jim. 2012–2019. "Open Broadcast Software." https://obsproject.com/de/download.

Kim, Youjin. 2008. "The Contribution of Collaborative and Individual Tasks to the Acquisition of L2 Vocabulary." *The Modern Language Journal* 92.1:114–30.

Manchón, Rosa, and Jessica Williams. 2016. "L2 writing and SLA studies." In *Handbook of second and foreign language writing*, edited by Rosa Manchón and Paul K. Matsuda, 567–86. Handbooks of Applied Linguistics [HAL]. Berlin, Boston: De Gruyter.

Manchón, Rosa M., and Julio R. de Larios. 2007. "On the Temporal Nature of Planning in L1 and L2 Composing." *Language Learning* 57.4:549–93.

Moodle-Dev Humboldt-Universitätzu Berlin. 2019. "Moodle Etherpad Lite." https://moodle.org/plugins/mod_etherpadlite.

Qi, Donald S., and Sharon Lapkin. 2001. "Exploring the role of noticing in a three-stage second language writing task." *Journal of Second Language Writing* 10.4:277–303.

Reinders, Hayo. 2009. "Learner uptake and acquisition in three grammar-oriented production activities." *Language Teaching Research* 13.2:201–22.

Roca de Larios, Julio, Rosa M. Manchón, and Liz Murphy. 2006. "Generating Text in Native and Foreign Language Writing: A Temporal Analysis of Problem-Solving Formulation Processes." *The Modern Language Journal* 90.1:100–14.

Sato, Masatoshi, and Susan Ballinger. 2012. "Raising language awareness in peer interaction: A cross-context, cross-methodology examination." *Language Awareness* 21.1–2:157–79.

Shehadeh, Ali. 2011. "Effects and student perceptions of collaborative writing in L2." *Journal of Second Language Writing* 20.4:286–305.

Sprachenzentrum der UniversitätMünster. 2019. "C-Test." https://www.uni-muenster.de/C-Test/.

Stapleton, Paul. 2010. "Writing in an electronic age: A case study of L2 composing processes." *Journal of English for Academic Purposes* 9.4:295–307.

Steinberger, Franz. 2017. *Synchronous collaborative L2 writing with technology*. München.

Storch, Neomy. 1999. "Are two heads better than one?: Pair work and grammatical accuracy." *System* 27.3:363–74.

Storch, Neomy. 2002. "Patterns of Interaction in ESL Pair Work." *Language Learning* 52.1:119–58.

Storch, Neomy. 2005. "Collaborative writing: Product, process, and students' reflections." *Journal of Second Language Writing* 14.3:153–73.

Storch, Neomy. 2008. "Metatalk in a Pair Work Activity: Level of Engagement and Implications for Language Development. (cover story)." *Language Awareness* 17.2:95–114.

Storch, Neomy. 2013. *Collaborative Writing in L2 Classrooms*. New Perspectives on Language and Education. Bristol, Buffalo: Multilingual Matters.

Storch, Neomy. 2016. "Collaborative writing." In *Handbook of second and foreign language writing*, edited by Rosa Manchón and Paul K. Matsuda, 387–406. Handbooks of Applied Linguistics [HAL]. Berlin, Boston: De Gruyter.

Swain, Merrill. 2010. "Talking it through: Languaging as a source of learning." In *Sociocognitive perspectives on language use and language learning*.2nd ed., edited by Rob Batstone. Oxford applied linguistics. Oxford: Oxford University Press.

Swain, Merrill, and Sharon Lapkin. 1995. "Problems in Output and the Cognitive Processes They Generate: A Step Towards Second Language Learning." *Applied Linguistics* 16.3: 371–91.

Swain, Merrill, and Sharon Lapkin. 1998. "Interaction and Second Language Learning: Two Adolescent French Immersion Students Working Together." *The Modern Language Journal* 82.3:320–37.

Uzawa, Kozue, and Alister Cumming. 1989. "Writing strategies in Japanese as a foreign language: Lowering or keeping up the standards." *Canadian Modern Language Review* 46.1:178–94.

Watanabe, Yuko, and Merrill Swain. 2007. "Effects of proficiency differences and patterns of pair interaction on second language learning: Collaborative dialogue between adult ESL learners." *Language Teaching Research* 11.2:121–42.

Wigglesworth, Gillian, and NeomyStorch. 2009. "Pair versus individual writing : Effects on fluency, complexity and accuracy." *Language Testing* 26.3:445–66.

Williams, Jessica. 2012. "The potential role(s) of writing in second language development." *Journal of Second Language Writing* 21.4:321–31.

Yoon, Choongil. 2016. "Individual differences in online reference resource consultation: Case studies of Korean ESL graduate writers." *Journal of Second Language Writing* 32:67–80.

Appendix

Descriptions and examples of writing behaviors and problem-solving strategies[a]

Code	Description	Example[b]
Writing strategies and behaviors: Content discussion / comments	Participants discuss their ideas, what they want to write, or they comment on the content of something that has been written.	Ok so my opinion is that there is a tendency towards a split in our society and so on. (P2 CW, 0:59–1:13)
Writing strategies and behaviors: Planning: Micro-level	Participants decide on what to do next.	Hm, what shall I do next? I don't know more. (P1 IW1, 39: 36–39:48)

(continued)

Code	Description	Example[b]
Writing strategies and behaviors: Planning: Macro-level	Participants decide on a general direction of their writing (for example, they create an outline, decide whether to finish writing or add an additional paragraph).	At least, now we have got a closing sentence (P2 CW, 44: 56–44:59)
Writing strategies and behaviors: Pre-formulating	Participants try to find a way to express an idea by saying it aloud (in English or in German).	More represented, how do you say it, erm. Or I would say, are, represented more by Trump or so. (P2 CW, 18:23–18:38)
Writing strategies and behaviors: Proof-reading	Participants read through their text or its parts. Often, this process is interrupted by making changes to the text.	Note: This is mostly visible when participants stop writing and move the cursor along the text, sometimes highlighting parts of the text.
LRE: Problem focus: Mechanics	The focus of an LRE is on spelling or punctuation.	[. . .] *free time. in the school iler* [. . .] *in the school ile*r*arned* (P1 IW1, 17:44–18:13)
LRE: Problem focus: Lexis: Does not know word	The focus of an LRE is on a word which the participants do not know.	[. . .] *In this nature state you would have an equilib*ri*urium between hunter and* leo.org – key word "beute"[. . .] *In this nature state you would have an equilibrium between* hunter and*predetor* [. . .] *In this nature state you would have an equilibrium between prede*to*rator and prey* (P2 IW2, 14:56–15:32)

(continued)

Code	Description	Example[b]
LRE: Problem focus: Lexis: Does not like word	The participants know a word but do not consider it ideal and are looking for a better alternative.	[. . .] *The first scenario is more interessting because it only eradicates the human race while the buildings and the nature is still ~~functioning~~ alive.* (P2 IW2, 9: 56–10:02) Stimulated recall: Researcher asks about the background of substituting "functioning" by "alive", P2 says he thought the word "functioning" would have needed more expansion and that the word "alive" refers to a state instead of a process, and this state stays intact to a certain extent; in addition, the word "functioning" does not go well with "nature". (P2 SR2, 8: 52–10:10)
LRE: Problem focus: Lexis: Uncertain about word	The participants are not sure whether the word they want to use is correct.	dict.cc – keyword "freizeit" (P1 IW1, 17:13–17:33) Stimulated recall: Researcher asks why P1 chose "free time" among many possible alternatives, P1 explains he came up with the word-by-word translation "free time" but wanted to check whether it was correct or whether there was a better alternative (P1 SR1, 7: 10–8:00)
LRE: Problem focus: Lexis: Forgot word	The participants forgot to write a word he actually planned to write	*the time*i *was in the school* (P1 IW1, 2:06–2:11)
LRE: Problem focus: Grammar + Word order	The participants are concerned about the word forms they use or the word order.	[. . .] *the teachers ~~was~~ were very* (P1 IW1, 16:18–16:26)

(continued)

Code	Description	Example[b]
LRE: Problem focus: Cohesion	The participants are concerned about the way their phrases / clauses / sentences are built and connected with each other	[. . .] *Since the industrial revolution* ~~there has been~~ a [. . .] *Since the industrial revolution* ~~a~~*more and more people* (P2 IW1, 2:05–2:11) Stimulated recall: Researcher asks what P2 wanted to write after "there has been" and why he deleted it; P2 says probably "there has been a tendency", but he did not know how to continue> (P2 SR1, 1150–12:30)
LRE: Problem focus: Cohesion: Avoiding repetition	The participants try to avoid repeating words or information.	[. . .] *and move to the cities, mostly due to the technical changes of the production process.* ~~The tec~~ (P2 IW1, 4:33–4:35) Stimulated recall: Researcher asks why P2 deleted "the tec", P2 answers "That's where I saw that I was being repetitive again." (P2 SR1, 18:34–18:52)
LRE: Problem focus: Content: Addition / specification	The participants add new content or specify what they have written.	[. . .] *But at the same time a increase in anonymity, seperation and exclusion from one's* ~~roots.~~ *cultural and social roots.* (P2 IW1, 12:02–12:08)

(continued)

Code	Description	Example[b]
LRE: Problem focus: Content: Substitution / reformulation	The participants are not happy with the content of what they have written and replace a part of their sentence.	[. . .] *The technic~~is used as~~tial changes are produced mostly because of concurrence* (P2 IW1, 13:16–13:40) Stimulated recall: Researcher asks what P2 was thinking about; P2 says "the technic is used" is too much top-down, but he wanted to express that there is a specific driving force for technical development (P2 SR1, 41:51–42:55)
LRE: Problem focus: Content: Deletion	The participants delete a part of what they have written and do not replace it, but continue writing something else.	[. . .] *Today or at the of the last century the world wide web has changed ~~the social, political and~~* [. . .] *Today or at the of the last century the world wide web has changed the social and political situation. Even the third sector* (P2 IW1, 6:10–6:29) Stimulated recall: Researcher asks what P2 was thinking while doing the change; P2 says he wanted to use the three examples from the task wording, but eating habits did not fit and he forgot other examples that he had in his mind. (P2 SR1, 23:23–24:01)
LRE: Problem type: Confirmatory	The participants check whether their intended wording is correct.	dict.cc – key word "leider" (P1 IW1, 42:11–42:16) Stimulated recall: Researcher asks why P1 chose "unfortunately" among many possible alternatives; P1 replies he knew the word and wanted to check whether it was correct (P1 SR1, 10:26–10:43)

(continued)

Code	Description	Example[b]
LRE: Problem type: Upgrading	The participants aim at improving their text in some way.	[. . .]*The video offers a scenario in which you should imagnee* leo.org – key word "imag" {the word "imagine" is offered in the drop-down menu} *The video offers a scenario in which you should imageine the d* (P2 IW2, 5:46–5:52)
LRE: Problem type: Compensatory	The participants need to compensate for lack of knowledge.	leo.org – key word "entwicklungen" (i.e. developments, trends)[. . .] *This is widely recognized and already down. Trends in india* (P2 IW2, 19:24–19:30)
LRE: Strategy type: Reasoning	The participants use their logical thinking to arrive at a solution of their problem.	[. . .] *In tThe video describes* [. . .] *In the video someone describes* (P2 IW2, 10:33–10:42) Stimulated recall: Researcher asks about the background of changing "The video describes" to "In the video, someone describes"; P2 says a video cannot describe anything, he either needed to change the verb (*darstellen* instead of *beschreiben*) or the formulation (P2 SR2, 10:14–10:47)
LRE: Strategy type: Rules / knowledge	The participants draw on their own knowledge to resolve a problem.	[. . .] *my most hatet subjects was* (P1 IW1, 39:53–39:54) Stimulated recall: Researcher asks P1 why he changed "subject" into "subjects"; P1 says there are more subjects, which is why he needs the plural form (P1 SR1, 22:41–23:40)

(continued)

Code	Description	Example[b]
LRE: Strategy type: Dictionary: Intuition[c]	The participants use a dictionary and intuitively pick a solution to resolve their problem.	dict.cc – key word "besonders" [. . .] *i am glad to live here without problems especially* (P1 IW2, 18:25–18:39) Stimulated recall: Researcher asks why P1 chose "especially" among many possible alternatives; P1: That fits best in this case. (P1 SR2, 10:28–10:44)
LRE: Strategy type: Dictionary: Frequency counts	The participants use a dictionary and use frequency counts to select a solution to their problem.	dict.cc – key word "bzw." {points with the cursor to various words} [. . .] *schools by our big brother e.trespectivel the sovietunion.* (P1 IW1, 23:12–23:42) Stimulated recall: Researcher asks why P1 chose "respectively" among many possible alternatives; P1 explains he did not know the word and decided for "respectively" based on the frequency (P1 SR1, 8:57–9:36)
LRE: Strategy type: Dictionary: Knowledge	The participants use a dictionary select a word they already know.	dict.cc – key word "fast" (P1 IW1, 18:21–18:30) Stimulated recall: Researcher asks why P1 chose "almost" among many possible alternatives; P1 replies he knew the word and wanted to check whether it was correct (P1 SR1, 8:18–8:46)

(continued)

Code	Description	Example[b]
LRE: Strategy type: Dictionary: Context	The participants use a dictionary and consider the context when selecting a solution to their problem.	leo.org – keyword "konkurrenz" [. . .] *The technicial changes are produced mostly because of* ~~concurrence~~*competion between the comp*(P2 IW1, 13:41–14:04) Stimulated recall: Researcher asks why P2 chose "competition" among other alternatives; P2 says he the only two possible words which he knew were "competition" and "rivalry". From these, "competition" is linked to economy which is what he wanted to express (P2 SR1, 42:57–43:48)
LRE: Strategy type: L1 / Cross-linguistic influence	The participants draw on knowledge from another language to find a solution to their problem.	[. . .] *russian language and "staatsbürgerkunde" and ESP.* (P1 IW1, 37:56–38:03) Comment: ESP is a German abbreviation and P1 did not attempt to translate it into English.
LRE: Strategy type: Intuition	The participants apply an intuitive or automatic solution to their problem, no explicit strategy is recognizable.	[. . .] *schools in the uk~~und~~and the us and that was we lerned* (P1 IW1,18:46–19:02)
LRE: Strategy type: Writing partner	The participants ask their writing partner for a solution (only applicable to the collaborative writing session)	P1: What does embraced mean? P2: Embraced, have welcome them, I would say. P1: Ok.(CW, 17:44–17:52)
LRE: Strategy function: Achievement	The participants arrive at a solution which corresponds in form and meaning to what they intended to express.	dict.cc – key word "schon"[. . .] is *already a long time ago* (P1 IW1, 2:22–3:10)

(continued)

Code	Description	Example[b]
LRE: Strategy function: Formal reduction	The participants keep the message, but simplify its form due to lack of linguistic resources.	[. . .] *but this do i to catch up on* Even though it probably sounds just terrible (P1 IW1, 44: 13–44:36)
LRE: Strategy function: Functional reduction	The participants change or abandon their message due to lack of linguistic resources.	[. . .] *Good examples are facebook, tinder, or jobs in which are*[. . .] *Good examples are facebook, tinder, or jobs which are.or tele*[. . .] *Good examples are facebook, tinder. ortelehomeoffice jobs.* (P2 IW1, 16:10–16:32) Stimulated recall: Researcher asks what P2 was thinking about when trying different alternatives before deciding for "homeoffice jobs"; P2 says he originally wanted to express something different, mentioning jobs where people work on the internet and single jobs take only a few minutes, for example picture editing for online photo shops; in the end, he decided to use the word "homeoffice jobs", changing what he originally wanted to say. (P2 SR, 47:16–48:36)

[a] Note that some codings require larger context to be correctly assigned.
[b] Utterances made in German were translated into English.
[c] The sub-codes in the dictionary code refer to the way in which the decision was made using the different options in the dictionary output.
CW: collaborative writing session
IW1: individual writing session 1 (before collaborative writing)
IW2: individual writing session 2 (after collaborative writing)
SR1: stimulated recall interview conducted after IW1
SR2: stimulated recall interview conducted after IW2
P1: participant 1
P2: participant 2
Oral utterances are typed in normal font, written text is typed in italics.
Underlined text is newly added text by participants, crossed text is text deleted by participants.

Fauzul Aufa and Neomy Storch
Learner interaction in blended collaborative L2 writing activities

1 Introduction

Collaborative writing has been claimed to be effective in L2 learning instruction (Storch 2011, 2013) because it offers authentic learning environments that orchestrate both L2 writing and L2 learning. A growing number of studies have thus set out to investigate the nature of collaboration and learning outcomes of collaborative writing activities in different instructional contexts (see review in Storch 2013, 2019). However, in most of these studies, collaborative activities were implemented either in a face-to-face or online mode (see also studies reported in this volume). Our study is the first to investigate the nature of collaboration when the collaborative writing activity is implemented in a blended approach, utilising both modes of communication.

Storch (2013) defines collaborative writing as the process of co-authoring or co-constructing a text by two or more writers, and "where there is a shared and negotiated decision-making process and a shared responsibility for the production of a single text" (p. 3). Bradley, Lindström, Rystedt, and Vigmo (2010, 71) also describe collaborative writing as an activity in which "learners produce a piece of text, and everyone is taking turns in contributing to the process of writing a joint text." Both definitions imply that the act of composing a text jointly entails interaction in every stage of the writing process (brainstorming, planning, drafting, revising, and editing). Interaction has been identified as key to language learning in both cognitive and sociocultural perspectives (e.g., Long 1996, Vygotsky 1978).

In Vygotsky's (1978) sociocultural theory, social interaction plays an essential role in all learning, including L2 learning. The negotiations learners engage in during collaborative writing accord with what Swain (2000) refers to as collaborative dialogues. Swain (2000) describes these as "dialogues with which the speakers are engaged in problem solving and knowledge building" (p. 102). The language related problems that L2 writers deliberate about during collaborative writing can stimulate cognitive processes (e.g., noticing gaps) and encourage learners to provide and consider peer feedback. In these deliberations about language, learners can also pool linguistic resources in a process termed 'collective scaffolding' (Donato 1994). Such deliberations and engagement in

---

Fauzul Aufa, Neomy Storch, The University of Melbourne

https://doi.org/10.1515/9781501511318-007

knowledge co-construction may result in language learning (Neumann and McDonough 2015, Wigglesworth and Storch 2012).

The units of analysis used in the literature to capture learners' deliberations about language are Language Related Episodes (LREs). According to Swain and Lapkin (1998, 326), LREs exemplify "any part of a dialogue where the students talk about the language they are producing, question their language use, or correct themselves or others".

The existing empirical studies have documented several factors that may impact on the quantity and quality of LREs during collaborative writing tasks, whether in face-to-face (FTF) or computer mediated forms. These factors include types or genres of writing task types in FTF (e.g., Abadikhah 2012, Lin and Maarof 2013, Sajedi 2014) and online collaboration (e.g., Díez-Bedmar and Pérez-Paredes 2012, Oh 2014), the proficiency level of L2 learners (e.g., Storch and Aldosari 2013), and the group size (e.g., Edstrom 2015, Fernández Dobao 2012). Another essential factor that has been examined is the patterns of interaction; that is, the relationships learners form when completing collaborative writing tasks.

2 Patterns of interaction in collaborative writing

Patterns of interaction have been investigated in research on collaborative writing in both FTF and online environments. Most studies have used Storch's (2002, 2013) model of dyadic interaction. In this model (reproduced in Figure 1 below), Storch identified four patterns (*collaborative, dominant/dominant, dominant/passive, and expert/novice*) based on the level of equality (i.e., the degree of contribution to group work and authority over the direction of the task) and mutuality (i.e., the degree of engagement with each other's contribution, see Kos this volume). The *cooperative* pattern appears in Storch's (2001) version of this diagram. It is placed in Quadrant 2, as this patterns also represents moderate to high equality but moderate to low levels of mutuality. Figure 1 shows how these patterns fit into the model which consists of equality and mutuality as two intersecting continua.

A *collaborative* pattern (Quadrant 1) is where the pair contribute to the joint task and engage with each other's contribution (a medium-high level of equality and mutuality). In Quadrant 2, a *dominant/dominant* or *cooperative* pattern is where the pair contribute to the task completion but does not engage very well with each other's suggestions. This may occur because there is a clear task division (medium-high level of equality, but medium-low mutuality).

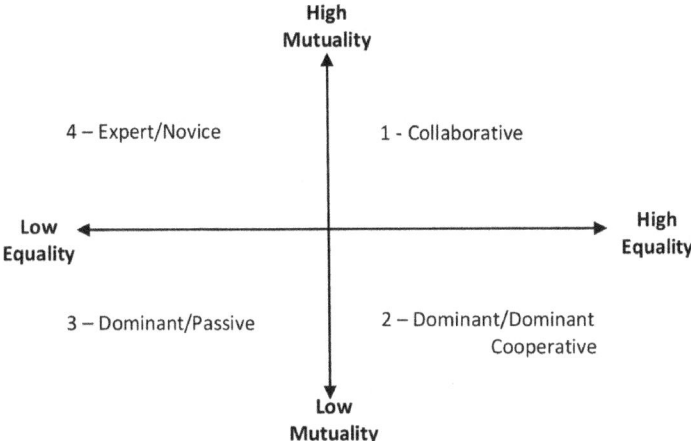

Figure 1: A model of dyadic interaction (Storch 2001, 2002, 2013).

A *dominant/passive* pattern is where one participant adopts an authoritative role and the other participant takes a more passive role which leads to little negotiation (medium-low level of equality and mutuality). Lastly, an *expert/novice* pattern is where one participant takes an 'expert' role and encourages the 'novice' participant to contribute to the task (medium-low level of equality, but medium-high mutuality).

Storch (2002) found that such interactional patterns affect the quantity and quality of LREs and their resolutions. While the pair talk data of collaborative and expert/novice pairs showed that both members of the dyad engaged in deliberations about language and produced a high ratio of correctly resolved LREs, this was not the case in dominant/dominant and dominant/passive pairs who showed a lack of such engagement. More importantly, Storch also reported that patterns of interaction had an impact on language learning. Pairs which formed collaborative and expert/novice patterns engaged in the co-construction of language knowledge during their pair work; knowledge which was subsequently internalised by members of the dyads. In comparison, dominant/dominant and dominant/passive pairs exhibited very limited transfer of knowledge since members of such dyads did not deliberate very much about language nor engage in pooling their linguistic resources and co-constructing language knowledge. Briefly, Storch's work suggests that collaborative and expert/novice patterns of interaction provide learners with more language learning opportunities, evident in more instances of collaborative dialogue (i.e., LREs) and collective scaffolding, than dominant/dominant and dominant/passive patterns do.

Building on the work of Storch (2002), an increasing number of studies have investigated the patterns of group and pair interaction in a range of L2 contexts (e.g., Edstrom 2015, Tan, Wigglesworth, and Storch 2010, Watanabe and Swain 2007). Some studies (e.g., Watanabe and Swain 2007) identified additional patterns such as expert/passive. Others applied these patterns to small groups rather than pairs (e.g., Edstrom 2015) and to collaborative writing projects completed online, using wikis or Google Docs (e.g., Arnold, Ducate, and Kost 2012, Li and Kim 2016, Rouhshad and Storch 2016). These studies identified additional patterns to describe relationships formed by small groups rather than dyads, and the distinct roles adopted by some members of the groups, such as leader or facilitator (see Arnold, Ducate, and Kost 2012). Moreover, studies which compared learners' interaction on collaborative writing tasks FTF and in online environments (e.g., Rouhshadand Storch 2016, Tan et al. 2010) have shown that a cooperative pattern is more likely to occur in collaborative writing in online environments compared to FTF.

Patterns of interaction learners form in collaborative writing tasks are clearly an important consideration when implementing such tasks in FTF or online environments. However, given the widespread use of collaborative writing platforms such as wikis and Google Docs in education, a blended approach is perhaps more likely to be used in the language classroom than just FTF or just an online format. According to Gruba and Hinkelman (2012, 4), blended learning is "the integration, or configuration, of global network technologies with technologies commonly used within FTF classrooms". Blended learning has also been defined as a pedagogical approach that incorporates the effectiveness of FTF classrooms with technologically mediated active learning opportunities of the online mode (Graham 2012, 2013). To date, very few studies (e.g., Zorko 2009) have investigated the nature of learners' interaction and the focus of learners' talk in blended collaborative writing activities. Therefore, our study set out to investigate the relationships formed in blended collaborative writing activities and LREs generated during the activities in an ongoing language classroom.

3 The study

This study drew on data from a larger study on peer interaction in blended collaborative writing activities. The study was conducted in the Department of English Language and Literature at a public university, situated in the western part of Indonesia. English writing is one of the compulsory courses in the English department. Of the three writing courses (i.e., Writing 1, 2, and 3) offered by the department, we selected Writing 2 (essay writing) to be the context of our study since the course involves regular collaborative writing activities and it integrates online learning into FTF classroom activities.

3.1 Participants

Data for this study was collected from 27 undergraduate students, in the second year of their degree course, who enrolled in a two-credit essay writing course. Most of the students have been learning English as an additional language since they were 8 years old (primary schools); that is, for more than 10 years (*Mean* = 9, *SD* = 0.39). It was difficult for us to accurately determine the students' level of English proficiency. In this university, English is not the medium of instruction and students are not required to take standardised English proficiency tests as part of the admission process. Nevertheless, in this context (and confirmed in discussion with the teachers) the students were considered low intermediate. All participants were Indonesian who shared similar cultural and language backgrounds. They spoke Indonesian (national language) and some also spoke Minang (local language). The students ranged in age from 18 to 21 years (*Mean* = 19, *SD* = 0.62). All participants' names (students and teachers) referred to in this study are pseudonyms.

3.2 Tasks

Over the course of the 16-week semester, the teachers, Salam and Yati, required the students to complete a number of collaborative writing tasks, each writing task dealing with a different genre. According to the course syllabus, the course aimed to develop students' ability to write coherently six different writing genres including narrative, explanation, analytical exposition, hortatory exposition, discussion, and reviews. Through their written work, the students were expected to demonstrate not only their creative, analytical, and critical thinking skills, but also their ability to understand and use writing conventions (e.g., rhetorical structures, lexico-grammar, and other textual components) associated with each text, and to recognize commonly shared attributes of these writing genres.

The collaborative writing activities were carried out in two modes: FTF and online. Both FTF and online collaborative work were done in groups and students self-selected their own group members, also choosing whether to work in dyads or triads. This selection occurred in the second week of semester. The students remained in the same groups for the entire semester. Originally, there were 11 groups composed of four pairs and seven triads. However, as one group (Group 2) withdrew from the course in Week 3, 10 groups were left.

At the beginning of each writing task cycle, which lasted one or two days, the students were given around 50 minutes to work FTF in class to brainstorm the topic and plan their task. They were then expected to continue working collaboratively on the writing tasks outside the class in their own time. Google Docs, a free web-based synchronous collaborative writing application, was set up for the students to use. Students were required to complete a joint text of about 700–1000 words for each of the six assigned writing tasks in the blended mode, with each task dealing with a different writing genre.

As seen in Figure 2, Google Docs provides collaborators with two windows. In the big window, collaborators write their joint texts whereas in the small window, on the right side, they can comment on any aspects of their texts.

Figure 2: A screenshot of Google Docs.

3.3 Data collection

Data was collected using a range of tools, including classroom observations, recorded group talk, computer log files, and the completed jointly produced texts. All classes, which met twice a week over the 16-week semester (i.e., a total of 32 classes), were observed by the first named author to gain a better understanding of the teaching environment in which the study was conducted and, in particular, the learners' behaviour during the FTF group interaction. Group talk was audio-recorded using recorders set up in the middle of each group (about 62 hours in total) and then transcribed.

3.4 Data analysis

Data analysis consisted of two stages. The first stage involved coding dyadic and triadic recorded FTF interactions and the online writing logs for patterns of interaction. The second stage involved coding the interactions for LREs.

3.4.1 Coding for patterns of interaction

In coding for patterns of interaction in our data, we drew on Storch's (2002) model and studies investigating patterns of interaction in the online mode (e.g., Li and Kim 2016, Li and Zhu 2017, Rouhshad and Storch 2016). When coding, and in line with other studies that coded for patterns of interaction, noted above, we considered the overall pattern that best captures the relationship the learners established when completing a particular task, whether in FTF or using Google Docs. Following a repeated reading of our data, we identified five typical patterns:
1. *collaborative*;
2. *cooperative*;
3. *facilitative/cooperative*;
4. *facilitative/cooperative/cooperative*
5. *cooperative/passive/passive*.

Some group members adopted the role of a facilitator who tended to lead the activity, directing how the task should proceed but also encouraging other group members to contribute. This role is perhaps somewhat similar to the 'expert' role in the expert/novice pattern in Storch's (2002) model, but differs in that the facilitator's role in this study seemed to move the task along rather than to provide scaffolded assistance to the novice. The following excerpts illustrate these five patterns. Translations are provided when L1 was used.

A *collaborative* pattern of interaction displays a high level of contribution of group members to the tasks and mutual engagement with each other's contribution (Storch 2002, 2013). Only one group (Group 1) consistently demonstrated a *collaborative* pattern during the six blended writing activities; that is in FTF and online modes. The following excerpt illustrates their pattern of interaction.

Excerpt 1. Collaborative pattern (Group 1, Task 1, FTF)
13 Titis: How about *kita* <we> review another film?
14 Nadia: [review *film apa* <what movie>? (waiting for the answer)
15 Rintan: [review *film apa* <what movie>?
16 Titis: *film apa* <what movie>?
           (Giggling while thinking of a movie without mentioning what the movie was. They all seemed to know what the movie was.)
17 Rintan: Oh.. No . . . no..no (looking at each other while smiling)
18 Titis: *Bukan masalah* sex-*nya*<not about the sex thingy>
19 Nadia: What? But? (smiling)
20 Titis: But it's more to do with the woman aspect.
21 Rintan: Lebih ke sisi perempuanya gitu <more to do with the woman aspect>?
22 Nadia: Okay. (giggling)
23 Rintan: because I didn't watch that film, how can we make it interesting without that film?
24 Nadia: Oh *gini* <like> . . . we talk about the human right, *tentang hak asasinya sebagai wanita*<about the human right as a woman>
25 Titis: Noo . . . it's about love, *tapi cintanya itu*<but the love is . . . > blind, *tapi bukan* <but not . . . > blind 100%. Kalau memang benar<If it's true>.
26 Rintan: So it's not like a review movie, it's like we make another story based on that movie. Is it right?
27 Nadia: make a story?
28 Rintan: No, you said that we don't see that film, we just make up about the story.
           We take the moral value.
29 Titis: We pay more attention for the glow side, and then, it means that
30 Rintan: we make a new story for it.
           Hmmm, yeah? (While thinking)
31 Nadia: It's like write a new story, isn't it? (While looking at Titis asking
32 Rintan: for agreement)

Excerpt 1 shows that these three female students – Titis, Nadia, and Rintan – were working well together completing the first given task, a narrative text requiring the learners to write their own short story. The discussion started with suggestions to review a movie (turn 13) and some optional topics to write about emerged from the discussion (turns 21, 25–26, 30). As can be seen in the excerpt, the students engaged with each other's suggestions, confirming (e.g., turns 26–27) or disagreeing with the suggestions made (turns 18, 27, 29). However, these disagreements seemed easily resolved. For instance, Rintan did not seem to agree with the idea proposed by Titis (turn 26), but rather than imposing her viewpoint, she sought confirmation from her peers to reach a mutually acceptable resolutions(turn 32).

We also identified a *collaborative* pattern of interaction displayed by Group 1 via Google Docs from the comment windows as shown in Excerpt 2.

Excerpt 2. Collaborative pattern(Group 1, Task 1, Google Docs)
1 Rintan: My suggestion on the title, sister. (with 'smile' emoticon)
2 Titis: About to write it. Still looking for inspiration on Webtoon (with 'smile' emoticon)
3 Nadia: Not that scary though (with 'flat face' emoticon)
4 Titis: Stuck *nih* <huft> (with 'sad' emoticon)
5 Nadia: Here I add the character dear
6 Rintan: a bit of revision, (laughing)
7 Nadia: already revised
8 Rintan: Sis, what is the moral value?
9 Titis: What about if there is a naughty character, Louisa or her
10 Rintan: friend?
11 Titis: Like a message if we can't interfere other people's life.
12 Rintan: Is it? A bit confused.
13 Nadia   Still unclear, very confused.
14 Rintan   Found any ideas on Webtoon Sister? wkwkwkkwkw (laughing)

The group members frequently engaged with each other's contributions via the 'comment' window. This excerpt illustrates how they worked collaboratively online to decide on the title of their story ("The White Bloody Bunny"), the characters, and the moral value of the story. For example, they provided suggestions on the title (turns 1–2, 3), additional characters (turn 5), and discussed content (turns 7–13). In general, their writing process was quite recursive as they usually returned to Google Docs to make further revisions on each other's work. Clearly, Group 1 showed a high degree of equality and mutuality in text construction via Google Docs.

A *cooperative* pattern is marked by an explicit division of labour, with interactions typically showing high equality but mid-low mutuality. With the exception of Group 1, this pattern predominated during online interaction via Google Docs. For instance, Group 8 – Ummul, Febrina, and Khairun – worked cooperatively on most tasks in the online mode. They divided not only the workload, but also roles in some stages during online interaction. In Task 1, for instance, once they came to work online, Ummul (Figure 2a) and Febrina (Figure 2b) suggested an outline of the text.

Outline

- Orientation:
    One sunny morning, the sun shone brightly. There was a girl who named Dini from Junior High school. She felt in love with her senior. He was Reno. She had three best friends. They were Ana, Feli, and Sisi.

- Conflict:
    1. Dini wanted give a present to Reno, but there was a girl who also loved Reno. Her name was Fei. She always disturbed Dini's plan
    2. Dini wanted to register dancing class but her teacher did not allow because she was ugly. She was very sad.
    3. It was impossible for her to make Reno interested to her.

Figure 2a: Screenshot of Google Docs 'History' of Group 8 – Ummul (Outlining).

- Resolution:
    1. Dini and her friends should follow Mrs. Leni's drama class, but in that occasion she met Reno and it made her really happy.
    2. Dini became very famous after joined in the drama and she got many presents on valentine day. She also got roses from Reno.
    3. .

Figure 2b: Screenshot of Google Docs 'History' of Group 8 – Febrina (Outlining).

Khairunthen wrote the whole text individually based on the suggested outlines (see Figure 3, regular font). Throughout the composing activity, there was little engagement with each other's contribution. As shown in Figure 3, unlike Febrina (bold font), Ummul (italics font) made some substantial changes in Khairun's text. Ummul also highlighted the changes she made (see shaded text) to draw other members' attention to these changes. However, her peers did not comment on these revisions. In general, Group 8 did not make further revisions once they posted their contributions to the joint text; that is, their work did not demonstrate recursivity. The division of workloads and roles were also commonly observed in other groups (e.g., Group 6) when drafting and revising their tasks on Google Docs.

> One sunny morning, the shone brightly. A girl walked under the shady tree. She looked very happy because it was her first day in Junior High School. ~~Dini was a first year student in Junior High School.~~ Her name was Dini. She was ~~fallelt~~ in love with her senior, Reno a first year student of Senior High School. Dini had tan skin with short hair, used glasses and also a shy girl. Moreover, Reno was very popular at school. Dini could do all the ways to see and speak with him. Dini's best friends ~~were~~ Ana, Feli and Sisi. *They* helped Dini to get Reno with "9 Love's recipe" and "how to date with your senior". Dini said that those book didn't make sense, but in secretly Dini did all the boooks' instruction.
>
> By following the instruction in the book, Dini started do all the methods. One day, Dini and her friends wanted to give Reno chocolate as a present. Dini put it on Reno's motorcvleecle. Suddenly, Fei cam and threw it away. She replaced it with hers. "She *was* a narrow girl, but she was beautiful", said Feli. As they were looking around, Reno came and Fei started her drama. She acted that her legs hurt. Unfortunaantelly, Reno offered a load

Figure 3: Screenshot of Google Docs 'History' of Group 8 (Drafting).

A *facilitative/cooperative* pattern is characterized by a moderate level of equality, yet mid-low mutuality. A *facilitative/cooperative* pattern, for instance, can be seen in Excerpt 3 formed by the pair Ridho and Yogi (Group 7) when they worked FTF on Task 2 (this task required them to write an explanation text).

Excerpt 3. Facilitative/cooperative pattern(Group 7, Task 2, FTF)
1 Ridho: *Cari topik dulu* <find a topic first>! (giving instructions)
2 Yogi: (writing down the word 'topic' on the paper)
3 Ridho: Process. (mentioning the structure of the explanation text)
4 Yogi: *Topiknya . . . apa tu ya* <itstopic . . . what>?
5 Ridho: *Cari aja dulu topiknya* <just find a topic first>!
6 Yogi: *Topiknya tentang* <its topic is about> . . . .
7 Ridho: How is rain happen? (giving a possible topic)
8 Yogi: *Hujan terjadi karena penguapan terus* <Rain happens because of the evaporation and then..(trying to answer the question)
9 Ridho: How is the storming happen? (giving another alternative topic)
       Kalau <if> storming? (looking confused)
10 Yogi: How is storm happen. (changing the word 'storming' to 'storm')
11 Ridho: *Jadi itu topiknya* <So that's the topic>? *Yakin* <Sure>?
       The process of storm. The process.. the process of storm
12 Yogi: The process of storm?
13 Ridho: Maybe this. The process of memories, . . . our memories, which
14 Yogi: explained by Mr. Juf (the name of a lecturer)
15 Ridho: *Oh yang dijelaskan sama Pak Juf* <Oh the one explained by Mr. Juf>?

16 Yogi: The cycle of memories. Circle? Cycle?
17 Ridho: CYCLE, not circle
18 Yogi: *Ya, itu aja* <yes, that's it>?*Terus body-body nya berapa* <then how many body paragraphs>?
19 Ridho: Four. Four body. We will make for body. Review, repeat, reinforce. (dictating what to write)
20 Yogi: *Catat gak ya* <Do I need to write it down>?
21 Ridho: Memorising, repeating, reviewing, reinforcing
22 Yogi: *Ininya . . . body-body nya* <these are . . . the body paragraphs>?
23 Ridho: Yes

As the excerpt shows, Ridho gave orders and interpreted instructions (turns 1, 3, 5), made suggestions about alternative topics (turns 7, 9, 11, 13, 15, 17) and the text organisation (turns 21) all seemingly in order to move the task along. Yogi participated in the task by taking on the role of the scribe. He also sometimes initiated suggestions (e.g., turn 10) and asked questions (e.g., turns 14).

In triads, the equivalent to the *facilitative/cooperative* pattern was the *facilitative/cooperative/cooperative* pattern. It is characterized by a moderate level of equality, yet mid-lowmutuality. Group 9 consisting of Stephanie, Rezi and Rizkid, for instance, displayed a *facilitative/cooperative/cooperative* pattern of triadic interaction when working on the tasks in the class, in the FTF mode.

Excerpt 4. Facilitative/cooperative/cooperative pattern (Group 9, Task 5, FTF)
7 Stephanie: *Pertama apa* <the first one is>? Hmm..
8 Rezi: *Pembelajaran bahasa Inggris* . . . <English learning>
9 Stephanie: *Aku ragu kalau ganti topik. Aaa . . . Anggaplah dulu ini topik ya. Kita..pokoknya intinya di sini kita maunya belajar bahasa Inggris di usia dini itu* . . . <I doubt if we change the topic. Aaa..just consider this as our topic. We..the main thing is..here we want the topic 'Learning English in early childhood'>
10 Rezi: *Kalau ini* <what about this> . . .
11 Stephanie: *Jadi gini, kamu gak usah bikin sulitlah . . . jangan dipikirkan itu sulit. Maksudnyo giko . . . Hmmm . . . hhmmm. Belajar bahasa Inggris di usia dini, tentu ada pro kontra. Apa penyebab pro kontra? Karena sebagian dari sekolah . . . hmmm . . . ada yang menghapus hmmm pembelajaran bahasa Inggris, ada yang tidak menghapus. Itu karena apa? Karena pro dan kontra. Pro nya apa [misal* . . . <So, you don't need to make it complicated . . . don't need to think if it's difficult. That's why . . . hmmm . . .

		hmmm. Learning English in early childhood must bring pros and cons. What makes pros and cons? Because some schools . . . hmmm . . . omit English subject. And some don't. Why is that? Because pros and cons. Pros, [for instance . . . >
12	Rezi:	[*ini di SD kan* <[this is elementary school, right>?
13	Stephanie:	*Aaa, iya SD, di usia dini. Maksudnya di..di . . . Yang paling dini apa selain TK?* <Aaa . . . yes Elementary school, early age. I mean . . . in..in.. what's earlier than Playground>?
14	Rezi:	(Giggling) *SD* <elementary school>
15	Stephanie:	*Ya udah kita ambil SD, karena dulu di SD aku diaktifkan . . . hmmm..pelajaran bahasa Inggris di kelas 4, 5, 6..*<alright, we pick elementary school, because once in my school English subject was included, in grade 4, 5, 6>
16	Rizkid:	*Trus kelas 1, 2, dan 3 gimana* <What about grade 1, 2, and 3>?
17	Stephanie:	*Ya belum dikasi pelajaran bahasa Inggris* <there was no English lesson>.
18	Rizkid:	*Oh gitu* <I see>.
19	Stephanie:	*Jadi gimana* <so how> ?*Pasti ada pro dan kontra. Ini aja* <there must be pros and cons. That's it>?
20	Rizkid:	*Ya gak papa* <that's fine>.

During the FTF interaction, as seen in Excerpt 4, Stephanie played a facilitative role, providing direction on how the group members should collectively complete the task (turns 7, 9, 11, 13, 15) and encouraging other group members' participation (turn 19). Rezi and Rezkid were quite cooperative as they developed some of the text independently at later stages of the tasks. They were also quite responsive to the explanations given by Stephanie (turns 8, 10, 12, 16). However, their engagement with each other's suggestions was quite limited.

A *cooperative/passive/passive pattern* of interaction is characterised by a low level of both equality and mutuality. This was frequently observed in the online mode in which only one student worked on the task and the others generally made no or minimal contributions or changes to the text created by the one group member. For example, when Group 10, comprising Rozi, Rifa and Rukmala, worked on Task 1 via Google Docs, Rozi just briefly outlined the text (see Figure 4), but seemed disengaged from the subsequent drafting and editing processes. Although the group had split the workloads in the FTF mode, Rozi and Rifa did not seem to have a strong commitment to complete their share in the online mode. At the beginning, there were occasions when Rukmala attempted to encourage her peers to work on their parts during the drafting stage, but the response was minimal, at most. Therefore, Rukmala

> Title: Scary House
> Introduction: It was Friday night on my last holiday in WTC mall Jambi.
> Thesis: After waited about fifteen minutes, finally it was our turn to enter the scary house.
> Conflict: I was too scary and just wanted to cancel getting in.
> Resolution: I asked him bravely the way to go out.

Figure 4: Screenshot of Google Docs 'History' of Group 10 – Rozi (Outlining).

> Scary House
>
> It was Friday night on my last holiday in WTC mall Jambi. To pass the time we wanted to play something that challenge our bravery. Then, my friends and I decided to get into a scary house. I stood in line to buy the tickets for us. We bought four tickets and waited for our turn to enter the scary house. After waited about fifteen minutes, finally it was our turn **to enter the scary house.**
>
> I leaded the way because my friends thought that I was brave even in fact I was too scary and just wanted to cancel getting in. I stepped my feet in. It It was too dark and frightening. I wanted to go back but it was late. The ghosts already started spooking us and closed the door. Spontaneously we ran over and were stucked further. We saw so many ghosts in that room. Some of their terrible eyes just looked at us. Of course it made us going to be insane.

Figure 5: Screenshot of Google Docs 'History' of Group 10 – Rukmala (Drafting).

assumed responsibility for drafting the text (Figure 5, regular font). Rifa (bold font) only made few simple changes to the draft. Overall, the passive members contributed very little to the writing task, and also showed little engagement with each other's contributions.

3.4.2 LRE analysis

In the second stage of analysis, we coded the transcribed data from the FTF prewriting activities and from the drafting and revising activities in the online mode for LREs. Given that the focus of this study was on dyadic and triadic interaction, self-corrections were not coded as LREs.

Once identified, LREs were coded for their linguistic focus, which can be categorised into three types (Storch 2013, Swain and Lapkin 1998): 1) Form-LREs (F-LREs), dealing with morphology and syntax; 2) Lexis-LREs (L-LREs), dealing with word choice and meaning; and 3) Mechanics-LREs (M-LREs), dealing with pronunciation, capitalisation, spelling, and punctuation. We then coded LREs for their resolution, distinguishing between correctly resolved, incorrectly resolved, or left unresolved. The following excerpts illustrate these distinct types of LREs.

Excerpt 5 deals with verb tense (F-LRE). Here, Group 3 wrote an outline for Task 2 in the FTF mode. Rahmi asked Ramita to write the outline for the first paragraph (turn 35). When Ramita wrote it down, she used the future tense with a past participle verb, instead of using the infinitive (turn 36). Risa questioned the use of the verb (turn 37) and Rahmi corrected and explained the need for the infinitive (turn 38). Ramita then changed it to the correct form, seeking confirmation from her group (turn 39), and Risa confirmed. This F-LRE was coded as correctly resolved. We note that it also showed evidence of collective scaffolding, with Risa noticing the error and Rahmi providing the correction and explanation.

Excerpt 5. Correctly resolved F-LRE (Group 3, Task 2, FTF)
35 Rahmi: *Paragraf partamo, tentang melanggar hak asasi manusia. Cubo tulis.* <the first paragraph, about breaching human rights. Please write it down!>
36 Ramita: 'it will broken the human rights' (writing it down while reading out loud)
37 Risa: Verb *partamolah nak*? <the first verb (main verb) right?>
38 Rahmi: *Itu kan* future tense. *Yo mah gantilah jo* verb *partamo*! <That's future tense. Change it with the verb infinitive!>
39 Ramita: Okay, break? (while changing it)
40 Risa: Yes

Excerpt 6 is an example of an L-LRE dealing with word meaning, coming from the data of Group 1 in the online mode. Rintan asked her peers the meaning of 'smudge' (turn 8) and Nadia responded (turn 9). However, Rintan realised that Nadia is providing the meaning of a different word (nudge), and sought further assistance from her group (turn 10). The other group members were focusing on the plot of the film they were narrating (turns 11–12) and did not respond to Rintan's request, despite her repeating it (turn 13). This L-LRE was coded as unresolved.

Excerpt 6. Unresolved L-LRE (Group 1, Task 1, Google Docs)
8 Rintan: 'Smudge' . . . what's the meaning of 'smudge'?
9 Nadia: 'smudge with elbow' *tu menyenggol gitulah* <it's like pushing something>

10 Rintan: 'nudge' *ndak*? <Isn't 'nudge'?>
            (Other members talked about something else and did not respond to Rintan)
11 Nadia: I'm still confused with the plot.
12 Titis: So? We changed the plot?
13 Rintan   So, what's the meaning of 'smudge'? (she's trying to ask the same question)

Excerpt 7 illustrates how Group 9 deliberated about the correct spelling of a word. Rezi was not certain how to spell the word curriculum and asked for help (turn 25). Rizkid provided the wrong answer (turn 26) and Rezi accepted it. This M-LRE was coded as incorrectly resolved.

Excerpt 7. Incorrectly resolved M-LRE (Group 9, Task 6, Google Docs)
25 Rezi: Hey guys, *tulisannyo* 'curricullum' *koba a*? <How do we spell 'curricullum'?
26 Rizkid   Pakai 'r' ciek se. <just use single 'r'>
27 Rezi: Okay.

To confirm reliability of analysis of interactional patterns and LREs, we invited another coder, an Indonesian EFL teacher at a university in Indonesia and a colleague of the first author. After a training session, a subset of the data (20% of the data set including the transcripts of verbal interactions and comment logs from Google Docs) was coded by the first author and the second coder. Inter-coder reliability was calculated as the number of agreements divided by the total number of ratings (i.e., agreements plus disagreements) as suggested by Miles and Huberman (1994, 64). The inter-rater reliability scores were 92% for interactional patterns and 90% for LREs. Discrepancies about patterns of interaction and LRE coding were resolved through further discussion.

4 Findings

Our first aim was to identify patterns of peer interaction in a blended setting. Overall, based on levels of equality and mutuality, we identified five distinct patterns of interaction formed by the ten groups of students when they completed six collaborative writing tasks which corresponded to six writing genres (i.e., narrative, explanation, analytical exposition, hortatory exposition, discussion, and reviews). These five patterns were: *collaborative (COL), cooperative*

Table 1a: Patterns of dyadic and triadic interactions across tasks (1–3) in the blended mode.

Group	Task 1		Task 2		Task 3	
	FTF	Online	FTF	Online	FTF	Online
1	COL	COL	COL	COL	COL	COL
3*	FAC/COP/COP	COP	FAC/COP/COP	COP	FAC/COP/COP	COP
4	FAC/COP	COP	FAC/COP	*Individual*	FAC/COP	*Individual*
5	FAC/COP/COP	COP/PAS/PAS	FAC/COP/COP	COP/PAS/PAS	FAC/COP/COP	COP/PAS/PAS
6	FAC/COP	COP	FAC/COP	*Individual*	FAC/COP	*Individual*
7	FAC/COP	COP	FAC/COP	COP	FAC/COP	COP
8	FAC/COP/COP	COP	FAC/COP/COP	COP	FAC/COP/COP	COP
9	FAC/COP/COP	COP/PAS/PAS	FAC/COP/COP	COP/PAS/PAS	FAC/COP/COP	COP/PAS/PAS
10	FAC/COP/COP	COP/PAS/PAS	FAC/COP/COP	COP/PAS/PAS	FAC/COP/COP	COP/PAS/PAS
11	FAC/COP/COP	COP	FAC/COP/COP	COP	FAC/COP/COP	COP

*Group 2 withdrew from the course in Week 3.
COL = Collaborative
FAC/COP = Facilitative/Cooperative
FAC/COP/COP = Facilitative/Cooperative/Cooperative
COP = Cooperative
COP/PAS/PAS = Cooperative/Passive/Passive

(COP), facilitative/cooperative (FAC/COP), facilitative/cooperative/cooperative (FAC/COP/COP), and cooperative/passive/passive (COP/PAS/PAS). However, as shown in Tables 1a and 1b, we also found a few instances where one member of the group completed the entire task on their own (e.g., Groups 4 and 6, Task 3) or that the group did not complete the task at all (e.g., Group 8, Task 5). These instances were labelled as 'individual activity' and 'no activity' respectively.

While the *cooperative* pattern was predominant in the online mode, when the groups drafted and revised their joint texts, the *facilitative/cooperative* and *facilitative/cooperative/cooperative* patterns were more frequent during the FTF pre-writing activities (task negotiation phase) in the classroom. Most groups also displayed shifting patterns of interaction predominantly across modes, rather than across tasks within the same mode. The following figure illustrates how the groups' patterns of interaction shifted across modes.

As shown in Figure 6, the majority of the groups displayed variations with regards to their patterns of interactions in this blended setting across the

Table 1b: Patterns of dyadic and triadic interactions across tasks (4–6) in the blended mode.

Group	Task 4		Task 5		Task 6	
	FTF	Online	FTF	Online	FTF	Online
1	COL	COL	COL	COL	COL	COL
3	FAC/COP/COP	COP	FAC/COP/COP	COP	FAC/COP/COP	COP
4	FAC/COP	COP	FAC/COP	COP	*No activity*	
5	FAC/COP/COP	COP/PAS/PAS	FAC/COP/COP	COP/PAS/PAS	FAC/COP/COP	*No activity*
6	FAC/COP	*Individual*	FAC/COP	COP	*No activity*	
7	*No activity*		FAC/COP	*Individual*	*No activity*	
8	*No activity*	COP	*No activity*		*No activity*	COP
9	FAC/COP/COP	COP/PAS/PAS	FAC/COP/COP	COP/PAS/PAS	*No activity*	
10	FAC/COP/COP	COP/PAS/PAS	FAC/COP/COP	COP/PAS/PAS	*No activity*	COP/PAS/PAS
11	FAC/COP/COP	COP	FAC/COP/COP	COP	*No activity*	COP

COL = Collaborative
FAC/COP = Facilitative/Cooperative
FAC/COP/COP= Facilitative/Cooperative/Cooperative
COP = Cooperative
COP/PAS/PAS = Cooperative/Passive/Passive

modes. For instance, Groups 4, 6, and 7 shifted from *facilitative/cooperative* in the FTF mode to a *cooperative* pattern in the online mode. Groups 3, 5, 8, 9, 10, and 11 shifted from a *facilitative/cooperative/cooperative* pattern to either *cooperative* (Groups 3, 8 and 11) or *cooperative/passive/passive* (Groups 5, 9 and 10) patterns. In the case of Groups 5, 9, and 10, the group members who played the facilitative role in the FTF mode tended to be *cooperative* in the online mode. Only one group (i.e., Group 1) consistently displayed a *collaborative* pattern across both modes when completing the six writing tasks. Briefly, dynamic patterns of interaction were evident in almost all the groups. Most of the groups approached each task in the two modes differently. Thus, the finding suggests that the integration of FTF and online modes in collaborative L2 writing activities may affect the patterns of peer interaction. Whereas in the FTF mode, the pairs and triads tended to form a cooperative pattern but with one member taking a leading role and facilitating the interaction; in the online mode, the pattern became cooperative or cooperative/passive/passive, with no member taking a leading role to move the task along. These patterns seemed to impact on attention to language (LREs).

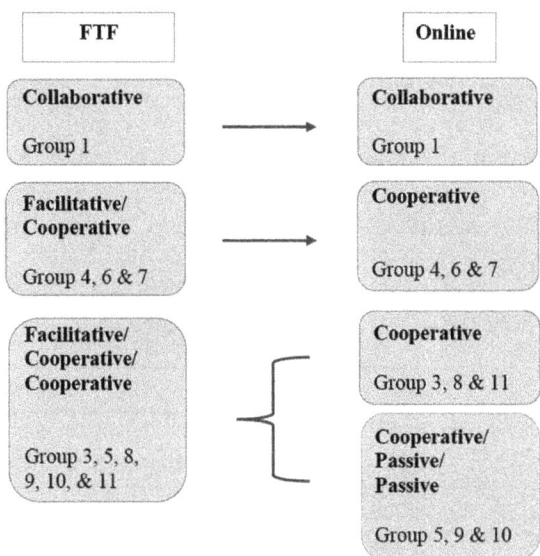

Figure 6: Shifting patterns of interaction across both modes.

Table 2 reports on the LRE findings. As can be seen, Group 1, forming a *collaborative* pattern in both modes, produced the highest number of LREs (49), with the vast majority of those LREs (39) produced when the group worked FTF. The next highest number of LREs were found in Group 7 (17 LREs) displaying *facilitative/*

Table 2: LREs across the patterns of interaction in the blended mode (frequency).

Group	FTF			Online			Subtotal
	COL	FAC/COP	FAC/COP/COP	COL	COP	COP/PAS/PAS	
1	39			10			49
3			11		0		11
4		10			0		10
5		6				0	6
6		12			0		12
7		17			0		17
8			14		1		15
9			5			0	5
10			3			0	3
11			14			0	14
Total		131			11		142

cooperative pattern and Group 3 (14 LREs) displaying *facilitative/cooperative/cooperative* pattern. The other groups generated very few LREs. These findings confirm that patterns of interaction affect the quantity of LREs generated.

Mode also impacted on the quantity of the LREs. There were considerably more LREs in the FTF (131) than in the online (11) mode. Even the group that collaborated in both modes (i.e., Group 1) produced significantly fewer LREs when working online than FTF. In both modes, however, and as shown in Table 3, L-LREs predominated.

Table 3: Focus of LREs in the blended mode (frequency and %).

	F-LREs	L-LREs	M-LREs	Subtotal
FTF	43 (33%)	68 (52%)	20 (15%)	131
Online	2 (18%)	9 (82%)	0	11
Total	45	77	20	142

The mode also influenced the resolution of LREs. As shown in Table 4, in the FTF mode, the majority of the LREs (61%) were resolved correctly, 17% of LREs were resolved incorrectly and 22% were unresolved. In contrast, of the total LREs in the online mode, only 27% were resolved correctly. An equal proportion was resolved incorrectly (36%) or left unresolved (36%). It should also be noted that the learners used their L1 to resolve most of the LREs.

Table 4: Resolutions of LREs in the blended mode (frequency and %).

	Correct	Incorrect	Unresolved	Subtotal
FTF	80 (61%)	22 (17%)	29 (22%)	131
Online	3 (27%)	4 (36%)	4 (36%)	11
Total	83	26	33	142

5 Discussion

We identified five different patterns of dyadic and triadic interactions in this study: *collaborative, cooperative, facilitative/cooperative, facilitative/cooperative/cooperative, and cooperative/passive/passive*. The patterns did not seem to be influenced by the writing genres, as found in Tan, Wigglesworth, and Storch (2010). Rather, they appeared to shift due to different modes. The shifting modes were also aligned with different phases of writing activities. Whereas in the FTF mode, the learners focused mainly on brainstorming the topic and discussing how to approach the writing, it was in the online mode that the composing and revision/editing took place. With the exception of Group 1 which displayed a *collaborative* pattern of interaction in both modes, other groups formed a shifting pattern across the modes. For instance, Group 7 forming a *facilitative/cooperative* and Group 8 forming *facilitative/cooperative/cooperative* pattern in the FTF mode, shifted to a *cooperative* pattern in the online mode. Similarly, Group 9 forming a *facilitative/cooperative/cooperative* pattern in the FTF mode, switched to a *cooperative/passive/passive* pattern in the online mode. This finding suggests that in most instances the FTF mode, in which task negotiation took place, seemed to encourage one member to assume a facilitative role to manage the task. One possible explanation for this finding is time pressure. The students had to complete the task FTF within 50 minutes (the duration of the lesson), whereas they had one to two days to complete each task online. The online mode offered some flexibility and autonomy and seemed to encourage a *cooperative* approach to the tasks (see Figure 6). Each group member could work on a particular section of the text based on the division of labour decided in the FTF meeting, and at their own pace without needing someone to tell them what to do. This at times, however, also resulted in some group members choosing to make no contribution to the task. For example, when Group 5 worked FTF, they formed a *facilitative/cooperative/cooperative* pattern, with the facilitative member encouraging the other two members to contribute to the task. In the online mode, the facilitative member relinquished responsibility for the task, and the other two became totally disengaged. As Lantolf and Thorne (2006) state, using computer-mediated communication technology does not automatically guarantee a more participatory mode of interaction.

Our findings that groups tended to cooperate in the online mode are consistent with the findings reported by Rouhshad and Storch (2016). However, the nature of cooperation in this study was different. In the Rouhshad and Storch (2016) study, the division of labour was mainly in terms of roles, with one member of the dyad taking on the role of the scribe and the other dictating the text. In this study, the group members often divided not only the roles but also workloads (i.e., dividing the composition of the joint text into separate sections). In the literature on cooperative learning, cooperation based on a division of roles is termed horizontal division, and one based on a division of contribution to the texts is termed stratified division (Lowry, Curtis, and Lowry 2004).

The tendency to cooperate in the online mode also impacted on attention to language. In general, the groups forming a *cooperative* pattern had limited engagement or interactions with their group members' contributions, including very little to no evidence of deliberations over language form, hence the very low frequency of LREs found in their data. This finding accords with findings reported by Oskoz and Elola (2012), who investigated learners' wiki discussion spaces, and Rouhshad and Storch (2016), who compared collaborative writing in FTF and Google Docs of the same set of pairs, suggesting that little deliberation about language use takes place in online collaborative writing.

The lack of attention to language perhaps can be attributed to the nature of the mode. In the online mode, group members tended to make direct changes to the evolving text rather than make suggestions and offer feedback to each other. These findings are similar to those reported in other studies (e.g., Kessler 2009). Although Google Docs provides spaces for the members to comment and deliberate in the small window, learners generally appeared reluctant to utilise these spaces (see also Rouhshad and Storch 2016).

We also found that the mode influenced the resolution of LREs, but not the focus of the LREs. Most of the LREs in both modes tended to be L-LREs, as was also found by Rouhshad and Storch (2016), perhaps not surprising given the meaning-focused nature of the tasks (see also Storch 2013). However, a higher number of LREs in the FTF mode was resolved correctly, compared to those in the online mode. This suggests that engagement in LRE resolution, where learners consider and evaluate counter-suggestions and pool their linguistic resources, can contribute to correct resolutions of LREs. As Chen (2017) remarks, mutuality is likely more significant than equality in providing learning opportunities since a high degree of mutuality enables students to provide feedback and assist each other in resolving LREs correctly.

6 Conclusions

Our study found that learners form distinct patterns of interaction when asked to co-author a text. In this learning context, where a blended approach was implemented with learners completing six texts (each representing a different genre) in FTF and online modes of interaction, the mode of interaction rather than the genre of the text impacted on the patterns formed. More importantly, the mode and the patterns formed seemed to influence whether learners engaged in deliberations about language. As had been shown by a small but growing number of studies (e.g., Rouhshad and Storch 2016), when co-authoring online learners seem less likely to engage in deliberations about language and persist in such deliberations to reach resolutions to the language problems they encounter. These findings have some implications for language pedagogy.

However, before discussing these implications, we need to acknowledge some of the limitations of the study. First, the study focused exclusively on examining blended collaborative L2 writing activities in one classroom at an Indonesian public university. Therefore, the findings might not be generalisable beyond this setting. Though we intended to collect data and provide thick descriptions about the students' experiences during their blended collaborative writing activities in order to enhance the transferability of our results to similar contexts, collecting such data proved difficult when conducting research in a naturalistic environment. Lastly, the first author's familiarity with the research site may raise potential issues of objectivity; that is, the first author's insider perspectives might have affected the process of data analysis and interpretation. To address this issue and to avoid bias, we checked for inter-coder reliability during the data analysis. A blended approach to collaborative writing may offer a potential setting for L2 learning, extending learners' interaction beyond the physical confines of the classroom and allowing students more flexibility. However, our findings suggest that in order to maximise the language learning benefits of blended collaborative writing tasks, teachers need to carefully design and implement the activities. Prior modelling of collaborative discourse in both modes may assist learners to participate more fully in the activities (Kim and McDonough 2011). Teacher intervention may also be important in order to encourage the students to form a collaborative relationship when completing the tasks (Chen 2018). Perhaps given that there were more LREs in the FTF mode, we can suggest having more such sessions in the blended approach.

References

Abadikhah, Shirin. 2012 "The Effect of Mechanical and Meaningful Production of Output on Learning English Relative Clauses." *System* 40: 129–43.

Arnold, Nike, Lara Ducate, and Claudia Kost. 2012. "Collaboration or Cooperation? Analyzing Group Dynamics and Revision Processes in Wikis." *CALICO Journal* 29: 431–48.

Bradley, Linda, Berner Lindström, Hans Rystedt, and Sylvi Vigmo. 2010. "Language Learning in a Wiki: Student Contributions in a Web-Based Learning Environment." *Themes in Science and Technology Education* 3: 63–80.

Chen, Wenxue. 2017. "The Effect of Conversation Engagement on L2 Learning Opportunities." *ELT Journal* 71: 329–40.

Chen, Wenxue. 2018. "Patterns of Pair Interaction in Communicative Tasks: The Transition Process and Effect on L2 Teaching and Learning." *ELT Journal* 72: 425–34.

Díez-Bedmar, María Belén, and Pascual Pérez-Paredes. 2012. "The Types and Effects of Peer Native Speakers' Feedback on Cmc." *Language Learning & Technology* 16: 62–90.

Donato, Richard. 1994. "Collective Scaffolding in Second Language Learning." In *Vygotskian Approaches to Second Language Research*, edited by James P. Lantolf and G. Appel. 33–56. Norwood, NJ: Ablex.

Edstrom, Anne. 2015. "Triads in the L2 Classroom: Interaction Patterns and Engagement During a Collaborative Task." *System* 52: 26–37.

Fernández Dobao, Ana. 2012. "Collaborative Writing Tasks in the L2 Classroom: Comparing Group, Pair, and Individual Work." *Journal of Second Language Writing* 21: 40–58.

Graham, Charles. 2012. "Blended Learning Systems: Definition, Current Trends, and Future Directions." In *The Handbook of Blended Learning: Global Perspectives, Local Designs*, edited by Curt. J. Bonk and Charles R. Graham. 3–21. San Francisco, CA: John Wiley & Sons.

Graham, Charles. 2013. "Emerging Practice and Research in Blended Learning." In *Handbook of Distance Education*, edited by Michael G. Moore. 333–50. New York: Routledge.

Gruba, Paul, and Don Hinkelman. 2012. *Blending Technologies in Second Language Classrooms*. London, UK: Palgrave Macmillan.

Kessler, Greg. 2009. "Student-Initiated Attention to Form in Wiki-Based Collaborative Writing.". *Language Learning and Technology* 13: 79–95.

Kim, Youjin, and Kim McDonough. 2011. "Using Pretask Modelling to Encourage Collaborative Language Learning Opportunities." *Language Teaching Research* 15: 183–99.

Lantolf, James, and Steven Thorne. 2006. *Sociocultural Theory and the Genesis of Second Language Development*. Oxford: Oxford University Press.

Li, Mimi, and Deoksoon Kim. 2016. "One Wiki, Two Groups: Dynamic Interactions across ESL Collaborative Writing Tasks." *Journal of Second Language Writing* 31: 25–42.

Li, Mimi, and Wei Zhu. 2017. "Good or Bad Collaborative Wiki Writing: Exploring Links between Group Interactions and Writing Products." *Journal of Second Language Writing* 35: 38–53.

Lin, Ong Poh, and Nooreiny Maarof. 2013. "Collaborative Writing in Summary Writing: Student Perceptions and Problems." *Procedia – Social and Behavioral Sciences* 90: 599–606.

Long, Michael. 1996. "The Role of the Linguistic Environment in Second Language Acquisition." In *Handbook of Language Acquisition*, edited by William C. Ritchie and Tej K. Bathia. 413–68. New York: Academic Press.

Lowry, Paul Benjamin, Aaron Curtis, and Michelle Lowry. 2004. "Building a Taxonomy and Nomenclature of Collaborative Writing to Improve Interdisciplinary Research and Practice." *Journal of Business Communication* 41: 66–99.

Miles, Matthew, and Michael Huberman. 1994. *Qualitative Data Analysis: An Expanded Sourcebook (2nd Edition)*. Thousand Oaks: SAGE Publications, Inc.

Neumann, Heike, and Kim McDonough. 2015. "Exploring Student Interaction During Collaborative Prewriting Discussions and Its Relationship to L2 Writing." *Journal of Second Language Writing* 27: 84–104.

Oh, Haejin. 2014. "Learner's Writing Performance, Revision Behavior, Writing Strategy, and Perception in Wiki-Mediated Collaborative Writing ." *Multimedia-Assisted Language Learning* 17: 176–99.

Oskoz, Ana, and Idoia Elola. 2012. "Understanding the Impact of Social Tools in the Fl Writing Classroom: Activity Theory at Work." In *Technology across Writing Contexts and Tasks*, edited by Greg Kessler, Ana Oskoz and Idoia Elola. 131–53. San Marcos, Texas: CALICO.

Rouhshad, Amir, and Neomy Storch. 2016. "A Focus on Mode: Patterns of Interaction in Face-to-Face and Computer-Mediated Contexts." In *Peer Interaction and Second*

Language Learning: Pedagogical Potential and Research Agenda, edited by Masatoshi Sato and Susan Ballinger. 267–89. Philadelphia/Amsterdam: John Benjamins.

Sajedi, Seyyede Paria. 2014. "Collaborative Summary Writing and EFL Students' Development." *Procedia – Social and Behavioral Sciences* 98: 1650–57.

Storch, Neomy. 2001. "How Collaborative Is Pair Work? ESL Tertiary Students Composing in Pairs." *Language Teaching Research* 5: 29–53.

Storch, Neomy. 2002."Patterns of Interaction in ESL Pair Work." *Language Learning* 52, no. 1: 119–58.

Storch, Neomy. 2011. Collaborative Writing in L2 Contexts: Processes, Outcomes, and Future Directions." *Annual Review of Applied Linguistics* 31: 275–88.

Storch, Neomy. 2013. *Collaborative Writing in L2 Classroom*. Bristol, UK: Multilingual Matters.

Storch, Neomy. 2019. "Time Line on Collaborative Writing ".*Language Teaching* 52: 40–59.

Storch, Neomy, and Ali Aldosari. 2013. "Pairing Learners in Pair Work Activity." *Language Teaching Research* 17: 31–48.

Swain, Merril. 2000. "The Output Hypothesis and Beyond: Mediating Acquisition through Collaborative Dialogue." In *Sociocultural Theory and Second Language Learning*, edited by J. Lantolf. 98–114. Oxford: Oxford University Press.

Swain, Merrill, and Sharon Lapkin. 1998. "Interaction and Second Language Learning: Two Adolescent French Immersion Students Working Together." *Modern Language Journal* 82: 320–37.

Tan, Lan Liana, Gillian Wigglesworth, and Neomy Storch. 2010. "Pair Interaction and Mode of Communication: Comparing Face-to-Face and Computer Mediated Communication." *Australian Review of Applied Linguistics* 33: 1–24.

Vygotsky, Lev. 1978. *Mind in Society: The Development of Higher Pyschological Processes (New Edition)*. Cambridge: Harvard University Press.

Watanabe, Yuko, and Merrill Swain. 2007. "Effects of Proficiency Differences and Patterns of Pair Interaction on Second Language Learning: Collaborative Dialogue between Adult ESL Learners." *Language Teaching Research* 11: 121–42.

Wigglesworth, Gillian, and Neomy Storch. 2012. "Feedback and Writing Development through Collaboration: A Socio-Cultural Approach." In *L2 Writing Development: Multiple Perspectives*, edited by R. M Manchón. 69–100. New York: Mouton de Gruyter.

Zorko, Vida. 2009. "Factors Affecting the Way Students Collaborate in a Wiki for English Language Learning." *Australasian Journal of Educational Technology* 25: 645–65.

Izaskun Villarreal, M. Camino Bueno-Alastuey and Raquel Sáez-León
Computer-based collaborative writing with young learners: Effects on text quality

1 Introduction

Writing has positioned itself as a valuable asset for language learning and numerous investigations have burgeoned in an attempt to ascertain which factors hasten the writing process. Within the writing-to-learn language approach (Manchón 2011b), collaborative writing, or the activity by which two or more students co-construct and co-own a written text (Storch 2013), has gained momentum, because negotiating for meaning in authentic tasks is considered essential for effective language learning (e.g. Long 1996; Pica 1994).

Numerous studies have underscored the linguistic benefits brought about by collaboration for students of diverse backgrounds and contexts (for a summary, see Storch 2013). Likewise, several factors such as learner grouping (Bueno-Alastuey and Martínez de Lizarrondo 2017; Fernández Dobao 2012; Villarreal and Munarriz-Ibarrola this volume), proficiency level (Kim and McDonough 2011), engagement level (Storch and Aldosari 2013), and task type (García Mayo and Azkarai 2016; McDonough and García Fuentes 2015) have been suggested to mediate the collaborative writing process. The expanding use of technology across educational contexts and levels has steered research analysing computer-mediated collaborative writing and its effects on the quality of the jointly written product (see Li 2018 for a research synthesis). The few studies that have contrasted different learner grouping effects in computer-mediated tasks have considered adult populations and have pointed towards slight text quality advantages for collaborating students over individuals (Elola and Oskoz 2010; Strobl 2014; Tare et al. 2014). However, whether these advantages will also be observed among secondary school learners, whose learning process has increasingly been influenced by technology, is still unexplored.

Technology-based L2 writing has stood out for its remarkable capacity to help students develop and integrate competences (Elola and Oskoz 2017). Foreign language learners seem to obtain linguistic benefits from these tasks (Bikowski and Vithanage 2016). Few studies, however, have focused on the

---

Izaskun Villarreal, M. Camino Bueno-Alastuey, Raquel Sáez-León, Public University of Navarre

https://doi.org/10.1515/9781501511318-008

mediating factors of mode and, to date, insufficient evidence has accumulated to draw strong conclusions about the role of writing mode in text quality. While face-to-face paper-based writing tasks have been shown to be more effective among secondary school students (Woodrich and Fan 2017), tertiary students who collaborate online seem to obtain higher scores after extended collaboration (Suwantarathip and Wichadee 2014). These contradicting results call for more investigations to understand the real effects of mode.

Therefore, situated within the writing to learn language approach (Manchón 2011b), this study seeks to explore the linguistic effects different groupings and different writing modes might have on text quality. This study adds to Second Language Acquisition (SLA) literature by examining the effects of collaboration and writing mode among young learners in school settings, a population that has received little attention even though they are increasingly exposed to technology-assisted learning and teaching pedagogies (Woodrich and Fan 2017) and constitute one of the largest and fastest growing populations of English learners in the world (Enever 2018; García Mayo 2017; Lázaro-Ibarrola and Villarreal 2019; Villarreal and Munarriz-Ibarrola this volume).

2 Literature review

The social constructivist theory of learning (Vygotsky 1978) establishes that cognitive and linguistic progress occur in socially embedded contexts through scaffolded interaction, and L2 learners have been shown to offer carefully attuned support to one another that helps to foster learning (De Guerrero and Villamil 2000; Donato 1994; Swain 2000). Although traditionally viewed as a solitary activity (Hyland 2011), more modern conceptions of learning to write (see Manchón 2011a) conceive writing as a social practice, which has been shown to be effective for L2 language development. For example, studies which have contrasted texts written by L2 adults working in pairs or groups with those written by L2 adults working on their own have overall obtained promising linguistic enhancement in the texts written collaboratively using complexity, accuracy and fluency (CAF) quantitative measures as well as analytic rubrics to analyse text features (e.g., Fernández Dobao 2012; Storch 2005; Wigglesworth and Storch 2009). However, to date few studies have focused on secondary school learners.

Web-based technologies have been claimed to transform teaching and learning (Wang 2015), and their use in foreign language instruction has led to higher student satisfaction and motivation (Chen and Brown 2012), more collaboration (Chao and Lo 2011; Cho 2017; Kukulska-Hulme and Shield 2008), and increased language use and language-related episodes (LREs) about all aspects of language (Bueno-Alastuey 2013; Chun, Kern, and Smith 2016). Since these technological tools are not neutral, investigations have begun to explore their affordances for writing skills development (Bueno-Alastuey and López Pérez 2014; López Pérez and Bueno-Alastuey 2015; Oskoz and Elola 2014).

Studies comparing online texts written by individuals and pairs have suggested that digital collaboration leads to improvements in the final written texts. Elola and Oskoz (2010) and Strobl (2014) reported improvements among collaborating advanced university students when CAF and content measures were contrasted. They concluded that those enhancements were the consequence of the in-depth discussions, the knowledge and skills shared, and the scaffolding dialogues with their peers (Storch 2005; Swain 2000). In a study involving intermediate L2 Russian learners, Tare et al. (2014) contrasted individual versus collaborative accuracy (one of the CAF quantitative measures) and lexical diversity scores obtained from two summaries written before and after an intensive six-week period of interactive or individual homework. Furthermore, the type-token ratio and the use of target words in the drafts written in the first and fourth week of the treatment were compared. The pre-post comparisons did not evince significant effects for the collaborating students, although slightly higher means were obtained. An advantage for collaborating students was observed, however, when the types and tokens of the ongoing drafts were compared, but not for the type-token ratio or the number of target words used. In line with Storch (2005) and Swain (2000), these authors attributed the gains to the peer modelling the students obtained through collaboration and interaction.

Some researchers have already signaled the value of online collaborative writing projects because compared with face-to-face collaborative writing, they represent a more authentic group writing activity as in the real-life professional career (Storch 2012). Nevertheless, whether different modes such as online versus paper-based writing might alter the trends observed in face-to-face interactions and affect writing in collaboration has hardly been explored. The scant studies contrasting face-to-face and digital collaboration processes have reported that learners in either mode collaborate actively, although the type and the nature of the collaboration seems to vary depending on mode and task (Ansarimoghaddam, Tan, and Yong 2017 for a Wiki essay; or Rouhshad, Wigglesworth, and Storch 2016 for a decision making task; see Li 2018; Storch 2019 for more studies).

Regarding the outcomes of written texts, research has reported inconclusive results. Wang (2015) examined the effects of mode among tertiary students in a 12-week experiment by contrasting letters written by groups of four students in Wiki versus paper-based modes. He concluded that Wikis were more effective tools to increase EFL students' performance as demonstrated by the higher scores obtained in the ratings of text features, such as text purpose and audience, organization, content and style, and structure and grammar. He concluded that Wiki collaboration enhanced peer to peer learning.

Similarly, Suwantarathip and Wichadee (2014) explored individual pre and post-writing test scores of Turkish university students learning English after 14 weeks of group practice in which they had to write either face-to-face on paper or on Google Docs. Student paragraphs were assessed for content, language use, and organization. Results showed that both groups of students improved their scores, but only the Google Docs group did so significantly. Increased opportunities for (more efficient) collaboration, availability of constructive feedback, increased involvement, and motivation were deemed the reasons for the success.

In contrast, Woodrich and Fan (2017) examined modality effects among elementary school students, in the only study including pre-university students. In groups of four, students were asked to compose three argumentative paragraphs which varied in mode (face-to-face on paper, Google Docs, Google Docs but anonymously). Drafts were scrutinized for participation and text features ratings obtained from the application of an analytic rubric with the following categories: thought, voice, or grammar/mechanics for the reading letter; bias, tone, grammar for the slant article; and finally, assertion, examples, explanation, significance, grammar/mechanics/formatting for the argumentative paragraph. Their results demonstrated that face-to-face on paper drafts promoted more equal participation and the ratings of the features analysed were significantly higher than those in the texts composed digitally. The researchers related these distinct results to the differences in design, population, and task.

All in all, a limited number of studies has compared the written products of individuals and pairs or groups, especially in secondary school contexts. Likewise, there is a scarcity of studies comparing how the mode of writing (face-to-face versus online) might affect the final product. Considering the increasing number of students involved in foreign language learning in compulsory education settings worldwide and the fact that technology seems to be firmly entrenched in the teaching and learning pedagogies of schools, how writing mode and learner grouping affect language learning, and more specifically, how they affect the quality of written texts, seems worth exploring. Consequently, the present study intends to examine those variables through the following research questions:

1. Is there any difference between the texts produced by EFL secondary school individuals and pairs in terms of quantitative accuracy and fluency indicators and text features ratings?
2. Does writing mode affect text quality as measured by fluency and accuracy indicators and text features ratings of adequacy, coherence, cohesion, grammatical accuracy, vocabulary range, and mechanics?

3 Methodology

3.1 Participants and instructional context

Participants were 28 EFL Spanish students (12 females and 16 males). They were an intact group enrolled in their first year of compulsory secondary education (12–13 years old) at a semi-private school located in Navarre (Northern Spain). The school is located in a middle-upper class neighbourhood in the centre of a small city.

Participants had begun learning English at school when they were 3 years old. At the time of data collection, students were receiving three 55-minute classes of English per week. As reported by the teacher and observed by the third author, the group was homogenous for their English proficiency level, which could be identified as high A1 or low A2 according to the Common European Framework of Reference for Languages (Council of Europe 2001).

The school followed a particular competence-based methodology aimed at students from Primary 5 (10–11 years old) to the second year of compulsory secondary education (13–14 years old). As part of the project, students from two same-year classes met face-to-face for about 12 hours a week with three teachers who were specialists in the areas of human sciences, natural sciences, and languages. Projects integrated these three areas in an authentic way through learner-centred activities which placed the learner at the heart of the learning process. The teacher served as a guide that accompanied students throughout the process helping them to think critically. Students worked on projects which targeted inclusion, equality, responsibility, and autonomy. Thus, students were used to working in groups in order to achieve a common goal.

For the English arts course, students followed the books Spectrum 1 Workbook and Student's Book by Oxford University Press designed for first year compulsory secondary education students. Students were arranged in groups of four and each of them owned a Chromebook they could use in class. Generally, classes followed a Presentation-Practice-Production model which focused heavily on grammar, although, occasionally, *Kahoot* or listening activities were completed. The teacher explained the grammar issues on the board and students took notes in their notebooks or Chromebooks. The teacher monitored the groups to solve any misunderstandings and to ensure they did not stray off-task. Writing tasks were done individually on paper, as observed by the third author.

For the present study, students were divided into 2 groups of 14 students each. Assuming that parallel level pairs collaborate better (Storch and Aldosari 2013), similar English level pairs were created based on the grades given by the English teacher to the last composition they had drafted in class, and randomly assigned to one of the groups. A Chi-square test confirmed that the two groups were comparable and that no differences between the groups existed at the outset of the study ($\chi2=18,000$, p=0.207).

3.2 Instruments

Three instruments of data collection were used in the study: (a) An individual composition about a book; (b) A collaborative writing activity: the description of a picture; and (c) A collaborative writing activity: a letter to a friend.

Students carried out a total of three writing tasks (two of them collaboratively and one of them individually). The first one, the individual task, was a 100–120 word summary of the book that they had read during the summer holidays, *The Adventures of Tom Sawyer* (Twain 2001). In the second one, students had to write a 100–120 word description of a family picture in pairs. The third and final activity was also a collaborative one and consisted on writing a letter of about 100 to 120 words about their summer holidays. The writing tasks and topics were suggested by their teacher, who thought they were appropriate because of the familiar content for the students. Writing letters was common and they had recently practiced physical descriptions and reviewed the past tense. Furthermore, these genres and their linguistic characteristics were aims of their course in the curriculum (Decreto Foral de Navarra 24/2015). The fact that they were different tasks eliminated any possible task repetition effect (Nitta and Baba 2014).

3.3 Procedure

The procedure involved three different sessions, which were carried out over two weeks. Google Docs was chosen as the digital platform to support collaboration because it posed no difficulty for students, as each student in the class owned a Google Chromebook which they had been using since the beginning of the year.

In the first session, students were asked to write the individual summary of the book by hand on paper. All students completed the task even though some of them had not read the book, which was obvious because some wrote summaries unrelated to its content.

In the second session, students had 50 minutes to write a 100–120 word description. Students were paired up and divided into two groups of 14 students to write the description. Seven pairs of students did the collaborative writing by hand on paper and 7 pairs did the collaborative writing in Docs. As students were going to swap writing modes in the tasks, the distribution of when to write by hand or in a computer was made at random. Dyads working online were arranged in such a way that hampered oral communication, which compelled them to communicate digitally and were asked to share the document with their teacher. Dyads working face-to-face sat together and were monitored by the teacher and the third author as recording them was not possible due to privacy issues.

In the third session, the procedure was repeated, but each group swapped the writing procedure so that students who had written on paper wrote in Google Docs and vice versa. This time, however, students had to write a letter to a friend about their holidays.

3.4 Data coding and analysis

The quantitative data used in this study was obtained from 56 texts: 28 individual summaries, 14 descriptions (7 paper-based and 7 online) and 14 informal letters (7 paper-based and 7 online).

3.4.1 Data coding

The texts were examined only for fluency and accuracy measures. Complexity indicators were excluded from the analysis in order to avoid any possibility of compromising task comparability as it has already been indicated that they might be affected by text genre (Pallotti 2009). Following previous studies (Storch and Wigglesworth 2007; Wigglesworth and Storch 2009), fluency was calculated as the total number of words. Accuracy was established by scrutinizing the drafts for three types of errors: (a) grammatical, (b) lexical, and (c) mechanical errors (e.g., Fernández Dobao 2012; Storch 2005; Wigglesworth and Storch 2009). For each type, the total number of errors was tallied and the means and the standard deviations were computed. Table 1 illustrates the different types of accuracy errors and includes examples from the texts written by our learners.

In order to evaluate the texts written on a computer and by hand in terms of overall quality and following previous research (McDonough, Crawford, and Vleeschauwer 2016; Storch 2005), the texts were rated using a 30-point analytic rubric created for this purpose, based on a rubric used by the English teacher. The rubric measured six factors – adequacy, coherence, cohesion, grammatical accuracy, vocabulary range and mechanics- on a five-point scale ranging from 5, very good, to 1, which was poor. Adequacy measured whether the topic was targeted, whether the text was well organized and if the minimum

Table 1: Coding scheme for accuracy.

Error type		Examples
Grammatical Error	Syntactical error	Errors in the order of words "A pair of jeans blue [sic]."
	Morphological Error	Errors in the verb tense "We have visit the holy family."
	Morphosyntactic Error	Errors in the use of articles "I'm eating burger and drinking a coke."
Lexical Errors	Word choice	Borrowings "José is happy because he *touched* [meaning 'won'] the lottery."
		Using Spanish words "I like this place more than *Inglaterra* [England].
Mechanical Errors	Spelling	Juan is esmol [small]."
	Punctuation	"Jose is fat and not very tall he wears a yellow shirt and a blue trousers."
	Capitalization	"(. . .) is very healthy and also good. i love surfing and sunbathing."

number of words had been reached. Text coherence was established by the clarity of the ideas reflected. Cohesion considered the development of ideas, and grammatical accuracy took into account the errors in the use of verbs, word order, articles, prepositions, and adjectives. Mechanics targeted errors on spelling, capitalization, and punctuation, and, finally, vocabulary range evaluated the use of words and the richness of the vocabulary.

3.4.2 Data analysis

The third author sent the compositions to the first two authors, who did not know which condition the texts belonged to, as the compositions had been typed for ease of analysis. The three authors rated 15% of the papers, 8 papers, and an agreement of 90% was reached. The instances where there was disagreement were discussed by the three authors until total agreement was reached, and, then, the third author coded the remainder of the data. Finally, the data were entered into an Excel spreadsheet and analysed using SPSS v25 for Windows.

Quantitative variables exhibited normal distribution and, thus, parametric T-tests were employed to test for statistically significant differences. In order to answer research question one addressing grouping condition effects, several two-tailed paired t-tests were carried out to calculate any possible significant differences among the various accuracy and fluency measures from the three tasks. T-tests were used so that inferential statistics between two variables could be explored. The text features ratings, however, were not normally distributed and, hence, the non-parametric equivalent of T-tests, Wilcoxon signed-rank tests, were used to compare rating differences.

The variables for the second research question, which dealt with writing mode condition differences, were created by combining data from tasks two and tasks three and, then, dividing the data by writing mode condition, Google Docs versus pen-and-paper. Then, as with the first research question, parametric T-tests and non-parametric Wilcoxon tests were conducted to analyse whether writing mode condition yielded any statistical difference for quantitative scores or text feature ratings. The confidence interval was established at 95%.

4 Results

4.1 Individual versus collaborative written texts

As Table 2 illustrates, the results for fluency and accuracy measures did not differ greatly when texts written in collaboration or individually were compared.

Table 2: Fluency and accuracy measures by task.

	Individual text		CW 1		CW 2	
	Mean	SD	Mean	SD	Mean	SD
Words	89.57	26.89	93.29	30.22	99.86	21.90
Gram. E	11.93	6.46	9.79	3.62	11.71	4.29
Lex. E	4.89	3.57	5.14	2.77	4.43	1.74
Mec. E	9.39	5.29	6.07	2.56	5.86	2.48
Total E	26.21	11.91	21.00	7.34	22.00	4.52

Gram = Grammatical. Lex = Lexical. Mec = Mechanical. E = Errors.
CW = collaborative writing task.

Students wrote slightly more words when they wrote in pairs than when they wrote individually (89.7 words vs. 93.29 or 99.86), although the difference was not significant. Regarding grammatical errors, individual texts had the highest number of errors (11.93), although the difference was not significant (see Appendix 1). Regarding lexical errors, one of the texts written collaboratively (CW1) had the highest number of lexical errors (5.14) followed by the individually written one (4.89) and the second text written collaboratively (4.43). Nevertheless, the difference in errors among the three texts was not statistically significant (see Appendix 1). Finally, mechanical errors dropped significantly when students wrote collaboratively (Individual vs. CW1: $t = 2.398$; $p = 0.033$; Individual vs. CW2: $t = 2.572$; $p = 0.023$). Overall, regarding accuracy, collaborative writing seems to be more favourable than individual writing as the total number of errors decreased when students wrote collaboratively in both tasks. Furthermore, two of the measures included in accuracy, grammatical and mechanical errors, decreased when students wrote in pairs, and the decrease was significant for mechanical errors (see Appendix 1), while the third element, lexical errors, only declined in the second collaborative task.

Text features ratings comparing both conditions also showed differences, which favoured writing collaboratively (see Table 3). All ratings, except adequacy and vocabulary in the first collaborative writing (−0.07 for adequacy and −0.21 for vocabulary), increased when students wrote in pairs in both tasks (CW1 and CW2).

Table 3: Text features ratings (max = 5) by writing task.

	Individual text		CW 1		CW 2	
	Mean	SD	Mean	SD	Mean	SD
Adequacy	3.21	1.23	3.14	1.03	3.64	.84
Coherence	2.43	.96	2.93	.73	3.21	.70
Cohesion	2.50	.92	2.50	.65	3.07	.47
Grammar	2.82	.82	2.86	.53	3.07	.62
Mechanics	2.93	1.02	3.07	.73	3.43	.65
Vocabulary	3.64	1.03	3.43	.65	3.79	.70
Total	17.53	3.48	17.93	2.50	20.57	2.71

CW = collaborative writing task.

Adequacy increased 0.43 in the second task (CW2) as compared to the individual task; coherence increased 0.5 in the first task (CW1) and 0.71 in the second task (CW2), and the difference between the individual task and CW2 was significant (t=−2.280; p=0.046); cohesion was the same in CW1 but increased 0.57 in CW2; grammar increased slightly in CW1 (0.04) and moderately in CW2 (0.25); mechanics also improved slightly in CW1 and moderately, 0.5, in CW2; and finally vocabulary also obtained higher scores but only in CW2 (0.15). Total text features ratings also improved in CW1 (0.4) and in CW2 (3.04), and in the case of CW2, the results were significantly higher (t=−2.288; p=0.040) as compared to the individual one (see Appendix 1). Summing up, writing in pairs improved all the text features ratings, especially in the case of the second collaborative writing task, although only two of the measures showed statistically significant differences (see Appendix 1).

4.2 Mode contrast: Computer vs. pen-and-paper written texts

When the effect of mode was explored, results (Table 4) did not show any statistically significant difference (see Appendix 1).

Table 4: Fluency and accuracy measures by writing mode.

	Google Docs		Pen and paper	
	Mean	SD	Mean	SD
Words	100.14	28.14	93.00	24.43
Gram. E	10.14	3.94	11.36	4.14
Lex. E	5.00	2.60	4.57	2.03
Mec. E	6.50	2.28	5.43	2.62
Total E	21.64	6.55	21.36	5.65

Gram = Grammatical. Lex = Lexical. Mec = Mechanical. E = Errors.

As can be seen in Table 4, texts written in Google Docs seemed somewhat more fluent (100.14 vs 93), and were grammatically more correct (10.14 vs. 11.36, −1.22 fewer errors). On the contrary, paper-based writing favoured more lexically (−0.42 fewer errors) and mechanically (−1.07 fewer errors) accurate texts. Furthermore, paper-based texts had slightly fewer errors in total (21.36 vs. 21.64, −0.28). In general, it can be stated that fluency and accuracy measures between both modes showed minor differences. Fluency was better when writing in Google Docs, while accuracy was better, but very slightly, when writing on paper.

A similar pattern is observable regarding the scores given to the text features assessed (Table 5). The differences between the six ratings awarded to each writing mode were very modest, and none of them was statistically significant (see Appendix 1), although in general paper-based writing obtained higher scores in most of the criteria. Coherence, grammar, mechanics, and vocabulary showed better scores when students wrote on paper (3.14 vs. 3.00, 2.86 vs. 2.71, 3.36 vs. 3.14, and 3.71 vs. 3.50, respectively), cohesion had the same score for both modes (2.79), and adequacy was the only criteria in which the Google Docs group surpassed the paper-based group (3.43 vs. 3.36). Considering these slight differences in results, mode does not seem to be a variable which triggers differences among collaborating pairs.

Table 5: Text features ratings (max = 5) by writing mode.

	Google Docs		Pen and Paper	
	Mean	SD	Mean	SD
Adequacy	3.43	.93761	3.36	1.01
Coherence	3.00	.67937	3.14	.77
Cohesion	2.79	.57893	2.79	.70
Grammar	2.71	.72627	2.86	.53
Mechanics	3.14	.66299	3.36	.74
Vocabulary	3.50	.75955	3.71	.61
Total	18.93	2.89467	19.21	3.02

5 Discussion and conclusions

The purpose of this study was to assess the effects of learner grouping and writing mode on texts written by young learners in secondary education by examining the quality of the texts produced in three writing tasks. The study was deemed necessary as writing collaboratively using technology and the linguistic benefits this might actually bring about have hardly been explored in secondary education settings.

Considering our results regarding accuracy, fluency, and holistic measures, collaboration resulted in texts that were, overall, more accurate and fluent, and of a higher quality. Although less robust than previous findings obtained from pairs who wrote exclusively by hand (e.g., Fernández Dobao 2012; Villarreal and Gil-Sarratea 2020; Wigglesworth and Storch 2009), our results support those studies which have compared individuals and pairs in computer-mediated tasks and defend the benefits of technology-based collaborative writing (Elola and Oskoz 2010; Strobl 2014; Tare et al. 2014). In fact, in the current research, significant differences were obtained when individual versus pair mechanical errors were contrasted, and also when the individual and the second collaborative texts were compared for cohesion and total quality scores. Although different genres in the texts were used to avoid possible task repetition effects (Manchón 2014), writing task effects (McDonough and García Fuentes 2015), or topic familiarity effects (McDonough and Crawford 2018) cannot be completely ruled out, even though McDonough and colleagues did not find accuracy differences.

Differences regarding writing mode, however, were very modest and most of them, with the exception of fluency and adequacy, favoured paper-based written texts. Unlike in previous research including tertiary learners (Suwantarathip and Wichadee 2014; Wang 2015), technology did not render notable benefits to the quality of the drafts. This is in accordance with the findings obtained by Woodrich and Fan (2017), who also targeted secondary learners completing a syncretic task, and obtained significantly higher scores for face-to-face writing tasks. However, their analysis lacked an investigation of text features. Our results seem to suggest that although texts written digitally seem to be slightly more fluent, paper-based texts written face-to-face seem to be more accurate and of a better quality. Other studies comparing the nature and type of collaboration seem to point in the same direction (Rouhshad, Wigglesworth, and Storch 2016) and face-to-face paper-based writing has been claimed to foster more and distinct collaboration.

A possible explanation for our results may be related to task design features as well as learner literacy and collaboration skills. A judicious task design and use might be needed so that students leverage the benefits of technology-based writing (Elola and Oskoz 2017). It seems that students are not sufficiently literate, understood as having the knowledge and skills to read, write, and communicate with others using digital technologies (Leu 2002), to collaborate and scaffold each other digitally. Consequently, it is important to realize that L2 learners need to be taught the potential of digital affordances and how to make use of them in the most effective manner (Elola and Oskoz 2017; Lomicka and Lord 2016). Teaching students how to take advantage of the affordances of technology to aid them in the writing process seems necessary. It is likely that since there was only a mode change without any training, there were no additional benefits to the students.

Although web-technologies can alter learning (Wang 2015), the nature of the task will influence students' interaction and collaboration (Li 2018) and effective collaboration will only occur if technological tools are used creatively (Elola and Oskoz 2017), not if we use them to repeat conventional uses (Bueno-Alastuey and Villarreal submitted; García-Valcárcel, Basilotta and López 2014). If the additional benefits of using technology are to be achieved, technology-appropriate genres (Elola and Oskoz 2017) should be used in which the tool is not just a means to complete the same tasks in a different mode. Technologically-tailored task design might be needed to unpack the full potential of the online mode. In fact, although more technologically adequate genres have already entered the curriculum and some recommendations have been made to diversify genres in writing, there seems to be still a clear preference for conventional academic genres (Kessler 2017).

Our learners seemed not to take advantage of the increased opportunities for interactive and meaningful practices offered by technology-based collaborative writing (Elola and Oskoz 2010). They most frequently directly edited the text for mistakes, and this change might have gone unnoticed for the peer that had written the original text. Students might need to be trained on the uses of Google Docs functions such as suggestions and comments, which could be the equivalent to oral languaging episodes in face-to-face interactions (Storch 2019), so that form-focused attention is increased. This shortcoming could be overcome by raising students' awareness of their role within the writing process, which would prepare them to be more reflective, thoughtful, and self-correcting in their future writing (Kessler 2017), impelling them to focus on form even when it does not compromise meaning.

The "bridging activities" framework (Thorne and Reinhardt 2008) has also been discussed to facilitate technology-mediated L2 teaching and learning. Just changing the mode seems to be insufficient and training to make the most of collaborative technology-mediated writing is needed as previous research has already claimed (Elola and Oskoz 2017). Furthermore, the whole paradigm needs to be shifted and teaching needs to be reshaped to help students master knowledge and competences needed for learning in the digital age (Zheng and Warschauer 2017). Maybe the benefits of technology-based writing are not observable using CAF measures or standardized tests (Zheng et al. 2016), but other aspects such as the development of students' digital literacy skills, the improvement of collaborative learning skills, the enhancement of the learning to learn competence (García-Esteban, Villarreal and Bueno-Alastuey 2019), and even the quality of students' interaction should be measured to explore the real potential of technology-mediated L2 writing. Additionally, alternative qualitative data sources (e.g., interviews or recordings of the interaction taking place when writing collaboratively) would be helpful to capture the benefits of technology-based writing.

Despite the encouraging findings for collaboration, this study has several limitations that need to be acknowledged. First, the study was carried out with a small number of secondary students, and, thus, the findings may not be generalizable to other educational settings, or to populations with different backgrounds. Secondly, there is no individual online text to compare initial measures of individual paper-based and online texts. Thirdly, due to personal data protection issues, investigators could not access data from the personal interaction and collaboration that had taken place among learners and, the only information available was the information provided by the third author, who was present throughout the data collection process and monitored the students while they were writing their texts. A final limitation relates to the comparability of the tasks and the fact that the researchers could not choose the text genres students had to write. However, this limitation also makes this research more ecologically valid because the genres selected are the ones used in secondary school contexts. Further research should also examine whether the integration of different tools would facilitate more negotiation (Liou 2016) and, thus, result in higher quality texts. Additionally, along the lines suggested by Elola and Oskoz (2017), more digitally oriented genres such as digital stories or blogs could be used to see whether collaboration is also mediated by task-type.

All in all, it seems that writing together is also beneficial for students in secondary contexts as evinced by the better overall texts they produced, most likely due to the pooling of knowledge of the students (Storch 2005) to assist one another, which produced incidental meaning focused attention to form (e.g., Storch 2013; Swain 2000; Villarreal and Gil-Sarratea 2020). Our results might be helpful for teachers who, because of lack of appropriate training in technology integration and use, simply shift modes and carry out the same tasks in the same way as when not using technology, and become frustrated because they do not observe the purported additional benefits technology can bring. The present study seems to suggest that additional actions need to be taken to reap the benefits of technology. Focusing on how to maximise technology for learning is increasingly relevant because, as stated by Woodrich and Fan (2017, 404), "there is an increasing impact of technology-assisted collaborative writing on student learning and teaching pedagogy" at schools.

Consequently, our study has yielded some insights for classroom practice as it has indicated that collaboration seems to be beneficial, but merely using Google Docs in a conventional manner is not enough to experience any further benefits. The results of this study point to four aspects which should be taken into consideration by teachers so that technology-based collaborative writing can be conducive to learning: (i) the writing task, its type and students' familiarity with the topic (McDonough and Crawford 2018; McDonough and García Fuentes 2015); (ii) the design of the task, which should take into consideration the affordances and possibilities offered by technology (Elola and Oskoz 2017); (iii) students' knowledge and skills using the technological affordances such as comments, dictionaries, language checkers (Cavaleri and Dianati 2016) and training on how to use those affordances effectively so that they are able to take advantage of technology; and (iv) students' awareness about their role in the writing process and about successful patterns of interaction (Kessler 2017; Li and Zhu 2017).

Both, students and teachers, would benefit from carefully structured training on how to thrive using technology in a foreign language classroom. First, teachers should be made aware of the affordances of different technological tools for the acquisition of writing skills and language, and on how to design tasks which leverage the functionalities and affordances of technology, and the possibility to combine various technological tools or the use of alternative genres. Teachers need to try to raise awareness and reflection among learners by instructing students on the affordances available in Google Docs such as the comments, editing, suggesting, explore function, and the revision history for collaborative writing, and those accessible online such as dictionaries, or grammar checkers so that they can maximise the use of technologies for collaborative writing. Moreover, teachers could show examples of successful and unsuccessful collaboration patterns, and of uses of (a combination of) tools and together they could even tailor the technological solutions that might help them to solve linguistic doubts and enhance noticing, and eventually, language learning. Above all, although current practices encourage the use of technologies in secondary school settings, more research is needed to determine what characteristics unpack the potential benefits of technologies for language learners. The present study, therefore, represents one of the first attempts to explore the effect of collaboration and technology on students' written performance, a research arena in need of further research.

Acknowledgements: The authors would like to thank the school Hijas de Jesús in Pamplona (Navarra) for granting permission to conduct the study and to the school teacher for donating his precious class time. Our most heartfelt gratitude to the students for their willingness to participate in the study. The first author would like to acknowledge grants FFI2016-74950-P (Spanish Ministry of Economy and Competitiveness, National Research Agency and European Regional Development Fund- AEI/FEDER/EU) and IT904-16 (Basque Government). Finally, the first and second authors would also like to acknowledge I-Communitas, Institute for Advanced Social Research (Public University of Navarre).

References

Ansarimoghaddam, Shokoufeh, Bee Hoon Tan, and Mei Fung Yong. 2017. "Collaboratively Composing an Argumentative Essay : Wiki versus Face-to-Face Interactions." *GEMA Online Journal of Language Studies* 17 (2): 33–53.
Bikowski, Dawn, and Ramyadarshanie Vithanage. 2016. "Effects of web-based collaborative writing on individual L2 writing development." *Language Learning & Technology* 20 (1): 79–99. http://dx.doi.org/10125/44447.
Bueno-Alastuey, M. Camino. 2013. "Interactional Feedback in Synchronous Voice-Based Computer Mediated Communication: Effect of Dyad." *System* 41 (3): 543–59. https://doi.org/10.1016/j.system.2013.05.005.
Bueno-Alastuey, M. Camino, and María Victoria López Pérez. 2014. "Evaluation of a Blended Learning Language Course: Students' Perceptions of Appropriateness for the Development of Skills and Language Areas." *Computer Assisted Language Learning* 27 (6): 509–27. https://doi.org/10.1080/09588221.2013.770037.
Bueno-Alastuey, M. Camino, and Patricia Martínez de Lizarrondo. 2017. "Collaborative Writing in the EFL Secondary Education Classroom Comparing Triad, Pair and Individual Work." *Huarte de San Juan. Filología y Didáctica de La Lengua*, no. 17: 254–75. https://dialnet.unirioja.es/servlet/articulo?codigo=6408523.
Bueno-Alastuey, M. Camino, and Izaskun Villarreal. Submitted. "Pre-service teachers' perceptions and training contributions towards ICT use"
Cavaleri, Michelle Rose, and Saib Dianati. 2016. "You want me to check your grammar again? The usefulness of an online grammar checker as perceived by students." *Journal of Academic Language and Learning* 10 (1): A223–A236.
Chao, Yu-chuan Joni, and Hao-Chang Lo. 2011. "Students' Perceptions of Wiki-Based Collaborative Writing for Learners of English as a Foreign Language." *Interactive Learning Environments* 19 (4): 395–411. https://doi.org/10.1080/10494820903298662.
Chen, Julian Chengchiang, and Kimberly Lynn Brown. 2012. "The Effects of Authentic Audience on English as a Second Language (ESL) Writers : A Task-Based, Computer-Mediated Approach." *Computer Assissted Language Learning* 25 (5): 435–454. https://doi.org/10.1080/09588221.2011.606224.
Cho, Hyeyoon. 2017. "Synchronous Web-Based Collaborative Writing : Factors Mediating Interaction among Second-Language Writers." *Journal of Second Language Writing* 36: 37–51. https://doi.org/10.1016/j.jslw.2017.05.013.
Chun, Dorothy, Richard Kern, and Bryan Smith. 2016. "Technology in Language Use, Language Teaching, and Language Learning." *Modern Journal of Language Teaching Methods (MJLTM)* S1 (100): 64–80. https://doi.org/10.1111/modl.12302.
Council of Europe. 2001. Common European Framework of Reference for Languages: Learning, Teaching, Assessment. Cambridge: Cambridge University Press. https://rm.coe.int/1680459f97
Decreto Foral 24/2015. Boletín Oficial de Navarra número 127, Pamplona, Navarra, 2 July 2015.
De Guerrero, Maria C. M, and Olga S. Villamil. 2000. "Activating the ZPD: Mutual Scaffolding in L2 Peer Revision." *Modern Language Journal* 84 (1): 51–68. https://doi.org/10.1111/0026-7902.00052.

Donato, Richard. 1994. "Collective Scaffolding in Second Language Learning." In *Vygotskian Approaches to Second Language Research*, edited by James Lantolf and Gabriela Appel, 33–56. Norwood, NJ: Ablex.

Elola, Idoia, and Ana Oskoz. 2010. "Collaborative Writing : Fostering Foreign Language and Wrigin Conventions Devleopment." *Language Learning & Technology* 14 (3): 51–71.

Elola, Idoia, and Ana Oskoz. 2017. "Writing with 21st Century Social Tools in the L2 Classroom: New Literacies, Genres, and Writing Practices." *Journal of Second Language Writing* 36: 52–60. https://doi.org/10.1016/j.jslw.2017.04.002.

Enever, Janet. 2018. *Policy and Politics in Global Primary English*. Oxford: Oxford University Press.

Fernández Dobao, Ana. 2012. "Collaborative Writing Tasks in the L2 Classroom: Comparing Group, Pair, and Individual Work." *Journal of Second Language Writing* 21 (1): 40–58. https://doi.org/10.1016/j.jslw.2011.12.002.

García-Esteban, Soraya, Izaskun Villarreal, and M. Camino Bueno-Alastuey. 2019. "The effect of telecollaboration in the development of the Learning to Learn competence in CLIL teacher training." *Interactive Learning Environments*. https://doi.org/10.1080/10494820.2019.1614960

García Mayo, María Pilar (ed.) 2017. *Learning Foreign Languages in Primary Schools. Research Insights*. Bristol: Multilingual Matters.

García Mayo, María Pilar, and Agurtzane Azkarai. 2016. "EFL Task-Based Interaction: Does Task Modality Impact on Language-Related Episodes?" In *Peer Interaction and Second Language Learning: Research Agenda and Pedagogical Implications*, edited by Masatoshi Sato and Susan Ballinger, 241–266. Amsterdam: John Benjamins.

García-Valcárcel, Ana, Verónica Basilotta, and Camino López. 2014. *Las TIC en el Aprendizaje Colaborativo en el Aula de Primaria y Secundaria* [ICT for Collaborative Learning in the Primary and Secondary Classroom]. *Comunicar* 42: 65–74.

Hyland, Ken. 2011. "Learning to Write: Issues in Theory, Research and Pedagogy." In *Learning-to-Write and Writing-to-Learn in an Additional Language*, edited by Rosa M. Manchón, 18–35. Amsterdam/Philadelphia: John Benjamins Publishing Company.

Kessler, Greg. 2017. "Language and Technology." *Language and Technology*, 1–13. https://doi.org/10.1007/978-3-319-02328-1.

Kim, YouJin Jin, and Kim McDonough. 2011. "Using Pretask Modelling to Encourage Collaborative Learning Opportunities." *Language Teaching Research* 15 (2): 183–99. https://doi.org/10.1177/1362168810388711.

Kukulska-Hulme, Agnes, and Lesley Shield. 2008. "An Overview of Mobile Assisted Language Learning: From Content Delivery to Supported Collaboration and Interaction." *ReCALL* 20 (3): 271–89.

Lázaro-Ibarrola, Amparo, and Izaskun Villarreal. 2019. "Questioning the Effectiveness of Procedural Repetition: The Case of Spanish EFL Primary School Learners." *Porta Linguarum* 31: 7–20.

Leu, Donald J. 2002. "The New Literacies: Research on Reading Instruction with the Internet." In *What Research Has to Say about Reading Instruction.*, edited by Alan E. Farstrup and S. Jay Samuels, 310–36. Newark, DE: International reading association.

Li, Mimi. 2018. "Computer-Mediated Collaborative Writing in L2 Contexts : An Analysis of Empirical Research." *Computer Assisted Language Learning* 31 (8): 882–904. https://doi.org/10.1080/09588221.2018.1465981.

Li, Mimi, and Wei Zhu. 2017. "Good or Bad Collaborative Wiki Writing: Exploring Links between Group Interactions and Writing Products." *Journal of Second Language Writing* 35: 38–53. https://doi.org/10.1016/j.jslw.2017.01.003.

Liou, Hsien-Chin. 2016. "CALL Tools for Reading and Writing". In *The Routledge Handbook of Language Learning and Technology*, edited by Fiona Farr and Liam Murray, 478–490. New York NY: Routledge.

Lomicka, Lara, and Gillian Lord. 2016. "Social Networking and Language Learning." In *The Routledge Handbook of Language Learning and Technology*. Edited by Fiona Farr and Liam Murray, 255–268. London: Routledge.

Long, Michael H. 1996. "The Role of the Linguistic Environment in Second Language Acquisition." In *Handbook of Second Language Acquisition*, edited by William C. Ritchie and Tej K. Bhatia, 413–68. New York: Academic Press.

López Pérez, María Victoria, and M. Camino Bueno-Alastuey. 2015. "Una Experiencia de Enseñanza Combinada En Un Curso Universitario de Español/L2: Percepciones de Los Estudiantes Sobre El Efecto de Las TIC En Sus Aprendizajes." *Revista Espanola de Linguistica Aplicada* 28 (1): 213–33. https://doi.org/10.1075/resla.28.1.10lop.

Manchón, Rosa M., ed. 2011a. *Learning-to-Write and Writing-to-Learn in an Additional Language*. Amsterdam: John Benjamins Publishing Company.

Manchón, Rosa M. 2011b. "Writing to Learn the Language." In *Learning-to-Write and Writing-to-Learn in an Additional Language*, edited by Rosa M. Manchón, 61–82. Amsterdam: John Benjamins Publishing Company.

Manchón, Rosa M. 2014. "The Distinctive Nature of Task Repetition in Writing. Implications for Theory, Research, and Pedagogy." *Estudios de Lingüística Inglesa Aplicada ELIA* 14: 13–41.

McDonough, Kim, and William J. Crawford. 2018. "Identifying Effective Writing Tasks for Use in EFL Write-to-Learn Language Contexts." *Language Learning Journal* 0 (0): 1–12. https://doi.org/10.1080/09571736.2018.1465990.

McDonough, Kim, William J. Crawford, and Jindarat De Vleeschauwer. 2016. "Thai EFL learners' interaction during collaborative writing tasks and its relationship to text quality." In *Peer interaction and second language learning: Pedagogical potential and research agenda*, edited by Sato, Masatoshi, and Susan Ballinger, 185–208. John Benjamins Publishing Company.

McDonough, Kim, and César García Fuentes. 2015. "The Effect of Writing Task and Task Conditions on Colombian EFL Learners' Language Use." *TESL Canada Journal* 32 (2): 67–79. https://doi.org/10.18806/tesl.v32i2.1208.

Nitta, Ryo and Kyoko Baba. "Task Repetition and L2 Writing Development: A Longitudinal Study from a Dynamic System Perspective" in *Task-Based Language Learning – Insights from and for L2 Writing* edited by Heidi Byrnes and Rosa M. Manchón. Amsterdam: John Benjamins Publishing Company.

Oskoz, Ana, and Idoia Elola. 2014. "Promoting Foreign Language Collaborative Writing through the Use of Web 2.0 Tools and Tasks." In *Technology-Mediated TBLT: Researching Technology and Tasks*, edited by Marta González-LLoret and Lourdes Ortega, 115–48. Amsterdam/Philadelphia: John Benjamins Publishing Company.

Pallotti, Gabrielle. 2009. "CAF : defining, refining and differentiating constructs." *Applied Linguistics* 30: 590–601.

Pica, Teresa. 1994. "Research on Negotiation: What Does It Reveal about Second-Language Learning Conditions, Processes, and Outcomes?" *Language Learning* 44: 493–527.

Rouhshad, Amir, Gillian Wigglesworth, and Neomy Storch. 2016. "The Nature of Negotiations in Face-to-Face versus Computer-Mediated Communication in Pair Interactions." *Language Teaching Research* 20 (4): 514–34. https://doi.org/10.1177/1362168815584455.

Storch, Neomy. 2005. "Collaborative Writing: Product, Process, and Students' Reflections." *Journal of Second Language Writing* 14 (3): 153–73. https://doi.org/10.1016/j.jslw.2005.05.002.

Storch, Neomy. 2012. "Collaborative Writing as a Site for L2 Learning in Face-to-Face and Online Modes." In *Technology across Writing Contexts and Tasks*, edited by Greg Kessler, Ana Oskoz, and Idoia Elola, 113–29. San Marcos, Texas: CALICO.

Storch, Neomy. 2013. *Collaborative Writing in L2 Classrooms*. Bristol: Multilingual Matters.

Storch, Neomy. 2019. "Collaborative Writing." *Language Teaching* 52 (1): 40–59. https://doi.org/10.1017/S0261444818000320.

Storch, Neomy, and Ali Aldosari. 2013. "Pairing Learners in Pair Work Activity." *Language Teaching Research* 17 (1): 31–48. https://doi.org/10.1177/1362168812457530.

Storch, Neomy, and Gillian Wigglesworth. 2007. "Writing Tasks: The Effects of Collaboration". In *Investigating Tasks in Formal Language Learning*, edited by María del Pilar García Mayo, 157–177. London: Multilingual Matters.

Strobl, Carola. 2014. "Affordances of Web 2.0 Technologies for Collaborative Advanced Writing in a Foreign Language." *CALICO Journal* 31 (1): 1–18. https://doi.org/10.11139/cj.31.1.1-18.

Suwantarathip, Ornprapat, and Saovapa Wichadee. 2014. "The Effects of Collaborative Writing Activity Using Google Docs on Students' Writing Abilities." *Turkish Online Journal of Educational Technology – TOJET* 13(2): 148–56. https://doi.org/10.5539/ies.v8n3p175.

Swain, Merrill. 2000. "The Output Hypothesis and beyond: Mediating Acquisition through Collaborative Dialogue." In *Sociocultural Theory and Second Language Learning*, edited by James Lantolf, 97–114. Oxford: Oxford University Press.

Tare, Medha, Ewa M Golonka, Karen Vatz, Carrie L Bonilla, Carolyn Crooks, and Rachel Strong. 2014. "Effects of Interactive Chat Versus Independent Writing on L2 Learning." *Language Learning & Technology* 18 (3): 208–27.

Thorne, Steven, and Jonathan Reinhardt. 2008. "New Media Literacies and Advanced Foreign Language Proficiency." *CALICO Journal* 25 (3): 558–72.

Twain, Mark. 2001. *The Adventures of Tom Sawyer*. Bendon Publishing.

Villarreal, Izaskun, and Nora Gil-Sarratea. 2020. "The Effect of Collaborative Writing in an EFL Secondary Setting." *Language Teaching Research* 24 (6): 874–897. https://doi.org/10.1177/1362168819829017.

Vygotsky, Lev S. 1978. *Mind in Society: The Development of Higher Psychological Processes*. Cambridge: Harvard University Press.

Wang, Yu-Chun. 2015. "Promoting Collaborative Writing through Wikis: A New Approach for Advancing Innovative and Active Learning in an ESP Context." *Computer Assisted Language Learning* 28 (6): 499–512. https://doi.org/10.1080/09588221.2014.881386.

Wigglesworth, Gillian, and Neomy Storch. 2009. "Pair versus Individual Writing: Effects on Fluency, Complexity and Accuracy." *Language Testing* 26 (3): 445–66. https://doi.org/10.1177/0265532209104670.

Woodrich, Megan, and Yanan Fan. 2017. "Google Docs as a Tool for Collaborative Writing in the Middle School Classroom" *Journal of Information Technology Education: Research* 16:

391–410. http://jite.informingscience.org/documents/Vol16/JITEv16ResearchP391-410Woodrich3331.pdf.

Zheng, Binbin, and Mark Warschauer. 2017. "Epilogue: Second Language Writing in the Age of Computer-Mediated Communication." *Journal of Second Language Writing* 36: 61–67. https://doi.org/10.1016/j.jslw.2017.05.014.

Zheng, Binbin, Mark Warschauer, Chin-Hsi Lin, and Chi Chang. 2016. "Learning in One-to-One Laptop Environments." *Review of Educational Research* 86 (4): 1052–84. https://doi.org/10.3102/0034654316628645.

Appendix 1

T-test and Wilcoxon test comparisons by task

	Individual text vs CW1		CW 1 vs CW2		CW 2 vs individual text	
Words	t=−.371	p=.716	t=−.595	p=.562	t=−1.330	p=.206
Gram. E	t=1.071	p=.304	t=−1.102	p=.290	t=−.401	p=.695
Lex. E	t=.132	p=.897	t=.746	p=.469	t=−.798	p=.439
Mec. E	t=2.389	p=.033	t=.236	p=.817	t=−2.572	p=.023
Total E	t=1.787	p=.097	t=−.377	p=.712	t=−1.868	p=.084
Adequacy	Z=−.193	p=.847	Z=−.975	p=.330	Z=−1.025	p=.305
Coherence	Z=−9.14	p=.361	Z=−.933	p=.351	Z=−1.999	p=.046
Cohesion	Z=−.265	p=.791	Z=−2.309	p=.021	Z=−1.811	p=.070
Grammar	Z=−.447	p=.655	Z=−1.000	p=.317	Z=−.921	p=.357
Mechanics	Z=−1.84	p=.854	Z=−1.155	p=.248	Z=−1.732	p=.083
Vocabulary	Z=−.884	p=.377	Z=−1.311	p=.190	Z=.000	p=1.000
Total	Z=−.252	p=.801	Z=−1.824	p=.068	Z=−2.033	p=.042

Gram = Grammatical. Lex = Lexical. Mec = Mechanical. E = Errors.

T-test and Wilcoxon test comparisons by writing mode

	Google Docs vs Pen-and-paper	
Words	t=−.836	p=.418
Gram. E	t=−.893	p=.388
Lex. E	t=.840	p=.416
Mec. E	t=1.184	p=.257
Total E	t=.130	p=.898
Adequacy	Z=−2.50	p=.803
Coherence	Z=−1.000	p=.317
Cohesion	Z=−.000	p=1.000
Grammar	Z=−.707	p=.480
Mechanics	Z= −1.134	p=.257
Vocabulary	Z=−1.000	p=.317
Total	Z=−.731	p=.465

Gram = Grammatical. Lex = Lexical. Mec = Mechanical. E = Errors.

Marta González-Lloret
Online collaboration through tasks for L2 pragmatic development

1 Introduction

Real authentic collaborative dialogue with speakers of the target language is an essential component of any language learning practice. As stated by García Mayo in the introduction to this volume, collaborative dialogue has been shown to lead to language learning in both second and foreign language contexts. However, in some geographical regions, this collaborative dialogue (or any other interaction) is difficult given the lack of speakers of the target language (L2). Moreover, this interaction needs to include different types of speakers and in different contexts for L2 learners to be able to gain sociopragmatic knowledge (the knowledge of the rules and behaviors that govern the interactions of a culture) and pragmalinguistic competence (the language associated with those rules and behaviors) to become appropriate users of the language. It is not only important that learners' L2 is fluent, accurate, and complex, but it also needs to be *appropriate*. That is, they need to use language that is suitable to their interlocutors, given their relationship, histories and backgrounds, in a given context to fulfill a purpose. In addition, this needs to be done in a dynamic and interactional manner, as the conversation evolves. This is not an easy skill to acquire and requires ample opportunities for practice. Therefore, when speakers of the target language are not readily available in the learners' context, computer-mediated communication (CMC) tools offer the possibility to connect speakers in remote locations, providing students with the needed contexts to engage in real, authentic, and meaningful interaction. This chapter proposes that technology-mediated tasks, in which L2 learners collaborate with speakers of the target language, are excellent spaces to provide these opportunities for rich, authentic, contextualized interactions that can promote L2 pragmatic learning.

2 The pragmatics of synchronous CMC

A decade of studies on the pragmatics of technology-mediated interaction or "cyberpragmatics" (Yus 2001) parallel those topics common in traditional pragmatic

Marta González-Lloret, University of Hawaii at Manoa

https://doi.org/10.1515/9781501511318-009

studies such as politeness (e.g., Mancera Rueda 2015); speech acts such as: advice (e.g., Tsai and Kinginger 2014), commiseration (González-Lloret 2011), openings and closings (e.g., Gonzales 2013; Markman 2009), requests (e.g., Alcón-Soler 2013; Cunningham 2017), and issues of identity creation (e.g., Yus 2014), coherence (e.g., Bou-Franch, Lorenzo-Dus, and Garcés-Conejos Blitvich 2012), humor and language play (e.g., Lazaraton 2014), face work (e.g., Stroinska and Cecchetto 2013), as well as descriptive studies of pragmatic interaction focusing on different CMC technologies such as text messages (e.g., Spagnolli 2012), email (e.g., Bou-Franch 2011), forums (e.g., Nishimura 2008), social networks (e.g., Locher 2014), chat (e.g., Blyth 2012) and video interaction (e.g., Jenks and Firth 2013). This research reveals the ability of learners to apply pragmatic norms (with more or less accuracy) in the medium in a similar way to face-to-face interaction.

As for studies focusing on whether CMC can be an effective tool to promote pragmatic *acquisition*, some studies investigated the development of addressivity, the use of formal and informal pronouns, politeness markers, familiarity, deference, etc. (e.g., Belz and Kinginger 2003; González-Lloret 2008; Kim and Brown 2014). These studies show that CMC is a useful tool to develop addressivity, but also that the development is not homogeneous among students. Even when students have a positive view of SCMC for L2 learning, learner's follow different developmental paths (Belz and Kinginger 2003; Cunningham 2016; Li, Taguchi, and Tang 2019). In addition, there seems to be a high degree of correlation between development and amount and quality of interaction, feedback, learner's language level, and their personal beliefs. These studies suggest that for L2 pragmatic development to occur, a sustained interaction with targeted feedback is necessary, as well as awareness of the feedback and willingness from the students to incorporate it to their interactions. When these conditions are met, learners' language becomes more target-like (Cunningham 2016; González-Lloret 2008, 2011), and learners incorporate sociopragmatic practices and pragmalinguistic formulae that were not in their repertoire before (Blattner and Fiori 2011; Kakegawa 2009). For a more detail view of the impact of technology on L2 pragmatics, see González-Lloret (2019a).

Within the field of L2 pragmatic development it is important to mention studies that focus on the development of interculturality. This line of work investigates the technologies, implementation, and effectiveness of telecollaborative projects (among students of different institutions learning each other's culture and language) to develop intercultural competence. Within telecollaboration projects, CMC has been the most employed technology, although there are also studies employing blogs (e.g., Elola and Oskoz 2008), wikis (e.g., Vinagre 2010) and virtual environments (e.g., Canto, de Graff, and Jauregui 2014). These investigations suggest that telecollaborating with peers promotes not only large amounts of L2 interaction, but in these spaces L2 learners are able to learn the sociopragmatic norms of the L2 while reflecting on the sociopragmatic and pragmalinguistic norms of their own culture. The use of technology seems to promote a language that is pragmatically more complex and sophisticated, with more mitigators, and interactional strategies. It also promotes student's self confidence in their communication abilities and promotes cooperative and collaborative work. For more information on the advantages of telecollaboration for L2 learning see Chun (2011), Guth and Helm (2010), Dooly and O'Dowd (2012), and O'Dowd (2014).

3 Technology-mediated tasks to promote collaboration

The benefits of collaboration in technology-mediated education are well documented. In educational contexts, collaboration refers to two or more learners forming a team to engage in planning or problem-solving by continuous and interdependent interactions (West 1990). It is important to note that collaborative group work is different from cooperative work. Collaborative learning implies a common group goal and individual accountability for the outcome which leads to more internal motivation and active involvement in the activity, and therefore, the development of higher order thinking capabilities (Slavin 1996) as well as interpersonal skills.

In line with other chapters in this volume and following Storch's (2013) idea of collaborative activities as those in which students interact, negotiate meaning, and make joint decisions, collaborative pedagogical tasks seem an ideal choice for organizing a telecollaborative project. Engaging students in tasks which are meaning and goal oriented, relevant, and as authentic as possible helps maximize student engagement and target language use, generating *collaborative dialogue* in which "speakers are engaged in problem solving and knowledge building" a source of language learning and development (Swain and Watanabe 2013 p. 1).

When creating collaborative tasks to maximize its effectiveness for language (or pragmatics, intercultural) learning, it is essential to pay attention to the task design (including issues of complexity) and task implementation. In the case of tasks to promote pragmatic development, as suggested by González-Lloret and Ortega (2018), these should be designed to provide learners with the interactional and social contexts necessary to develop L2 pragmatic competence, with a focus on pragmatics as part of the required language to accomplish the task. This would help learners succeed in the interaction and establish and maintain rapport with their interlocutors to secure future interactions. It is also important to consider that the mediation of technology as well as the focus on pragmatics may change the nature of a task, that is, when tasks "leverage the mediation of new technologies, the pragmatic specifications may become even more complex, but the tasks will also become all the more authentic and motivating, hence supporting rich pragmatic learning, and rich overall language learning." (p. 209). For more information on tasks and L2 pragmatics see Taguchi and Kim (2018) and González-Lloret (2019b).

4 L2 Conversation closings

The management of politeness is clearly an essential component for the maintenance and opportunity for future social relations (Spencer-Oatey 2005). Among all the possible sequences where politeness is an essential component, conversation closings are frequent and essential in the interaction because they are not only used to terminate conversations, but also to reinforce relationships, and support future interactions (Button, 1987; Hartford and Bardovi-Harlig 1992; Schegloff and Sacks 1973). However, conversation closings are not common in the language classroom, and when they are employed, they are reduced to a few formulae. For L2 speakers, conversation closings are difficult and complex sequences since they must consider not just the language used, but also additional elements such as contextual norms, sociopragmatic and pragmalinguistic conventions, and fundamental cultural values.

Although conversation closing differ among cultures (Firth 2007), according to Schegloff and Sacks (1973) all closing sequences share some universals (at least in oral conversation).

1. All conversation closings involve a ritual familiar to the members of a particular community.
2. Closings occur in rapid succession, often with few pauses but considerable overlap and latching.
3. The sequential structure of closings may vary, with multiple opportunities for participants to go in and out of the closing sequence

4.1 Conversation closings in Spanish

Several studies have looked at the realization of closing sequences in Spanish face-to-face conversation (e.g., Fitch, 1990; García, 1981), phone interactions (e.g., Márquez Reiter, 2011; Placencia, 1997; Valeiras Viso 2002), and online environments (e.g., Codina-Espurz and Salazar-Campillo 2019; Félix-Basdefer

2012; Gonzales 2013; Kuriscak and Luke 2009). The research done on closings in Spanish has shown that Spanish speakers use different formulae to closing conversations which are affected by factors such as power, social distance, age, etc. Young speakers tend to use more simple forms such as *chau* rather than *hasta mañana* (see you tomorrow) (Ferrer and Sánchez Lanza 2002).

Fitch (1990) described Colombian Spanish leave-takings as "*salsipuedes*" sequences, ('get out if you can'). Fitch emphasizes the sensitive importance that closing sequences place on social events for Spanish speakers in comparison to North Americans. Her data showed that the typical pattern of a closing sequence when leaving a social gathering is:
1. Guest(s) announce intentions to leave, sometimes thanking host(s) for the invitation.
2. Host asks why the guest is proposing to leave and protests timing of departure.
3. Guest repeats intention to leave and/or offers account for needing to leave.
4. Host rejects account and/or suggests alternative.
5. Finally the host accepts the leaving

Although, according to Goffman (1971), supportive interchanges, such as leave takings, are more important for relations between people who know each other than those who do not, leave takings seem to be pervasive in all types of conversations, from service encounters to family conversations, which makes them an important target for L2 learning. In a study on leave takings in Spanish, Márquez Reiter and Placencia (2004) show that speakers in service encounters employ similar sequences, including pre-closing tokens such as *well* and *okay*, indirect questions like *are you busy?* and other closing devices (promises to come back and shop, expressions of gratitude, apologies, and leave-taking utterances). Placencia (1997) also shows how closings in a family setting in Quito include pre-closing devices (similar to those in English conversations) that serve to close the interaction in a way that the interactant does not feel offended. Placencia emphasizes how age and the relationships of the interactants affect the choice of formulae to thank and farewell expressions and discusses those mechanisms the speakers use to mark connectedness, showing how many of the procedures used in Quiteño Spanish are similar to those in English but with some distinctive differences.

4.2 Technology-mediated closing sequences

Although there are few studies of closing sequences in synchronous CMC (SCMC), other media of communication can shed some light on their sequential patterns.

This is the case with telephone conversations (although the media is different, they share in common the lack of non-verbal interacting clues) and asynchronous CMC such as email.

Previous work by Schegloff and Sacks, (1973) and Clark and French, (2010) has shown that phone calls contain three components in their closing sequences:
1. The closing of the topic, which can involve a pre-closing statement, often characterized by a particle such as *well*, *so*, and *ok*;
2. The leave-taking, which can include a summary of the conversation, future plans for contact, expressions of thanks or pleasure for having had the conversation, justification for ending the conversation, expression of well-wishing, and the leave-taking itself; and
3. The hang-up

This structure seems to apply to both Spanish and English with some variation on length and linguistic forms, with Spanish including more variation of form (Valeiras Viso 2002, *bye, bye-bye, bye now, cheers, see you- adiós, hasta luego, hasta lueguito, un beso, un besito, nosvemos, chau, etc*). This variation may be due to the importance of physical contact in maintaining social relations in Spanish culture (Valeiras Viso, 2002) and therefore there may be a verbal compensation for the lack of embodiment when on the phone. This sequence was also found in Márquez Reiter's (2011) investigation of service encounters over the phone. In her data, arrangement making was the most frequent closing strategy (part of the institutional culture) and extended closing sequences were more frequent that short ones, including more than one turn-construction unit such as an expression of appreciation and good wishes or an expression of willingness to serve the client. The data also showed a preference for the use of *hasta luego* (bye for now), *chau* (bye), and *bai bai* (bye bye) over a more neutral *adios* (good bye), showing that even in service encounters, building relationships and expressing familiarity in closings is important. In addition, Márquez Reiter (2011) demonstrates how people from different cultures (Colombia and Argentina) understand closings differently, even when they speak the same language.

Researching email conversations, Bou-Franch (2011) explored Spanish (as L1) openings and closings in emails in an academic context. She analyzed 240 individual emails (consisting of two or three email exchanges). The most frequent moves in closings were thanking, leave-takings, and signatures. One of the interesting results of the study was that although closings have been regarded as optional, closings appeared in 97% of the emails and the closings did not decrease (or did it slightly) in email exchanges (while the openings did). The amount of closings was not affected by power relationships. Finally, closings included expressions of distance and respect (more than greetings), showing patterns of respect-building practices, consistent with the institutional setting.

Also using emails, but with L2 learners, Salazar-Campillo (2018) shows similar politeness and respect practices in closings by students both in their L1 (Spanish) or their L2 (English). However, Salazar-Campillo and Codina-Espurz (2018) and Codina-Espurz and Salazar-Campillo (2019) show that L2 learners, although polite in their closings, tend to transfer their pragmatic practices from their L1 to their L2 emails, resulting in language that is more informal and may not be appropriate in the L2. Finally, Félix-Brasdefer's (2012) data suggests that there is no difference in politeness between male and female L2 learners in their closing moves in emails.

Focusing on synchronous interaction, Markman (2009) investigated closings in chat among virtual student teams (in English, their L1). The study shows that closing a conversation is not easy and requires several attempts, often disrupted, requiring repetitive work to bring the conversation to a closing. The author suggests the lack of embodied action and the impossibility of monitoring the ongoing progress of turns as reasons for this difficulty. Exploring the closing sequences of CMC tasks for three proficiency levels of Japanese learners of English in Japan, Abe and Roever (2020) found that in low-level (according to TOIC scores) proficiency learners' terminal exchanges, their social actions when closing the task ranged from achieving agreement to confirming the end of the talk. Mid-level learners were similar but displayed less explicit marking of the end of the task and more steps between the task and the task closing. In contrast, high-level learners produced more internal sequential expansion disrupting the adjacency of the posts, which according to the authors suggests a prioritization of social relations over transactional task-talk.

Finally, two studies have previously focused on closing sequences in CMC conversation produced by L2 learners of Spanish in *Livemocha* (Gonzales 2013) and *Second Life* (Kuriscak and Luke 2009). Gonzales (2013) presents the case of a 33-year-old learner of Spanish engaged in *Livemocha* and the evolution of his chat closing strategies during one academic year (adding to eight hours of chat). The student's closings evolved from abrupt closings (which can lead to rapport neglect) to the use of extended preclosing sequences. In addition, at the end of the interactions, the learner was able to initiate closings that included rapport enhancement strategies. Gonzales' results suggest that sustained interaction leads to closings that are more appropriate and can hep maintain rapport. Finally, Kuriscak and Luke (2009) investigated the attitudes and language produced by fourth-semester learners of Spanish engaged in *Second Life*. Students were allowed to engage in conversation with classmates or seek native Spanish speakers. The data showed a variety of closings in length, content and level of directness. Pre-closings were more elaborated when initiated by the native speakers, and the native speakers never corrected the learners during closing sequences.

The results of both studies suggest that L2 learners perceive these environments as authentic places of interaction, even when they attend to the activities as language classroom tasks. The results of both studies suggest that learners pay careful attention to closings, using same resources as the ones used in face to face interaction, even when not having done so in this medium would have had no communicative consequences for these learners. This fact suggests the importance that pragmatic norms have from communication, independently of the medium, highlighting the commonality between face and face and CMC conversation (also confirmed by data from Thai L2 English learners interacting in *Second Life* in Pojanapunya and Jaroenkitboworn 2011). The results also show that a sustained participation and a favorable disposition to engage with the internet tools were decisive factors in the participants' improvement of their closing sequences, and that participants learned to engage in lengthier closing sequences, although they still produced shorter, less detailed pre-closings and less indirect discourse strategies (in Kuriscak and Luke 2009) and they never managed to have the last word in their leave-taking acts with NSs (in Gonzales 2013).

4.3 Conversation Analysis (CA) for language learning (CA-SLA)

Conversation Analysis (CA), in its ethnomethodological origins, was developed as an approach to the analysis of social interaction for the study of ordinary conversation and not as a theory of learning, however, there is now more than a decade of robust research successfully employing CA for the study of language development (CA for SLA) (e.g., González-Lloret 2008; Kasper and Wagner 2014; Markee 2008; Pekarek Doehler and Pochon-Berger 2015; Tudini 2010). This view of CA for SLA adopts a wide definition of 'learning' that includes not only the acquisition of linguistic forms but also the development of interactional patterns and behaviors necessary to become competent users of the language. Learning is therefore associated with the deployment of "intersubjective resources to co-construct with their interlocutors locally enacted, progressively more accurate, fluent, and complex interactional repertoires in the L2." (Markee 2008, 406). CA has also been employed for the study of pragmatic features and intercultural communication since "CA studies of speaking practices across languages and cultures can provide a basis for comparison of L2, or language learner, speaking practices with L1 speaker norms in both L1 and L2" (Schegloff, Koshik, Jacoby, and Olsher 2002, 16).

Computer-mediated interactions are not new for conversation analysts who have investigated the nature of sequence organization and the turn-taking system in SCMC and compared them to well established findings of sequence organization in oral communication. Thanks to these studies we have a picture of how phenomena such as turn taking and organization (e.g., Herring 1999), repair (e.g., Lazaraton 2014; Tudini 2013), conversation openings and closings (e.g., Markman, 2009), negotiation of face (e.g., Golato and Taleghani-Nikazm, 2006), and identity construction (e.g., Stommel 2008) are manifested in chat environments. We also know that participants in text-based CMC display an orientation toward the interactions as being fundamentally conversational (e.g., Markman 2005) but the online environment plays a crucial role in the interaction. The establishment of the MOOD (Microanalysis of Online Data) network, an interdisciplinary association of academic researchers using CA to investigate online interaction (Giles, Stommel, Paulus, Lester, and Reed 2015), demonstrates the importance that the study of online interaction has within CA.

As for the investigation of language learners' SCMC data, we now know that learners are able to recognize pragmatic norms in CMC and produce interactionally appropriate speech acts (e.g., Chun 1994). Despite that the interactions seem chaotic, learners are able to produce turns in an appropriate way and their sequences are as elaborated as those of expert speakers. They use similar resources to those of native speakers and they are able to organize the interaction and develop and maintain new topics (González-Lloret 2009; Tercedor Cabrero 2013; Tudini 2010). In addition to text-based CMC, we now have a growing body of studies employing video and audio CMC (e.g., Jenks 2009; Jenks and Firth 2013). Research also points out that learners tend to ignore linguistic issues in favor of maintaining social interaction. That is, instead of engaging in discussion or negotiation about the language, they try to establish mutual understanding and convergence with the other speaker(s), which requires complex interactional work, highly organized and collaborative (Jenks and Brandt 2013; Tsai and Kinginger 2014; Vandergriff 2013). For more on CA in technology-mediated environment, see González-Lloret (2015).

5 The study

The present study is part of a larger study investigating whether text-based telecollaborative interaction can help L2 learners develop their interactional competence. The data presented here focuses on one particular aspect of interactional competence: the ability to produce appropriate closing sequences.

The participants in this study were 15 L2 Spanish intermediate high learners (according to ACFL proficiency guidelines) at a US University engaged in telecollaboration with L1 Spanish speakers (university students, learners of English in Spain) as part of their L2 learning curriculum. The learners engaged in a task using Spanish (the target language of the US students) for six weeks and in another task in English (the target language of the students in Spain) for five weeks (not described in this chapter). The telecollaboration projects and time frameworks were negotiated by the instructors of both language classes.

The task in Spanish consisted in developing a travel itinerary with a given budget to travel together as a group in Spain, including lodging, transport, things to do, restaurants, and places to visit. Groups of two or three students (one from each institutions) met synchronously online and also shared documents and messages asynchronously via email. The participants connected at least once a week using text chat outside the classroom. The groups were formed according to their time availability and the students negotiated a time to meet. Learners saved their conversations and emailed them to the researcher (the author) and their teachers for credit. The task was part of their class assignments and the outcome was a document with the itinerary and photos to illustrate their trip and budget.

6 Data analysis

The data consisted of 10 pairs (one student from each institution) and two groups of three students (two from US and one from Spain). This chapter presents the interaction of the two pairs and a group of three that interacted at least four times.

The longitudinal data was analyzed using CA. The closing sequences for each group and each interaction across the six weeks were microanalayzed to find whether there was any development in the way the participants produced their closing sequences. As in any CA analysis, attention was placed to the sequence of the interaction (the turn-taking system), who initiated and closed the sequence, how participants oriented to the sequence, and what interactional resources they used to manage and co-construct their closings.

In spoken interaction, adjacency pairs are the basic building blocks of sequences (Schegloff and Sacks 1973). These adjacency pairs are composed of two turns, produced by different speakers next to each other in the conversation. In technology-mediated interactions, these adjacency pairs may not be placed next to each other. They form what Schönfeldt and Golato (2003) termed "virtual adjacency pairs" but they can still be identified for analysis. Most of the time this disrupted turn adjacency is not problematic for the participants or cause miscommunication (Meredith 2017).

7 Results

The microanalysis of data showed that the L2 learners developed their closing sequences in three main aspects:
1. They started to initiate the closing sequence (which in their first interaction was done exclusively by the expert speaker),
2. Their closing sequences became more similar to those of the expert speakers in length and amount of terminal components, and
3. They included thanking as part of the sequence, demonstrating an orientation to the activity as institutional talk for learning.

7.1 Initiation of closing sequences

In the following extracts, to illustrate how learners developed their ability to initiate closing sequences, we follow Mary, a Spanish language student, engaged with Juan a student of English in Spain and her evolution on the initiation of closing sequences. Although this is their first chat interaction, they have exchanged several emails introducing themselves, their likes and dislikes, and discussing times when they could connect outside the language classroom.

Interaction #1. Week 1. Mary=Language learner, Juan=L1 Spanish speaker

30.	Mary (10:07:54 AM): wow! Temenos mucho en common!	*wow! We have a lot in common!*
31.	Juan (10:08:04 AM): eso parece	*it seems so*
32.	Juan (10:08:06 AM): bueno mary	*well mary*
33.	Juan (10:08:16 AM): me tengo q ir, podemos quedar mañana una hora antes?	*I have to go, can we meet tan hour earlier?*
34.	Mary (10:08:18 AM): si, si	*yes, yes*
35.	Mary (10:08:21 AM): a que hora	*what time?*

36.	Mary (10:08:36 AM): a las 8? tengo clases a las 9:00	*at 8? I have class at 9:00*
37.	Juan (10:08:44 AM): a la misma hora que hoy, una hora antes,	*same time as today, one hour earlier*
38.	Juan (10:08:57 AM): a las 8. hora española?	*at 8. Spanish time?*
39.	Mary (10:09:04 AM): si...	*yes...*
40.	Juan (10:09:10 AM): ok	*ok*
41.	Mary (10:09:17 AM): gracias juan....	*thank you juan*
42.	Mary (10:09:27 AM): hasta manana![1]	*see you tomorrow* (mañana)
43.	Juan (10:09:46 AM): hasta mañana	*see you tomorrow*

In interaction 1, Juan stars the closing sequence in turn 32 with a pre-closing token (*bueno Mary*) followed by an explicit closing move: an overt announcement of leaving (*me tengo que ir*) followed by a sequence to make arrangements for a later meeting, a common element in oral closing sequences (Schegloff and Sack 1973). The conversation ends with a thanking turn in line 41 by the learner (which will be addressed in 6.3 below) and a very minimal terminal exchange composed of an adjacency pair: farewell-farewell.

In interaction 2 is also Juan, the expert speaker, who initiates the closing, but we can already see a longer ending to the closing sequence, incorporating two terminal exchanges, one initiated by Mary and the other by Juan.

Interaction #2. Week 3. Mary=Language learner, Juan=L1 Spanish speaker

56.	Mary (8:59:50 AM): pero en Hawaii, las personas conducen muy, muy lento... estamos en "Hawaiian time"	*but in Hawaii, people drive very very slowly...we are in "Hawaiian time"*
57.	Juan (8:59:56 AM): jaja	*haha*
58.	Juan (9:00:50 AM): mary, si no te importa podríamos quedar otro día, porque quiero ir me a recostar un poquito... :-&	*mary, if you don't mind could we meet another day, because I want to go to lay down a bit... :-&*

---

1 Errors in the chat have been kept intact. The correct word is provided in parenthesis next to the translation on the right column.

59.	Mary (9:01:05 AM): si..si	*yes..yes*
60.	Mary (9:01:19 AM): claro que si	*of course*
61.	Juan (9:01:22 AM): ok	*ok*
62.	Juan (9:01:27 AM): el miércoles?	*Wednesday?*
63.	Mary (9:01:34 AM): si...a qué hora?	*yes...at what time?*
64.	Mary (9:01:46 AM): 8:30 o 9:00?	*8:30 or 9:00?*
65.	Juan (9:01:46 AM): pon tu la hora	*you decide the time*
66.	Juan (9:01:49 AM): ok	*ok*
67.	Mary (9:02:13 AM): sientes mejor!	*feel better!*
68.	Mary (9:02:17 AM): adios	*good bye*
69.	Juan (9:02:23 AM): adios y...	*good bye*
70.	Juan (9:02:24 AM): aloha	*good bye and..*
71.	Juan (9:02:30 AM): gracias mary! ;)	*thank you mary! ;)*
72.	Mary (9:02:32 AM): aloha	*aloha*

Juan opens the closing sequence in line 58 using a pre-closing token (the vocative Mary) followed by an indirect request to finish the conversation. The student orients to it as an invitation to close the conversation and accepts it. It is also the expert speaker who initiates a sequence to arrange a future meeting from line 62 to 66. The final part of the closing in this interaction is already longer than the previous one. It incorporates two terminal exchanges, the first one initiated by Mary in line 68 and the second one by Juan in line 70. This terminal exchange is closer to those found by Garcia (1981) in expert speakers' encounters.

It is in interaction 3 that the Spanish learner initiates the closing sequence for the first time.

Interaction #3. Week 4. Mary=Language learner, Juan=L1 Spanish speaker

86.	Mary (9:06:28 AM): si...pero mi esposo quiere ser un médico y él tiene 10 años mas	*yes...but my husband wants to be a doctor and he has 10 more years*
87.	Juan (9:06:57 AM): buff	*buff*
88.	Juan (9:07:03 AM): estas cansada?	*are you tired?*
89.	Mary (9:07:14 AM): si un pocito...	*yes a Little* (poquito)
90.	Mary (9:07:28 AM): creo que hemos hablado pr una hora si?	*I think we have spoken for* (por) *an hour, right?*
91.	Juan (9:08:12 AM): si, mas o menos	*yes, more or less*

92.	Juan (9:08:56 AM): mary, una cosita, tienes e-mails divertidos en ingles?	mary, one thing, do you have fun emails in English?
93.	Mary (9:09:15 AM): si a veces.. porque?	yes sometimes..why?
94.	Juan (9:09:58 AM): me podrías mandar los que tengas...?	could you send me what you have...?
95.	Mary (9:10:29 AM): si...es to email xxxxxxx@yahoo.com?	yes...it is (your) email xxxxxx@yahoo.com
96.	Mary (9:10:40 AM): yahoo.es	yahoo.es
97.	Juan (9:10:44 AM): .com	.com
98.	Juan (9:10:55 AM): pero creo q da igual	but I think it is the same
99.	Mary (9:11:00 AM): okay...no problema!	okay.....no problem!
100.	Juan (9:11:22 AM): muchiiiiiiiiiiiiiiiiiiiiiiiiiiiiiisimas gracias	manyyyyyyyyyyyyyyyyyyyy thanks
101.	Mary (9:11:38 AM): :Dcuando podemos reunirnos próximo?	:D when can we meet next (la próxima vez)?
102.	Juan (9:12:01 AM): viernes?	Friday?
103.	Mary (9:12:52 AM): lo siento...tengo que trabajar hasta 12:00...el sabado tal vez? o durante la mañana o tarde para ti?	I am sorry...I have to work until 12:00...Saturday perhaps? or during the morning or evening for you?
104.	Juan (9:13:08 AM): ok el sabado, por la tarde mejor	ok Saturday, in the evening better
105.	Mary (9:13:30 AM): que hora es mejor para tí?	what time is best for you?
106.	Juan (9:13:56 AM): sobre esta hora?	about this time?
107.	Mary (9:14:46 AM): 9:30? bien..nos vemos el sabado a las 9:30 de la noche en España.	good..see you on Saturday at 9:30 night time in Spain.
108.	Juan (9:15:14 AM): un poquito antes...	a little bit earlier...
109.	Mary (9:15:20 AM): sisi	yes yes
110.	Juan (9:15:30 AM): a las 8.30	at 8.30
111.	Juan (9:15:33 AM): o 9.00	or 9.00

112.	Juan (9:15:36 AM): decide tu	*you decide*
113.	Mary (9:16:09 AM): okay 8:30 es bien...probablamente quieres salir con tus amigos...	*okay 8.30 is well....you probably want to go out with your friends...*
114.	Juan (9:16:23 AM): muchas gracias!!! eres un sol	*thank you very much!! you area sun [common compliment]*
115.	Mary (9:16:36 AM): adios juan!	*good bye juan!*
116.	Juan (9:16:43 AM): aidos mary	*good bye* (adios) *mary*
117.	Juan (9:16:50 AM): y gracias	*and thank you*
118.	Mary (9:16:55 AM): de nada	*your welcome*
119.	Juan (9:16:59 AM): --- y aloha	*--and aloha*
120.	Mary (9:17:06 AM): :)	*:)*
121.	Juan (9:17:40 AM): :D	*:D*

In their third interaction, Juan, the expert speaker, utters a question in line 88 as the initiation of a closing sequence (are you tired?) a common practice in oral conversation (Schegloff and Sacks 1973). The student orients to the question as a closing sequence, answering briefly and providing herself a possible closing sequence (since their conversations were usually about 1 hour long). At this point, the expert speaker starts a move out of the closing by bringing out a new topic (found also often in oral data). When the inserted sequence finishes, it is the student who initiates the arrangement of a future meeting (which had previously always been done by the expert speaker), and it is also the student who initiates the terminal exchange in line 115 (*adios Juan*). This terminal exchange is also longer than the previous one, including two terminal exchanges and an exchange of emoticons, frequent CMC indicators of emotion (González-Lloret 2016; Vandergriff 2014).

In the last interaction, 6 weeks later, we can see how the student is actually the one initiating most of the sequences in the closing of the conversation.

Interaction #4. Week 6. Mary= language learner Jaun=Expert speaker

87.	Mary (10:27:41 AM): es pachangeo el nombre para el pop?	*is pachangeo the name for pop?*
88.	Mary (10:30:32 AM): juan? Estás aqui?	*juan? Are you here?*
89.	Juan (10:30:45 AM): si, si	*yes, yes*
90.	Juan (10:30:49 AM): si mas o menos	*yes more or less*
91.	Mary (10:31:08 AM): estas cansado?	*are you tired?*

92.	Mary (10:31:47 AM): podemos terminar nuestra conversasion si quieres...	*we can finish our conversation if you want...*
93.	Juan (10:31:48 AM): un pokillo	*a little bit (poquillo)*
94.	Mary (10:32:42 AM): yo aprendo.... cuando quieres hablar próximo?	*I understand (entiendo)...when do you want to talk next?*
95.	Juan (10:33:00 AM): lunes	*Monday*
96.	Juan (10:33:02 AM): ?	*?*
97.	Mary (10:33:03 AM): okay...	*okay...*
98.	Mary (10:33:14 AM): a qué hora?	*at what time?*
99.	Juan (10:33:31 AM): 8.00	*8.00*
100.	Juan (10:33:34 AM): ?	*?*
101.	Juan (10:33:36 AM): pon tu hora venga	*you can decide the time*
102.	Mary (10:33:43 AM): okay..	*okay..*
103.	Juan (10:33:54 AM): ok	*ok*
104.	Juan (10:34:09 AM): bueno, iré a cenar algo...	*ok, I am going to have some dinner*
105.	Mary (10:34:11 AM): hasta el lunes...tal vex mar puedo hablar con nosotros	*see you on Monday...may be* (vez) *mar can* (puede) *talk to us*
106.	Mary (10:34:21 AM): puede	*can (self-repair)*
107	Mary (10:34:29 AM): adios!	*good bye!*
108.	Juan (10:34:31 AM): quizás	*maybe*
109.	Juan (10:34:33 AM): aloha	*aloha*
110.	Juan (10:34:35 AM): jejej	*heheh*
111.	Mary (10:34:45 AM): aloha!	*aloha!*

After a very long pause of 3 minutes and a lack of answer to her question in line 86, Mary, the learner, initiates in line 88 a summons sequence to find out whether Juan is still part of the conversation (a common practice in text-based CMC). After making sure that her interactant is still connected, she initiates the closing sequence with a two-turn direct question in line 91, similar to the one the expert speaker had used in their previous interaction (are you tired?), followed by a suggestion to close the interaction. It is also the student who initiates in line 94 the arrangement of their next meeting, finishing the sequence with the reinvocation of earlier made arrangements, a common resource in regular conversation (Schegloff and Sacks 1973). It is also the student who initiates the terminal component by initiating in line 107 a terminal exchange, to which Juan responds with another terminal exchange.

7.2 Longer terminal sequences

After six weeks, students managed to produce very complicated and sophisticated closing sequences that incorporated up to four terminal components before the closing. In the case of Mary (above), from their second interaction two terminal sequences were employed. Other students' closings grew even longer. This is the case of Valery interacting with Antonio and Jeff (another L2 learner).

Interaction #5. Week 6. Valery & Jeff = L2 students, Antonio = Expert speaker

167.	Valery (2:07:46 AM): cuando hablamos otra vez?	*when do we talk again?*
168.	Antonio (2:08:05 AM): esta en catalan. No se si lo entendereis. Son canciones diferentes.	*it is in catalan. I don't know if you'll understand it. They are different songs*
169.	Valery (2:08:08 AM): la mismo tiempo, la mismo dia?	*the* (el) *same time, the* (el) *same day?*
170.	Jeff (2:08:27 AM): no cuido	*don't care* (no me importa)
171.	Jeff (2:08:51 AM): la mismo tiempo	*the* (el) *same time*
172.	Valery (2:08:54 AM): ?	*?*
173.	Antonio (2:08:55 AM): El 17-03-2005 a la 01:00?	*17-03-2005 at 01:00?*
174.	Antonio (2:09:04 AM): AM.	*AM.*
175.	Valery (2:09:13 AM): ok	*ok*
176.	Antonio (2:09:15 AM): de ahí	*over there?*
177.	Antonio (2:09:18 AM): Ok	*OK*
178.	Jeff (2:09:27 AM): 1 aqui?	*here?*
179.	Jeff (2:09:30 AM): o alli?	*or there?*
180.	Antonio (2:09:35 AM): ahi	*there*
181.	Jeff (2:09:42 AM): ok	*ok*
182.	Jeff (2:09:45 AM): bueno	*good*
183.	Antonio (2:10:01 AM): media hor a ante tambien puedo	*I can also half an hour earlier*
184.	Antonio (2:10:05 AM): si quereis	*if you want*

185. Valery (2:10:08 AM): bueno... entonces...habia una buen almuerzo...	good...then...have (que tengas) a (un) good lunch
186. Valery (2:10:39 AM): adios	good bye
187. Jeff (2:10:39 AM): si, gracias para su tiempo	thank you for your time
188. Valery (2:10:49 AM): si gracias!!!!!!!!!	yes thank you!!!!!!!!
189. Antonio (2:10:51 AM): adios y gracias a vosotros	good bye and thank you to you two
190. Jeff (2:10:56 AM): adios amigos	good bye my friends
191. Valery (2:11:00 AM): !!!!!!!!!!!!!11	
192. Antonio (2:11:03 AM): adios guapos	good bye good looking
193. Jeff (2:11:04 AM): como weeeee!	what weeeee!
194. Antonio (2:11:08 AM): y guapas	and good looking (fem)
195. Valery (2:11:16 AM): adios!!	good bye!!!
196. Jeff (2:11:19 AM): gracias, adios	thank you, good bye
197. Antonio (2:11:29 AM): Buenas noches, supongo.	good night, I guess.
198. Antonio (2:11:35 AM): Me voy a comer	I am going to have lunch
199. Valery (2:11:47 AM): Que vas a comer?	What are you going to eat?
200. Antonio (2:12:02 AM): Si "i Have the lunch"	Yes
201. Valery (2:12:08 AM): ok then	
202. Valery (2:12:13 AM): bye	
203. Antonio (2:12:17 AM): Adios	Good bye/bye
204. Valery (2:12:24 AM): final adios	final good bye
205. Antonio (2:12:29 AM): Ok	Ok

In this interaction we can see how the terminal exchanges occur in succession, initiated both by the student and the expert speaker. The closing sequence starts in line 167 with a pre-closing initiated by Valery attempting to make arrangements for a future meeting (the most common pre-closing move found in Márquez Reiter's 2011 data). The negotiation continues until line 184. Valery then initiats a first terminal component in line 185 with a two-turn sequence, placing the terminal component '*adios*' (goodbye) in a visually prominent position. However, this does not end the conversation since Jeff initiated another terminal component in line 192 and 194 to which Jeff and Valery also orient by answering with farewells in line 195 (*adios*) and 196 (*adios!!*). It is interesting here that Valery also includes exclamations marks to her terminal turn, usually employed in CMC to create emphasis. Antonio then, in line 197, starts a new terminal component that results in an inserted sequence that moves the conversation out of the closing (197–200). In line 201, Valery attempts again to close the conversation, this time code-switching to English (possible to emphasize her turn and make sure everybody understands it). When Antonio answers to her terminal component, in line 204, Valery orients to this accumulation of terminal exchanges by stating '*final adios*-final goodbye', making sure this way her contending turn actually closes the conversation. This explicit orientation to a need for a final terminal exchange suggests this accumulation of terminal exchanges as a non-normative pattern of interaction for her as an English speaker, one that she is willing to produce, approximating herself to the target language norm, but only to a certain extent.

7.3 Thanking sequences

In all the previous excerpts, we have seen that the participants engaged in a thanking sequence inside the conversation closing. This thanking was frequently uttered by the expert speakers and the students. According to Schegloff and Sacks (1973) this occurs as recognition of a special type of conversation. Similar to this data, Bou-Franch (2011) found an abundance of thanking sequences embedded in the closing sequences of Spanish speakers in an educational institution.

In the present data, although at times the interaction was very similar to a conversation among friends, some features, such as these appreciation sequences, show how students oriented to the activity as a learning activity. These are some more examples in the data incorporating thanking sequences.

Interaction #5. Week 6. Valery & Jeff = L2 students, Antonio = Expert speaker

186.	Valery (2:10:39 AM): adios	*bye*
→ 187.	Jeff (2:10:39 AM): si, gracias para su tiempo	*yes, thank you for your time*
→ 188.	Valery (2:10:49 AM): si gracias!!!!!!!!!	*yes thank you!!!!!!!!!!*
→ 189.	Antonio (2:10:51 AM): adios y gracias a vosotros	*good bye and thank you to you two*
190.	Jeff (2:10:56 AM): adios amigos	*by my friend*

Interaction #3. Week 3. Shoji =L2 student, Ana= Expert speaker

	333	Ana: bueno llego mi hermana y quiere ver su correo	*well my sister has arrived and she wants to look at her email*
	334	Ana: así aprovecho y ceno	*that way I can have dinner also*
	335	Ana: luego si puedo me conecto otra vez	*if I can I will connect later again*
	336	Shoji: Tal vez no yo	*may be I cannot*
→	337	Ana: gracias por tus cumplidos!!	*thank you for your compliments!!*
	338	Shoji: me quedo aquí.	*I have to stay here*
→	**339**	Shoji: gracias por charlear conmigo.	*thank you for talking* (charlar) *with me.*
	340	Ana: bueno pues sino nos vemos otro dia	*well if not we'll meet another day*
	340	Ana: ciao	*bye*
	341	Shoji: disfruta cenar.	*enjoy to dinner*
	342	Shoji: Hasta luego.	*see you later*
	343	Shoji: Aloha.	*aloha*

Interaction #3. Week 4. Mary=Language learner, Juan=L1 Spanish speaker

	116	Juan (9:16:43 AM): aidos mary	*good bye (*adios*) mary*
→	117	Juan (9:16:50 AM): y gracias	*and thank you*
	118	Mary (9:16:55 AM): de nada	*your welcome*
	119	Juan (9:16:59 AM): --- y aloha	*--and aloha*

7.4 Terminal components

It was interesting to find in the data a variety of terminal components employed by the L2 learners to finish the conversation (*chau, adios, hasta mañana, nos vemos*). This finding is in line with Valeiras Viso's (2002) data who also found a large variety of endings by Spanish speakers (larger than by American speakers) and suggests students' pragmalinguistic development towards the target norm.

A very contextualized terminal component (adopted very early in the interactions) used by both L2 students and expert speakers was "*aloha*". In addition, in the interactions of one student (L1 Japanese, L3 Spanish) "*namaste*" was used frequently by both, the student and his Spanish partner. Students also employed a variety of forms that in previous research have been attributed to older populations such as "*hasta mañana*" (Ferrer and Sánchez Lanza 2002).

This may be due to the influence of textbooks and lack of interaction that these L2 learners have with younger expert speakers of the L2, which highlights the importance of connecting students with speakers of their own age in the L2 classroom for the acquisition of age appropriate pragmalinguistics. Differently from Gonzales (2013), the data in this study shows that the L2 students did often produced the last closing statement of the interaction.

8 Discussion

This study does not intend to answer the question of 'why' learners' interaction changed but rather 'how do L2 learner's closings change when interacting with an expert speaker in a telecollaborative online environment'. The learners in this study were taking part in a regular face-to-face class and, as expected, their language ability improved as a result. What the study shows is that these students, already in their fifth semester of language classes, were not producing target-like closings when they started the telecollaborative project. It was during the online interaction that their closing sequences developed without any teaching or practice of closings in class. We cannot claim any causality and results cannot be generalized from this small group of students, but the data suggests that through the six-week engagement in the telecollaborative task, participants were able to develop their competence to produce closing sequences that approximated those of expert speakers. They started to initiate the closing sequences themselves, their closing sequences became longer and more elaborated, and they used a variety of terminal components. It was during these collaborative dialogues that learning happened. The data also revealed that students oriented to this activity as a language learning activity (rather than a regular conversation) by including thanking sequences in their closings.

In addition, the study shows how the analysis of longitudinal online interaction using CA can allow for the investigation of the L2 development of interactional practices. These results add to the existing literature on the organization of different communicative contexts, including those mediated by technologies, providing a view of how telecollaborative tasks can impact our communicative practices.

As always, further research can clarify these results and explain whether the task itself had any effect on the results (by employing different types of task in the design of the study), whether it was the interaction with native speakers that triggered the development of the learners' closing sequences (by comparing the results with the same task but conducted among learners only), and/or if the technology and its affordances played a role (by comparing these results with a face-to-face group engaged in the same task). All and all, the task used in this study promoted telecollaborative engagement between language learners and expert speakers of their L2. It helped them improve their closing sequences and therefore their interactional competence. The activity helped them clarify sociopragmatic norms of closing sequences in Spanish and increase their pragmalinguistic repertoires, while providing them with a chance to meet and interact with other language learners like themselves.

References

Abe, Makoto, and Carsten Roever. (2020). "Task Closings in L2 Text-Chat Interactions: A Study of L2 Interactional Competence." Edited by Julie M. Sykes and Marta González-Lloret. *CALICO Journal*. Special Issue on Exploring the Interface of Interlanguage (L2) Pragmatics and Digital Spaces.

Alcón-Soler, Eva. 2013. "Pragmatic Variation in British and International English Language Users' Email Communication: A Focus on Requests." *RESLA* 26: 25–44.

Belz, Julie A., and Celeste Kinginger. 2003. "Discourse Options and the Development of Pragmatic Competence by Classroom Learners of German: The Case of Address Forms." *Language Learning* 53 (4): 591.

Blattner, Geraldine, and Melisa Fiori. 2011. "Virtual Social Network Communities: An Investigation of Language Learners' Development of Sociopragmatic Awareness and Multiliteracy Skills." *CALICO Journal* 29 (1): 24–43.

Blyth, Carl S. 2012. "Pragmatics of Chat." In *The Encyclopedia of Applied Linguistics*, edited by Carol A. Chapelle. Oxford, UK: Blackwell Publishing Ltd. http://doi.wiley.com/10.1002/9781405198431.wbeal0940.

Bou-Franch, Patricia. 2011. "Openings and Closings in Spanish Email Conversations." *Journal of Pragmatics* 43 (6): 1772–85. https://doi.org/10.1016/j.pragma.2010.11.002.

Bou-Franch, Patricia, Nuria Lorenzo-Dus, and Pilar Garcés-Conejos Blitvich. 2012. "Social Interaction in YouTube Text-Based Polylogues: A Study of Coherence." *Journal of Computer-Mediated Communication* 17 (4): 501–21. https://doi.org/10.1111/j.1083-6101.2012.01579.x.

Button, Graham. 1987. "Moving out of Closings." In *Talk and Social Organisation*, edited by Graham Button and John R. E. Lee, 101–51. Intercommunication 1. Clevedon: Multilingual Matters.

Canto, Silvia, Rick de Graff, and Kristi Jauregui. 2014. "Collaborative Tasks for Negotiation of Intercultural Meaning in Virtual Worlds and Video-Web Communication." In *Technology-Mediated TBLT: Researching Technology and Tasks*, edited by Marta González-Lloret and Lourdes Ortega, 183–212. Task-Based Language Teaching 6. Amsterdam; Philadelphia: John Benjamins.

Chun, Dorothy M. 2011. "Developing Intercultural Communicative Competence through Online Exchanges." *CALICO Journal* 28 (2): 392–419.

Chun, Dorothy M. 1994. "Using computer networking to facilitate the acquisition of interactive competence". *System* 22: 17–31.

Clark, Herbert H, and Wade J. French. 2010. "Telephone Goodbyes." *Language in Society* 10 (1): 1–19.
Codina-Espurz, Victoria, and Patricia Salazar-Campillo. 2019. "Openings and Closing in Emails by CLIL Students: A Pedagogical Proposal." *English Language Teaching* 12 (2): 57. https://doi.org/10.5539/elt.v12n2p57.
Cunningham, Joseph. 2016. "Request Modification in Synchronous Computer-Mediated Communication: The Role of Focused Instruction." *The Modern Language Journal* 100 (2): 484–507. https://doi.org/10.1111/modl.12332.
Cunningham, Joseph. 2017. "Second Language Pragmatic Appropriateness in Telecollaboration: The Influence of Discourse Management and Grammaticality." *System* 64: 46–57. https://doi.org/10.1016/j.system.2016.12.006.
Dooly, Melinda Ann Dooly, and Robert O'Dowd, eds. 2012. *Researching Online Foreign Language Interaction and Exchange: Theories, Methods and Challenges*. Telecollaboration in Education 3. Bern; New York: Peter Lang.
Elola, Idoia, and Ana Oskoz. 2008. "Blogging: Fostering Intercultural Competence Development in Foreign Language and Study Abroad Contexts." *Foreign Language Annals* 41 (3): 454–77. https://doi.org/10.1111/j.1944-9720.2008.tb03307.x.
Félix-Brasdefer, J. Cesar. 2012. "Email Openings and Closings: Pragmalinguistic and Gender Variation in Learner-Instructor Cyber Consultations." *Utrecht Studies in Language & Communication*. 24: 223–48.
Ferrer, María Cristina, and Carmen Sánchez Lanza. 2002. *Los Actos de Habla*. Rosario: UNR Editora.
Firth, Raymond. 2007. "Verbal and Bodily Rituals of Greeting and Parting." In *The Interpretation of Ritual: Essays in Honour of A. I. Richards*, edited by Jean S. La Fontaine and Audrey I. Richards, Reprinted, transferred to digital print, 1–38. Religion, Rites and Ceremonies, in 5 volumes; 5. London: Routledge.
Fitch, Kristine. 1990. "A Ritual for Attempting Leave-Taking in Colombia." *Research on Language& Social Interaction* 24: 209–24. https://doi.org/10.1080/08351819009389339.
Garcia, Mary Ellen. 1981. "Preparing to Leave: Interaction at a Mexican-American Family Gathering." In *Latino Language and Communicative Behavior*, edited by Richard P. Duran, 195–215. Norwood, NJ: Ablex.
Giles, David, Wyke Stommel, Trena Paulus, Jessica Lester, and Darren Reed. 2015. "Microanalysis Of Online Data: The Methodological Development of 'Digital CA.'" *Discourse, Context & Media* 7: 45–51. https://doi.org/10.1016/j.dcm.2014.12.002.
Goffman, Erving. 1971. *Relations in Public: Microstudies of the Public Order*. New York: Harper & Row.
Golato, Andrea, and Carmen Taleghani-Nikazm. 2006. "Negotiation of Face in Chats." *Multilingua* 25: 293–322.
Gonzales, Adrienne. 2013. "Development of Politeness Strategies in Participatory Online Environments: A Case Study." In *Language Learning & Language Teaching*, edited by Naoko Taguchi and Julie M. Sykes, 36:101–20. Amsterdam: John Benjamins. https://doi.org/10.1075/lllt.36.06gon.
González-Lloret, Marta. 2008. "Computer-Mediated Learning of L2 Pragmatics." In *Investigating Pragmatics in Foreign Language Learning, Teaching and Testing*, edited by Eva Alcón Soler and Alicia Martinez-Flor, 114–32. Clevedon, UK: Multilingual Matters.

González-Lloret, Marta. 2009. "CA for Computer-Mediated Interaction in the Spanish L2 Classroom." In *Talk-in-Interaction: Multilingual Perspectives*, edited by Hanhn Nguyen and Gabrielle Kasper, 281–316. Honolulu, HI: NFLRC and University of Hawai'i Press.
González-Lloret, Marta. 2011. "Conversation Analysis of Computer-Mediated Communication." *CALICO Journal* 28 (2): 308–25.
González-Lloret, Marta. 2015. "Conversation Analysis in Computer-Assisted Language Learning." *CALICO Journal* 32 (3): 569–94. https://doi.org/10.1558/cj.v32i3.27568.
González-Lloret, Marta. 2016. "The Construction of Emotion in Multilingual Computer-Mediated Interaction." In *Emotion in Multilingual Interaction*, edited by Matthew T. Prior and Gabriele Kasper, 291–313. Pragmatics & Beyond New Series 266. Amsterdam; Philadelphia: John Benjamins. DOI:10.1075/pbns.266.12gon.
González-Lloret, Marta. 2019a. "Pragmatics in Technology-Mediated Contexts." In *Learning Second Language Pragmatics beyond Traditional Contexts.*, edited by Ariadna Sánchez-Hernández and Ana Herraiz-Martínez, 15–45. S.l.: Peter Lang.
González-Lloret, Marta. 2019b. "Task-Based Language Teaching and L2 Pragmatics." In *Routledge Handbook of SLA and Pragmatics*, edited by Naoko Taguchi, 338–52. London: Routledge.
González-Lloret, Marta, and Lourdes Ortega. 2018. "Pragmatics, Tasks, and Technology: A Synergy." In *Task-Based Approaches to Teaching and Assessing Pragmatics*, edited by Naoko Taguchi and YouJin Kim, 191–214. Task-Based Language Teaching. John Benjamins.
Guth, Sarah, and Francesca Helm, eds. 2010. *Telecollaboration 2.0: Language, Literacies and Intercultural Learning in the 21st Century*. Telecollaboration in Education, v. 1. Bern; New York: Peter Lang.
Hartford, Beverly S., and Kathleen Bardovi-Harlig. 1992. "Experimental and Observational Data in the Study of Interlanguage Pragmatics." *Pragmatics and Language Learning* 3: 33–52. Available at https://files.eric.ed.gov/fulltext/ED395520.pdf
Herring, Susan. 1999. "Interactional Coherence in CMC." *Journal of Computer-Mediated Communication* 4 (4). http://jcmc.indiana.edu/vol4/issue4/herring.html.
Jenks, Christopher. 2009. "Getting Acquainted in Skypecasts: Aspects of Social Organization in Online Chat Rooms." *International Journal of Applied Linguistics* 19 (1): 26–46. https://doi.org/10.1111/j.1473-4192.2009.00211.x.
Jenks, Christopher, and Adam Brandt. 2013. "Managing Mutual Orientation in the Absence of Physical Copresence: Multiparty Voice-Based Chat Room Interaction." *Discourse Processes* 50 (4): 227–48. https://doi.org/10.1080/0163853X.2013.777561.
Jenks, Christopher, and Alan Firth. 2013. "Interaction in Synchronous Voice-Based Computer-Mediated Communication." In *Pragmatics of Computer-Mediated Communication*, edited by Susan C. Herring, Dieter Stein, Tuija Virtanen, and Wolfram Bublitz, 209–34. Handbooks of Pragmatics, ed. Wolfram Bublitz; Vol. 9. Berlin: de Gruyter Mouton.
Kakegawa, Tomomi. 2009. "Development of the Use of Japanese Sentence-Final Particles through Email Correspondence." In *Pragmatic Competence*, edited by Naoko Taguchi, 301–34. Mouton Series in Pragmatics 5. Berlin; New York: Mouton de Gruyter.
Kasper, Gabriele, and Johannes Wagner. 2014. "Conversation Analysis in Applied Linguistics." *Annual Review of Applied Linguistics* 34 (March): 171–212. https://doi.org/10.1017/S0267190514000014.

Kim, Eun Young Ariel, and Lucien Brown. 2014. "Negotiating Pragmatic Competence in Computer Mediated Communication: The Case of Korean Address Terms." *CALICO Journal* 31 (3): 264–84. https://doi.org/10.11139/cj.31.3.264-284.

Kuriscak, Lisa M., and Christopher Luke. 2009. "Language Learner Attitudes toward Virtual Worlds: An Investigation of Second Life." In *The next Generation: Social Networking and Online Collaboration in Foreign Language Learning*, edited by Lara Lomicka and Gillian Lord, 173–98. CALICO Monograph. Series. San Marcos, Tex: Computer Assisted Language Instruction Consortium (CALICO).

Lazaraton, Anne. 2014. "Aaaaack! The Active Voice Was Used! Language Play, Technology, and Repair in the Daily Kos Weblog." *Journal of Pragmatics* 64: 102–16. https://doi.org/10.1016/j.pragma.2014.02.002.

Li, Qiong, Naoko Taguchi, and Xiaofei Tang. 2019. "Pragmatic Development via CMC-Based Data-Driven Instruction: Chinese Sentence Final Particles." In *Learning Second Language Pragmatics beyond Traditional Contexts.*, edited by Ariadna Sánchez-Hernández and Ana Herraiz-Martínez, 256: 47–84. Studies in Language and Communication. Bern: Peter Lang.

Locher, Miriam. 2014. "Electronic Discourse." In *Pragmatics of Discourse*, edited by Klaus P. Schneider and Anne Barron, 555–81. Handbooks of Pragmatics, volume 3. Boston: De Gruyter Mouton.

Mancera Rueda, Ana. 2015. "Los Estudios Sobre (Des)Cortesía y Actividades de Imagen En Las Redes Sociales: Notas Para Un Estado de La Cuestión." *Textos en Proceso* 1 (1): 50–70. https://doi.org/10.17710/tep.2015.1.1.3man.

Markee, Numa. 2008. "Toward a Learning Behavior Tracking Methodology for CA-for-SLA." *Applied Linguistics* 29 (3): 404–27.

Markman, Kris. 2005. "To Send or Not to Send: Turn Construction in Computer-Mediated Chat." *Texas Linguistic Forum* 48: 115–24.

Markman, Kris. 2009. "'So What Shall We Talk About': Openings and Closings in Chat-Based Virtual Meetings." *Journal of Business Communication* 46 (1): 150–70. https://doi.org/10.1177/0021943608325751.

Márquez Reiter, Rosina. 2011. *Mediated Business Interactions: Intercultural Communication between Speakers of Spanish*. Edinburgh: Edinburgh University Press.

Márquez Reiter, Rosina, and María Elena Placencia. 2004. "Displaying Closeness and Respectful Distance in Montevidean and Quiteño Service Encounters." In *Current Trends in the Pragmatics of Spanish*, edited by R. Márquez Reiter and Maria Elena Placencia, 121–55. Amsterdam; Philadelphia: John Benjamins.

Meredith, Joanne. 2017. "Analaysing Technological Affordances of Online Interactions Using Conversation Analysis ." *Journal of Pragmatics* 115 (July): 42–55. https://doi.org/10.1016/j.pragma.2017.03.001.

Nishimura, Yukiko. 2008. "Japanese BBS Websites as Online Communities: (Im)Politeness Perspectives." *Language@Internet* 5: article 3.

O'Dowd, Robert. 2014. "Intercultural Communicative Competence through Telecollaboration." In *The Routledge Handbook of Language and Intercultural Communication*, edited by Jane Jackson, Paperback ed., 340–56. Routledge Handbooks. London: Routledge.

Pekarek Doehler, Simona, and Evelyne Pochon-Berger. 2015. "The Development of L2 Interactional Competence: Evidence from Turn-Taking Organization, Sequence Organization, Repair Organization and Preference Organization." In *Usage-Based Perspectives on Second Language Learning*, edited by Teresa Cadierno and Søren Wind

Eskildsen. Berlin, München, Boston: DE GRUYTER. http://www.degruyter.com/view/books/9783110378528/9783110378528-012/9783110378528-012.xml.

Placencia, Maria Elena. 1997. "Opening up Closings – the Ecuadorian Way." *An Interdisciplinary Journal for the Study of Discourse* 17 (1): 53–81.

Pojanapunya, Punjaporn, and Kandaporn Jaroenkitboworn. 2011. "How to Say 'Good-Bye' in Second Life." *Journal of Pragmatics* 43 (14): 3591–3602. https://doi.org/10.1016/j.pragma.2011.08.010.

Salazar-Campillo, Patricia. 2018. "Student-Initiated Email Communication: An Analysis of Openings and Closings by Spanish EFL Learners." *Sintagma: Revista de Lingüística* 30: 81–93. https://doi.org/10.21001/sintagma.2018.30.05.

Salazar-Campillo, Patricia, and Victoria Codina-Espurz. 2018. "Politeness in First and Follow-up Emails to Faculty: Openings and Closings." In *Learning Second Language Pragmatics beyond Traditional Contexts*, edited by Ariadna Sánchez-Hernández and Ana Herraiz-Martínez, 85–106. Peter Lang AG. https://doi.org/10.3726/b14949.

Schegloff, Emanuel, and Harvey Sacks. 1973. "Opening up Closings." *Semiotica* 8 (4): 289–327.

Schegloff, Emanuel, Irene Ann Koshik, Sally Jacoby, and David Olsher. 2002. "Conversation Analysis and Applied Linguistics." *Annual Review of Applied Linguistics* 22: 3–31.

Schönfeldt, Juliane, and Andrea Golato. 2003. "Repair in Chats: A Conversation Analytic Approach." *Research on Language and Social Interaction* 36 (3): 241–84.

Slavin, Robert E. 1996. "Research on Cooperative Learning and Achievement: What We Know, What We Need to Know." *Contemporary Educational Psychology* 21 (1): 43–69. https://doi.org/10.1006/ceps.1996.0004.

Spagnolli, Anna. 2012. "Pragmatics of Short Message Service." In *The Encyclopedia of Applied Linguistics*, edited by Carol A. Chapelle. Oxford, UK: Blackwell Publishing Ltd. http://doi.wiley.com/10.1002/9781405198431.wbeal0943.

Spencer-Oatey, Helen. 2005. "Rapport Management Theory and Culture." *Intercultural Pragmatics* 2 (3): 335–46. https://doi.org/10.1515/iprg.2005.2.3.335.

Stommel, Wyke. 2008. "Conversation Analysis and Community of Practice as Approaches to Studying Online Community." *Language@Internet* 5 [Available at http://www.languageatinternet.de/articles/2008/1537].http://www.languageatinternet.org/articles/2008/1537.

Storch, Neomy. 2013. *Collaborative Writing in L2 Classrooms*. Multilingual Matters.

Stroinska, Magda, and Vikki Cecchetto. 2013. "Facework in Intercultural E-Mail Communication in the Academic Environment." In *Language and Intercultural Communication in the New Era.*, edited by Farzad Sharifian and Maryam Jamarani, 160–80. [Place of publication not identified]: Routledge.

Swain, Merrill, and Yuko Watanabe. 2013. "Languaging: Collaborative Dialogue as a Source of Second Language Learning." In *The Encyclopedia of Applied Linguistics*, edited by Carol A. Chapelle. Oxford, UK: Blackwell Publishing Ltd. https://doi.org/10.1002/9781405198431.wbeal0664.

Taguchi, Naoko, and YouJin Kim, eds. 2018. *Task-Based Approaches to Teaching and Assessing Pragmatics*. Task-Based Language Teaching. John Benjamins.

Tercedor Cabrero, Marta. 2013. "Developing Interactional Competence through Video-Based Computer-Mediated Conversations: Beginning Learners of Spanish." PhD dissertation, University of Iowa. http://ir.uiowa.edu/etd/4918/.

Tsai, Mei-Hsing, and Celeste Kinginger. 2014. "Giving and Receiving Advice in Computer-Mediated Peer Response Activities." *CALICO Journal* 32 (1): 82–112.
Tudini, Vicenza. 2010. *Online Second Language Acquisition. Conversation Analysis of Online Chat*. London, New York: Continuum.
Tudini, Vincenza. 2013. "Form-Focused Social Repertoires in an Online Language Learning Partnership." *Journal of Pragmatics* 50 (1): 187–202. https://doi.org/10.1016/j.pragma.2012.12.005.
Valeiras Viso, Jesús. 2002. "'Deja Tu Mensaje Después de La Señal': Despedidas y Otros Elementos de La Sección de Cierre en Mensajes Dejados en Contestadores Automáticos en Madrid y Londres." In *Actos de Habla y Cortesía en Español*, edited by Maria Elena Placencia and Diana Bravo, 209–32. Munich: LINCOM Europa.
Vandergriff, Ilona. 2013. "Emotive Communication Online: A Contextual Analysis of Computer-Mediated Communication (CMC) Cues." *Journal of Pragmatics* 51: 1–12. https://doi.org/10.1016/j.pragma.2013.02.008.
Vandergriff, Ilona. 2014. "A Pragmatic Investigation of Emoticon Use in Nonnative /Native Speaker Text Chat." *Language@Internet* 11: Article 4.
Vinagre, M. 2010. "Intercultural Learning in Asynchronous Telecollaborative Exchanges: A Case Study." *The Eurocall Review* 17: Availableat: http://www.eurocall-languages.org/uploaded/EUROCALL_Review/review17.pdf.
West, J. Frederick. 1990. "Educational Collaboration in the Restructuring of Schools." *Journal of Educational and Psychological Consultation* 1 (1): 23–40. https://doi.org/10.1207/s1532768xjepc0101_2.
Yus, Francisco. 2001. *Ciberpragmática. El Uso Del Lenguaje En Internet*. Barcelona, Spain: Ariel.
Yus, Francisco. 2014. "El Discurso de Las Identidades En Línea: El Caso de Facebook." *Discurso y Sociedad* 8 (3): 398–426.

Mimi Li
Participation and interaction in wiki-based collaborative writing: An Activity Theory perspective

1 Introduction

Informed by sociocultural theory, collaborative writing, as an instructional activity encouraging interaction throughout the writing process, has been increasingly implemented in second language (L2) classes. It provides valuable opportunities for students to pool language resources collectively and co-construct knowledge and writing through scaffolded interactions (Donato 1994). Ede and Lunsford (1990) initially defined collaborative writing as the writing involving multiple writers co-producing written texts, so-called a *singular text/plural authors* approach. Storch (2013) later clarified that collaborative writing refers to a writing activity in which students interact, negotiate meaning, and make joint decisions throughout the writing process and produce a single text with shared responsibility and co-ownership. Collaborative writing has supported L2 learning and writing development in multiple aspects, including enhanced audience awareness (Storch 2012), increased attention to language forms and discourse (Swain and Lapkin 1998) and opportunities to apply newly-learned knowledge (Hirvela 1999).

With the development of Web 2.0 tools that afford participation and collaboration at an unprecedented level, computer-mediated collaborative writing has captured increasing attention in L2 contexts. Computer-mediated collaborative writing provides more affordances for learning due to time/space independence, wider interaction, and deeper level of reflection. The wiki, a collaborative web site that allows users to freely create and edit the contents of web pages, has gained wide acclaim in English as a second language (ESL)/English for Academic Purposes (EAP) settings. The wiki has four distinctive functions that assist writing and collaboration: "Edit" enables users to freely write and revise the wiki page in terms of texts, images, or hyperlinks; wiki "Discussion" allows users to communicate and negotiate writing tasks via asynchronous messaging; "Comment" allows users to provide comments or raise questions regarding specific texts via pop-up boxes; "History" reveals all the changes that the wiki page has gone through with the color coding of additions and deletions. A few researchers (e.g., Kessler and Bikowski 2010; Li and Kim 2016) have examined peer interactions

---

Mimi Li, Texas A&M University-Commerce

https://doi.org/10.1515/9781501511318-010

during task-negotiation and text-construction using wikis, but no research explores the complex nature of students' participation in collaborative wiki writing, viewed as a collective, artifact-mediated and object-oriented activity system (Engeström 1987). That is, research that adopts activity theory as a heuristic to study collaborative writing activities is very much needed. This book chapter, therefore, reports on a study that utilizes Engeström's Activity Theory as an evolutionary lens to analyze peer interactions and explicate essential interconnected components (including tools, rules, community, division of labor, objects, and outcome) within a wiki group writing activity. Also, informed by scholarship maintaining that contradictions may arise with regard to an activity system (Engeström 1987) and that activities are always in the process of working through contradictions (Kuutti 1996), this chapter discusses the contradictions that occur among the interconnected components of the activity system.

Two research questions guide this inquiry: 1) How do the components of collaborative wiki writing activity afford and/or constrain ESL students' participation and learning? and 2) What contradictions occur among the components of the activity system of wiki-based collaborative writing?

2 Activity theory

This study is theoretically informed by sociocultural theory, particularly activity theory. According to Vygotsky (1978), human cognitive development is inherently a socially situated activity. Mediation is a mechanism through which external sociocultural activities are transformed into internal mental functioning (Vygotsky 1978). Language learning is a mediated process that involves mediation by artifacts, by self, and by others in social interactions (Lantolf 2000; Vygotsky 1978). In group or pair work, peers provide mutual scaffolding, an assisting process that enables an individual to "solve a problem, carry out a task, or achieve a goal which would be beyond his [or her] unassisted efforts" (Wood, Bruner, and Ross 1976, 90). Language, also as a critical source of mediation, assists learners to co-construct language and solve problems through interaction in collaborative tasks (Swain 2000). Engeström (1987, 1999) later proposed the Activity System model (Figure 1) and further developed the conceptualization of mediation.

Going beyond Vygotskian concerns with the individuals, their goals, and mediation by tools, Engeström (1987, 1999) explained how individual actions and goals are interconnected with other factors within the sociocultural context. He identified the activity system as a collective unit composed of tools, subject, object, outcome, community, division of labor, and rules. This framework of activity

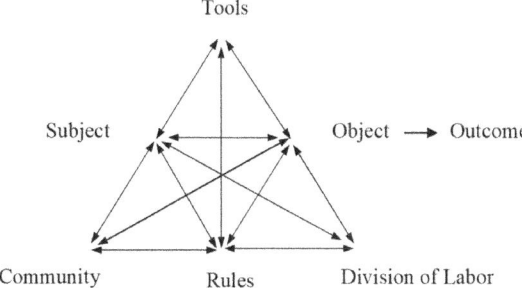

Figure 1: Activity System Model (Engeström 1987, 1999).

theory provides a broad theoretical basis for studying different kinds of human practices, specifically the wiki-based collaborative writing in this case. The upper axis helps analyze how mediating artifacts regulate the construction of the activity system to achieve an object and ultimately accomplish an outcome. The lower axis reflects the "deep social structure of the activity" (Engeström 2008, 90) by portraying the division of labor, the community, and the rules. Within the "collective, artefact-mediated and object-oriented activity system" (Engeström 2001, 136), all components constantly interact with one another, which may lead to the process of working through contradictions. That is, the subjects may face emerging contradictions in varied ways while pursuing the outcome. These contradictions can force individuals to re-conceptualize the object and motive of the activity, which creates expansive transformation within the activity system (Engeström 2001). The contradictions are therefore perceived as a "driving force of change and development" rather than conflicts (Engeström 2001, 135).

3 Method

This study came from a larger wiki writing project (Li 2014) that explored and interpreted peer interactions in wiki-based small group writing via a multiple-case study approach. The project was conducted in an EAP class in the English Language Institute at a southeastern public university in the USA. The class aimed to develop ESL students' academic English skills through academic writing and presentation tasks. In a team project, students formed small groups of three on their own, and slight adjustments were then made in light of mixed ESL proficiency levels and mixed L1/cultural backgrounds (there were still some small groups comprised of only Chinese students due to the large enrollment of this population). The students in small groups jointly worked on two collaborative wiki writing tasks (i.e., research proposal and annotated bibliography) addressing the broad topic of globalization (displayed in Figure 2). The students were required to communicate in the L2 (English) on the wiki site, as previous literature suggests that languaging in the L2 during collaborative tasks affords L2 learning (Storch 2013; Swain 2000). In addition, private permission for each group was set, so students focused on their own group writing and were not able to see other groups' writing throughout the project.

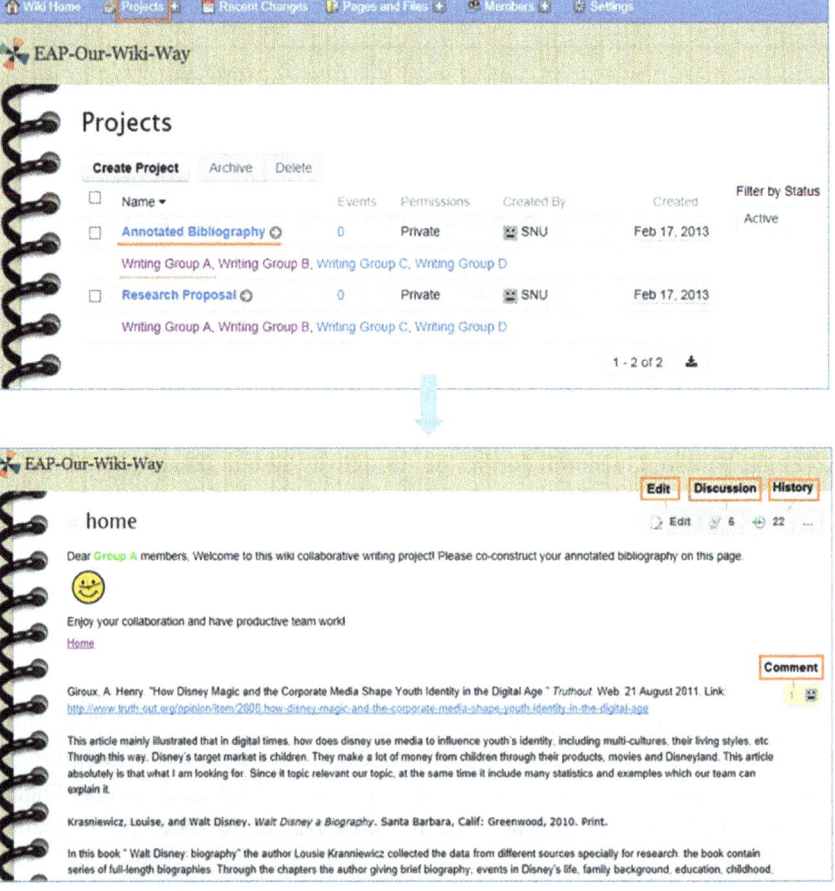

Figure 2: Screenshots of the Wikispaces Site.

The larger wiki project explored how four small groups of ESL students negotiated writing tasks and co-constructed wiki writing, and examined what factors mediated dynamic peer interactions and how the interactions influenced wiki writing products and connected with students' reflections on collaborative wiki writing. Triangulated data sources included archived wiki records (involving wiki writing processes and products), pre-task and post-task questionnaires, post-task and follow-up interviews, students' reflection papers, and instructors' assessment of students' wiki group writing. The study reported in this chapter focused on two small groups from the larger project. By reanalyzing the relevant data of interviews and reflection papers, the present study innovatively examined interconnected components regarding the two small groups' interactions, drawing on the framework of activity theory (Engeström 1987, 1999).

3.1 Participant profile and patterns of interaction

The two groups (i.e., Group A and Group B in this study) were selected because their group members shared insights on the mediating factors that had both afforded and constrained collaborative writing activities in a post-task interview. The two cases also provide a thick description (Lincoln and Guba 1985) and enhance validity of my interpretations through comparing findings across cases (Yin 2009). Table 1 displays the participant profile, collected from a pre-task questionnaire survey in the larger project.

Table 1: Participant Profile.

	Pseudo Name	Gender	Nationality	Study Area	English Proficiency	Attitude to teamwork
Group A	Xia	F	China	TESOL	Intermediate-high	Positive
	Hai	M	China	Civil engineering	Intermediate	Positive
	Ali	M	Iraq	Electronic engineering	Intermediate	Very positive
Group B	Mei	F	China	Finance	Intermediate	Neutral
	Lan	F	China	Finance	Intermediate	Positive
	Ju	F	China	Finance	Intermediate	Positive

Group A consisted of three members: two Chinese students and one Iraqi student, and Group B was composed of three Chinese students. After examining the two indexes of "equality" and "mutuality" (Kos, this volume; Storch 2002) through three focused aspects, i.e., language functions, writing change functions, and scaffolding strategies, it was concluded that the two groups demonstrated distinctive patterns of interaction in wiki-based collaborative writing: Expert/novice for Group A (mid-low equality, high mutuality) and Cooperating-in-parallel (high equality, low mutuality) for Group B (See Li 2014, Li and Zhu 2017 for details). Group A members Xia and Hai shared the role of "expert," leading the writing direction together, and encouraging the participation of Ali, the "novice". Ali acknowledged group partners' "expert" role and was responsive to their guiding behaviors. In contrast, members of Group B equally divided the workload into three parts and each conducted the assigned sub-tasks in parallel; no sufficient evidence showed group members' engagement with one another's contributions.

3.2 Data analysis

In order to address the first research question of the study, the analysis of interconnected components of the wiki writing activity regarding the two selected small groups was conducted. Interviews (see Appendix A for interview questions) and reflection papers (See Appendix B for writing prompts) in relation to Group A and Group B constituted the primary data sources. Using Engeström's Activity System (1987, 1999) as the methodological framework, the researcher coded the data in terms of the themes that emerged from the study regarding mediating components within the activity system, i.e., tools, object, rules, community, and division of labor. The operational definitions of these components are displayed in Table 2.

Students' comments obtained from the interviews were coded with key words that could represent the gist of their response. After checking and rechecking the codes, the researcher derived themes by merging the codes, which were afterwards connected to the constructs of the mediating components. For instance, in terms of the construct of tool, the students reported wiki benefits in the post-task interview. After reading and rereading the interview transcripts, the researcher identified codes such as "convenience", "efficiency" and "usefulness", based on which the theme of affordance was derived. To take another example, regarding the aim of wiki writing revealed from the post-task interviews, the participants used words/ phrases such as "collaboration", "work together" and "do homework". In vivo coding was used as the lexicons captured the gist of the students' comments. Then the relationship among the coded terms was analyzed, and two contrasting themes

Table 2: Operational definitions of the components of the collaborative wiki writing system.

Component	Operational Definition
Tools	All the artifacts that mediate small groups' task negotiation and writing participation
Object	Wiki-based collaborative writing as the overall object, plus each member's specific goals
Rules	Regulations and conventions regarding writing and communication required by the instructor
Division of labor	How group members take on specific workload and roles to achieve the goal of collaborative wiki writing
Community	Group of people involved in the construction of the collaborative wiki writing system

were derived: *collaboration-oriented goals* and *participation-oriented goals*. Since these codes and themes reflected what these students hoped to accomplish, they were labelled "Object," as a component of the activity system. To further interpret the affordances or constraints of the mediating components for collaboration and learning, the researcher drew on the findings of joint writing processes (i.e., language functions and writing change functions) and writing products (i.e., overall rhetorical structure, coherence, and accuracy of papers), which were reported in Li and Zhu (2017). Regarding writing processes, examining types and frequency counts of language functions and writing change functions that each group member performed helped evaluate the "equality" of peer interaction, and examining *initiating* vs. *responding* language functions and *self* vs. *other* writing change functions helped evaluate the "mutuality". Regarding writing products, rhetorical elements, coherence breakdowns, and error distributions were specifically analyzed (please refer to Li and Zhu 2017 for details).

In order to address the second research question, the contradictions within the collaborative wiki writing system, based on Engeström's (1987) discussion of multilevel contradictions, were examined. The students' interview transcripts and written reflections were repeatedly read and coded for recurrence of emergent themes in terms of internal contradictions that occurred among multiple components in relation to the two cases. A grounded approach (Strauss and Corbin 1998) was then adopted to analyze the triangulated data in an iterative and holistic manner and comparisons of the data between the two cases were established until three areas of contradictions were derived: division of labor-object, tool-object, and rules-tool-object.

4 Results

4.1 Interconnected components in the collaborative wiki writing system

Multiple components of collaborative wiki writing activity were found to have afforded and/or constrained these ESL students' participation and learning, including mediating tools, object, division of labor, rules, and community.

4.1.1 Mediating tools

Table 3 presents an overall picture of students' perceptions on the main mediating tool-wiki in this collaborative writing project.

Table 3: Perceived affordances and constraints of the wiki.

	Group A (N: 3)	Group B (N: 3)
Affordance	*Xia*: Convenience & Efficiency *Ali*: Asynchronous communication (flexible time and location); Wiki transparency stimulating participation *Hai & Xia*: Comments from both peers and the instructor	*Mei & Lan*: Usefulness of Wiki *Ju*: Convenience; easy communication compared with email exchange
Constraint	*Xia*: Format restriction	*Lan*: Lack of immediate response → switch to synchronous communication tool WeChat *Mei*: Format restriction → Use Word doc

The members of Group A acknowledged the affordances of the wiki for collaborative writing and learning. All the members commented on the convenience of wikis in the interviews (please note that all the quotes below were transcribed verbatim from the student's comments). Xia had the following positive comments:

> Wikis are convenient tools for collaboration. The traditional way is time-consuming. We have to save time and be efficient. [. . .]We do not have to make a schedule when we will be there. When we have ideas, we posted on the wiki, and some other people have idea and time, they come to, we can see. (3/8/2013)

Ali also commented that "anytime anywhere we can work on the wiki, even if some of members cannot be on wiki in the same time"(3/8/2013). Both Xia and Hai particularly acknowledged the usefulness of wiki "Comment". As Hai remarked, "I like the "Comment" function. There is some problem with my teammate's work, I can leave comments. They can see. I can also receive the comments from the instructor [. . .] not only the connection between me and my group partners, but connection with our instructor" (Interview, 3/7/2013). This viewpoint was coincidently shared by Xia, who stated that "Comment is a good module. The instructor can leave comment: which part to revise, which part to change" (Interview, 3/8/2013). Ali, on the other hand, communicated the usefulness of the wiki "Discussion" in the interview (3/8/2013): "If I was not able to participate in time, I could go through what they discussed and I was able to join the conversation via "discussion" module even not at the same time."

Moreover, Ali pointed out that the wiki enabled the group members to have more equal participation. Unlike Warschauer's (1997) argument that wikis provided participants with more time for thinking and expressing their ideas, thus leading to more equal participation, Ali shared his distinct perspective.

> In wikis, I have the opportunity/chance to review all my knowledge, my ability, my participation compared with other group members. [. . .] See my weak points. Revise and my participation [. . .] Wiki is transparent. If some member did not do that much, you can see his level of participation in the wiki. You can see the information is valuable or not valuable, you can see your skills and others' skills. (Post-task interview, Ali, 3/8/2013)

As Ali indicated, Wiki's transparency spurred him on to contribute to the group writing. However, Xia stated a constraint of the wiki in relation to a particular task (i.e., annotated bibliography) in the post-task interview (3/8/2013), "The biggest disadvantage is format. Annotated bibliography we needed a certain MLA format; wiki cannot keep the format."

Members of Group B echoed the affordance of wikis that Group A discussed. Mei stated in the reflection paper (4/5/13) that "Wiki is very useful to discuss with each other. We can communicate with each other frequently. We all share our own opinions on wikis and we enjoy that." Ju addressed the superiority of wikis to emails for collaborative writing. She stated that "It [the wiki] is good, it is very convenient for the team project. Before, we use emails. We cannot collaborate easily. [. . .] It's convenience and we can exchange our work directly through wiki, rather than email back and forth" (Interview, 3/8/13). With regard to the usefulness of wiki modules, Lan commented in the interview (3/8/13) that "wikis record our discussion. Discussion on the wiki can recorded all information we wrote through the communication and that would be the evidences and supports of our team research. [. . .] Comment is also useful."

Despite their acknowledgement of the wiki's convenience, the members of Group B noted that the asynchronous tool wiki may delay peer communication. As Lan said in the interview (3/8/13), "We cannot know each other's opinion immediately. I have to wait for them to answer." To solve this problem, the members switched to a synchronous tool during the wiki writing project. Ju elaborated in the reflection paper (4/5/13) on how they used another communication tool in the wiki project:

> We divided our group task for later jobs, and use cellphone Group Chat App [. . .] When we have ideas and different opinions, we can leave our message on the App, and team members can immediately saw the message and give reaction.

As Xia from Group A did, Mei addressed the technical problem of the MLA formatting. Mei told in the interview (3/8/13), "To avoid the problem of the format, I like to write on Word first, and copy and paste it on the wiki."

4.1.2 Object

Students' wiki writing activities entail multiple goal-oriented actions. The overall object of this wiki writing project is for group members to collaborate on and complete wiki writing tasks. The goals which each student hoped to accomplish, suggested in the interviews, helped the understanding of the personalized object. Table 4 summarizes each member's goal(s) regarding both groups.

Table 4: Goals for Group A and Group B.

Group A (N: 3)	Group B (N: 3)
Collaboration-oriented goals	*Participation-oriented goals*
Xia: Work together; Monitor collaborative task	*Mei*: Do assignments as a team
Hai: Practice writing and collaboration skills	*Ju*: Do homework as a team; practice writing skills
Ali: Collaborate equally	*Lan*: Equally do assignments

For Group A, Xia commented that the purpose of the wiki project for her is to "work together" as the course required. Driven by this goal, she dutifully conducted collaborative writing tasks to meet the instructor's expectation. Xia recalled her duty of being a group leader, "I used emails to give instruction. [. . .] I remind the partners of the schedule and deadlines set by the professor" (Interview, 3/8/13). Hai seemed to be motivated more intrinsically in the wiki project; he stated in the interview, "I like computer. I enjoy learning online" (Interview, 3/7/13). For Hai, the goal of wiki-based collaborative writing tasks is to practice his writing skill, and learn how to collaborate in the online community. Driven by the motive of enhancing writing skills, he invested many efforts in negotiating writing tasks and constructing texts in wikis. Also, to create learning community, Hai was not only highly engaged in wiki writing himself but also provided effective assistance via multiple scaffolding strategies to the "novice" Ali (Li 2014).

Hai's goal "to collaborate" was echoed by Ali. Ali emphasized group members' collaboration and active participation, in his words, "Members can equally collaborate with each other" (Interview, 3/8/2013). The motive to "equally collaborate" with his group partners accounted for Ali's active participation throughout the wiki writing activities. On one hand, Ali accepted scaffolds provided by his group partners and reacted responsibly to their suggestions. On the other hand, as he became more familiarized with the research topic, he participated in the wiki project at an increasing scale. He exclaimed that "I feel more involved in the annotated bibliography. [. . .] I get familiarized with the topic and can do better" (interview, 3/8/2013). Overall, the convergent collaboration-oriented goals, which occurred in Group A, positively mediated the wiki writing process.

In terms of Group B, the members coincidently expressed identical goals and used similar phrases (e.g., "do assignments") to describe their perceived goals in the interviews. Mei stated that the purpose of wiki-based collaborative writing was "to do some assignments as a team" (Interview, 3/8/2013). Similarly, the goal for Ju was "to do the homework as a team, and practice English and writing skills" (Interview, 3/8/2013).Their perspectives were echoed by Lan, who addressed her goal of "equally doing the assignments" (Interview, 3/8/2013). Thus, the overall participation-oriented goal (i.e., completing the tasks) motivated the group members to dutifully participate in the wiki writing project. The motive of equal participation in particular made them divide the workload equally into three parts, and they each completed their respective individual part timely. This group, however, showed a relatively low degree of mutuality of engagement in one another's writing efforts while rather stressing the completion of individual workload.

4.1.3 Division of labor

Division of labor exhibited in Group B seemed to have constrained the students' participation and collaboration in the group wiki writing. As addressed in the earlier text, this group demonstrated a cooperative-in-parallel pattern. The three members equally divided the tasks and had equal participation in text construction. Little evidence showed that the group members were actively engaged with one another's contribution. For example, when they worked on their research proposal, each member performed a few instances of writing change functions, among which three were changes made to one's own texts while only one to other's texts. The group members' limited individual contribution and little engagement of each other's texts led to a low degree of coherence and accuracy in their wiki paper (Li and Zhu 2017).

Different from Group B, Group A did not show a clear-cut division of workload, although each member agreed to be responsible for researching a different part of the research topic in the brainstorming stage. The expert/novice pattern was featured with experts' engaging the novice's writing efforts, reflected in the high ratio of responding /initiating language functions (Li 2014). Interactions between "experts" and "novice" focused on the negotiation of the research topic, which supported the novice's contribution of rhetorical components required of the writing task. Therefore, Group A completed a wiki paper of good quality, particularly in the area of rhetorical structure (Li and Zhu 2017).

4.1.4 Rules

In the interviews and reflection papers, students indicated two rules regarding the group wiki writing tasks that constrained their participation and learning. These rules were the MLA formatting and no L1 allowed. In this study, students learned two new research genres: research proposal and annotated bibliography. The task-related skill required included the grasp of MLA format for the annotated bibliography. However, according to Group A member Xia, it was rather difficult to arrange an accurate MLA format using the wiki. As Xia commented in the post-task interview (3/8/2013), "Annotated bibliography we needed a certain MLA format, wiki cannot keep the format. [. . .] I cannot solve the problem." Members of Group B agreed that the format was one of the big technical problems. Mei told in the interview (3/8/13), "To avoid the problem of the format, I like to write on Word first, and copy and paste it on the wiki." The rule of the MLA format, to a certain extent, constrained students' participation in wiki writing.

In addition, the rule of L1 not allowed impacted the way of group interaction. As discussed earlier, members of Group B resorted to the other technology tool to communicate in L1 about the wiki writing tasks outside the class. According to Lan, the course instructor would not like them to communicate using their L1 Chinese in the wiki, so they ended up adopting another Computer Mediated Communication (CMC) tool, namely WeChat, a popular chatting application tool used among Chinese people, when they wanted to communicate in Chinese.

In this sense, the L2 only rule constrained the wiki participation from the members of Group B.

4.1.5 Community

The last component in the wiki group writing system identified in the study was community, which was believed to afford students' participation and learning. As discussed earlier, Ali worked hard to demonstrate his presence and contribution to the small group community. His writing action was mediated by the community where each individual member's writing contribution is "transparent". Another Group A member Hai bore in mind that the goal was to "collaborate in the online community" (interview, 3/7/13). To create the online community, Hai was actively engaged in wiki writing as well as providing scaffolding to the novice member Ali. Hai also demonstrated a high sense of agency by overseeing the group work to foster online community. Going beyond the small group community, Hai pointed out the importance of the larger class community for the wiki writing project. In addition to interaction occurring within the small group, Hai hoped that the wiki papers from all small groups were accessible to him so that he could view diverse perspectives and make comments on other groups' writing. His sentiment was echoed in Zorko (2009), which argued that the visibility of all the groups' work afforded more learning opportunities, and knowing their group work was accessible to other groups would also motivate the students to work the best.

4.2 Contradictions

The results of this study showed that contradictions occurred between/among the components of the activity system. The contradictions lied in three relationships: division of labor-object, tool-object, and rules-tool-object.

4.2.1 Division of labor-Object

The contradiction between division of labor and object was nuanced in group interaction of Group B. The overall object of the wiki project was for group members to collaborate on two papers using the wiki. Collaboration, different from cooperation featured with division of labor, entails individuals' coordinated effort to complete a task collectively throughout the writing process (Storch 2013). A collaborative writing product, meanwhile, is a jointly produced text that cannot be easily reduced to the separate input of individuals (Stal 2006; Storch 2013). Group B did not achieve collaboration in the wiki writing project, as the three members, bore "equally doing the assignment" in mind, equally divided the writing tasks and equally participated in text construction. The writing product was combination of each member's equal efforts, which was featured with quite a few instances of coherence breakdowns (Li and Zhu 2017). Therefore, division of labor contradicted with the object of collaborative writing, which led to unsatisfactory outcome.

4.2.2 Tool-Object

Despite students' acknowledgement of the affordances of wikis for collaborative writing, some degree of tension between the tool and the object occurred. The wiki, being an asynchronous CMC tool, is not designed to support students' simultaneous communication. To facilitate communication, Members of Group A innovated their collaborative writing activity by having a synchronous use of the asynchronous tool. The archived wiki records revealed that they frequently discussed the writing tasks almost "synchronously" via the "Discussion" module after arranging for a time to virtually meet in the wiki. As Hai remarked in the interview (3/8/13), "We always finish the teamwork, put on our ideas like chats." This group responded to the constraint of the wiki: transformation was thus created due to the "driving force of change" (Engeström 2001). Dissimilar to Group A, members of Group B gave up the wiki and switched to the chatting tool WeChat to discuss about the writing tasks when they feel a need for immediate correspondence using the L1. Accordingly, the tool of wiki did not support the students' object of collaboration fully in their group writing activity.

4.2.3 Rules-Tool-Object

Moreover, the tension emerged among the rules, the tool, and the object. The MLA formatting rule for the task of annotated bibliography was hard to comply with on the wiki site, as the wiki did not support particular academic formats. Students reported that they could not save the version with the formats and fonts that they needed. Group A member Xia reckoned that the annotated bibliography was not well suited for the wiki collaborative writing, because this genre highly demanded the accuracy of formats (interview, 3/8/2013). Group B member Mei also pointed out that she could not produce a good-quality annotated bibliography by using merely the wiki tool. Instead, she wrote on the Word document first, and then copied and pasted it into the wiki.

For members of Group B which consisted of all three Chinese students, the rule of L2 (English) only in the wiki contradicted with their desire to facilitate communications in the L1. To respond to this issue, they resorted to the chatting tool WeChat to communicate in L1 about wiki writing tasks outside the class, which was against the object of collaborative writing using the wiki in L2. For this case, it seems that the requirement of using only the target language for wiki writing assignments decreased group members' participation levels and learning opportunities in the wiki. Actually, the use of L1 during the prewriting stages of L2 writing can be helpful for students to organize their composition (Lally 2000). However, the use of L1 is still debatable in L2 classes, as L1 use can deprive students of L2 input and decrease opportunities for students to foster L2 competence (Duff and Polio 1990).

5 Discussion

This study illustrates how activity theory can be used to understand the processes of wiki-based small group writing activities. Figure 3 depicts the activity system that two small wiki writing groups were engaged in, from the participants' viewpoints. The ESL students worked on collaborative wiki writing tasks in small groups in an EAP class. Wikis and L2 (English) were the main mediating tools, supplemented by the use of word doc (for the sake of good formatting), L1 (Chinese) and WeChat from Group B. Their participation and interaction in the wiki writing activity were constrained by rules such as using L2 to communicate and adopting the MLA style. Division of labor emerged from both groups: Group A exhibited an expert/novice pattern and Group B was featured with equal parallel work.

Of particular note, Figure 3 displays three cross-component contradictions. Both groups experienced tensions among tool, rules, and object. Specifically, for Group B, the wiki is an asynchronous CMC tool and cannot support students' simultaneous communication, which somewhat constrained the object of smoothly completing the writing tasks. For both groups, the wiki does not support the specific documentation format (MLA) editing, which constrained their writing a high-quality annotated bibliography paper (adhering to MLA style is one of the task requirements). Moreover, the rule of only L2 (English) use in the wiki did not meet with Group B's desire to facilitate communication in L1 (Chinese), which consequently contradicted with the object of successfully completing the wiki writing tasks. Moreover, the clear-cut division of labor with little evidence of mutual scaffolding in Group B, furthermore, constrained the object of team work and collaborative wiki writing.

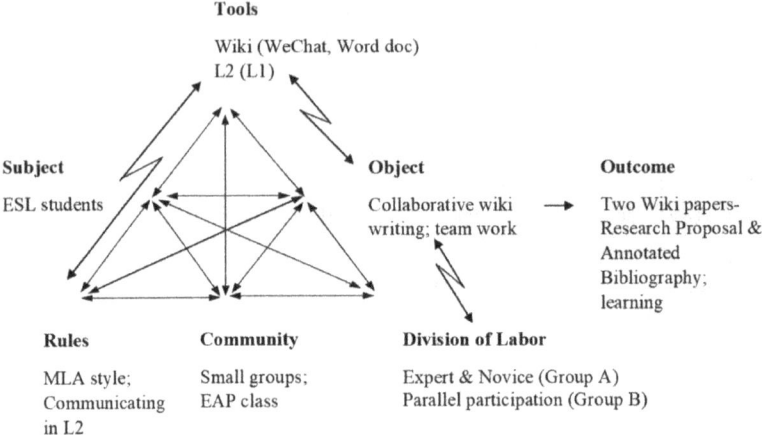

Figure 3: Activity System of Wiki-based Collaborative Writing.

The research results, in general, confirmed the wiki as a good artifact for collaboration reported in previous studies (e.g., Li and Zhu 2013; Bradley, Lindströmand Rystedt 2010; Lund 2008). Members of both groups believed that the wiki was a convenient collaboration tool; one participant particularly exclaimed at the motivated participation due to the wiki's transparency. The members drew on "Discussion" and "Comment" and negotiated the writing tasks through multiple language functions such as greeting, encouraging and acknowledging during the pre-writing and writing stages. The finding also echoed the wiki's constraint being an asynchronous communication tool as discussed in previous studies (e.g., Lee and Wang 2013; Zorko 2009). In Lee and Wang (2013), students complained that they have to even wait for a couple of days to receive their group partners' comments on their posts. To overcome the disadvantage of the wiki tool, researchers added a chatting tool to assist with participants' synchronous communication in addition to wiki communication (e.g., Elola and Oskoz 2010).

This study also helped us understand how/why contradictions arise and what possibilities might exist to alleviate or remove them in wiki-based collaborative writing. For instance, although using L2 rather than L1 is highly encouraged to maximize opportunities for students to practice the target language, the rule of exclusive L2 use in this study somewhat constrained Group B's wiki participation and interaction. Thus, the use of L1 can be allowed at a specific stage (i.e., prewriting stage) for collaborative tasks. Previous research (e.g., Alegría de la Colina and García Mayo, 2009; Antón and DiCamilla 1998, Azkarai and García Mayo, 2015; Brooks and Donato, 1994; García Mayo and Hidalgo, 2017; Storch and Wigglesworth 2003) suggested that the L1 may be a useful tool for learning the L2; it plays a critical role in L2 students' collaborative interaction, including mutually defining and clarifying task elements, developing strategies to manage difficult tasks, commenting on L2 use, providing scaffolding, and externalizing inner speech.

Division of labor, as an essential component of the wiki group writing system, also deserves our attention. The results of the larger project revealed that Group B produced the wiki paper of low writing quality due to equal division of labor and lack of mutuality (Li and Zhu 2017). This finding, to some extent, is in conflict with Lee and Wang (2013)'s argument that an even share of workload is an important factor facilitating wiki collaborative writing. As Li and Zhu (2013) pointed out, although equality and mutuality have been used as two important indexes for collaborative writing, group relationship of high mutuality may be more important than a relationship which emphasizes high equality. We definitely encourage group members' share of workload, but discourage the clear-cut division of workload without members' mutual scaffolding, because the simple division of labor cannot facilitate the collaborative writing task.

6 Conclusion

This chapter reports on an initial study that used Activity Theory as a heuristic to examine computer-mediated collaborative writing activities. This study addresses the general topic of the book "working collaboratively in second/foreign language learning" by taking an in-depth examination into collaboration in ESL wiki-based small group writing. It enhances our understanding of how collaboration or non-collaboration occur in online asynchronous writing task environments, and provides both theoretical and pedagogical insights on implementing collaborative work in second/foreign language writing classes. In particular, this study first examined interconnected mediating components within the wiki-based collaborative writing activities, and explored the aspects of these components that afforded or constrained collaborative wiki writing. Moreover, the study illustrated three areas of contradictions identified as embedded in the system, namely *division of labor-object*, *tool-object*, and *rule-tool-object*. In short, this research study innovatively explored the activity system of wiki-based collaborative writing from the perspectives of subjects, tools, rules, community, division of labor, objects, and outcome, and put forth the role of Engeström's Activity System in explaining peer interactions in the online collaborative task environment.

6.1 Limitations of the study

This study views the collaborative writing activities taking each small group interaction as a unit of analysis, and did not look at each individual student's wiki writing system. As different students working on the same task may have different activity systems motivated by their differing goals (Coughlan and Puff 1994), examinations of each individual's activity system and comparing these systems within small groups may shed further light on the interaction and contradiction that occur in wiki small group writing activities. Also, Engeström (1987) proposed two inner contradictions within the activity system: 1) contradictions embedded in the individual components of the activity system (e.g., as to mediating tools, contradictions can occur between L1 and L2), and 2) contradictions between constituent nodes of the system (e.g., contradictions between the tools and object). This study only focused on examining the second type of contradictions; with inquiry of the first type of contradiction added, the picture of the wiki group writing activities would be clearer and more comprehensive. Moreover, as contradictions can be sources of development, and innovations occur along with the resolving of contradictions (Dayton 2000; Kuutti 1996), more thorough investigations of how contradictions make individuals re-conceptualize the object of activity and utilize specific strategies to resolve different types of tensions would be important.

6.2 Pedagogical implications

This study has shed important pedagogical insights on computer (wiki)-based collaborative writing. The wiki has proved to be a good potential tool for group writing projects, allowing for learning within the small or big community. Wiki sites provide teachers with options to set the writing project either public (wide community) or private (small community). In this study, a few students expressed their willingness to view other groups' writing products and would appreciate the opportunity to comment on other groups' writing. Since the visibility of all groups' work afforded more learning opportunities (Zorko 2009), and the wiki, as a popular Web 2.0 tool, aims to enhance a sense of audience and foster online learning community, the open permission of group pages would be necessary at some points in the collaborative writing project. Hereupon, as echoed by

Wang, one of the participants in this study, a way to take wikis to full advantage may be the combination of two rounds of writing activities: collaborative writing within small groups and peer response among small groups. In that case, the permission of small group wiki pages can be set as private when students construct their joint group essay. After small groups complete their drafts, the permission status switches to "open" so that all the participants will be able to read the co-products completed by other groups and further interact within a wider community and allow more mutual scaffolding to occur.

Also, training is essential in computer-mediated collaborative writing. Instructors should enable students to understand the object/goal of a collaborative wiki writing project. Students need to learn the nature of collaborative writing (i.e., interaction and collaboration throughout the writing process and co-producing a single text with co-ownership), and be reminded that sheer division of labor can be an obstacle to accomplishing the collaboration goal. Moreover, students need to be guided to take advantage of the technology tool; for instance, teachers should highlight the distinctive features of the wiki in use, such as asynchronous communication leading to more thoughtful responses/reflection and affording recursive writing process. While emphasizing the affordance of asynchronous discussion via the wiki, teachers may consider embedding a chatting application to the wiki site for students to have synchronous communication in the brainstorming stage and editing stage so that collective decision based on negotiation about the group writing can be made more easily.

Moreover, teachers should design tasks that are aligned with wiki affordances. That is, instructors need to ensure that the wiki tool allows students to accomplish all task requirements. In this study, students experienced the rule-tool-object tension. Students were concerned about constructing the annotated bibliography using the wiki (i.e., tool), because this task required an accurate documentation format (i.e., rule), which proved difficult to achieve in the wiki page. Instructors will need to ensure that the technology tool matches task objectives before implementing wiki-based collaborative writing. For instance, the tasks such as picture book creation and cultural exploration conducted in previous studies (Ducate, Anderson, and Moreno, 2011; Lee and Wang 2013) are good examples, due to the wiki's affordance of multimodality. In addition, although we encourage students to communicate in L2 throughout the collaborative writing process, it can be reasonable to allow L1 use in the prewriting stage for ESL students with lower language proficiency so that they can brainstorm writing tasks more smoothly. Nevertheless, the use of the L2 should be emphasized for the actual joint writing processes so as to foster students' L2 competence. All in all, the activity system of wiki-based collaborative writing can lend insights into the nature of students' online participation and interaction, which would help instructors adopt online collaborative writing tasks to its most potential.

References

Alegría de la Colina, Ana, and María del Pilar García Mayo. 2009. "Oral Interaction in Task-based EFL Learning: The Use of the L1 as a Cognitive Tool" *International Review of Applied Linguistics* 47: 325–345.

Antón, Marta, and Frederick DiCamilla. 1998. "Socio-cognitive functions of L1 collaborative interaction inthe L2 classroom." *The Canadian Modern Language Review* 54: 314–342.

Azkarai, Agurtzane and María del Pilar García Mayo, 2015. "Task Modality and L1 Use in EFL Oral Interaction" *Language Teaching Research* 19: 550–571.

Bradley, Linda, Berner Linstrom, and Hans Rystedt. 2010. "Rationalities of Collaboration for Language Learning on a Wiki." *ReCALL* 22 2: 247–265.

Brooks, Frank and Richard Donato. 1994. "Vygotskian Approaches to Understanding Foreign Language Learner Discourse during Communicative Tasks." *Hispania* 77: 262–274.

Coughlan, Peter, and Patricia A Puff. 1994. "Same Task, Fifferent Activities: Analysis of SLA Task from an Activity Theory Perspective." In *Vygoskian Approaches to Second Language Research*, edited by James P. Lantolf and Gabriela Appel, 173–191. Norwood, NJ: Ablex.

Dayton, David. 2000. "Activity Theory: A Versatile Framework for Workplace Research." In *Proceedings of the 47th Annual Conference of the Society for Technical Communication*, 298–304. Arlington, VA: Society for Technical Communication.

Donato, Richard. 1994. "Collective Scaffolding in Second Language Learning." In In *Vygoskian Approaches to Second Language Research*, edited by James P. Lantolf and Gabriela Appel, 33–56. Norwood, NJ: Ablex.

Ducate, Lara, Lara Anderson, and Nina Moreno. 2011. "Wading through the World of Wikis: An Analysis of three wiki Projects." *Foreign Language Annals* 44: 495–524.

Duff, Patricia, and Charlene Polio. 1990. "How Much Foreign Language is there in the Foreign Language Classroom? *The Modern Language Journal* 74:154–166.

Ede, Lisa, and Andrea Lunsford, eds. 1990. *Singular Texts/Plural Authors*. Carbondale, IL: Southern IllinoisUniversity Press.

Elola, Idoia, and Ana Oskoz. 2010. "Collaborative Writing: Fostering Foreign Language and Writing Conventions Development." *Language Learning & Technology* 14: 51–71.

Engeström, Yrjö. 1987. *Learning by Expanding: An Activity Theoretical Approach to Developmental Research*. Helsinki: Orienta-Konsultit.

Engestrom, Yrjö. 1999. "Activity Theory and Individual and Social Transformation." In *Perspectives on Activity Theory*, edited by Yrjö Engestrom, Reijo Miettinen, and Raija-Leena Pulamaki, 19–38. New York, NY: Cambridge University Press.

Engestrom, Yrjö. 2001. "Expansive Learning at Work: Toward an Activity Theory Reconceptualization." *Journal of Education and Work* 14:133–156.

Engestrom, Yrjö. 2008. "Enriching Activity Theory without a Shortcut." *Interaction with Computers* 20: 256–259.

García Mayo, María del Pilar, and María de los Ángeles Hidalgo. 2017. "L1 Use among Young EFL Mainstream and CLIL Learners in Task-supported Interaction". *System* 67: 132–145.

Hirvela, Alan. 1999. "Collaborative Writing Instruction and Communities of Readers and Writers." *TESOL Quarterly* 8: 7–12.
Kessler, Greg, and Dawn Bikowski. 2010. "Developing Collaborative Autonomous Learning Abilities in Computer Mediated Language Learning: Attention to Meaning among Students in Wiki Space." *Computer-Assisted Language Learning* 23: 41–58.
Kuutti, Kari. 1996. "Activity Theory as a Potential Framework for Human-computer Interaction Research." In *Context and Consciousness: Activity Theory and Human-computer Interaction*, edited by Bonnie A. Nardi, 17–44. Cambridge, MA: MIT Press.
Lally, Corolyn Gascoigne. 2000. "First Language Influences in Second Language Composition: The Effect of Pre-writing." *Foreign Language Annals* 33: 428–532.
Lantolf, James. 2000. "Introducing Sociocultural Theory." In *Sociocultural Theory and Second Language Learning*, edited by James Lantolf, 1–26. Oxford: Oxford University Press.
Lee, Hsiaochien, and Peiling Wang. 2013. "Discussing the Factors Contributing to Students' Involvement in an EFL Collaborative Wiki Project." *ReCALL* 25: 233–249.
Li, Mimi. 2014. Small Group Interactions in Wiki-Based Collaborative Writing in the EAP Context. (Doctoral Dissertation, University of South Florida). Retrieved from https://scholarcommons.usf.edu/cgi/viewcontent.cgi?article=6450&context=etd
Li, Mimi, and Kim Deoksoon. 2016. "One wiki, Two groups: Dynamic Interactions across ESL Collaborative Writing Tasks." *Journal of Second Language Writing*, *31*, 25–42.
Li, Mimi, and Zhu Wei. 2013. "Patterns of Computer-Mediated Interaction in Small Writing Groups Using Wikis." *Computer Assisted Language Learning*, *26*(1), 62–81.
Li, Mimi, and Zhu Wei. 2017. "Good or Bad Collaborative Wiki Writing: Exploring Links between Group Interactions and Writing Products." *Journal of Second Language Writing*, *35*, 38–53.
Lincoln, Yvonna, and Egon G. Guba. 1985. *Naturalistic Inquiry*. Newbury Park, CA: SAGE.
Lund, Andreas. 2008. "Wikis: A Collective Approach to Language Production." *ReCALL* 20: 35–54.
Stahl, Gerry. 2006. *Group Cognition: Computer Support for Building Collaborative Knowledge*. Cambridge, MA: MIT Press.
Storch, Neomy. 2002. "Patterns of Interaction in ESL Pair Work." *Language Learning* 52: 119–158.
Storch, Neomy. 2012. "Collaborative Writing as a Site for L2 Learning in Face-to-Face and Online Modes." In *Technology across Writing Contexts and Tasks*, edited by Greg Kessler, Anna Oskoz, and Idoia Elola, 113–129. Texas State University, TX: CALICO.
Storch, Neomy. 2013. *Collaborative Writing in L2 Classrooms*. Bristol, UK: Multilingual Matters.
Storch, Neomy, and Gillian Wigglesworth. 2003. "Is there a Role for the Use of the L1 in an L2 Setting?" *TESOL Quarterly* 37: 760–770.
Strauss, Anselm, and Juliet Corbin. 1998. *Basics of Qualitative Research* (2nd ed.). Newbury Park, CA: Sage.
Swain, Merrill. 2000. "The Output Hypothesis and Beyond: Mediating Acquisition through Collaborative Dialogue." In *Sociocultural Theory and Second Language Learning*, edited by James P. Lantolf, 97–114. Oxford: Oxford University Press.
Swain, Merrill, and Sharon Lapkin. 1998. "Interaction and Second Language Learning: Two Adolescent French Immersion Students Working together." *Modern Language Journal* 82: 320–337.

Vygotsky, Lev. S. 1978. *Mind in Society: The Development of Higher Psychological Processes.* Cambridge, MA: Harvard University Press.
Warschauer, Mark. 1997. "Computer-mediated Collaborative Learning: Theory and Practice." *Modern Language Journal* 81:470–481.
Wood, David, Bruner, Jerome, and Gail Ross. 1976. "The Role of Tutoring in Problem-Solving." *Journal of Child Psychology and Psychiatry* 17: 89–100.
Yin, Robert K. 2009. *Case Study Research Design and Methods* (4th ed.). Thousand Oaks, CA: Sage Publications.
Zorko, Vida. 2009. "Factors Affecting the Way Students Collaborate in a Wiki for English Language Learning." *Australasian Journal of Educational Technology* 25: 645–665.

Appendix A: Interview questions

(Only part of the interview protocol used in the larger study, which is relevant to this study, has been included.)
- What do you think of the wiki-based collaborative writing tasks?
- What do you think is the purpose of the wiki-based collaborative writing tasks? What is your aim in these tasks?
- What do you think is your role in the wiki-based collaborative writing tasks?
- What do you think influence the ways your group members interacted on the wiki writing tasks?
- What suggestions would you have to make the wiki-based collaborative writing tasks more effective for the students in future EAP classes?

Appendix B: Reflection Paper Writing Prompts

(Only part of the prompts used in the larger study, the ones pertinent to this study, have been included.)
- How did you/your group approach the two wiki writing tasks, i.e., research proposal and annotated bibliography?
- Did your group divide group tasks and labor? Did each group member play a distinct role? If yes, in which ways?
- What do you think influence the ways the group members interacted on the two wiki writing tasks?

Hyeyoon Cho
Factors mediating small-group interactions during synchronous web-based collaborative summary writing using Google Docs

1 Introduction

Collaborative writing is defined as an activity in which two or more writers coauthor a text (Storch 2011). As informed by sociocultural theory and studies underlining the importance of peer interaction in language development (Donato 1994; Storch 2002; Swain and Lapkin 1998), collaborative writing has become a common pedagogical practice in the second language (L2) classroom setting. Further, the potential of Web 2.0 tools such as wikis and blogs (Storch 2011) have attracted scholarly attention to web-based collaborative writing in the L2 learning context. While many studies have examined web-based collaboration and writing processes from the learner's perspective, relatively few have investigated the interaction patterns associated with computer-mediated communication (CMC) (see Storch 2013, Chapter 7). Nevertheless, the limited number of studies on these interaction patterns have found that collaboration is potentially conducive to language learning (e.g., Li and Zhu 2013; Tan, Wigglesworth, and Storch 2010).

Similar to scholarly findings on face-to-face interactions, studies of computer-mediated interactions revealed that not all pairs or groups work collaboratively via CMC (e.g., Bradley, Linstrom, and Rystedt 2010; Li and Zhu 2017b). While some studies have suggested that different CMC modes such as text-chat and voice-chat contribute to these results (Li and Zhu 2013; Tan et al. 2010), few have investigated why or how this may be (e.g., Li and Zhu 2017a; Storch 2004). Such research would be crucial to understanding how learners interact during collaborative writing in order to design and facilitate related web-based activities more effectively.

This case study addressed these research gaps by investigating why the abovementioned small-group interaction patterns vary in the context of web-based collaborative writing. More specifically, this study compared two separate synchronous modes of CMC to determine whether and how they fostered different types of collaboration. As informed by activity theory and previous related studies (Li and Zhu 2017a; Storch 2004), this study hypothesized that collaborations would be influenced by

Hyeyoon Cho, The University of Toronto

https://doi.org/10.1515/9781501511318-011

participant goals and goal-directed actions. Most prior studies on collaborative writing have focused on classroom contexts, in which student goals may be influenced by pedagogical priorities and assessments. This study instead investigated collaborative writing activities in a voluntary context outside the classroom among English as a second language (ESL) learners; participants, therefore, had the opportunity to experiment with their interaction and negotiation processes in order to write summaries.

2 Relevant literature

2.1 Collaborative writing and patterns of group and pair interaction

Face-to-face collaborative writing studies (e.g., Storch 2002; Watanabe 2008) have shown that interaction patterns can influence both writing performance and learning outcomes. Drawing upon Damon and Phelps's (1989) indices of mutuality and equality, Storch (2002) investigated interaction patterns during paired work in a college-level ESL class. In this context, mutuality is defined as the level of engagement each participant has with the other's contribution, while equality refers to the degree of task control or authority. Storch (2002) arranged mutuality and equality along perpendicular axes, thus resulting in the four following distinct interaction patterns: *collaborative, dominant/dominant, dominant/passive,* and *expert/novice* (Figure 1). She concluded that only the collaborative and expert/novice patterns contributed to language learning among students.

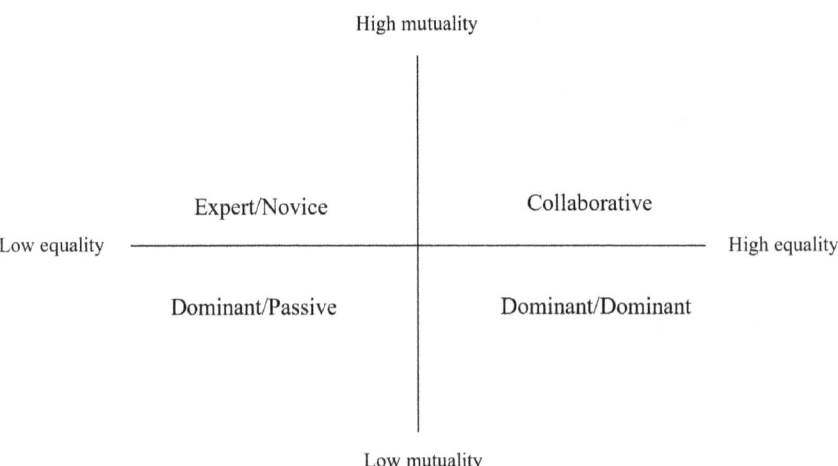

Figure 1: Storch's pattern of dyadic interaction model (2001, p.113).

Watanabe (2008) adopted Storch's interaction model to demonstrate that language learners of different proficiency levels could provide each other with learning opportunities if they were willing to share ideas and equally contribute to tasks. Watanabe also identified another pattern called *expert/passive,* which differs from Storch's expert/novice pattern of interaction. Here, the novice remains passive despite the expert encouraging their participation.

There has been an increasing amount of scholarly interest around interaction patterns in the CMC context. To date, studies of web-based collaborative L2 writing have focused on five main strands (Storch 2013, p.142): (a) L2 learners' perceptions of online collaboration (e.g., Kost 2011; Lee 2010; Li and Zhu 2013); (b) the nature of learners' contribution and engagement (e.g., Kessler and Bikowski 2010; Lee 2010; Mak and Coniam 2008); (c) focus on language (e.g., Elola and Oskoz 2010; Kost 2011; Mak and Coniam 2008); (d) interaction patterns (e.g., Li and Zhu 2013, 2017a; Tan et al. 2010; Rouhshad and Storch 2016); and (e) the quality of the collaboratively produced texts (e.g., Elola and Oskoz 2010; Mak and Coniam 2008). Relatively few studies have investigated interaction patterns of pair/small group in online collaborative writing (Storch 2013). Studies on interaction patterns have found evidence that collaborative patterns are potentially beneficial to language learning (e.g., Li and Zhu 2013; Rouhshad and Storch 2016). To design and facilitate online collaborative writing activity effectively, it is essential to understand how students interact during a collaborative task.

The studies investigating learner interactions in CM have mainly compared different communication modes and examined their influences on interaction patterns. Some have found unique interaction patterns related to text-based CMC. For instance, Tan et al. (2010) investigated interaction patterns among beginner-level Chinese language learners to compare face-to-face and delayed text-chat interactions. A *cooperative* pattern was only found in the text-chat context, in which participants focused on composing and revising their own writings without seeking interaction. Similarly, Rouhshad and Storch's (2016) comparison of face-to-face and text-chat interactions found that the modes of communication influenced both the interaction pattern and level of student attention to language learning. Participants who tended to interact collaboratively while in face-to-face mode were more apt to work cooperatively during text-chat interactions.

Li and Zhu (2013) examined small-group interaction of college-level English language learners' wiki collaborative writing. Their investigation revealed a *dominant/withdrawn* pattern. Here, the delayed nature of asynchronous text-based CMC allowed students to postpone their responses (or refrain from responding) while remaining detached or withdrawn from the task. Cooperative patterns were also observed in synchronous text-based CMC.

Some studies have investigated the factors influencing pair/group interactions during collaborative writing activities. For example, Storch (2004) argued that, while previous related studies considered personality differences (e.g., Villamil and de Guerrero 1996) and L2-proficiency variation (e.g., Kowal and Swain 1994) to explain interaction-pattern variations, they failed to consider how students were orientated to writing tasks. Storch (2004) used Leontiev's activity theory to investigate how participant goals and motives explained variations in face-to-face collaborative writing activities in a college-level ESL class. She concluded that interaction patterns were influenced by the nature of learners' goals and whether and how group members engaged in goal-sharing.

In a CMC context, Li and Kim (2016) examined the nature of interaction among two groups of ESL writers during wiki collaboration. They specifically analyzed language functions, writing-change functions, and scaffolding strategies to find that learners interacted differently in relation to their attitudes and preferences during collaborative writing activities. These findings supported Storch (2004) regarding the importance of affective factors in explaining how and why participants act in certain ways during paired or group work. Most recently, Li and Zhu (2017a) investigated interaction patterns while ESL learners worked on collaborative wiki writing tasks. They identified sociocultural factors that helped explain variations in the interaction patterns. For instance, the *collective pattern* involved convergent goals, collaborative agency, and positive emotions, whereas the *dominant/defensive* pattern involved divergent goals, individual agency, and negative emotions.

2.2 Activity theory

Activity theory emerged from Vygotsky's (1978) concept of mediation as a collection of actions taken to achieve desired outcomes that are mediated by psychological or material tools. Swain, Kinnear, and Steinman (2010) explained, "activity theory conceptualizes human cognition in relation to human physically and socially motivated activities" (97). The original theory was further developed by Leontiev (1978) and Engeström (2015).

Leontiev's version of activity theory emphasized individual goals, motives, and the connections between motives and behaviors while acknowledging the social nature of activity (Kaptelinin 2005). He defined the level of activity to strengthen the analytic power of the theory (Lantolf and Thorne 2006) by looking at the same activities through different analytical perspectives (Wells 1999). Here, an activity is driven by an object-related motive, while an action instantiates the motives by orienting toward a goal (i.e., the objective of an action taken by an individual or group). Goal-directed actions are realized by operations that are "automatized or habituated actions that respond to the immediate social-material conditions at hand" (Lantolf and Thorne 2006, 216).

Engeström (2015) further developed Leontiev's concepts of collective activity by shifting the focus from activities occurring at the individual level to human behaviors as they exist in collective activity systems (Kaptelinin 2005). Engeström (2015) introduced *community* as the third component of interaction to describe a three-way interaction among subjects, the object, and community. An activity model is represented as a triangular diagram describing the relationship between these components, as illustrated in Figure 2:

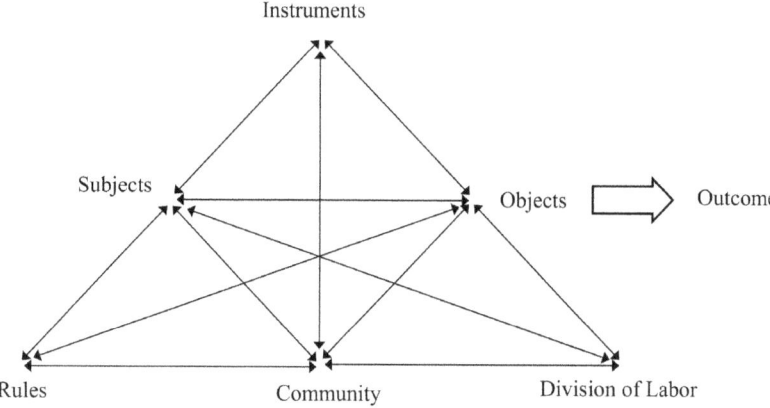

Figure 2: The structure of the human activity system (Engeström 2015).

People who share the same general objective become a community. With the emergence of a community, social mediators (i.e., *rules* and *divisions of labor*) also influence activity. The actions and interactions of subjects within an activity are regulated and guided by rules. The division of labor refers to how tasks are shared within the community. Engeström (2015) also emphasized that continuous construction among the components of an activity system are ongoing and that the components reconstruct themselves by reciprocally influencing one another.

Guided by Engeström's activity model, this study responded to the need for research on variation of interaction patterns in CMC contexts. By investigating the mediating factors of peer interactions in synchronous web-based collaborative writing, it captured how each element of the model shapes writing activities and reconstructs itself from influences of other elements.

This study directly addressed three research questions:
1. What interaction patterns occur when small-group L2 writers engage in synchronous web-based collaborative writing tasks?
2. How and to what extent are group interactions influenced by individual participant goals and, conversely, how do group interactions influence these goals?
3. In addition to individual goals and goal-directed actions, what factors influence peer interactions during web-based collaborative writing?

These questions were designed to generate information on how collaborative writing operates and why collective performance is found to vary between groups.

3 Method

3.1 Research setting and participants

Participants were recruited from an English debate club that the author organized over a two-year period at a Canadian university. The debate club was a voluntary group in which members met weekly to practice their English communication skills. All members were adult ESL learners from East Asia. The author anticipated that participants would be highly motivated because of the voluntary nature of the program. Groups were formed according to participant availability with one condition. That is, each group required at least one member with a different first language than the other two. This practice was based on previous studies involving L2 voice-based CMC (Bueno Alastuey 2011; Cheon 2003) in which findings indicated that ESL communication among peers who shared an L1 was inauthentic or not meaningful. Table 1 summarizes participant profiles.

3.2 Writing tasks

Participants wrote debate summaries using web-based writing tools while working in groups. The debate summaries were collaborative in nature because participants had already shared information during the debate meeting; they were required to reconstruct this information into a consensual summary. This writing task resembled some aspects of the dictogloss tasks that have been suggested in prior studies to promote peer collaboration and language-related episodes (Storch 1999; Swain and Lapkin 1998). Dictogloss refers to a pedagogical activity in which students

Table 1: Participant profiles.

Group	Pseudonym	First language	Gender	Length of stay in Canada	Length of participation in the debate club	Language proficiency test score	Participant language proficiency[1]
A	Lauren	Korean	Female	2 years	2 months	N/A	Upper-Intermediate
	Yuko	Japanese	Female	11 months	2 months	TOEIC[2] 825/990	Independent user
	Carey	Korean	Female	2 years, 5 months	3 months	IELTS[3] 6/9	Competent user
B	Scott	Korean	Male	1 year, 1 month	1 month	TOEIC 785/990	Independent user
	Ryan	Korean	Male	2 years, 2 months	1 month	TOEFL iBT[4] 80/120	Intermediate
	Victoria	Chinese	Female	5 years, 3 months	1 month	N/A	Advanced

listen to a short text a few times before reconstructing it based on memory and notes while working in pairs or other small groups (Wajnryb 1990). However, the summary tasks used in this study involved authentic, naturally-generated topics and contexts rather than prescribed language-learning exercises.

This study was a part of a bigger research project (n=12) on two groups (n=6). The general project alternated the order of texts and voice-chats by group to counterbalance any effects of the task order. The two groups examined

---

[1] All terms describing participant English proficiency were based on the scoring rubrics for each test. If a participant did not have an English language proficiency test score, her language proficiency was estimated based on her English learning history (e.g., length of studying English and stay in Canada) and performance during debate meetings.
[2] *TOEIC* refers to the Test of English for International Communication. Total scores are on a scale from 10 to 990.
[3] *IELTS* refers to the International English Language Testing System. IELTS scores are based on each for the four language skills on a scale of 1 to 9.
[4] *TOEFL iBT* refers to the Test of English as a Foreign Language Internet-Based Test. The maximum score is 120.

in this study wrote debate summaries (about an hour each) three times. For Task 1, they used Google Docs and voice-chat (Skype), and then Google Docs and text-chat for Task 2. Task 3 enabled all participants a free choice of modality (both groups chose voice-chat).

3.3 Procedure and data collection

Groups were recruited one at a time from the debate club. Each group completed a training session to become familiar with Google Docs, built-in text-chat, and voice-chat. They also learned to create real-time recordings of activities performed on the computer screen. This involved creating a video file that captured everything displayed on the screen. These files allowed the researcher to unobtrusively observe participant writing behavior (Cohen 2014) and access their computer-based activities independently of Google Docs (e.g., their use of online dictionaries and debate-resource websites). Google Docs revision histories of the debate summaries were retrieved and pasted into spreadsheets to further document screen-recording data. Text-chats were copied from Google Docs chat windows and voice-chats were transcribed verbatim; these elements were also added to the spreadsheets. All excerpts presented in this chapter were directly taken from text and voice-chat logs; no language errors were removed.

Participants responded to a questionnaire regarding their profile information and goals for the writing task. They were also asked to write debate summaries collaboratively. In addition, all participants completed one-hour stimulated-recall interviews within 48 hours of completing the task (Bloom 1954 as cited in Gass and Mackey 2016, 15). They were specifically asked to comment on the collaboration process and provide other details about their interactions while watching screen-recorded data from the project. The stimulated-recall interviews were designed to ascertain what the participants thought was particularly important about the writing process, which offered insights into relevant aspects the researcher may have overlooked. Finally, participants were asked to elaborate on their responses to the questionnaire. All resulting interview data were audio-recorded and transcribed verbatim.

3.4 Data analysis

Storch's (2001) dyadic interaction model was used to identify the interactional patterns of each group. Group-contribution equality was assessed by quantifying the writing portions of each participant in contributing to the tasks. That is, word counts were recorded and turns taken during text and voice-chats were quantified. Group mutuality was determined by investigating decision-making episodes (i.e., how and by whom episodes were initiated and resolved) (Storch 2001). Decision-making episodes were defined as those in which participants made decisions about the summary writings. All decision-making episodes were evaluated according to the degree of interactivity each participant contributed in resolving the related issues (Storch 2001). These contributions were then given ratings of *interactive/low, interactive/medium,* or *interactive/high* (Table 2).

Table 2: Level of engagement in the decision-making process.

Level of engagement	Definition
Interactive/low	Minimal interaction was evident (e.g., phatic utterances) or requests for assistance were dismissed (e.g., "I don't know").
Interactive/medium	There was some participant involvement (e.g., a confirmation request was followed up).
Interactive/high	Participants were substantially involved in providing interactive suggestions to generate ideas.

The overall qualitative analysis process related to assessing these interaction patterns was informed by Storch's (2001) patterns of dyadic interaction and associated traits. This involved locating the results of mutuality and equality analyses along two axes. The researcher therefore iteratively read all screen-recording transcripts while noting patterns of interaction as well as any salient features.

Participant goals were investigated based on an assessment of their responses to the questionnaire survey. This helped determine how their goals influenced group interactions. Episodes indicating participant attempts to achieve these goals were determined using the constant comparative method (Strauss and Corbin 1980). The influences of participant goals and goal-directed actions on group interactions were then examined according to Leontiev's activity theory, which defines actions as goal-oriented activities. The factors mediating group interactions were identified based on seven components of Engeström's (2015) activity model. All transcripts of screen recordings and stimulated-recall interviews were then iteratively reviewed to classify cases in which these components mediated the collaborative writing activities.

A second rater coded the derived interaction patterns by utilizing the results of the mutuality and equality analyses and Storch's (2001) patterns of dyadic interaction and associated traits. This was done to establish a reliable data coding process. The primary researcher and second rater agreed on the patterns of interaction in eight of 11 cases (73%) in the larger project (Cho 2018). Regarding the three cases where raters disagreed, the researcher placed them in the same quadrant with the expert/novice pattern but identified them as different patterns while the second rater identified them as expert/novice patterns. The second rater commented that the description of expert/novice did not fit perfectly to those three cases. Disagreements were resolved through discussion.

4 Results

4.1 Equality and mutuality

This chapter only provides a brief summary of the equality and mutuality analysis due to word limits (see Cho 2018, Chapter 5, for a detailed discussion). The following section provides a discussion on the excerpts by elaborating on the distinctive features of the interaction patterns. Table 3 displays participants' verbal and written contributions to the writing activities. Tables 4 and 5 present information on this study's analyses of the decision-making episodes.

Table 3: Participants' verbal and written contributions.

Task	Group	Member (pseudonym)	Total number of turns (% of turns)	Total number of words in turns	Words per turn	Total number of words in Written summaries
1 Voice-chat	A	Yuko	153 (46%)	598 (41.4%)	3.91	235 (38.1%)
		Lauren	106 (31.8%)	511 (35.4%)	4.82	247 (40%)
		Carey	74 (22.2%)	336 (23.3%)	4.54	135 (21.9%)
2 Text-chat	A	Yuko	32 (33.3%)	169 (27.1%)	5.28	412 (43.7%)
		Lauren	30 (31.3%)	270 (43.3%)	9.0	352 (37.4%)
		Carey	34 (35.4%)	184 (29.5%)	5.41	178 (18.9%)
3 Voice-chat	A	Yuko	126 (39.8%)	582 (36%)	4.62	384 (46%)
		Lauren	95 (30 %)	498 (30.8%)	5.24	278 (33.3%)
		Carey	96 (30.2%)	538 (33.3%)	5.60	173 (20.7%)
1 Voice-chat	B	Scott	84 (35.7%)	934 (41.4%)	11.10	483 (41.0%)
		Ryan	112 (47.7%)	784 (35.4%)	7	256 (21.8%)
		Victoria	39 (16.6%)	130 (23.3%)	3.33	438 (37.2%)

Table 3 (continued)

Task	Group	Member (pseudonym)	Total number of turns (% of turns)	Total number of words in turns	Words per turn	Total number of words in Written summaries
2 Text-chat	B	Scott	42 (35.3%)	314 (47.2%)	7.48	804 (52.1%)
		Ryan	42 (35.3%)	180 (27.1%)	4.29	318 (20.6%)
		Victoria	35 (29.4%)	171 (25.7%)	4.89	420 (27.2%)
3 Voice-chat	B	Scott	72 (25.3%)	650 (36.5%)	9.03	719 (46.1%)
		Ryan	130 (45.6%)	787 (44.2%)	6.05	331 (21.2%)
		Victoria	83 (29.1%)	344 (19.3%)	4.14	510 (32.7%)

Table 4: Initiation and resolution of decision-making episodes (DME).

Group	Task	Initiation of DME			Total	Resolution of DME		
A		Yuko	Lauren	Carey		Yuko	Lauren	Carey
	1	2	4	7	13	5	3	5
	2	5	8	5	18	9	6	3
	3	5	7	6	18	4	8	6
B		Scott	Ryan	Victoria		Scott	Ryan	Victoria
	1	8	14	1	23	18	3	2
	2	6	5	0	11	6	3	2
	3	7	3	4	14	7	6	1

4.1.1 Group A

In terms of equality, Yuko took the most turns in both Tasks 1 and 3, while Carey took the most in Task 2 (Table 3). Lauren distinctively spoke the most words per turn during Tasks 1 and 2. She took longer turns to provide information from her notes, which she took during the debate meeting. Regarding written contributions, Lauren wrote the most words in Task 1, while Yuko wrote the most in Tasks 2 and 3. Carey wrote about half the amount of what Yuko and Lauren wrote across all three tasks. In terms of mutuality, Group A initiated a similar number of decision-making episodes across tasks (Table 4). All three participants initiated and resolved similar numbers of episodes (i.e., no single person dominated the tasks). Decisions were primarily made in the medium-to-high interactivity range across all three tasks (Table 5).

Table 5: Level of engagement in the resolution of decision-making episodes.

Group	Task	Interactive/Low	Interactive/Medium	Interactive/High	No Response	Total
A	1	0 (0 %)	9 (69.2%)	4 (30.8%)	0 (0%)	13
	2	0 (0%)	12 (66.7%)	4 (22.2%)	2 (11.1%)	18
	3	1 (5.6%)	11 (61.1%)	6 (33.3%)	0 (0%)	18
B	1	0 (0%)	13 (56.5%)	10 (43.5%)	0 (0%)	23
	2	0 (0 %)	4 (36.4 %)	7 (63.6%)	0 (0%)	11
	3	0 (0%)	9 (64.3%)	4 (28.6%)	1 (7.1%)	14

4.1.2 Group B

Regarding equality, Scott wrote the most and took the longest turns across the tasks. Ryan took the most turns for all three tasks, but contributed to the summary writing the least. Victoria contributed to communication the least. However, her percentage of number of turns distinctly increased in Tasks 2 and 3 when compared to Task 1. In terms of mutuality, Scott initiated and resolved the most episodes across all three tasks. However, Victoria's initiation of decision-making episodes noticeably increased in Task 3. Ryan and Scott resolved a similar number of decision-making episodes. Most such episodes were resolved in the medium or high interactivity ranges.

4.2 Interaction patterns

Group A's interaction patterns were identified as collaborative for all three tasks, while Group B revealed leader/participants patterns for Tasks 1 and 2 and a collaborative pattern for Task 3.

4.2.1 Collaborative

For Task 1, Group A wrote a collaborative summary (i.e., each member took turns as a scribe and dictate or (re)organized what others had said for inclusion in the summary). Excerpt 1 demonstrates how Yuko took on the role of scribe while the others complemented each others' ideas to co-construct the summary.

Excerpt 1 (Group A, Task 1, voice-chat)

	((On Google Docs))
1 Carey: °Uh, they have to°, they have to	Since they made the rules, they
2 show, they have to show-	have to **show good behavior.**

3   Yuko: Oh, okay. Show?
((Yuko wrote, "show."))
4   Carey: Behavior. Hhhh. I don't know.
5   Yuko: Uh, hhh.
6   Lauren: They . . . they have to . . . well
7   behaved?
8   Yuko: They have to-
9   Carey: Show . . . uh . . . good
10   behavior.
11 Lauren: Yeah.
12 Yuko: Is it right?
13 Carey: Yeah.
((Yuko wrote "good behavior."))

Carey suggested what to include in the summary (Lines 1 and 2). Yuko then wrote "*show*" on the Google Docs following Carey's proposal. Carey suggested that Yuko write "(good) behavior," but she was unsure (Line 4). Lauren then proposed the following: "They have to well behaved" (Lines 6 and 7). Yuko repeated "they have to" (Line 8). Finally, Carey suggested the words "show good behavior" (Lines 9 and 10). Lauren agreed with Carey's proposal (Line 11). Yuko requested a confirmation on what she wrote (Line 12); Carey confirmed this (Line 13). This episode was identified as a collaborative completion according to Storch's (2001) terms (i.e., a behavior that is evident in collaborative pairs).

Group A decided to divide parts of the writing and review them together in Task 2. Members often suggested or asked others about their courses of action. Group A members also closely assisted each other when help was requested across all three tasks. Group B also exhibited this behavior during Task 3.

Excerpt 2 (Group B, Task 3, voice-chat)
1   Ryan: Scott, do you remember what Eunbie say about the . . . .
2   pesticide?
3   Scott: Uh . . . no. How about Victoria?
4   Ryan: Victoria?
5   Victoria: Can you say the question again?
6   Ryan: Yeah, Eunbie . . . mentioned about pesticide.

7	Victoria:	What does that mean?
8	Ryan:	Uh-
9	Scott:	Pesticide, special, special medicine which kills=
10	Ryan:	Bugs [or something.
11	Scott:	[=bad stuff. Yeah.
12	Victoria:	You, you mean Eunbie mentioned that?
13	Ryan:	Yeah.
14	Victoria:	I don't remember.
15	Ryan:	I think, ah, she mentioned about we should endure that situ-,
16		we can endure that situation without the GMO
17		(genetically modified organism).
18	Victoria:	Oh, I see! Do you mean that uh, she say . . . we have to reduce
19		. . . using pesticide?
20	Ryan:	Oh, and then?
21	Victoria:	Then, to use GMO food . . . We have to reduce using . . . uh . . .
22		pesticide rather=
23	Ryan:	[Uh-huh.
24	Victoria:	[=than eating GMO food.
25	Ryan:	Okay. Thanks.

In Excerpt 2, Ryan asked Scott if he remembered what Eunbie (another debate club member) said during the debate (Lines 1 and 2). Scott did not remember, but asked Victoria (Line 3). Victoria asked Ryan to repeat the question (Line 5) and inquired about the meaning of "pesticide" (Line 7). Scott intervened to explain the meaning of "pesticide" (Lines 9 and 11). Ryan also tried to explain the meaning of "pesticide" (Line 10). Victoria seemed unable to recall what Eunbie said. However, she remembered after Ryan provided more information (Lines 18 and 19). Finally, Victoria explained Eunbie's argument (Lines 21, 22, and 24). By interacting with Victoria, Ryan was able to collect the information he needed to write the summary (Line 25).

4.2.2 Leader/participants

Group B's interaction patterns during Tasks 1 and 2 were identified as *leader/participants*. Scott (who was identified as the leader by other group members) contributed the most to discussing the process of writing and the actual writing. He led the writing procedure by making relevant suggestions, answering related member questions, and creating headings to outline the summary (see Excerpt 4).

Once a group decision was made, Scott focused on his share of the writing and paid little attention to other members. For instance, a stimulated-recall revealed that Scott could not identify Victoria's contribution because she had remained quiet during that time. The expert in Storch's expert/novice pattern would check on Victoria to encourage her participation.

Scott made most decisions about the writing activity, but decision-making episodes were initiated by everyone in the group. For example, Ryan asked about the style of the summary in Excerpt 3 (Lines 1 and 2). Scott suggested that Ryan write what he recalled then, but to add more details later (Lines 3, 5, 7, and 8). Ryan clarified his question (Lines 6, 9, and 10). Scott thus suggested that Ryan write the summary using full sentences (Line 11).

Excerpt 3 (Group B, Task1, voice-chat)

1	Ryan:	Hmm, first they mentioned about . . . we don't, we don't need to
2		make a full sentence? Right?
3	Scott:	But if you, if you can, but really don't remember about it=
4	Ryan:	Uh-huh.
5	Scott:	=just put the . . . simple form-
6	Ryan:	No, [I-
7	Scott:	[And we can make, we can add the, another sentence and some
8		full . . . some yeah back up thing later.
9	Ryan:	No, I mean our final result, like summary thing like, we don't need,
10		we don't write down about essay, right?
11	Scott:	Uh! No, no. The, the final form, we need to make full sentence.
12	Ryan:	Uh, like essay?
13	Scott:	I don't know, but I will check with Hyeyoon (the researcher) later,
14		but I think it is gonna be, looks like essay after it.
15	Ryan:	Oh, okay.

In sum, this study found both collaborative and leader/participants patterns. Table 6 summarizes the related characteristics of each interaction pattern.

Table 6: Description of patterns found during small group interactions.

Interactional pattern	Description
Collaborative	– All group members contribute equally to the task. – Decisions are made mutually; most participants reached agreement. – Group members are willing to help one another. – They are willing to offer and engage with each other's ideas.
Leader/ participants	– The leader takes over the task and contributes the most. – Other participants recognize the leader and support his/her leadership. – The leader leads the task by making frequent suggestions about the writing procedures. – Decision-making episodes are initiated by everyone, but the leader primarily makes the decisions

4.3 Participant goals and goal-directed actions

In addition to participant goals and goal-directed actions shaping interaction patterns of groups as reported in previous studies (Li and Zhu 2017a; Storch 2004), the reverse was also observed.

The following section displays examples of individuals' goals and goal-directed actions (Scott's) influencing the group interaction and participants' goals and actions being affected by the dynamics of the group (Carey's and Victoria's).

4.3.1 Scott's goal of leading the writing activities

During the stimulated-recall interview, Scott said that people tended to waste time determining their courses of action. Whereas it was not his initial goal to be the leader, he quickly decided to lead the group as soon as the first task started. Scott created a heading for each section of the summary to serve as an outline.

Excerpt 4 (Group B, Task 1, voice-chat)

			((On Google Docs))
1	Scott:	Okay, so I, I will write the . . . so,	1.P
2		here's the start. One, one proposition,	1.O
3		1P . . . and one opposition 1O and two	2.P

4	proposition, 2P, 2 opposition, 2O.	**2.O**
	((Scott wrote "1.P, 1.O . . . " on Google Docs as he spoke.))	**3.P**
5	Ryan: Uh-huh.	**3.O**
6	Scott: Three proposition and three	
7	opposition.	
8	Ryan: Okay.	

In Excerpt 4, Scott read what he was writing on Google Docs aloud (Lines 1 to 4). Ryan responded to Scott indicating that he was following what he was saying (Line 5). Scott explained what "3P" and "3O" meant (Lines 6 and 7); Ryan acknowledged an understanding (Line 8). Scott's attempts to lead Group B shaped its interaction patterns as leader/participants.

4.3.2 Carey's goal of communicating with others more effectively

The process of writing collaborative summaries influenced Carey's goals and goal-directed actions during writing tasks. Before engaging in the first task, Carey thought she could simply work on her share of the writing. She accordingly took fewer turns than other members while focusing on writing the summary. However, Carey came up with a new goal of communicating more effectively during Task 2. She thus paid closer attention to what others were saying during that task. For example, Carey often monitored the text-chat window and responded to others.

Excerpt 5 (Group A, Task 2, text-chat)

1	Lauren:	I'll do [E]unbie['s arguments] then
2	Carey:	(24) okay
3	Yuko:	(205) I've done Steve's part, but I guess it's not perfect so plz add
4		later.
5	Carey:	(10) okay.

Lauren informed others that she would work on the arguments Eunbie presented in the debate meeting in Excerpt 5 (Line 1). After 24 seconds, Carey responded positively to Lauren (Line 2). For a total of 205 seconds, all members worked on the summary (no text-chat messages were sent). Yuko then requested that others add more details to Steve's (another debate club member's) arguments (Lines 3 and 4). Carey responded to Yuko (Line 5) as soon as she noticed this message. As for Task 2, Carey retained the goal of communicating better for Task 3. During the stimulated-recall interview, she said that paying attention to what others were saying helped her to communicate with them more effectively.

Carey often requested clarifications and confirmations when navigating and negotiating the writing procedures. In Excerpt 6, Carey deleted "*And it is not*" to revise Steve's part. However, she also noticed that Lauren was working on the same part. Carey asked Lauren if she was working on Steve's argument (Lines 1 to 3). Lauren responded positively (Line 9); Carey told her to keep working on Steve's arguments (Lines 10 and 11) and then moved on to a new section.

Excerpt 6 (Group A, Task 3, voice-chat)

((Carey deleted "And it is not."))
((Lauren deleted "be aware of" and inserted "realizing more about."))

((On Google Docs))
Steve: . . . . . . **And it is not** It's already being helpful, many people are **realizing** ~~be aware~~ more abou~~t~~of fair trade by this movement

1	Carey:	Uh! Lauren . . . so . . . uh,
2		Lauren?
3		Are you typing here?
4	Lauren:	Hm?
5	Carey:	Lauren? Are you typing
6		here?
7	Lauren:	Where? Steve's part?
8	Carey:	Yeah.
9	Lauren:	Yes.
10	Carey:	Okay, you can type what he
11		said.

4.3.3 Victoria's goal of interacting more with others

Victoria contributed more to the summary writing process than verbal communication during Task 1. Including Victoria, all group members commented that she did not talk much during Task 1. However, her patterns of contribution changed throughout the last two tasks as she developed the new goal of learning how to communicate with others. She took almost twice as many turns (in percentage) during Tasks 2 and 3 when compared to Task 1. Victoria initially said she did not need to talk to others much because she had gained nearly all the information required to perform the related activities by taking extensive notes during the debate meeting. However, she attempted to recall the debate content by interacting with others instead of relying on her notes during Tasks 2 and 3.

4.4 Mediating factors influencing group interactions

Each activity component was identified and analyzed to determine which one played a mediating role. Consider Figure 3:

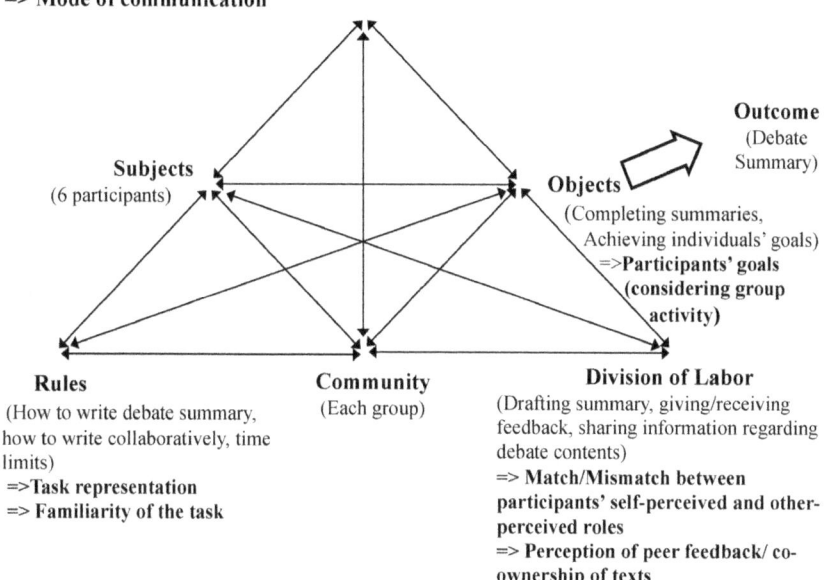

Figure 3: The structure of collaborative writing activities.

4.4.1 Modes of communication

Participant engagement was encouraged during the collaborative summary writing process in terms of interaction quantity by switching the mode of communication. The quantity of turns and speech among both groups tended to increase by two to three times when they communicated through voice-chat as compared to text-chat (Table 3).

While most participants preferred to use voice-chat, Carey and Victoria expressed their preferences for text-chat. Carey said that using text-chat pushed her to clarify her comments. She also found it easier to read written texts than listen and attempt to understand spoken phrases. Carey also said it was convenient to refer to text-chat messages. Indeed, Carey took a higher percentage of turns during group discussions in Task 2 when using text-chat as opposed to her voice-chat participation levels during Task 1.

Victoria desired text-chat because she preferred typing over talking. She identified herself as a quiet person that preferred interpersonal interactions through texting rather than talking (e.g., on the telephone). Victoria also said that she was not a multitasker; she had to stop writing when someone was talking. However, her number of turns almost doubled in percentage during Task 1 (voice-chat) when compared to Task 2 (text-chat).

4.4.2 Matches/mismatches between self and other-perceived roles

Matches/mismatches between self and other-perceived roles also influenced how participants interacted. In Group A, Lauren tried to facilitate the writing activity, but her efforts were not recognized by other group members. Lauren said that she did not typically prefer to take the lead during group work, instead preferring to focus on her individual part. However, she noticed that everyone in her group had similar working styles to her own. She thus decided to help organize the summary writing activity. Lauren's attempts at task organization were observable through the screen-recording data. For instance, she facilitated the writing activities by saying, "Shall we start?" and "Should we move on to the next section?" Although Lauren initiated a few facilitating turns, Yuko and Carey did not seem to register her leadership attempts.

On the other hand, Scott's leadership role was recognized by others in Group B. Ryan said that Scott seemed to prefer leading tasks. Victoria similarly commented with the following: "I think Scott is the leader and tells us what to do." Their recognition and positive attitude toward Scott's leadership allowed him to play a leadership role.

4.4.3 Learner perceptions about peer feedback/co-ownership

Some participants hesitated to fix or edit the writings of other group members. For example, Lauren was worried about editing others' writings because she thought she could thereby hurt their feelings. At the same time, she tried to remain open-minded to both editing others' work and receiving editing since the purpose of writing the collaborative summary was to help each other achieve a positive result. Similarly, Scott did not mind when Ryan fixed his part and informed him about the revision. Scott even thought that it was not necessary for

Ryan to report what he had fixed because they had a mutual understanding of the problem and if one of them fixed it, then the job was done.

4.4.4 Task representation

Participants had different understandings of what constituted summary writing. They resolved these discrepancies by frequently discussing the needed summary structure. For example, Ryan was not sure whether a debate summary should be written in full sentences or point form (Excerpt 3). He also wondered if it was okay to place additional information that was not presented during the debate to make the summary more complete. Scott and Victoria told him it was okay to do this. Reflecting on Ryan's comment, Victoria explained that she wrote the summary with additional details because she thought people who were not present during the debate meeting would not otherwise understand.

Victoria presented an idea of what constituted a summary based on her experiences writing class-discussion summaries for her university courses. She thought that her group's final product was not a summary because they wrote almost everything recalled from the debate rather than condensing the information. However, she did not address this issue with other group members.

4.4.5 Task familiarity

Both groups performed Tasks 1 and 3 using voice-chat, while Task 2 was performed via text-chat. As previously mentioned about Task 1, most participants in both groups took two to three times the number of turns than in Task 2 due to the instant nature of voice-chat. Although they communicated with one another using the same mode of communication (i.e., voice-chat), most participants took fewer turns in Task 3 than they did in Task 1. It seemed that participants had become more familiar with the task in general. The writing procedure had become routine so that discussions were not as frequently needed. For instance, in Group B, Scott said that he did not need to lead the group during Task 3 because members had become familiarized with the task and knew what to do. Victoria also stated the following: "I think we are getting better [with the task] because we already know what we should do." Ryan tended to maintain previously agreed-upon procedures from earlier tasks as part of an established routine. For instance, he mentioned that, because all group members had agreed to work on their arguments first during Task 1, he had begun to write his argument soon after Scott wrote summary headings for

Task 2. Ryan also requested that Scott create the headings for Task 3 since he had done so for earlier tasks.

5 Discussion

This study examined interaction patterns and mediating factors among two groups of ESL learners during web-based collaborative writing activities. By showcasing web-based collaborative writing activities, this chapter contributes to a better understanding of how online collaborative writing operates and why collective performance varies according to group.

Collaborative and leader/participants patterns were identified in this study. The collaborative pattern was predominant across all four groups in the larger project. This may be because the participants in this study were highly motivated language learners who had engaged in voluntary debate meetings and collaborative summary activities. Besides sharing their writings with debate club members, participants were not under pressure to score high marks. This may have encouraged them to focus more on the writing process than the product of writing.

As guided by activity theory, the study examined how participant goals prompted them to take certain actions, how these individual goal-directed actions interacted with the goals of other members, and how individual goals influenced group interaction patterns. For example, Scott set the goal of leading group work. This shaped the pattern of group interactions. Participant interactions also reciprocally influenced goals and goal-directed actions (e.g., for Carey and Victoria).

In addition to individual goals and goal-directed actions, this study found five factors that mediated small group collaboration. First, voice-chat seemed to facilitate participant collaboration due to its instantaneous nature when compared to text-chat. These findings support those of previous studies that revealed how face-to-face and voice-chat interactions facilitated collaboration during paired and group work (Loewen and Wolff 2016; Rouhshad and Storch 2016) better than text-chat interactions. Second, members were encouraged and influenced to shape interaction patterns when their self-perceived roles matched other-perceived roles. However, a mismatched role was found to discourage (or render unrecognized) such interaction and did not influence the interaction pattern. Third, as previous studies on online peer feedback (e.g., Guardado and Shi 2007; Lee 2010) have reported, participants hesitated to provide peer feedback to avoid hurting the feelings of other members. Although this study's participants engaged in collaborative writing so that "all writers [shared] in the ownership of the text produced" (Storch 2013, 2), it may still be challenging for students to relinquish the idea that writing is an individual and private activity (Bruffee 1983). Fourth, participants had different understandings of the summary writing tasks. This created disturbances during collaborative writing activities so that participants needed to resolve issues through group discussions. Finally, all participant interactions may have been influenced by their familiarity with the task. That is, participants developed a routine by completing a series of similar tasks.

In addition to observing patterns of collaborative interaction as reported in previous studies, this study also found a leader/participants pattern (a variation of Storch's expert/novice pattern). Here, the difference between a leader and an expert is that the leader mostly focuses on dividing shares of the writing and indicating how to proceed with the summary task, while the expert encourages novices participate in the task. This variation may have been observed because this study examined triadic rather than dyadic interactions. For example, Group B may have exhibited different interactions if only two of its members had worked as a pair. That is, three members may have created more opportunities than were possible in a pair.

This study provides important pedagogical insights into how teachers can collaborate to assist students to develop interaction patterns conducive to successful out-of-the-classroom collaborative writing activities by discussing the characteristics of different interaction patterns and their influences on group dynamics. For instance, it is important for teachers to discuss the characteristics and purposes of collaborative writing with their students. Students are then better informed about what they are expected to produce during collaborative writing tasks. For example, a teacher may discuss the concept of co-ownership with students before a writing activity to promote their understanding that collaborative writing is not simply about dividing shares of writing among members and combining individual texts into a whole (see Storch, this volume). Students may further be encouraged to set group goals to improve collaboration during these tasks in this way. Indeed, Storch (2004) observed that paired/group work was only beneficial when learners shared goals or when goals were complementary.

The communication modes used in collaborative writing should carefully be selected according to both the task purpose and language proficiency among learners. This study's participants generally preferred voice-chat because of its interactive and instantaneous nature. They mostly had upper-intermediate to advanced English language proficiency, and therefore they had stronger verbal communication skills than beginners in English would. Text-chat could be more effective for lower-proficiency learners because the pace of conversation is slower when compared to voice-chat. Group members can also see what others have previously expressed by referring to earlier interactions in the text-chat window.

It may be helpful to have a group leader (Li and Zhu 2017a). In this study, some participants volunteered to take leadership roles, which mediated group collaboration. However, it is necessary to educate leaders on how to monitor and facilitate group activities. Finally, teachers should provide feedback on language forms. As in many previous studies, participants were not always confident about the decisions they made in that regard.

This study has several limitations worth addressing in future research. First, it was conducted within a relatively short period of time with a small sample of participants. Second, participants were highly motivated. This may have been due to the voluntary, self-defined context outside the classroom setting (learner goals and motives may have this differed from those seen in such a setting). Systematic comparisons between natural contexts involving synchronous web-based collaborative writing and those in the classroom may thus be useful. Third, only two synchronous CMC modes were investigated in this study. A more extensive comparison of the different communication modes would therefore provide insight into how (web-based) collaborative writing activities can be designed and facilitated in the L2 classroom context. Fourth, this study's participants performed the same type of writing activity three successive times. It is thus worth investigating how different genres of writing contribute to learner interaction patterns.

References

Bloom, Benjamin. 1954. "The Thought Processes of Students in Discussion." In *Accent on Teaching: Experiments in General Education*, edited by Sidney J. French, 23–46. New York, NY: Harper.

Bradley, Linda, Berner Lindström, and Hans Rystedt. 2010. "Rationalities of Collaboration for Language Learning in a Wiki." *ReCALL* 22(2): 247–65.

Bruffee, Kenneth A. 1983. "Teaching Writing through Collaboration." *New Directions for Teaching and Learning* 1983(14): 23–29.

Bueno, Alastuey M.C. 2011. "Perceived Benefits and Drawbacks of Synchronous Voice-Based Computer-Mediated Communication in the Foreign Language Classroom." *Computer Assisted Language Learning* 24(5): 419–32.

Cheon, Heesook. 2003. "The Viability of Computer Mediated Communication in the Korean Secondary EFL Classroom." *Asian EFL Journal* 5(1): 1738–1460.

Cho, Hye Yoon. 2018. "Synchronous Small-group Collaborative Writing via Web-based Word Processing: What Facilitates or Constrains Learners to Achieve their Goals in Summary

Reports?" PhD thesis, University of Toronto. Retrieved from http://hdl.handle.net/1807/91892
Cohen, Andrew D. 2014. *Strategies in Learning and Using a Second Language*. Florence: Taylor and Francis.
Damon, William, and Erin Phelps. 1989. "Critical Distinctions among Three Approaches to Peer Education." *International Journal of Educational Research* 13(1): 9–19.
Donato, Richard. 1994. "Collective Scaffolding in Second Language Learning." In *Vygotskian Approaches to Second Language Research*, edited by James P. Lantolf and Gabriela Appel, 33–56. Norwood, NJ: Ablex.
Elola, Idoia, and Ana Oskoz. 2010. "Collaborative Writing: Fostering Foreign Language and Writing Conventions Development." *Language, Learning and Technology* 14(3): 51–71.
Engeström, Yrjö. 2015. *Learning by Expanding: An Activity-Theoretical Approach to Developmental Research*. Second edition. New York, NY: Cambridge University Press.
Gass, Susan M., and Alison Mackey. 2016. *Stimulated Recall Methodology in Second Language Research*. Mahwah, NJ: L. Erlbaum Associates.
Guardado, Martin, and Ling Shi. 2007. "ESL Students' Experiences of Online Peer Feedback." *Computers and Composition* 24(4): 443–61.
Kaptelinin, Victor. 2005. "The Object of Activity: Making Sense of the Sense-Maker." *Mind, Culture, and Activity* 12(1): 4–18.
Kessler, Greg, and Dawn Bikowski. 2010. "Developing Collaborative Autonomous Language Learning Abilities in Computer Mediated Language Learning: Attention to Meaning among Students in Wiki Space." *Computer Assisted Language Learning* 23(1): 41–58.
Kost, Claudia. 2011. "Investigating Writing Strategies and Revision Behavior in Collaborative Wiki Projects." *CALICO Journal* 28(2): 606–620.
Kowal, Maria, and Merrill Swain. 1994. "Using Collaborative Language Production Tasks to Promote Students' Language Awareness." *Language Awareness* 3(2): 73–93.
Lantolf, James P., and Steven L. Thorne. 2006. *Sociocultural Theory and the Genesis of Second Language Development*. Oxford Applied Linguistics. Oxford, NY: Oxford University Press.
Lee, Lina. 2010. "Exploring Wiki-mediated Collaborative Writing: A Case Study in an Elementary Spanish Course." *CALICO Journal* 27(2): 260–276.
Leontiev, A.N. 1978. *Activity, Consciousness, and Personality*. Englewood Cliffs, NJ: Prentice Hall.
Li, Mimi, and Deoksoon Kim. 2016. "One Wiki, Two Groups: Dynamic Interactions across ESL Collaborative Writing Tasks." *Journal of Second Language Writing* 31: 25–42.
Li, Mimi, and Wei Zhu. 2013. "Patterns of Computer-Mediated Interaction in Small Writing Groups Using Wikis." *Computer Assisted Language Learning* 26(1): 61–82.
Li, Mimi, and Wei Zhu. 2017a. "Explaining Dynamic Interactions in Wiki-based Collaborative Writing." *Language Learning and Technology* 21(2): 96–120.
Li, Mimi, and Wei Zhu. 2017b. "Good or Bad Collaborative Wiki Writing: Exploring Links between Group Interactions and Writing Products." *Journal of Second Language Writing* 35: 38–53.
Loewen, Shawn, and Dominik Wolff. 2016. "Peer Interaction in F2F and CMC Contexts." In *Peer Interaction and Second Language Learning: Pedagogical Potential and Research Agenda*, edited by Masatoshi Sato and Susan Ballinger, 163–184. Amsterdam: John Benjamins.
Mak, Barley, and David Coniam. 2008. "Using Wikis to Enhance and Develop Writing Skills among Secondary School Students in Hong Kong." *System* 36: 437–455.

Rouhshad, Amir, and Neomy Storch. 2016. "A Focus on Mode: Patterns of Interaction in Face-to-face and Computer-mediated Contexts." In *Peer Interaction and Second Language Learning Pedagogical Potential and Research Agenda*, edited by Masatoshi Sato and Susan Ballinger, 267–290. Amsterdam: John Benjamins.

Storch, Neomy. 1999. "Are Two Heads Better than One? Pair Work and Grammatical Accuracy." *System* 27(3): 363–74.

Storch, Neomy. 2001. "An Investigation into the Nature of Pair Work in an ESL Classroom and its Effect on Grammatical Development." PhD thesis, University of Melbourne. Retrieved from https://minerva-access.unimelb.edu.au/handle/11343/38809

Storch, Neomy. 2002. "Patterns of Interaction in ESL Pair Work." *Language Learning* 52(1): 119–58.

Storch, Neomy. 2004. "Using Activity Theory to Explain Differences in Patterns of Dyadic Interactions in an ESL Class." *Canadian Modern Language Review* 60(4): 457–80.

Storch, Neomy. 2011. "Collaborative Writing in L2 Contexts: Processes, Outcomes, and Future Directions." *Annual Review of Applied Linguistics* 31: 275–88.

Storch, Neomy. 2013. *Collaborative Writing in L2 Classrooms*. New Perspectives on Language and Education, v 31. Bristol; Buffalo: Multilingual Matters.

Strauss, Anselm L., and Juliet M. Corbin. 1990. *Basics of Qualitative Research: Grounded Theory Procedures and Techniques*. Newbury Park, Calif: Sage Publications.

Swain, Merrill, Penny Kinnear, and Linda Steinman. 2010. *Sociocultural Theory in Second Language Education: An Introduction through Narratives*. Second edition. MM Textbooks 11. Bristol, Buffalo: Multilingual Matters.

Swain, Merrill, and Sharon Lapkin. 1998. "Interaction and Second Language Learning: Two Adolescent French Immersion Students Working Together." *The Modern Language Journal* 82(3): 320–37.

Tan, Lan Liana, Gillian Wigglesworth, and Neomy Storch. 2010. "Pair Interactions and Mode of Communication: Comparing Face-to-Face and Computer Mediated Communication." *Australian Review of Applied Linguistics* 33(3): 27.1–27.24.

Villamil, Olga S., and Maria C.M. de Guerrero. 1996. "Peer Revision in the L2 Classroom: Social-Cognitive Activities, Mediating Strategies, and Aspects of Social Behavior." *Journal of Second Language Writing* 5(1): 51–75.

Vygotsky, Lev S. 1978. *Mind in Society: The Development of Higher Psychological Processes*, edited by Michael Cole, Vera John-Steiner, Sylvia Scribner, and Ellen Souberman, Cambridge: Harvard University Press.

Wajnryb, Ruth. 1990. *Grammar Dictation*. Oxford: Oxford University Press.

Watanabe, Yuko. 2008. "Peer–Peer Interaction between L2 Learners of Different Proficiency Levels: Their Interactions and Reflections." *Canadian Modern Language Review* 64(4): 605–35.

Wells, C. Gordon. 1999. *Dialogic Inquiry: Towards a Sociocultural Practice and Theory of Education*. Learning in Doing. New York: Cambridge University Press.

Index

accuracy 90, 93–94, 99–100, 102–103, 108–109, 111, 178–180, 183–188
Activity Theory 1–2, 3, 4, 5, 8–9, 15, 22
adolescent participants VIII
age VIII
agency 3
Arabic 3
asynchronous collaboration VIII
attitudes 3, 94–96, 100, 103, 107, 109–110
authentic 199, 201–202, 206

Basque 3, 5, 10
blended environments 3

CAF 90, 178–179, 190
case studies 3
closing sequences 202–210, 215, 217, 219
closings 200, 202–208, 215, 219
computer-mediated communication 199
cognitive maturity 91, 108
cognitive mechanisms 1
collaboration 201
collaborative dialogue 1, 4
Collaborative learning 1
collaborative pattern 152, 157, 159, 168–169, 171
Collaborative pattern 158
collaborative wiki writing 1–3, 5, 7–8, 15–17, 19
collaborative work 1, 3–6, 9
collaborative writing 1–2, 3, 4, 5, 6, 7, 8, 9, 10, 11, 13–29, 151–152, 154–156, 166, 172–173
collective scaffolding 15–16, 19
community 2–3, 6, 8, 11, 13, 18
comparison group 38, 49, 52
composing strategies 121, 125n6, 128
computer-mediated collaborative writing 18, 177
computer-mediated-collaborations VII
contradiction 13, 18
contradictions 2–3, 7, 13, 15–18
control group 43, 49–50

Conversation Analysis 206
Conversational Analysis 8
cooperative pattern 152, 154, 159, 161–162, 167–168, 170–171

Decision-making 9
decision-making episodes 9–12, 15
deliberations 19
design 40–45, 49–52
dialogue 1, 3–4
dictogloss 6
digital literacy skills 190
division of labor 2, 6–7, 8, 13, 15, 17, 19

EAP 1, 3, 15, 22
ecologically-valid VII
effect size 41–42, 51
EFL 91–93, 95, 110, 179–181
email 204, 208
English 3
English as a second language 1
English for Academic Purposes 1
equality 2, 8–12
ESL 1–3, 5, 8–9, 15, 17, 19
experimental task 96–98, 98n1, 102
exposure 45–46, 48–49, 52

face-to-face collaborative writing 179
facilitative 157, 161–163, 167–171
familiarity effects 189, 192
fluency 90, 99, 102, 108–109, 178, 180, 183, 185, 187–189
form-focused 98

German 3, 6
goal-directed actions 2, 6, 9, 16–17, 22
goals 3, 9
Google Docs VIII, 8, 13, 16–17, 18, 154, 156–157, 159–161, 163–166, 172, 180, 182–183, 185, 187–188, 190–192, 198
grammatical knowledge VIII
groups 90, 92–94, 96–97, 100–102, 104, 106–109

individual texts 97, 102
individual writing 118–119, 136
individual writing 117–119, 123–124, 123n2, 128, 130–132, 131n11, 134–140, 150
interaction 1–2, 6–7, 12–13, 15, 17–20
interaction patterns 1–2, 3, 4, 5, 6, 9–10, 12, 14, 16–17, 22–24
interactionist 48
interactionist approach 47
intercultural competence 200
interculturality 200

Japanese 3

Korean 3

L2 pragmatics 200, 202
language learning opportunities 13, 16, 24
Language related episode 70, 76
languaging 2, 4, 7
learner interaction 117
learner setup 90, 107, 109
learning opportunities VII
lexico-grammatical features VIII
lexis-focused episodes 98
LREs 60, 67, 69–70, 71, 72, 73, 76, 79, 81–84, 91–92, 95, 98–101, 107, 109, 152–154, 157, 164, 166, 168–170, 172–173

mechanics-focused 98
mediating tool 8, 15, 18
metalinguistic awareness 89, 91
metatalk 89
microgenetic investigations 4
mixed-age 59, 63
modality effects 180
mode 178–180, 185, 187–190, 198
Moodle platform VIII
motivation 103
mutuality 2–3, 5, 8–12, 59–61, 64, 67, 69–83
mutuality 61–62, 74, 80, 82, 84

negotiation of meaning 1
noticing 118

object 2, 6–7, 8, 10, 13–15, 17–19
omission 45, 51
online collaborative writing 172, 179
online interaction 159
ownership 2–3, 4, 9, 13–14, 19–29

pair work 1
pairs 92–94, 96–97, 100–102, 106–109
paper-based writing 178–179, 187–189
Participation 10
participation 1–2, 6–9, 11–13, 15–17, 20
passive 152–154, 157, 163, 167–168, 170
patterns of interaction VII, 3, 7–8, 19, 152, 154, 157, 166–168, 172
peer interaction 67, 81–84
peer interactions 5–6
perceptions 94, 96–98, 103, 109
pragmalinguistics 219
pragmatic *acquisition* 200
pragmatic competence VIII
pragmatic development 200–201
pre-post 179
pre-writing activities 167
problem-solving 117–121, 123, 127–128, 130–132, 136, 138, 140, 142
problem-solving strategies 117, 119–121, 123, 127–128, 131, 136, 138, 140
proficiency level VIII

qualitative measures 90, 93–94, 109
Quantitative measures 93, 99, 178–179
questionnaire 96–98, 100

ratings of text features 180
resolution 91–92, 100, 102, 108
rubric 180, 183
Rubrics 94
rule 12, 14–17, 19

sample size 44, 50–52
scaffolding 1
screen recording 123
screen-recording 8–9, 20
second languages VIII
secondary school 177–178, 180, 191–192
small group 1, 5, 9

sociocultural theory 1–2, 14, 47
sociopragmatic 199–202, 220
Spanish 3, 5, 8
stimulated recall interviews 123–124, 138–139
stimulated-recall interview 16, 18
stimulated-recall interviews 8–9

tailor-made 38–39
tailor-made items 44
tailor-made test 38–41, 44
tailor-made test items 38–41, 44
task effects 189
task type 38–39, 41, 46
technology-based collaborative writing 189–191

tellecollaboration 8
terminal component 215–216, 218
terminal components 209, 215, 218–219
text quality 177–178, 180
thanking 203–204, 209–210, 217, 219
topic 183, 189, 192

Vygotsky 47

web-based collaborative writing 1, 5
wiki 1–2, 3, 5–19, 22
written text quality VIII

young FL learners 94
young learners 95, 108–110
young learners 178, 188

www.ingramcontent.com/pod-product-compliance
Lightning Source LLC
Chambersburg PA
CBHW071737150426
43191CB00010B/1605